# STRATEGIC CYCLE INVESTING

# STRATEGIC CYCLE INVESTING

Richard Coghlan

McGRAW-HILL BOOK COMPANY

**London** · New York · St Louis · San Francisco · Auckland
Bogotà · Caracas · Lisbon · Madrid · Mexico
Milan · Montreal · New Delhi · Panama · Paris · San Juan
São Paulo · Singapore · Sydney · Tokyo · Toronto

Published by
McGRAW-HILL Book Company Europe
Shoppenhangers Road, Maidenhead, Berkshire SL6 2QL, England
Telephone 0628 23432
Fax 0628 770224

**British Library Cataloguing in Publication Data**
Coghlan, Richard
Strategic Cycle Investing
I. Title
332.6

ISBN 0-07-707596-X

**Library of Congress Cataloging-in-Publication Data**
Coghlan, Richard (Richard T.)
Strategic cycle investing / Richard Coghlan.
p. cm.
Includes bibliographical references and index.
ISBN 0-07-707506-X
1. Investments. 2. Business cycles. 3. Investment analysis.
I. Title.
HG4521.C5293 1993
332.6—dc20                                                                                  93-16272
CIP

*Part of the series:*
The Economics of the Financial World and Stock Markets
*Series Editor:* Dr H. Motamen-Scobie

1234 CUP 9543

Typeset by BookEns Ltd, Baldock, Herts.
and printed and bound in Great Britain at the University Press, Cambridge

# CONTENTS

# PREFACE

This book has been written with the aim of providing investors with a way of increasing returns while at the same time reducing risk. There is no promise of instant wealth with no work and no risk, but there are ways to improve investment decision-making by taking account of changes in the business cycle. This may seem a modest objective by comparison, but it is, at least, achievable. The ideas and analysis were developed over the past 20 years, resulting in indicators that have been refined and tested in the real world over a long period of time. I hope that others will find them to be equally interesting and rewarding.

When it comes to investing, there are a great number of different risks, and the greatest of all is the possibility of a coordinated decline that drags down all prices. Investment returns, and investor confidence, will be greatly improved by anticipating such periods, and that is the main focus of this book. Strategic decision-making of this type can be used on its own, or combined with other specific approaches, such as emphasis on growth or value stocks, selecting bond maturities/duration, market indexing, domestic or international portfolios, etc. Even short-term speculators will benefit from understanding the direction of the main trend. The major asset markets are all covered, with assessments of how to weight each market within a diversified portfolio according to changing economic conditions.

The study of cycles in asset markets has become increasingly technical. Most discussion of cycles ignores the influence of other markets or the rest of the economy, assuming that market prices are determined independently of such inconvenient distractions. Books on the long wave inevitably have predicted the imminent and devastating collapse of financial markets, which can be very unsettling at times of increased uncertainty and can easily result in very bad decisions being made.

This book takes a more balanced view and provides some unexpected conclusions. At one level, it builds bridges between the markets and the economy, making it clear that each depends on the other in crucial ways. It makes no sense to consider markets in a vacuum. As far as the long wave is concerned, the discussion has been so one-sided that there seem to be only two alternatives: that a catastrophic depression and financial collapse is imminent, or that the long wave does not exist. The evidence supports an alternative view, that a long wave does, in fact, exist, but that a down wave has recently passed unnoticed. The turn has been missed because history, as usual, did not repeat in exactly the same way. The downturn in the 1930s was short and sharp and was accompanied by deflation. The latest downturn was shallow and much more drawn out, concealed behind high inflation.

One objective of this book is to draw attention to the international linkages that exist between economies and markets, and include the possibility of international diversification. The United States is treated as the domestic economy, but many examples are used to show how the analysis can be, and has been, extended to other countries.

Many people, in different countries and covering various aspects of economics and markets, have contributed to the development of my current views. It is impossible to implicate everyone, although I shall always appreciate the part they played. Tony Boeckh helped me make the transition from theory to practice, while Bank Julius Baer provided invaluable experience of institutional fund management. The Investment Committee and senior analysts at the bank were most helpful, and I particularly appreciate the encouragement I received from Henri Looser and Helmut Saurer. Special thanks are due to Richard J. Fox whose professional support and friendship have enabled me to develop many of the indicators included here.

The production of a book like this requires help from a number of people, and I would like to thank Suzanne Grant, Jennifer Harnish, Elisabeth Legge, Nancy Mullin, Jessie Rae, June Riley and Jill Webster for their assistance with the many drafts, the data and the charts. Simon Ward, and an anonymous reviewer, read an early draft and provided useful comments. Finally, I would like to thank the editors for their support and encouragement.

Richard Coghlan

# Introduction

## *INVESTING IN THE FUTURE*

The aim of this book is to improve investment performance through understanding the cyclical behavior of the economy and the financial markets. There are many different markets and types of investing, and the business cycle touches all of them. In all cases, the most important piece in the jigsaw is a forecast of what is happening to the business cycle. With that background, investors should be able to take part in the upswings while avoiding the cyclical downturns, and to structure a portfolio that keeps risk to a minimum. Understanding the markets requires an understanding of how they interact with the rest of the economy. Action and reaction are important ingredients in the cyclical process.

This is not a disaster-round-the-corner book. In fact, a strong case is made that a long-term bull market started in 1982. There is no doubting the critical importance of avoiding a smash in asset values, and that is a major objective of this book, but it is also necessary to consider the counter danger of crying wolf at every turn in the stock market. Such fears have stopped many investors buying at the bottom of numerous cyclical downturns. The missed opportunities add up to considerable numbers; in sum, they certainly exceed any loss that might have been incurred. No bells were rung, no mass hand wringing or panic, but the lost opportunities have been equally dramatic. Even more dangerous is the possibility that investors will become inured to the constant warnings of catastrophe and ignore the one that matters.

Complacency is the enemy of caution and can lead to careless decisions. Improbable things do occur, and sometimes the impossible, but careful planning should eliminate most problems and reduce the impact of the rest. Avoid over-confidence, but also beware of the terminal bear. To this pessimistic animal everything is either bearish, or will result in some change that will be bearish. Excessive pessimism can mean losses just as much as excessive optimism.

In the short term, the business cycle is not dead and investment profits are not inevitable. The bad news is that asset markets are highly related to

1

the rest of the economy; if the economy goes into recession stock prices will fall. The good news is that asset markets are highly related to the rest of the economy. When the economy recovers, stock prices will go up. Asset prices do not move in a vacuum, somehow independent of what is happening within the rest of the economy. All markets are interrelated and need to be considered together.

Markets, both economic and financial, are highly complex. The financial markets are part of the mechanism that helps to drive the economic machine and hold it together. Taken outside of this context the financial markets have no meaning and no existence. They are both explained by what else is going on in the economy, and provide part of the explanation for outcomes elsewhere. In analysing behavior and forecasting the future, it is essential to recognize that the various markets are highly interrelated.

To state that everything depends on everything else may overstate the case, but it is a lot closer to the truth than the alternative extreme that each market is independent. One of the interesting implications of this extensive interdependence is that positive effects invariably have negative reactions. There is no one-for-one relationship, and it is possible for not very good news to have very bad effects, and vice versa. Failure to recognize the likely reactions to current events and policies results in a great deal of confusion, bad policy and poor investment decisions. Increasing awareness of the linkages that exist is the greatest single way that investors can improve their results.

Economics is above all about human behavior. It is about how people, on average rather than individually, react to the various incentives and constraints with which they are faced—how they make the choices that determine the allocation of resources. With that understanding it is at least possible to start realistically considering the possibilities.

Many investors view the financial markets like a casino, some win and some lose, and the stories that are told encourage the myths, mysteries, miracles and mirages of the markets. There is nothing like a good story, but it is not very helpful in making money. Fear makes good press—'the end is nigh' packaged up a lot more convincingly. This is understandable when so many investors are looking for a quick fix, and if financial markets are treated like a casino it is quite right to be afraid.

Like any other business, success is more likely through hard work and understanding. Hard work is necessary but understanding does not necessarily follow. This book aims to improve understanding in as easily digestible a form as possible. Strong conviction of a particular future path can result in spectacular gains and equally spectacular losses. The long-term survivors put greater emphasis on diversification; they recognize that it is a game of relatives rather than absolutes.

Investors should constantly challenge old thinking, look for flaws in the most obvious conclusions, question the assumptions and consider the alternatives. If all this seems like hard work, that is right, but it should not be cause for despair. Toynbee (1947) pointed out that civilization prospers under adversity; when challenge disappears decline sets in. In the same way, it is dangerous for investors to become complacent. Conditions are constantly changing, partly as lessons are learnt, and there are no rewards for replaying the same old game over and over.

The objective for any investor is to be in a position to anticipate major turns in markets and the economy. This requires taking the opposite view of majority opinion—what might be called a contrarian approach. By the time anything is obvious, i.e. has become the majority opinion, it will inevitably be too late to profit from the information. Contrarian, in this sense, does not mean doing the opposite of the majority just for the sake of it. After all, if the majority are *buying*, prices will go up. The time to sell is when the majority have *bought*. At that time, sentiment is extremely bullish, because the majority are long the market, but there is very little buying power left.

A key element of successful investment is the management of risk, avoiding the sharp stock price declines associated with cyclical downturns or, even more importantly, super-cycle downturns. This is achieved by adopting a consistent method to the process of investing and having reliable guidelines, or indicators, to provide discipline and signposts to the future. The indicators that will be discussed here have been tested under heavy fire, and have survived.

Investment recommendations are often made on the basis of a simple repetition of past successes or failures. The most common mistake is to draw conclusions from a particular event out of context. What happened in the past is plain enough to everyone, and common knowledge is rarely helpful for the future, since it is already discounted in market behavior. Much more important is understanding *why* things happened.

Increasingly, also, investors need to be aware of what is happening in other countries. Risks and rewards in the domestic market, even one as large as the United States, are dependent to some extent on events else- where. In addition, there will be opportunities in other countries that are not available within the domestic markets. By diversifying into other countries, investors are able to improve returns and reduce risk.

Most mutual funds have opted out of the market selection process alto- gether. The individual investor has been given the responsibility to decide what market, what country, etc., to invest in, and then the professional fund manager takes over the details. At one level this is an efficient way to achieve diversification within a market, but it leaves the individual with the hardest decision of all. It may seem easy in a prolonged bull market, but not so great during a downturn.

Essentially what has happened is that the mutual funds have provided a way of reducing what might be called micro-risk, i.e. the individual risk of any one company doing very badly, possibly even going bankrupt. The way to handle this risk is through company research and diversification. Diversification is essential, since even the best research may miss some important change that will ultimately undermine profits.

What this approach by the mutual funds does not do is avoid the macro-risk, conveniently passing that responsibility onto the individual investor. The macro-risk is the risk of every sector in every country synchronizing on the downside. This risk is associated with the business cycle, and longer-term economic cycles. Typically, investors find it difficult to deal with these macro-risks, while mutual funds have successfully found a way of avoiding the responsibility, although, not the reality—which does not change the conclusion that the hardest decision lies with the individual investor not the fund manager. This book is designed to help make these allocation decisions.

A popular suggestion to avoid this macro-risk is through various permanent hedging techniques. However, these are very expensive to operate and, as the experience in 1987 showed, do not always provide the insurance promised. The alternative solution offered here is to anticipate trouble before it arrives and take action in advance.

## Lies and damn lies

When it comes to considering the whys and the hows, and using the past to predict the future, it is important to keep history in the right perspective. Visual impressions can be very deceptive, as can a verbal description of those same events. Figure I.1(a) shows what has happened to the Dow Jones Industrial Average, nominal GNP and M2 over the course of this century. Charts like this are frequently reproduced in order to show how far con-ditions have deteriorated. The rise in money, prices, or whatever is shown, will clearly appear to be explosive, as in this example. But appearances can be deceptive. There are *lies, damn lies and statistics*, but the deception is even greater when those statistics are put into chart form.

To begin with, all these series are nominal, and higher nominal values in the present, and the past, do not necessarily imply anything about the future. Just because they have risen so high does not mean they have to fall. There is absolutely no justification for such a view. If the Dow had been plotted on its own it might have seemed much too high, but when shown with nominal income and money, it is clear that nominal stock prices have, if anything, lagged behind.

The chart itself is also very deceptive. As numbers get bigger, it requires more and more of an increase to achieve the same percentage change. For

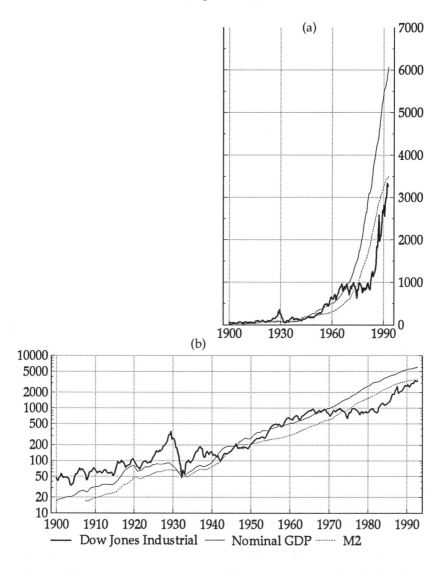

**Figure I.1** Money, the economy and stock prices (quarterly); (a) arithmetic, (b) logarithmic

example, an increase from one to two is 100 per cent, but starting at 50 the same percentage increase would require a move to 100. Figure I.1(b) shows exactly the same series as Fig. I.1(a), but plots them on a logarithmic scale. All that means is that percentage changes of the same size will measure the same distance up the side scale, thereby eliminating nominal size as a factor. The contrast with the chart of Fig. I.1(a) is striking. Now, everything looks to be back in proportion, and the apparent excesses have been eliminated.

Investors should beware of arguments, or charts, that are based on nominal series, particularly when considered in isolation. This also applies when buying stocks, or anything else. A one dollar stock is not necessarily cheap. It will be necessary to buy 100 times more shares of a one dollar stock than a 100 dollar stock in order to have the same effect on the portfolio. What makes a stock cheap is if there are good reasons to expect that the price will rise in the future. The starting price is not important.

## Back to the future

To invest is to make an assessment about the future. Each decision that an investor takes implies a view, a forecast, of the future. That may seem to be so obvious as not to be worth saying, but it is important since most investors do not usually see themselves as forecasters; many in fact are sceptical of professional forecasters—often with justification. But it remains the case that forecasts of the future are being made, and explicit recognition of that fact should result in better forecasts. The purpose of this book is to improve understanding of economic and market behavior as a way of improving the forecasting that is an indispensable part of investing profitably, and to enable timely decision making.

The essential characteristic of the future is uncertainty. A basic feature of the economy, and life in general, is that decisions are made under conditions of uncertainty—the future is unknowable. Market prices do not depend on the actions of a single individual but are determined in the aggregate, and it is impossible to know with certainty how the majority will act in the future. Frustration with this limitation of the human condition has caused some people to believe in crystal ball gazing, or divine guidance, despite otherwise rational behavior in other aspects of their lives. In essence, however, the only way to make a reasonable forecast of the future is by looking back at the past.

Unfortunately, interpreting what has happened often seems as difficult as forecasting what will happen. Past 'facts' are frequently revised, often substantially, and most statistical series are incomplete and require substantial estimation. Consequently, it is important to have a consistent framework for analysis, and to understand the relationships involved.

Only in that way can an individual have the confidence to make decisions at the crucial turning points: to extend a shaking hand to make the call to buy when all around are selling.

Even under normal circumstances, investment decisions have to take into account the expectations of the majority, and these, of necessity, will be short-term in nature. The further one looks into the future the more uncertain it becomes. For this reason, investment horizons are kept fairly short, and investors are usually prepared to get out of positions should market conditions change—even if the long-term expectation is un-affected. This flexibility, essentially the desire for liquidity, adds to the vola-tility of market prices.

There are those who take a long-term view and try to make decisions based solely on that expectation. However, that is not easy, since it means ignoring short-term fluctuations in the market value of their portfolios, and these can sometimes be extreme. The difficulty in staying true to one's long-term expectations stems from the existence of uncertainty. And the greater the uncertainty the harder it becomes to hold on to a consistent longer-term view.

One of the major effects of rapid, accelerating inflation is to raise the level of uncertainty about the future. This happened with the accelerating inflation of the 1970s, and was clearly evident in the German hyperinflation of the 1920s. As a result, investment horizons were shortened. Under these circumstances, long-term values receive less and less attention, and speculation is given increasing emphasis. Without a firm foundation in value, trend following becomes the norm, until that in turn becomes obvious and loses value. Such an environment increases volatility and raises the possibility of dominant trends in the market dictated by the latest fad to grip the imagination.

A long-term approach in this environment can prove highly profitable—in the long run. It is, however, a trader's market, and it will be difficult to hold on to an expectation, and a position, when faced with such short-term volatility. The majority will be traders and the majority will probably lose money, but enough will make spectacular gains to keep the promise alive. To survive, it is necessary to remain acutely aware of the risks involved, as well as the potential gains to be had.

There has been a dramatic increase in the emphasis given to the tech-niques of technical analysis over recent years, using past market behavior to identify trends in the future, and this bias has been reflected in the pro-liferation of technical books on markets. Such an approach works well when markets move in broad trends, and these trend-following techniques can play a role in the attempt to maximize investment profits. For this reason the principles of technical analysis are discussed in Chapter 10. However, one chapter clearly falls well short of making technical analysis the central focus of this book. In addition, it is argued in that chapter that many of the *technical* indicators are actually measuring economic conditions. The main objective here is also to identify and follow trends, but emphasizing a fundamental approach. When used properly, fundamental analysis will not only identify and explain trends, it can also provide important leading indicators of turning points.

## Understanding the system

This book sets out to explain how markets work. It describes and analyses the short-term and long-term cyclical behavior of the economy, and the major asset markets. The approach is based on the belief that knowledge is strength and assumes that any serious investor, or student of the markets, is prepared to invest some time in understanding the basic underlying forces that are at work in the economy.

Individuals are endowed with different strengths and weaknesses, but no Olympic runner ever won his or her race without a lot of effort, training and dedication. The same principle applies to life, work and the markets. There are certainly the lucky ones, who achieve big profits in the markets with no apparent effort. In some cases it is just that the effort is well disguised, but it is also the case that the law of averages must always favor a few. These lucky winners are not confined to the financial markets; there are also those who win the lottery, back the right horse, or beat the casino. There is no consistent pattern, no guarantee, and the odds are enormous. Even knowing that, however, does not diminish the magnetic attraction of easy money—no matter how illusory it is in reality.

While the majority are chasing dreams, the real winners are those who understand their own area of expertise; whether it is real estate, marketing, design, seventeenth-century furniture, French art glass, municipal bonds, low capitalized companies, gas turbine engines, or whatever. The particular specialization here is the behavior of the economy and markets over the business cycle. It will be shown how an understanding of these relationships can lead to a substantially improved profit performance.

Considerable emphasis over recent years has been given to the use of rules of trading, which run from the obvious, 'buy low, sell high' to recommendations not to meet margin calls, set stops on all positions, etc. There are many of these *rules* and they are not always consistent. These, moreover, do not constitute a total investment approach. At best they are little more than the basic rules of the road, like the highway code, and in many cases the rules do not apply. In addition, there is more to being able to drive than knowing the code of the road; and even the ability to drive is only one part of the skills and information needed on a journey from one point to another. And so it is when following the path towards higher profits.

By taking a position in the markets, an investor is betting on what will happen in the future. There is a great deal of information available on the interrelationships between one market and another, and between economic developments and the markets. By ignoring this information, investors are stacking the odds against themselves. Even the great speculators of history concentrated on the details of economic and political events. In the 1920s, the legendary Jesse Livermore employed a great many people, sifting a mass of information from around the world. He had a reputation as a great tape reader, i.e. technical analyst, but he knew that information was the key to profitable trading, and this was slotted into his own model of the world.

One lever to open a crack through which to catch a glimpse of the future is market action itself. It is, however, fatal to ignore what is happening to inflation, interest rates, growth, money, credit, the balance of payments or political trends. What has already happened is important for taking into account the effects these changes will have on investment opportunities. But it is also possible to go further and consider how changes in one sector will have repercussions elsewhere, which will in turn impact on other markets. A good example is the likely effect of accelerating growth of money and credit on short-term interest rates, and the reaction they have on stock and bond prices, the exchange rate and the economy generally.

Ultimately, prices are determined by fundamental forces. Stock prices anticipate profits, and interest rates reflect the demand for credit relative to the supply of money. The difference between understanding these fundamental forces at work and ignoring them can be compared to the difference between a trained soldier using the latest, most modern techniques of warfare, and an unarmed person wandering into the midst of battle. With extreme luck the naïve approach may produce a hero, but the odds are long, and a corpse is more likely. For the unwary the markets can be just as deadly.

The first priority is to understand the way the business cycle works. Understanding the causality involved allows early identification of turning points in the economy. This is important in itself, but more than that, being able to explain what is going on adds a degree of confidence that should improve decision making. One constant feature of turning points is that there are always many conflicting opinions about, and strident voices proclaiming, these views in the strongest possible terms. At exactly that point when clear thought and a steady hand are most needed, the air is filled with confusion and uncertainty. Not only is it necessary to have a view of where the economy and markets are headed, it is also necessary to have sufficient confidence in your opinion to make decisions when faced with strong appeals to the contrary, which too easily take root and feed upon uncertainty.

An independent view will be more easily maintained if the linkages which exist between the economy and the financial and commodity markets are well understood. There are clear relationships that have existed over history, firmly grounded in human psychology, and based upon responses to the incentives created. Market psychology plays a crucial role—a role that is missing in nature. Maintaining confidence is crucial in an uncertain world. A world in which the investor is faced with a wide range of competing pressures, reinforced by conflicting views, opinions and advice. If the behavior of a particular market can be related to what is going on in other markets and the economy in general, this will make it easier to act rather than wait, when action is what is demanded. At other times it will provide the confidence to stay your hand from the phone when others are proclaiming the certainty of massive profits, but only to those prepared to act *now*. Often the hardest decision to make is to do nothing.

Consistent expectations require some formal structure. The human mind is the most powerful computer available, but it is also highly flexible. The need to keep an open mind and avoid prejudice, and yet not be persuaded by each new piece of conflicting information, requires a discipline of some sort. The way to do that is by developing indicators of future market trends based on a thorough analysis of the past. This is by way of introduction to the indicators presented in this book.

Most of the indicators presented here have been in use for a long time, with little if any modification. These are discussed in the appropriate chapters. The different indicators are designed to improve decision making under conditions of uncertainty. The forecasts result from a careful study of history, using well-understood statistical techniques. However, the approach itself is unconventional. Everything is here to increase understanding of how the different markets interact together. Understanding that is essential to achieving consistent investment returns over the longer term, while at the same time controlling the amount of risk involved.

## Turning point behavior

Not everyone acts in the same way. Even in a panic liquidation there are some buyers, otherwise there would be no prices at all. What matters is the way the majority behaves; that is, the majority of those actually taking some action. The important reaction is at the margin, which tips the scales in one direction or the other. In the early stages of a market turnaround, it is not necessarily the case that the majority actually get bullish; it is usually only that sellers stop selling, or buyers stop buying.

The same pattern of behavior can be observed in economic decision making generally. In the early stages of economic recovery, manufacturers, distributors and retailers stop reducing inventories, or simply have to replace worn-out capital equipment, to maintain rather than expand production. At the margin, these reversals can be dramatic, gathering momentum as the incomes generated feed through to a wider range of producers and consumers. The opposite pattern shows up during the early stages of a slowdown in the economy.

At major cyclical turning points, it is not that people suddenly become bullish or bearish, that comes later. At the bottom the majority will be bearish, but will have already sold, and the selling pressure will have dried up. The reverse will happen at the top of a market. Under such conditions, when the majority has already committed themselves, a small number can easily become a majority as far as active buyers and sellers are concerned. Despite the fact that the volume of business will be small, this activity at the margin can have a large effect on prices. Small residual buying or estate liquidation, with no strong bullish or bearish bias, can, at such times, send prices sharply in one direction or the other. There is, of course, no way of knowing how any single person will react in a particular situation. Economics is not about the psychology of an individual but is all about the psychology of groups—how the majority will react at the margin to a given set of circumstances. Economics is often presented as abstract theory which seems to bear little relation to the real world. That is unfortunate, for it could not be further from the truth. Economics is, or should be, about how decisions are made in the real world, and how these impact on other people and markets. In its essence, economics is about the behavior of groups; about all the aspects of decision making in the aggregate.

Economists start by assuming rationality, which should not mean by assuming that the majority act like the particular economist doing the analysis. What it does mean is that people *on average* will behave in predictable ways when faced with particular incentives. For example, it is assumed and tested that, if nothing else changed, people would generally buy more of something the lower is the price (there can be certain exceptions); or that businessmen try to maximize profits (although other objectives like power and prestige are allowed); or that consumers will spend more the higher is their income, and so on—basic human forces and basic incentives and constraints. Clearly, each individual will react differently, but as a group it is possible to observe certain patterns of behavior that repeat over time and place.

While it is reasonable, in fact necessary, to assume that group behavior is rational, in the same way that when driving a car it is assumed that everyone will drive on the correct side of the road and stop at the traffic lights, it also has to be recognized that people in groups sometimes act in extreme, seemingly irrational, ways. There are times when people panic, and the emotion can spread through a crowd like wildfire. Under these conditions, a peaceful crowd can be turned into an unruly mob—a stampeding herd. Any who try to go against the herd are likely to be badly trampled, and it becomes rational to be irrational. No matter how rational an investment may seem on paper, and may actually be under normal circumstances or over the long term, it is foolish and very dangerous to go against the market at such times.

Such moments of irrationality are actually quite rare, despite the opinions of those who have been caught on the wrong side of the market, and they are extremely dangerous for precisely that reason. The silver speculation in 1979 fits into this category, as does the stock market mania in the 1920s. The crash in 1929 converted the hysteria into panic, but cannot properly be understood except in terms of the euphoria that preceded it. Other examples from history include the Mississippi scheme, originated by John Law, the South Sea Bubble and the tulip mania in the early seventeenth century. In Chapter 7 some of the major manias and crashes that have occurred in the past are considered in order to identify common characteristics for the future.

## Incentives versus controls

Adam Smith (1776) talked about 'the invisible hand' that guided the economy. Market economists since then have accepted the fact that the process of change can be described, and the forces involved can be understood. However, it has also been recognized that there is a secret ingredient, what John Maynard Keynes called 'animal spirits', that is essential to growth but which can never be fully understood or replicated artificially. For some people that is not acceptable. Rather than try to understand the workings of the economy better, they have tried to control it. The most extreme example has been the Soviet experiment in central planning, but it is also the nature of western governments to try to extend their control. Such attempts are only natural if some political body has accepted responsibility for particular sectors of the economy. Thus there have developed agricultural support programs, minimum wages, and a whole range of tax and incentive programs designed to achieve one objective or another. Inevitably, the result is not the one that had originally been intended. Even in controlled environments, the invisible hand is still at work.

The Soviet economy was plagued by inefficiencies resulting directly from the system of central controls, which is why it finally had to change direction. One of the classic examples is the true story of nail production. When orders came down that results were to be measured in terms of the number of nails produced, the factory produced millions of tiny nails which were no use to anyone. When the orders were changed to measure results by weight, the factory produced one huge nail, thereby fulfilling its quota with one enormous, unusable nail. The managers of the factory were probably shot, but they were, in fact, responding to the incentives created. Had profitability been used as the measuring rod these same managers would probably have led the field, but the scope for such initiative was squashed flat in the regime of directives from above. Another major example of the mischief worked by the invisible hand was in the appalling state of agriculture in the Soviet Union. Stories abound about the greater productivity of the small private agricultural sector, and the gross inefficiency and waste of the massive controlled sector. Finally, these inefficiencies were recognized and belated attempts made to allow a more competitive and efficient productive economy to emerge from the stifling cocoon of state stewardship, but it was too late.

Supporters of the market economy recognize that it is impossible to plan an economy; impossible to forecast which products and sectors will grow the fastest and which will fail. It is the same recognition, although not always explicit, which underlies the resurgence of interest in small businesses. Although it is a fact of life that a great many small companies declare bankruptcy each year, this is also where the large companies of the future are born. No government edict could plan the range of diversity, could think up the millions of ideas or take the total risk involved. Free competition allows individuals to experiment. Many of the ideas may well be crackpot, but the marketplace will quickly sift out the potential winners from the outright failures. And that process of sifting will continue all through the growth of these companies. *The freedom to succeed is inseparable from the freedom to fail.*

The decision of the marketplace can be cruel and harsh, and may even be unjust in some cases. The individual may suffer but the economy in general will benefit. The process is the economic equivalent of natural selection among plants and animals. Nature may be cruel and arbitrary in the case of the individual, but the surviving species are those best suited for their environment. The same thing is true of businesses in a market economy. The companies that survive and grow are those that are best suited to their environment. Governments should pay less attention to trying to achieve growth directly, and more on providing the right environment for growth. If the environment is too protective then the companies that have been protected by it will be placed at high risk when they are finally faced with competition. Even more harmful to long-term welfare is the fact that such a protective environment can only be maintained at the expense of smothering opportunities for new, as yet unborn, companies and industries.

Problems are also created, for example, in the shift from an inflationary to non-inflationary environment. Those best suited to grow with accelerating inflation are not the same ones that will do best once more stable conditions are re-established. Such shifts can be highly destabilizing to investors and businessmen alike. This is one way in which macro-economic mismanagement can have a negative impact on economic growth and prosperity.

There is a persistent demand from all sides for perfect forecasts of the future, but it should be clear that such knowledge is impossible. Its ability to surprise is the very heart and substance of a market economy. Fortunately, while it is impossible to determine the exact details of economic development far into the future, it is possible to identify some aspects of near-term trends. Also, although it is not possible to create growth artificially, it is possible to identify certain characteristics which, if they exist, are normally associated with success. Most importantly, it is possible to forecast macro-economic trends; imperfectly, to be sure, but at least with some success.

Most macro-economic forecasts assume that interest rates, government policies, exchange rates, etc. are given, and these have value in a planning context. However, in a dynamic forecast it is necessary to take these factors into account, and include the reactions of the authorities and these other markets as part of the forecast. Only in that way will the forecast be of value to investors and businessmen who are having to operate in the real world, and not in the refined atmosphere of a *what if* economy.

## Controlling risk

A first priority of any coherent investment strategy must be concerned with avoiding high-risk situations which can wipe out a large proportion of, if not total, wealth. There is an emotional aspect to any investment which is generally ignored when positions are taken on and optimism is high. Emotions frequently dictate actions and confuse clear thinking at the very time it is most required. Good decisions are more likely to be made if you can keep your head when all around are losing theirs. That is as true now as it was at the time of the French Revolution. Risk control is an essential requirement for all investors. The way to do this is always to hold a diversified portfolio, and consciously to consider the stage and condition of the business cycle. The greater the understanding of how the cycle works and the types of behavior involved, the more reliable expectations or forecasts are likely to be. Understanding the longer-term trends, and where we are in the process, will also raise the level of confidence.

In addition to the normal uncertainty of the market, there is also the risk of some unexpected or unknowable element changing the course of the economy and the markets. Some allowance can be made for the possibility of a particular event, but it is impossible to forecast earthquakes and other natural disasters with any accuracy. San Francisco has supposedly been falling into the sea every year since the great earthquake of 1906. A massive earthquake in Tokyo would have a devastating effect.

Understanding how people react to economic incentives over the business cycle will be a great help, even in these circumstances, in determining which direction the markets will follow and for how long. Just realizing that the markets are reacting to exceptional events that will be reversed adds to confidence, and makes it easier to make decisions. The business cycle is a regular phenomenon, although not in a mechanical way, and its movements can be forecast with a reasonable degree of accuracy. Armed with such knowledge there is no doubt that investors and businessmen can improve the profitability of their investments and, more important still, avoid the major risks which can wipe out their existing capital.

It is easy, much too easy, to devote exclusive attention to the investment opportunities that exist, while forgetting about the risks involved. With each new fad, some groups or individuals will attract attention with their wild claims for the price appreciation potential of the asset of their choice. It is always made to seem so obvious, and so easy, that values will double in hardly any time at all. What receives little or no mention is the potential for asset values to be cut in half equally quickly.

## The business cycle

The business cycle—the rhythmic behavior of the economy and market prices—is a well-known fact of life. These regular patterns of behavior were studied at great length by early economists, but have ceased to be the focus of attention of economists over the post-war period. The more recent emphasis has been on mathematical theory and econometric practice. One feature of econometric models has been that they tend to underestimate the cyclical behavior of the economy. Like the techniques of technical analysis, they are better at following trends than identifying turning points. Consequently, there is a tendency to extrapolate trends rather than anticipate changes in direction. A mathematical approach, on the other hand, tries to force cycles into a fixed, unchanging formula.

Investment would be easy if business cycles were uniform in length and amplitude—but they are not. For all their apparent regularity, each cycle has its own distinguishing characteristics that differentiate it from the others. There are innumerable cyclical and extra-cyclical forces at work against a changing background of economic, social, political and international pressures. Cycles are determined by the aggregate of individual reactions to the incentives created. The regularity is in the pattern of these reactions, not in the cycle itself. And each time, new factors have to be taken into account, as these have an effect on the timing and direction of the economy. Remarkably, the cycle still shows up but each time in a different form; this accounts for the ability of what is really a regular phenomenon continually to surprise.

A basic objective of this book is to show how the financial markets are linked to the economy, a simple fact sometimes forgotten in a world that has become increasingly technical. It might sometimes seem that the price of stocks or bonds, or whatever, today depends only on what happened to them yesterday. Yet it can be shown that prices in these financial markets follow similar cyclical patterns to economic events. There are cycles in all markets, and these are linked together through behavioral interactions. What happens in the financial markets, and other asset markets, are inseparable from the economy; they are, in fact, part of the economy. The relationships are complicated, which means that investment is also complicated. There is seldom any money to be made by doing anything that is obvious.

One of the many complicating factors is the existence of lags. There are lags between one thing happening and the repercussions elsewhere. Furthermore, just looking at the timing of events will not necessarily help. A well-known relationship that is misleading is that between stock prices and the economy. Stock prices change first and only later does the economy follow, and even then not always, and this had caused nearly everyone to conclude that changes in stock prices cause changes in economic activity. While there is some linkage, it is in fact very slight, and the reality is that both are responding to other cyclical forces. Understanding why, and how the cyclical process works, is essential to improving investment returns.

The up-phase of the cycle is associated with economic growth, increased employment, upward pressure on prices and improving stock prices. Initially, interest rates will be falling then stable, and finally the increased demand will start to raise credit demands and interest rates—leading to, among other things, a less positive or possibly inverted yield curve, as short-term interest rates rise relative to long-term bond yields. At some point, the economy becomes over-extended and starts to slow down, possibly moving into recession. A business cycle is typically thought to end with a recession. This is partly a question of definition, in that the cycle is only completed when a recession occurs. In reality, there are more periodic cycles, which I have called behavioral cycles. Sometimes the down-phase will result in a recession, while at other times there will only be a slow-down in the growth rate.

In the case of a recession, this first of all feeds upon itself, as demand is withdrawn from the economy. Companies consolidate and all groups reduce expenditure on durable goods. At an initial stage of recovery, demand stabilizes which sets up the conditions for eventual replacement demand of worn-out durables to make a significant impact on overall demand. The conditions are finally put in place by a fall in interest rates which reduces costs of production, and the cost of buying on credit; i.e. there is a beneficial effect on both demand and supply conditions.

Recovery of the economy will also be anticipated by the financial markets, with a large part of any cyclical move occurring before the economy has even turned up, let alone been identified as such. For example, the stock market started a cyclical bull phase in August 1982, but the economy did not bottom out until November of that year, and economists, politicians and everyone else were still arguing whether the recovery had started through the first quarter of 1983. By that time the Dow Jones Industrial index had risen by 44 per cent from its low point and was, in fact, in the process of hitting a short-term peak. Clearly, it is important for investors to anticipate the cycle rather than wait for confirmation from the economy itself, and that is what the indicators included in this book are designed to do.

## Beyond the cycle

While the business cycle is a major fact of life that investors ignore at their peril, there are important forces extending beyond that time frame which have to be taken into account. These are secular or long-term trends, often considered, quite reasonably, as part of a long-term, or super, cycle. Despite the long-term nature of such trends they still have a significant impact on the outcome of short-term investment decisions.

These secular, or super-cycle, trends are considered in this book as important inputs into investment decisions. Joseph Schumpeter, considered by many to be the major authority on the long wave, placed responsibility for the super-cycle on the waves of invention and innovation. From an investment point of view there is a clear association. The mass use of electricity created new markets and new companies, some of which produced phenomenal gains. Steel and heavy industry generally had a long run, but are now being replaced as the foundations of a modern economy. The secular shift towards a service-oriented economy has created major new opportunities, while telecommunications and computers have now embarked on a new accelerated phase in their cycle.

Each of these economic trends has created important investment opportunities, but also significant risks. The risks arise because each new development is usually at the expense of some traditional practice—tradition in the sense of expectations and the existence of entrenched interests. The introduction of the railways and the motor car devastated the horse-carriage trade, steamships replaced clippers, planes replaced ocean liners, plastics replace steel. New processes replace old, and so it goes on; for each winner there is generally a loser—if not in absolute terms, at least relatively. These effects have been felt across whole industries. Also, new products mean new industries and new companies, with no guarantees as to which will lead and which will fail.

Exceptional risks are created during the exhaustion phase of the long-wave cycle, when the economy can turn down sharply. There are some commentators who are very aware of this devastating potential. They are standing around the edge, waiting for the economy to fall into the pit. So far they have been disappointed but they keep waiting. Chapter 6 contains evidence that the downturn has been completed. The pessimists have been, and are, basing their expectation of disaster on a repeat performance from the 1930s. This is a classic example of looking at the symptoms and not the substance of what has been, and is, happening.

The negative side of the Kondratieff long wave has received so much attention that the long wave is now, almost exclusively, seen as meaning financial collapse, stock market crash, deflation and depression. If some-one mentions the long wave, it is automatically assumed they mean that they expect something very bad is about to happen. It is, however, a cycle, and is as much about growth and development as the other thing. There is need for an antidote for pessimism.

## The rest of the world

The dramatic improvement in communications, both physical and elec-tronic, has brought markets in different countries much closer together. Some decisions are made purely on the basis of local conditions, but increasingly there is an international pool of capital that moves around regardless of physical borders. Even what are thought of as local conditions may well be determined by decisions made thousands of miles away. For example, a farmer in the mid-west may be looking only at his local area, but the price for his output could well depend ultimately on demand in Russia or floods in China.

Just considering the more quantifiable risks opens up a world of new opportunities: gold mines in Australia and Canada, luxury automobile manufacturers in Germany, chemicals in Germany and the United King-dom, banks and other financial institutions in a variety of countries, etc. Not only does international diversification give access to different types of companies, different styles of management and different cost structures, etc., it also provides exposure to different economic conditions. Countries have their own tax structures, labor laws, regional policies, inflation rates, interest rates, etc., on top of which there are changes in exchange rates affecting international competitiveness and the return to international investors.

The market integration taking place in Europe represents a classic example of the opportunities available to investors only if they are prepared to look beyond the borders of their own country. First, there is the accelerating trend towards economic integration within western Europe. Second, there is the even more dramatic overthrow of communism, and the rapid movement towards democracy and free markets. How is it even conceivable to develop a consistent investment strategy without taking these changes into account?

International diversification is often seen as an activity that increases risk as the cost of increasing opportunity. But that would only be true if economic conditions were always better in the domestic economy, if government policies and tax laws were always more rational and the managers were always the best. Maybe the home economy is not always the best. Maybe the government will make mistakes, maybe the economy will go into recession or have relatively high and rising inflation. Under those sorts of conditions, international diversification provides an essential means of improving investment returns, while at the same time reducing risks.

Studies have shown that international diversification of both equities and bonds increases the average rate of return and reduces the standard deviation. Weighting portfolios in favor of the best performing markets can greatly increase the returns available. Of course, the ability to do that assumes a lot. However, as a rule of thumb, stocks do relatively better in the countries growing the fastest, and bonds do better where inflation is falling most rapidly. Country and market selection requires the sort of cyclical indicators for the different countries that are presented in this book. Selective diversification based on relative performance can be a very positive way to improve portfolio returns.

When it comes to international investing, movements in exchange rates can have a critical impact on the total return achieved in terms of dollars, or whatever the home currency might be. For stocks, there is an offsetting influence through the effect on competitiveness, whereas bond prices often move in the same direction. A significant decline in the exchange rate improves the external competitiveness of domestic companies. This may be reflected in higher sales or higher prices; either way, profit margins should improve. The total effect will be complicated further if the downward pressure on the exchange rate is resisted and interest rates are forced up. Also, imported inflation is likely to rise, which may put pressure on wages and prices in general. In the case of bonds, there are usually no beneficial offsets, although it obviously depends on the underlying currency and specific conditions at the time.

A falling currency lowers the total return to foreign holders, and will often be accompanied by higher yields, i.e. falling bond prices as well, but that is far from universal. The counterpart to this lower return to foreigners is that the return to domestic investors on their foreign holdings will be increased. International bond returns can, therefore, be very volatile, but it is still the case that combining these together through diversification yields increased returns and reduced standard deviation. An alternative, for those who wish to avoid the currency volatility, is to hedge their international bond exposure by selling the currency forward. This tends to reduce the standard deviation even further while still boosting the return available in the domestic market. Currency hedging is also possible, but more difficult and less justified, in the case of stocks.

Risk is minimized and return maximized when investment horizons are extended to include overseas markets. However, even those who wish to keep their money cocooned within national borders will make better investment decisions if they take external developments into account. The approach adopted in this book considers the United States as part of the world economy, and also includes separate chapters on the balance of payments, the dollar and other exchange rates and investment trends in international markets. While the emphasis in this case is on the United States as the domestic economy, a number of examples are included from other countries, and the same arguments apply for other industrialized economies.

# Section I

## *THE ECONOMIC BACKGROUND*

There are natural rhythms to the economy; just as a wave builds up, eventually spending its power on the beach, but remaining part of the process that creates the next wave. The process is not always obvious because there are waves within waves, and the underlying tide—like the trend of the economy—serves to complicate everything. In the case of the economy, these cycles are determined by human behavior. Understanding the cyclical fluctuations in the economy greatly enhances the potential for profiting in the financial markets, and can be used in conjunction with other more specific market approaches.

This first section sets out to provide an outline of the economic cycle, inflation, the role of money and credit. Also covered is the build-up of debt, and whether this is as frightening as it sometimes seems. The final chapter in this section deals with the long wave, or super-cycle. Some of the greatest and most irrational fears are associated with such long-term behavior, when a bear market becomes a blood-bath, and a recession turns into a depression. It is not irrational to fear the repeat of such periods in history, which can easily destroy wealth, but the basis for most expectations are more often founded on superstition than fact. Some examples of famous crashes are discussed in the next section, but here the long-wave cycle, with which these times are associated, is presented to round out the economic background. The conclusion is that there is evidence of a long-wave cycle, but that the downturn is already completed. The economy, and financial markets, are well into a long-term recovery phase.

The financial markets are intimately related to the rest of the economy. No great investigation is required to prove the basic point that cycles in stock and bond prices move in sympathy with the cycles of the economy and inflation. Stock prices may anticipate rising profits and/or falling interest rates but they do not typically rise ahead of falling profits, or to the accompaniment of sharply rising interest rates. The relationships are not absolutely precise but are still very close. There are short-term aberrations due to exceptional circumstances or, more usually, because forecasts of the underlying economic conditions were wrong. A precise link would only exist if the future were known with absolute certainty—a totally unrealistic and uninteresting condition.

A key element in these interactions is time. It takes time to recognize and accept that changes have taken place, and then to feed this new information into expectations. Then there is the time it takes to make decisions and carry them out. The results of these decisions may then take time to be completed. The decision to construct a new building, for example, will require planning permission, raising finance, etc., and then there is the actual construction, all of which could take a very long time. The same would be true of a decision to expand production facilities. Time is an essential element of a modern, market economy, and that introduces uncertainty. There is no escaping it; the future is not known by anybody.

The cycles in the economy and the markets interact, and are actually part of the continuing process. Continued economic expansion and higher inflation lead to higher interest rates which eventually slow demand and the economy, allowing inflation to fall and setting up conditions for a fall in interest rates. This simplest of illustrations does still show the importance of the interrelationships that exist. These movements will also react on the stock market, property, the exchange rate and the balance of payments, and may even affect political elections, thereby complicating the picture immensely, but that still covers only a fraction of the real world interactions.

# 1

## THE BUSINESS CYCLE
### (it just keeps turning)

Over the period of a few years, economic activity typically rises, falls, then rises again in a wave-like motion which has been categorized as the business cycle. It is important for investors and businessmen to be aware of what stage of the cycle they are in before they can properly evaluate the potential risks and rewards they face. Even more importantly, they need to be able to anticipate the timing and magnitude of the next stage of the cycle.

The business cycle is a regular phenomenon, but not so regular that it can be assumed to follow a fixed path that repeats in mechanical fashion over time. That is not the nature of human actions, and it is not the nature of the business cycle. There are many different events that affect the timing of the cycle, but remarkably it continues. Even the massive intervention of large-scale government has failed to eliminate the cyclicality of the market economy although, as we shall see, it has caused some changes.

The recurring nature of the business cycle is very impressive, and has caused most attention to be focused on the similarities of cycles over time. This is to some extent understandable, since it is the regularity of the cycle that has made it notable, and worthy of discussion at all. However, this effort has sometimes been so intense as to force the facts to fit the theory, by requiring greater regularity than could ever exist in the real world. This amounts to forcing square pegs into round holes, and has led to the neglect of some important changes that have taken place in the underlying character of the cycle.

Over time, explanations of the business cycle have changed, with emphasis shifting from one sector to another, but then the cycle itself has also changed. The fact that cycles have persisted despite major changes in the structure of the economy is a big clue that specific explanations which depend on the behavior of a particular sector are bound to be only partially correct at best, and misleading at worst. The persistence is also a major incentive to look for some general influence which has been present throughout.

Most descriptions of cyclical behavior fail to explain why the cycles in the different sectors are synchronized. This is a major weakness in such explanations. There is a normal presumption that effects, alternately positive and negative, flow from one sector to another through the technical pipelines of multipliers and accelerators. But why should the weakness in one sector spread to the rest of the economy, rather than the other way around? Recognizing a universal linking force provides important insights into the behavioral foundations of the business cycle.

There is definitely an observable cyclical pattern to economic activity and the financial markets, but not in an automatic or predetermined way. The secret to the business cycle is in the relationships that exist between the different parts of the economy, and the financial markets are an important part of the transmission mechanism. The actual cycles we observe are the result of a combination of circumstances, which differ from cycle to cycle. All have their origin in the fact that the process of change and growth takes time, and that the future is unknown. A consistent element is the behavioral relationships that persist over time. There are, in fact, cycles within cycles which are systematic, but behavioral rather than automatic.

There is no single pattern that is repeated every time; nothing in life is that easy. Not that important lessons cannot be learned from the past. Expectations feed on experience, good or bad, and are also cyclical. The learning process only affects the timing, it does not eliminate the cyclicality. What it does do is ensure that each new cycle is different from the last. This learning process, which is an integral part of human behavior, is a major reason why it is unrealistic to expect the business cycle to follow the same regularity that is found in nature. It is partly this learning process that determines differences in cycles. In addition, it is necessary to recognize that the players change; there is a constant process of renewal and replacement, and one constant feature of each new generation is that it has to learn for itself. The body of knowledge that is passed on increases all the time, but the practice of life has to be learned by each individual.

The differences between cycles affect the timing, and keep the uncertainty alive. Sometimes these differences are very important from an investment point of view. They could arise because of the timing of elections, domestic or international political events, an assassination, extremes of weather, a major earthquake, etc. Some of the effects of these particular circumstances will be slight, in other cases they could be quite significant. The bigger the initial economic effect, and the greater the surprise involved, the greater the reaction is likely to be in the financial markets. These are all items that ensure that the future remains uncertain.

In any economic downturn certain groups will suffer badly. The most obvious will be those industries or skills which are in decline anyway, but where the trend may have been disguised by general strong growth or direct government support. These experiences can be quite devastating, and over time cause major shifts from one industry to another. Modern support programs have slowed down adjustment and delayed change. On the other hand, the process of change is sped up by rapid population growth, a socially and geographically mobile labor force, a large pool of liquid capital and the entrepreneurial drive to innovate and initiate change. The existence of these conditions in the United States has enabled the economy to change and keep growing. Growth disguises the pockets of weakness, but these are exaggerated during recessions. The pain and dislocation of recession is also the knock of opportunity which opens doors to change and growth in the future.

In this chapter, some background to the business cycle is provided, with an explanation as to the importance of interest rates in synchronizing the different cycles. There is a description of a typical synchronized cycle, and an explanation of the behavioral cycles that underlie the whole process. The question of how the stock market fits into the business cycle is given special attention. Stock prices lead the economy but do not determine the cycle. In Chapter 2 there is a discussion of the way in which inflation has changed within the cycle. An important change has taken place in the way in which the monetary authorities respond to the cycle, and this has altered the cyclical relationships. In particular, the world has shifted from attempts, generally unsuccessful, to achieve price stability to achieving inflation stability.

## Mechanical cycles

Business cycles come and go, that is their nature. Repetition is a constant that can be relied upon, but so too is the fact that each new cycle is different from the one just ended. Cycles come in many different shapes, sizes and types. There are long cycles and short cycles, shallow cycles and high cycles, fast–slow, broad–narrow, thin–fat; there are noisy cycles and quiet cycles, inflationary cycles and deflationary cycles. Some cycles start explosively but end on a whimper, others start slowly but end suddenly and dramatically. Still others go straight up and then straight down.

Despite this diversity, it is possible to identify a pattern to economic activity which clearly justifies being called a cycle. From that observation, which is remarkable enough, have developed attempts to justify and prove the existence of a constant, mathematical regularity which can be plotted with the precision of the earth revolving around the sun, or the moon around the earth. Such constancy in human behavior would be truly fantastic, and attempts to prove it have inevitably been doomed to failure. However, attempts to establish such mechanical rules still continue.

To follow fixed signposts along an unchanging, pre-charted course is a journey to disaster. The business cycle is not determined by a mechanistic formula, operating with the regularity of a cuckoo clock. In order to profit from the regularities of the business cycle it is necessary to understand what causes certain patterns of behavior to be repeated, and combine this information with the secular trend. It is no use simply expecting the past to be repeated in exactly the same way over and over again in the future, comforting as such a prospect might be. In fact, a little thought shows that such repetitiveness is impossible. Once precise regularity had been identified, people would attempt to profit from it by trying to anticipate events. These actions would themselves change behavior and the cyclical pattern. For example, if bond yields were widely expected to rise over the next year on the basis of past cycles, then no one would wait; everyone would sell today, with the result that yields would rise immediately.

The growth cycle of plants and animals, and the many general cycles which exist in nature do not depend upon the expectations of those involved. The ability to think generates expectations and these in turn cause reactions in human behavior. This feedback to decision-making creates a loop that is missing in nature, and it is this more than anything which ensures that the economy does not follow fixed, mechanical cycles.

A listing of recorded business cycles through the nineteenth and twentieth centuries clearly fails to demonstrate a repeating cycle of mechanical regularity. The various writers who have chronicled the business cycle do not show unanimous agreement on exactly when the cycles occurred in every case. But that provides additional support for my contention that there are cycles within cycles, wheels within wheels. Table 1.1 provides a chronology of business cycles according to some of the senior analysts who have documented them. The average of all of these is approximately five years, but that does not mean a lot. There has been a wide dispersion around this mean value, while the severity of the recessions and strength of the recoveries have hardly been uniform.

What is constant is not the precise timing of the cycle, but rather the economic and investment behavior of individuals in aggregate. From what was said above, it is necessary to allow for the fact that the majority will learn from experience. For example, they may not react initially to an acceleration of inflation, because it is expected to be temporary and quickly reversed. However, if the inflation continues, falsifying the original assumption, then expectations will soon change. And as we shall see, the change in expectations is itself an important piece in the jigsaw explaining the cyclicality of the economy and financial markets.

## Sun spots, agriculture and construction

One early explanation of the business cycle was the *sun-spot* theory advanced by Stanley Jevons. This had the attention-grabbing attraction of

Table 1.1 Recorded business cycles over the nineteenth and twentieth centuries

| AYRES† | Duration | HICKERNELL† | Duration | MITCHELL† | Duration | NBER† | Duration | DEPARTMENT OF COMMERCE | Duration |
|---|---|---|---|---|---|---|---|---|---|
| | | 1819–1822 | 8 | 1822 | | | | 1949(10)–1954(5) | 4.5 |
| | | 1823–1833 | 11 | 1825 | 3 | | | 1954( 5)–1958(4) | 4 |
| | | 1834–1838 | 5 | 1837 | 12 | | | 1958( 4)–1961(2) | 3 |
| | | 1839–1843 | 5 | | | | | 1961( 2)–1970(11) | 9 |
| | | 1844–1849 | 5 | 1847 | 10 | | | 1970(11)–1975(3) | 4.5 |
| | | 1849–1854 | 6 | | | | | 1975( 3)–1980(7) | 5 |
| | | 1855– | | 1857 | 10 | | | 1980( 7)–1982(11) | 2 |
| | | –1860 | 6 | | | | | 1982(11)– | (7+) |
| | | 1861– | | | | 1867(12) | 3 | **Average** | **4.5** |
| | | –1867 | 7 | 1873 | 16 | 1870(12) | 8 | | |
| | | 1868–1878 | 11 | | | 1879( 3) | 6 | | |
| | | 1879–1885 | 7 | | | 1885( 5) | 6 | | |
| | | 1886– | | 1884 | 11 | 1888( 4) | 3 | | |
| | | | | 1890 | 6 | 1891( 5) | 3 | | |
| | | –1894 | 9 | 1893 | 3 | 1894( 6) | 3 | | |
| | | 1895–1897 | 3 | | | 1897( 6) | 3 | | |
| | | 1898–1900 | 3 | | | 1900(12) | 3 | | |
| | | 1901–1904 | 4 | 1903 | 10 | 1904( 8) | 3.5 | | |
| | | 1904–1908 | 4 | 1907 | 4 | 1908( 6) | 4 | | |
| | | 1908–1911 | 3 | 1910 | 3 | 1912( 1) | 3.5 | | |
| | | 1911–1914 | 3.5 | 1913 | 3 | 1914(12) | 3 | | |
| 1834(10)–1838(5) | 3.5 | | | | | 1919( 4) | 4.5 | | |
| 1838( 5)–1843(2) | 5 | 1915–1922 | 7.5 | 1920 | 7 | 1921( 7) | 2 | | |
| 1843( 2)–1848(12) | 6 | **Average** | **6** | **Average** | **7.5** | 1924( 7) | 3 | | |
| 1848(12)–1854(12) | 6 | | | | | 1927(11) | 3 | | |
| 1854(12)–1858(1) | 3 | | | | | 1933( 3) | 5.5 | | |
| 1858( 1)–1861(9) | 3.5 | | | | | 1938( 6) | 5 | | |
| 1861( 9)–1865(12) | 4 | | | | | 1945(10) | 7 | | |
| 1865(12)–1870(10) | 5 | | | | | 1949(10) | 4 | | |
| 1870(10)–1879(3) | 8.5 | | | | | **Average** | **4.0** | | |
| 1879( 3)–1885(9) | 6.5 | | | | | | | | |
| 1885( 9)–1888(7) | 3 | | | | | | | | |
| 1888( 7)–1891(4) | 3 | | | | | | | | |
| 1891( 4)–1894(6) | 3 | | | | | | | | |
| 1894( 6)–1896(9) | 2 | | | | | | | | |
| 1896( 9)–1900(11) | 4 | | | | | | | | |
| 1900( 4)–1904(8) | 4 | | | | | | | | |
| 1904( 8)–1908(5) | 4 | | | | | | | | |
| 1908( 5)–1911(6) | 3 | | | | | | | | |
| 1911( 6)–1914(12) | 3.5 | | | | | | | | |
| 1914(12)–1919(3) | 4.5 | | | | | | | | |
| 1919( 3)–1924(7) | 5 | | | | | | | | |
| 1924( 7)–1933(3) | 8.5 | | | | | | | | |
| 1933( 3)–1938(5) | 5 | | | | | | | | |
| **Average** | **4.5** | | | | | | | | |

† AYRES—L. P. Ayres (1940), *Turning Points in Business Cycles*, The Macmillan Company, New York.
HICKERNELL—W. F. Hickernell (1928), *Financial and Business Forecasting*, Bureaus of Business Conditions.
MITCHELL—W. C. Mitchell (1923), *Business Cycles and Unemployment*, National Bureau of Economic Research.
NBER—National Bureau of Economic Research, as reported by R. C. O. Mathews (1959), *The Trade Cycle*, Cambridge Economic Press.

linking human activity to a physical phenomenon. There was probably an element of truth in the sun-spot theory. It is instructive to understand why it may have been valid, and why it is no longer, since this will help to emphasize the persistent elements of the cycle.

The sun-spot theory, which was defined by Jevons (1875; 1878), was based on a crop cycle. Jevons measured the typical cycle to be 10.3 years (note that this is double the historical average identified above), while sun spots averaged 10.45 years. The link was made through the proposition that rainfall and general atmospheric conditions were dependent on solar variations caused by the 'alternate increase and decrease of area of the sun spots'. The size of harvests in turn determined the confidence of merchants and bankers, and the size of credit demand and supply.

It is easy to see how sunspots might have affected an agriculturally based economy. What is even more understandable is why people would have *thought* there was a relationship. Ancient civilizations that depended on the weather had elaborate theories about the relationship that existed between human actions and the weather. Many of these involved rituals and, quite often, sacrifices which would allow them, in turn, to influence the weather. Figure 1.1 shows the pattern of monthly sunspot behavior since 1900. Also plotted there is the rate of change of industrial production and the stock market. The relationship between these two and sunspots is very poor throughout the whole period, not only over the more recent period when the character of the economy has clearly changed.

There is no longer a close relationship between business cycles for the economy as a whole and the cycles in agriculture. Certain areas will suffer badly when harvests are bad or prices depressed, but the overall economy is little affected. Not only has agriculture become a smaller and smaller portion of the economy, but also the improvement in communications has made a sudden shortage of domestic raw materials less important. At the time Jevons was writing, agriculture at home and abroad was still widely recognized as an important determinant of general economic prosperity, although that connection had already been reduced substantially by rapid industrialization.

Warren F. Hickernell noted, 'The dependence of employment conditions and manufacturing prosperity in Great Britain upon the harvests in India was an accepted fact' in the nineteenth century. However, agriculture has long since ceased to dominate the rest of the economy, at least within the developed countries. Even at that time, the importance was almost certainly exaggerated. Events within the United States during the first half of the 1980s provided dramatic evidence of the independence between agriculture and the rest of the economy. The farming sector suffered nothing short of a depression, during which time the rest of the economy enjoyed a strong recovery.

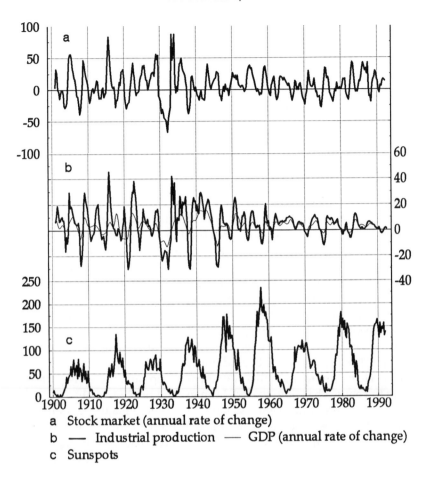

a   Stock market (annual rate of change)
b   —— Industrial production   —— GDP (annual rate of change)
c   Sunspots

**Figure 1.1** Sunspots and the economy

As agriculture became less important and manufacturing industry came to dominate, so theories of the business cycle adapted. Emphasis shifted to the production of durable goods, including housing. In the case of long-lasting goods, of which construction is the longest, changes in demand and supply have the greatest cyclical effect. An increase in supply, as the result of a rise in demand, will stay in existence and raise the quantity available. Purchases of durable goods can be postponed relatively easily by continuing to use the existing stock for longer or more intensively. If demand falls back to the old level, supply will be too high and production will, therefore, have to be cut back.

It has often been argued that the real estate cycle is particularly significant for the overall cycle, since there are many important side-effects. New houses, and even old ones, have to be furnished; roads have to be built; new communities require shops, libraries, schools, hospitals, etc. There is a whole infrastructure associated with housing that is missing with other forms of investment, and which may help to generate a full-fledged business cycle. In fact, the real distinction is between the scale of the investment. Any large-scale investment must be associated with similar infrastructure arguments. Massive investment in airplanes requires airports and transport facilities to service them. A huge investment in automobiles requires roads, gas stations, garages, etc.; and so it goes on. Housing is really no different except in the size of the sector and the scale of the investment involved.

A real estate cycle of 18.3 years was identified through the nineteenth century which appeared to work well until the 1950s, but then seemed to break down. Interestingly, there was also an 18.2 year cycle in marriage rates, and an 18.2 year cycle of immigration into the United States. The real estate cycle did not exist in isolation and was, therefore, likely to change if these inputs changed. What is missing is population growth through births, which would become a more important influence as immigration slowed down. Also, rising living standards, and a more equal distribution of income and wealth, will have the effect of increasing the demand for housing. These trends have been dominant over the post-war period.

The cycle of immigration that was apparent up until the early part of the twentieth century has now ceased. Immigration peaked, in absolute terms, in the early years of this century. There were three major peaks from the 1850s to the 1910s which were at or above 1.5 per cent of the population. Since the lows in the 1940s and 1950s the percentage has risen gradually, but remains below 0.3 per cent of the population. The cyclical pattern has gone. Here was another physical phenomenon that could well have imparted a cyclical influence in the past, but which has now changed.

In addition to the 18.2 year real estate cycle, a residential construction cycle has also been identified, lasting 33 months. Dewey (1971) called this 'one of the best substantiated cycles in our files', at least up until 1955. This cycle showed up in the rate of change of residential construction. Since that time, a clear cycle has shown up in the actual construction levels. This is, after all, the change in the stock of housing which is actually what is important. The rate of change of the flow follows a similar pattern, and it does not fit into a 33 month cycle.

Figure 1.2 shows three measures of the construction industry along with a leading indicator of the cycle. Housing starts and private housing building permits move together. It is often argued that permits are a leading indicator of starts, but there is little evidence of such a relationship. Commercial and industrial building contracts (shown at the top) do, however, lag behind

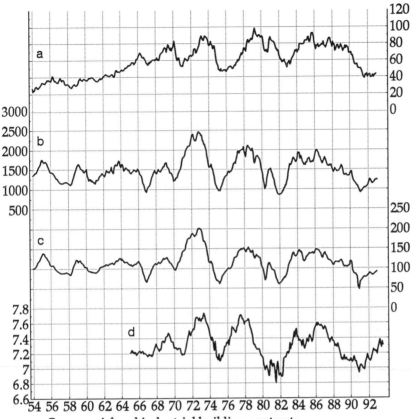

a Commercial and industrial building contracts
b New private housing starts
c Building permits for private housing
d Building cycle indicator

**Figure 1.2** Housing starts and building permits

housing starts and permits by approximately six to nine months. There are
good reasons for the existence of this lag. The corporate sector reacts more
to profits than it does to interest rates and credit conditions directly. The
main effect is only felt once these economic effects have spread through to
the bottom line. The cycles are very clear over this period, but they are not
33 months long and they are not uniform in length.

## Synchronizing cycles

The process of expansion and contraction can be observed for particular sectors throughout history, but that does not explain why the whole economy should go through periodic cycles. There are links between sectors, but that alone is not sufficient to explain macroeconomic cycles, since the links work in *both* directions. A downturn in one sector will have a negative impact on other sectors, but if the major part of the economy is still growing this will have positive feedbacks on the weak sector. Practically all explanations of the business cycle assume a degree of synchronization that has itself to be explained. In reality, there are cycles within cycles, moving at different speeds and with different patterns.

Keynesian explanations of the cycle, the so-called 'multiplier-accelerator' models, essentially assume a degree of synchroneity rather than prove it. In these models, demand spreads through different sectors as additional incomes are spent, creating new incomes which are spent, etc., and this interacts with companies that respond to expanding activity by increasing investment spending which raises incomes, etc. And, of course, the whole process also works in reverse.

These linkages clearly do work in this way, and the models make an important contribution to understanding how the process continues once it gets under way. These are often combined with floors and ceilings, as proposed by Hicks (1950), but this only provides physical restraints on explosive behavior. What these models do not do is explain how the process gets started in the first place: why the synchronization? Multiplier and accelerator models were originally designed to explain the interaction between companies and with overall demand. These have since been applied to the economy in aggregate, assuming a degree of uniformity that need not exist, but which is central to the cycle working in the way suggested. If companies started off at different times so that the timing of their cycles overlapped, it would be possible to create an example in which increases in demand in one area were being offset by downturns elsewhere. In each case the multiplier and accelerator effects could work, but in opposite directions, so there would be no cycle. Output under these conditions would simply follow the trend rate of growth, even though the individual sectors might be highly volatile.

When talking about the business cycle, there is a tendency to think that all businesses are moving in the same direction, but that is clearly not the case. This is true of other, more specific, explanations of the business cycle. There are always new products being created and new companies formed. What causes the cycle is the behavior of the majority. The Keynesian multiplier/accelerator models fail in their prime task of showing how the business cycle works. Once a general contraction, or recovery, is underway then the multiplier/accelerator effects will be observed; they are influencing the extent of the cycle but not determining it.

The existence of a business cycle in particular sectors does not necessarily mean that there will be an observed cycle in the economy as a whole. Certain industries may be depressed, and on more than a short-term cyclical basis, e.g. the making, and servicing of horse-drawn carriages in the early years of the twentieth century, but these need not pull the rest of the economy down. Superimposing secular trends, as in the example above, makes it clear that it is impossible to draw conclusions for the economy as a whole on the basis of a single sector.

A clear example of the confusion is given by Mitchell (1950), who said that, 'Even when a revival of activity is confined at first within a narrow range of industries or within a single section of the country, it soon spreads to other parts of the business field'. He then goes on to describe the sort of demand and supply effects that were outlined above. But why should the effects from one sector be dominant, and determine the outcome for the economy generally? If one sector is growing and another declining, while others are in different stages of development, why should any one dominate? And which one? Feedback effects will be working in all directions.

In the major part of the 1980s, the US economy in aggregate experienced a sustained recovery, but the agricultural sector was left behind totally. Agriculture, in fact, was in the depths of a depression during the first half of the decade, which was only slightly alleviated by the growth of demand. The sector was suffering from the extreme over-expansion which took place in the 1970s, in response to the incentives of rapidly rising commodity and land prices, and low real interest rates. This was followed by the return of high real rates of interest and an extremely strong dollar.

The crucially important point to realize here is that, despite the depressed state of the agricultural sector, the rest of the economy experienced a strong cyclical recovery, and also that, despite the strong economy, agriculture still did not join in. This experience, better than anything else, should illustrate the error of assuming that the influence of one sector is automatically transmitted to the rest of the economy. Other examples can be found in the contrary behavior of the oil sector, or housing in large parts of the country.

All sectors exhibit cyclical patterns but not always at the same time. There are times when certain sectors will follow a different cycle to the majority. That has always been the case and always will be. Despite that, there is still a business cycle which affects the majority, and the question is, why? The fact that all sectors have inherent cyclical tendencies built into them is not a satisfactory explanation of itself, although it does reinforce the cyclical movement once it has been created.

Some sectors are more cyclical than others, and these are the ones that use large amounts of capital in one form or another, which include some types of agriculture in its present form, and those that produce capital goods for others to use. These sectors experience the widest swings and are the most sensitive to changes in interest rates. The link with interest rates is not coincidental and introduces the single most important influence behind the business cycle. Changes in interest rates have a pervasive effect over a wide range of the economy; not only do they impact on demand, they also have an important effect on the cost of production and, therefore, supply.

There was a time, in the period of high Keynesianism, when interest rates were largely ignored. When they were introduced they were incidental to the main story. Businessmen, when interviewed, reinforced this belief by claiming that interest rates did not influence decision making. That just meant that they were employing a poor model of the world. They waited until rising interest rates reduced profitability, by which time emergency action was required. Monetarists further de-emphasized interest rates by concentrating attention exclusively on the growth of money. Gradually interest rates are coming to be recognized as an important determinant of economic behavior, but their true significance is still not fully appreciated.

A recession hits when more than a few of the different sectors synchronize on the downside. When this happens it is not normally an accident, but results from a deterioration in financial conditions. The normal, and expected, effect works through an increase in the cost of credit or money, i.e. the rate of interest. A worse reaction is created by an actual breakdown in confidence in the financial system altogether, such as happened in the 1930s.

*Interest rates are the key to synchronizing enough different sectors of the economy to produce a business cycle.* Cycles will differ depending on the changing composition of the economy, and the cyclicality of the dominant sectors. The final outcome will also be determined by the force that is driving interest rates. They could rise because of an excessive budget deficit, a crisis in external confidence, accelerating inflation, etc. There is no set rule, and the originating pressure is likely to be different in each cycle. That is to a large extent because of the learning process.

Hawtrey (1928) came closest to describing an interest rate model of this type, but within the context of his time. The financial system was much more unstable in the period Hawtrey was looking at, but the feast or famine reactions of the credit markets, and the banks in particular, can still be found today. Interest rates will affect a wide range of different sectors of the economy, producers and consumers, and provide the missing link to make an accelerator/multiplier model apply to the economy overall. The rate of return, interest, played a key role in agriculture even before the development of sophisticated credit markets. The rate of return demanded on deferred consumption would rise if inventories were in short supply. Future production required saving some of the crops in order to provide seed for the next planting.

The essence to understanding the business cycle is understanding the significance of rates of change. Typically, a fall in interest rates will result in increased spending—investment or consumption. The important thing has been the change in interest rates, not the new level. So, unless interest rates continue to fall, the rate of change comes back to zero and interest-sensitive spending will follow it, at least at the margin. Production gears up to produce in anticipation of continued growth only to find that demand has actually started to slow. As a result, inventories rise, costs increase and production will soon turn down as well. That will mean lower incomes, possibly more unemployment and still lower demand. This opens up the possibility of an overshoot on the downside, and the creation of a cyclical motion.

## Defining the cycle

The more basic an economy, i.e., the closer it is to nature, the more likely it is to be subject to some natural cycle. The yearly cycle of spring, summer, fall and winter is the most obvious cycle of all. However, the cycles that we are interested in are man-made, and result from changing supply and demand conditions. These exist even in an agricultural economy once it has extended beyond basic subsistence, and has become part of a market economy, where the output is sold on the open market.

Each cycle has its own special characteristics, differing in terms of depth, duration and detail. At the same time, however, there are many common elements, and it is possible to identify four major stages, like the seasons of the year; these are:

1. Recession—winter
2. Base building—spring
3. Recovery—summer
4. Maturity—autumn

When it comes to describing the business cycle there is always the problem of where to start. While any such position is arbitrary, the usual approach is to begin with the recovery. It is actually easier to begin with the recession phase, and that is the starting point here. Figures 1.3 to 1.6 show the movement of the main cyclical series discussed here.

Interest rates will have been rising for some time before the onset of recession, particularly in real terms, i.e. after taking account of expected inflation. In this period interest rates will normally continue to rise, and now have an increasingly negative effect on demand and corporate costs.

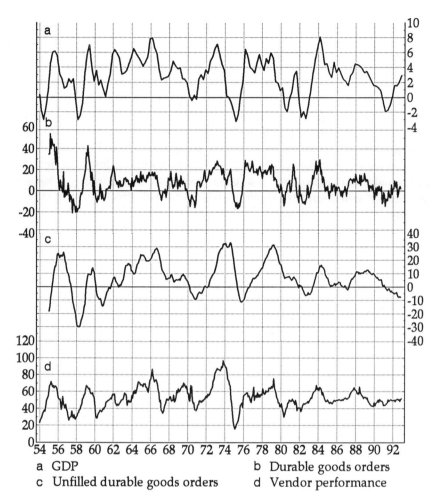

a  GDP                                    b  Durable goods orders
c  Unfilled durable goods orders          d  Vendor performance

**Figure 1.3** Durable goods and vendor performance (12-month rates of change, except vendor performance)

Companies are caught in the jaws of a powerful pincer, with the power of the force directly proportional to the capital intensity of the products they sell and the production process used.

Higher interest rates will have a direct negative effect on a wide area of the economy, and the effects will feed from one sector to another, both through the reduced spending of workers laid off, and the reduced spending of corporations faced with declining demand and revenue, and rising inventories and costs. The hardest hit industries will be those that typically use capital-intensive methods of production, sell on credit and are

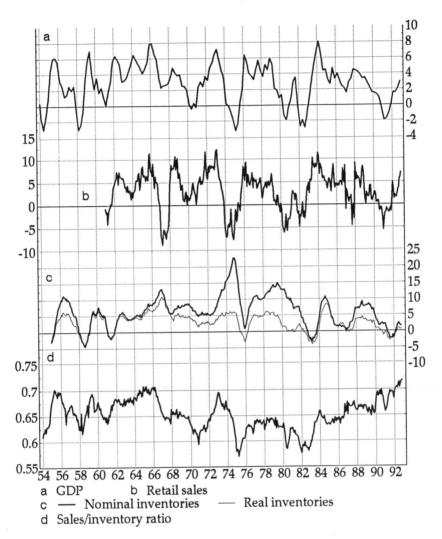

a  GDP          b  Retail sales
c  —— Nominal inventories   —— Real inventories
d  Sales/inventory ratio

**Figure1.4** Inventories and sales (12-month rate of change,
except sales/inventory ratio)

required to hold large inventories, e.g. the automakers, steel, machine
tools, construction, etc. Demand in these sectors can fall a long way and
very quickly. Being large items, it is often possible to postpone purchases,
as, for example, in the decisions whether to purchase a new automobile or
not. Moreover, there are generally highly active secondary markets for
most used durables. As a result, these generally exhibit very pronounced
cyclical patterns.

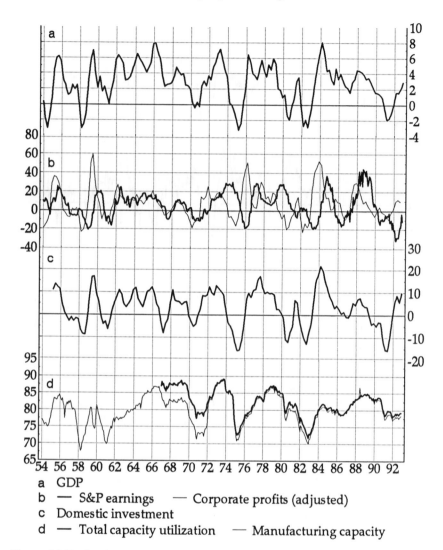

a   GDP
b   — S&P earnings    — Corporate profits (adjusted)
c   Domestic investment
d   — Total capacity utilization    — Manufacturing capacity

**Figure 1.5** Profits, investments and capacity use (12-month rates of change, except capacity utilization)

At the same time, costs in these capital-intensive industries will increase sharply as interest rates rise, making it hard to earn a profit even if demand remains high. However, demand does not remain constant, it actually falls, again under the powerful influence of higher interest rates, thereby

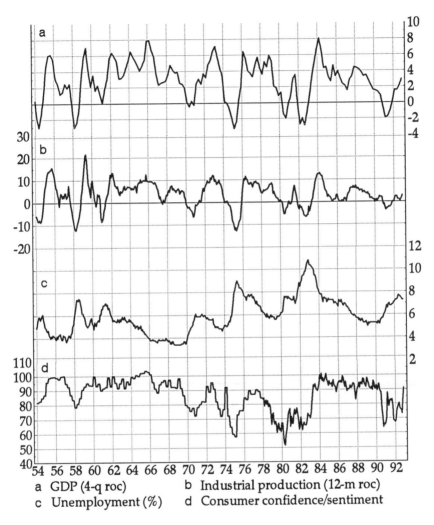

a  GDP (4-q roc)             b  Industrial production (12-m roc)
c  Unemployment (%)      d  Consumer confidence/sentiment

**Figure 1.6** Production, unemployment and confidence

squeezing margins even more. Mass production techniques require high volume, so that reduced output will generally result in a substantial increase in unit costs. If that were not enough, the dynamics of the situation are such that inventory levels are likely to rise significantly, counter to the desires and intention of management. The result is a sharp increase in inventory/sales levels. These inventories then have to be financed at the higher level of interest rates, adding still further to the already mounting costs.

Most past theories of the business cycle have relied heavily on the existence of an inventory cycle to explain the cycle in the overall economy. This represents a confusion of symptoms with causes. Rising inventory levels in a recession is not the cause of the recession, but is the result. They can play a role in the transmission mechanism but, as recent experience shows, recessions are not dependent on high inventory levels. If inventories increase significantly in the recession, these will have to be drawn down before production kicks in, thereby delaying the recovery. Better inventory control will take away this buffer between production and demand. Production will, therefore, respond more quickly both on the downturn and upturn phases.

Even with better inventory control methods it is impossible to avoid inventory effects completely, particularly in capital-intensive industries. Successful attempts to anticipate an increase in inventories only accelerate the cut-backs in production and speed up the cycle—they certainly do not eliminate it. What this means is that attempts to control inventories could help determine the cycle, even with only small changes in actual inventory levels, if producers anticipate the changes correctly, rather than wait for them to happen; it is the difference between reacting *ex ante* or *ex post*. There is an inventory control cycle, in effect, even if observed inventories fail to increase.

The effect of this combination of circumstances on corporate profitability and cash flow is likely to be devastating, and attention will increasingly become focused on ways to improve the situation. A major priority has got to be cutting back on the swollen inventory, or reacting quickly enough to prevent it increasing in the first place. The quickest way to do this is by slashing production and laying off workers. In addition, attempts will be made to cut costs wherever possible, and any postponable purchases will be postponed.

The actions will slow production directly and will spread the downward pressures to other companies. The effect of cutting production is obvious, but that in turn lowers the spending power of workers, and of those earning profits, and reduces orders for goods and services. This reduction in orders may well extend beyond normal operating supplies to include the cancellation or non-ordering of plant and machinery. If the downturn in demand was concentrated within a single sector, the negative effects would almost certainly be offset by positive developments elsewhere. The point about higher interest rates is that the effects extend across a wide cross-section of the economy, affecting both demand and supply. With enough sectors infected, recession becomes a contagious disease which can seriously affect otherwise healthy businesses. It is higher interest rates that destroy the natural immunity of the otherwise healthy sectors.

At this stage in the cycle, interest rates are being pushed up by the continued expansion of short-term business borrowing hitting against a limited supply of reserves, as the monetary authorities restrict availability. Consumer loans respond early to rising interest rates, and so does planned corporate borrowing. However, as demand falls and costs rise, companies are forced to borrow more in the short term. The emphasis on the short end is accentuated by the high cost of long-term borrowing, or of equity financing. This results in a significant build-up of short-term loan demand, which is capable of producing a sharp increase in interest rates even though new, discretionary borrowing has fallen dramatically.

Other visible signs normally seen at this time are declining money growth brought about by the high level of interest rates; housing and construction declines sharply for exactly the same reason; inflation will generally be accelerating fairly rapidly at this time, but will usually have peaked out before the recession phase has run its course; the stock market will be in sharp decline to begin with, as investors anticipate falling profits, and the amount of money available for investment is reduced just at the time when the demand for liquidity is increasing, both because of fear over what is to come and because of the high yields available on highly liquid assets. As demand falls and unemployment increases there will also be an increase in government spending, and a reduction in receipts, resulting in a sharp widening out of the budget deficit.

In addition, there will be a reduction in new stock offerings by existing and new corporations, and very little takeover activity. Declining share prices and falling investor confidence do not produce the ideal circumstances to float new issues or new companies and, anyway, it makes the cost much higher than most companies want to pay. New company formation generally falls off as profit opportunities are reduced, and the risks become more obvious with the evidence of rising bankruptcies. At this point, confidence evaporates and is replaced by extreme pessimism. Talk turns to the possibilities of financial collapse, destruction and ruin. These feelings definitely have real effects, as they feed back on actions. Plans for expansion and growth are replaced by retrenchment and concerns about survival. In this environment, bad news is interpreted as even worse, and good news as a mistake, an aberration or soon to be revised.

In the base-building period, expectations are still firmly down in negative territory, but conditions are in the early stages of starting to improve. The economy is still declining, but the rate of decline is slowing down. However, these early signs of improvement are generally not perceived, because of the negative outlook that has taken hold. Demand is still weak in the aggregate, but is starting to pick up in some sectors, and a few industries are already beginning to experience improved cash flow and profitability. There are a number of factors contributing to this improvement. Basically, the cost-cutting efforts undertaken during the recession are starting to have an effect. Companies cut out a lot of non-essential spending and wasteful expenditures, and introduce new controls and operating systems, working towards the objective of restoring profitability at a lower level of operation. The budget deficit will still be rising sharply as unemployment continues to rise, and this, at least, provides a cushion to total demand. This support, however, would never be sufficient to turn the economy on its own. A number of factors start to come together as companies improve efficiency, and as existing capital equipment wears out and finally needs replacing. In addition, new inventions and innovations raise the possibility of reducing costs by expanding investment spending, thereby increasing the possibility of additional demand.

The key factor, however, is the fall in interest rates which comes as short-term loan demands finally start to fall and the central bank injects liquidity in response to the recession. Loan demand falls and supply increases. That in itself is an important development. The fall in interest rates is crucial, but it is also necessary to ask why loan demands have fallen. At this stage in the cycle the reason is that corporate and individual cash flows have improved. Some companies will have gone bankrupt and have therefore stopped borrowing, but the main reason will be the cost cutting and retrenchment that has been underway. More efficient production and lower interest rates will also allow profits and cash flow to improve ahead of the economy.

There are, therefore, already signs of improved economic conditions for those who know where to look. The fall in interest rates then reinforces this improving trend. Now the effects are reversed. Falling rates stimulate demand and reduce costs still further, but against the background of recession, when expectations are still highly negative. In fact, it is at this time, just before the recovery takes hold, that expectations become the most negative. Consequently, cyclical bear markets in bonds and stocks frequently, in fact usually, end with a sharp sell-off, to be followed almost immediately by a dramatic reversal and a sudden improvement in prices.

The recovery begins against the background of highly negative sentiment and extreme uncertainty. The pace of the economy starts to quicken and this eventually leads to increasing employment, but there is still considerable scepticism about the sustainability of the recovery. As the recovery continues and accelerates, so the evidence accumulates and eventually becomes overwhelming. Expectations generally follow this improvement rather that anticipate it.

Profits will improve ahead of the economy, although these will not be reported immediately, and stock prices will move to anticipate this improvement. The point to emphasize is that stock prices are moving on the expectation of what will happen in the economy, and to the lower interest rates. Stock prices lead the economy but are not a major cause of cyclical activity, as often suggested.

The recovery is started by the combination of a number of forces which have come together during the period of base-building. Inventories have been reduced; interest rates have started to come down; a period of low demand has raised the potential for replacement needs by individuals and corporations; the continuing development of new products has created the potential for new demand to come into the markets; costs of production have been reduced, thereby improving profit margins at low levels of output; and the levelling out of demand, following its period of steep decline, works like an increase in demand on companies that are still cutting back. This change in momentum can be very significant. Here again, the key force linking the different sectors will be lower interest rates.

Increasing demand first of all reduces inventory levels on top of the cutbacks planned by management. Shortages appear and companies react by gearing up production. At this point, additional powerful forces come in to reinforce the improving trend and to propel the economy up at a very fast rate. To take an example from nature, the period of base-building has prepared the ground and planted the seeds. Now comes the sun and rain to stimulate the growth.

Companies have cut back in order to reduce costs and improve liquidity. Success in that direction, combined with a more relaxed attitude by the monetary authorities, allows the early fall in interest rates. As demand picks up, a high proportion of this will flow through to the bottom line, and companies stand to benefit substantially. With these gains in corporate profitability and cash flow, liquidity is further enhanced, which allows interest rates to fall still further, at least for a while longer. Falling interest rates in such an improving environment will serve to further reduce costs, while at the same time increasing demand. The vicious circle that had fed on itself, creating the downward spiral, is replaced by a virtuous circle which now works in the opposite direction. Now is the time when confidence returns, and with it a reduced demand for liquidity. This should rightly be seen as releasing a scarce resource for productive use, and as it comes back into use so it allows interest rates to fall further.

Large volume producers find it very hard to make money when demand falls. Being highly capital intensive they find that unit costs increase dramatically when capacity utilization rates decline. They consequently have to struggle hard and cut deep in order to survive under these conditions. However, once having got themselves into this position, any increase in capacity utilization will greatly reduce unit costs, quickly improving cash flow and profitability.

In the early stages of recovery, shortages quickly show up and companies start adding to inventory levels, but not as fast as sales, so that the inventory/sales ratio is typically still falling. Under these conditions, production starts to accelerate sharply, since it is now going to meet increasing demand and rising inventory needs. This is the take-off phase of the recovery, when the economy moves ahead at high speed, generally well above the average historical growth rate, and productivity growth accelerates. Employment improves slowly, but substantial gains should be made during the recovery, as long as labor has not become uncompetitively priced. During this period confidence improves slowly, but by the end the transition is complete. Contrary to popular opinion, confidence is not a good leading indicator. At best, it is coincident and more often lags the cycle.

In the same way that it is not possible to remain young forever, so it is not possible for the economy to continue growing at its recovery pace. At some point, the momentum has to slow down. This is a critical time, for the economy becomes more vulnerable to policy mistakes or outside shocks. The mature stage contains high risks for the unwary, but also great potential for those prepared to take risks.

For those observing the economy it often seems that nothing has changed, that the underlying structure is just as conducive to growth as it was in the recovery phase. In fact, the fundamentals have deteriorated significantly, but this is not recognized because of the more optimistic out-look that has been created. In the early stages of recovery there is a certain amount of pent-up demand and under-utilized resources. This combination provides a powerful impetus for a while, but one which cannot last. When maturity is reached there is only a slowing of growth, but it remains positive, just as during the basing period the rate of decline slowed down. Like then, this is a period of transition from one extreme to the other.

Whereas there had been a number of positive forces adding demand and cutting costs, so now these forces are reversed. The increase in confidence which initially improved liquidity has by now resulted in increased loan demand; first by households and then by corporations. Now liquidity is starting to become scarce again and interest rates are on the increase. Another factor putting pressure on liquidity is the behavior of prices. In the early stages of recovery, costs are low and going lower. There is a pool of skilled labor, and rising demand allows unit costs to fall even with the addition of new employees. As the recovery continues, workers are taken on and less productive equipment is brought into use. This first of all stops costs from falling, and then starts to reverse the process. Commodity prices will also pick up if there is a general world-wide recovery, and inflation at the consumer level is likely to accelerate. If domestic demand is rising faster than in the rest of the world, part of this excess will be reflected in rising net imports: imports rising faster than exports.

As demand and prices have recovered, so profitability will have increased. In the rapid growth phase, this profit will generally be in excess of that required for producers to engage in business initially. As these excess profits persist, so existing producers or new producers will respond by increasing output. Farmers will respond in this way, and so will other producers. As long as these excess profits can be earned so output will be increased. But there are lags between the planting and harvesting of crops, or between the addition of production facilities and increases in output. Thus, excess profits will still be earned even after productive potential has increased sufficiently to eliminate them in the future. The additional productive potential in aggregate is not obvious to each individual producer. Producers will be spread across the country, or even across many countries, and the published information they have available for decision making will reflect the past, while present prices are still independent of current, and many past, decisions to expand. As far as the individual is concerned, profit maximization requires further expansion.

It is easy to see how producers will continue to expand beyond the level that would eliminate the excess profit. By the time that point has been reached there will already be extra productive capacity in place waiting to come on stream. As the additional output continues to flood the market so profits are cut back generally, and marginal producers find red ink at the end of their accounts. As part of this process, inventory levels increase, resulting also in an increase in the ratio of inventories to sales. Changes in inventories have been given the leading role in explaining the business cycle by some economists. The swings in inventories to sales is an important step in the process, but, as discussed above they are only one link in the chain, and are more of a symptom than a cause. Much more important are the wide fluctuations in profitability.

For any given supply of money and credit, more is required to pay high prices and less to finance higher output. The Federal Reserve could, of course, supply the added reserves necessary to keep growth going, and that is what it has often done in the past. Nowadays there is greater awareness of the danger of accelerating inflation—an example of the changes in expectations which take place over time—and it is much less likely that the Federal Reserve will react in this way. The alternative danger is that the Federal Reserve will drain liquidity, thereby accelerating the onset of recession.

The effect of the recovery is to raise incomes and profits generally. That is the first effect, and it is easy to see how this further reinforces the expansion. However, there is a secondary effect which pushes taxpayers into higher tax brackets, and raises the *proportion* of taxes paid. This influence is reinforced by any acceleration of inflation. Some countries index tax exemption levels to inflation, but higher real growth will still push taxpayers into higher tax brackets. With rising revenues and declining cyclical expenditures, the budget deficit starts to decline, and under ideal circumstances should fall close to zero or even become a surplus. The drain on aggregate demand will act as an added restraint on rapid expansion, but will go unnoticed during the recovery phase.

Firmer interest rates, higher unit costs, rising inventories and imports, and a slowdown in the growth of real demand, all add up to slower growth in profits. This reduces the potential for stock prices to rise, and increases the risk of falling prices. The actual outcome will also depend on forces outside the business cycle, as in the 1950s, when stock prices began the decade still substantially undervalued following the disruptions caused by the war.

Increased volatility is a characteristic of this stage of the cycle, as conflicting forces come into contact. Confidence generally remains high but becomes frayed around the edges. In the latter part of this phase, there are bouts of enthusiasm followed by bouts of despair. In general, the outlook appears good, if only this, that or the other problem would be resolved. Underneath the surface the supports for growth are giving way, setting the scene for a return to recession.

## Behavioral cycles

The description of the business cycle presented here is fairly standard, and is easily recognizable, but with added emphasis on the pervasive role played by interest rates. What is less well understood is that there are many more embryonic business cycles, which never quite make it. All the stages are as described except that the cycle does not end in recession. Because of this, the cycle is never officially pronounced as completed.

This is really just a question of definition. A completed cycle is identified as the period between recessions. This is a convenient description, but it falls short of the true cyclical patterns that exist. The essence of the persistent cyclicality is the behavioral relationships that underlie it. These produce cycles that are much shorter than are typically thought of as making up the measured business cycle. What is more, these behavioral cycles are much more regular than the recorded cycles.

The economy and the various asset markets are closely related. Each action causes a reaction somewhere else within the system, echoes that reverberate through the markets. The ties that bind the separate parts together are strong but also elasticated. The same patterns keep repeating but with some slight variation each time. This elasticity is not entirely random, but very largely dependent on other developments.

Sometimes the pressure from rising interest rates becomes so great that the slowdown in growth leads to an actual fall in output generally and turns into a recession. More often, however, the excesses are driven out of the system without the need for a full-blown recession. Because these periods are not classified as any particular point in the cycle their significance has been missed, but they are crucial to understanding the financial markets. And it is this underlying behavioral cycle that forms the basis of the cyclical indicators employed here.

What turns weakness into recession is the continuation of high interest rates beyond the point where the economy has started to lose momentum. If interest rates start to ease early enough, a recession will generally be avoided. This is more likely to happen if there is confidence in the monetary authorities and the action they are taking. If the economy seems to be out of control, then interest rates will have to be kept higher, and for longer than necessary just to slow the economy. When doubters are in the majority, and concern has turned to fear, a recession becomes virtually inevitable. Alternatively, cautious behavior by business, resisting over-expansion and inventory accumulation, and cautious reactions by the monetary authorities, are likely to keep the cycle from ending.

Each cycle can, therefore, be split up into a number of sub-cycles, or what I prefer to call behavioral cycles. These are the true cycles of the economy which link the various sectors of the economy through their behavioral responses to what is going on elsewhere. Sometimes a recession will be avoided and at other times not.

A better feel for the concept behind behavioral cycles can be obtained by looking at Figs 1.7 and 1.8. Figure 1.7 gives some indication of the cyclical relationship between the financial markets and the rest of the economy. Charts of *ideal* cycles between various elements are often published, and it is helpful to see what the real thing looks like over a long period of time. Reality is, not surprisingly, a little messy. The cycles are not perfectly synchronized, as in the *ideal* world, but that does not prevent the basic underlying relationships showing through.

The similarity in cycles between different markets needs to be emphasized. Unfortunately, the creation of *ideal* cycles over-emphasizes that one point, and encourages the belief that there is an all-powerful, mechanical, force at work, producing neatly packaged cycles of uniform length. Reality is not like that; it is untidy, ragged around the edges. This presentation draws attention to the human element, the behavioral nature, of the business cycle.

Real-world disturbances knock the cycle off its path. Changes in taxation, and government, natural disasters and many other things produce changes in a particular cycle, but the behavioral responses keep the relationship alive even if a particular cycle is knocked off-course. The really big disturbances over this century are the two world wars and the depression. In each case, however, once the world got back to normal, the old patterns started to show up again. The chart in Fig. 1.7 just covers the post-war period in

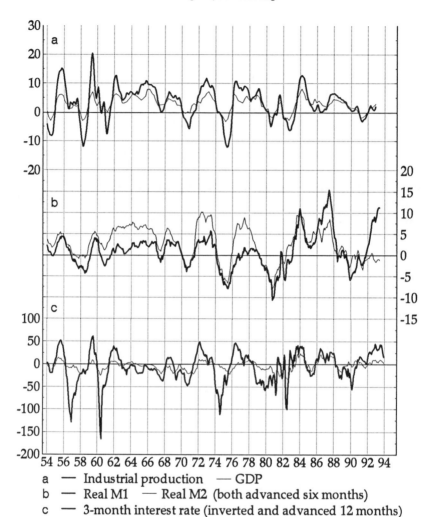

a    —  Industrial production    — GDP
b    —  Real M1    —  Real M2  (both advanced six months)
c    —  3-month interest rate (inverted and advanced 12 months)
     —  Aaa corporate bond (inverted and advanced 12 months)

**Figure 1.7** Behavioral cycles (12-month rates of change)

order to show the cycles more clearly. The scale on the century-long chart gets a little compressed, but the same patterns show up.

Money growth and the economy are related. The middle lines show the growth of real money advanced six months. The last two lines in the chart are the rate of change of short-term and long-term interest rates. This again shows a cyclical relationship with the growth of real money and industrial production, with an approximate six-month lead on money growth. Now it

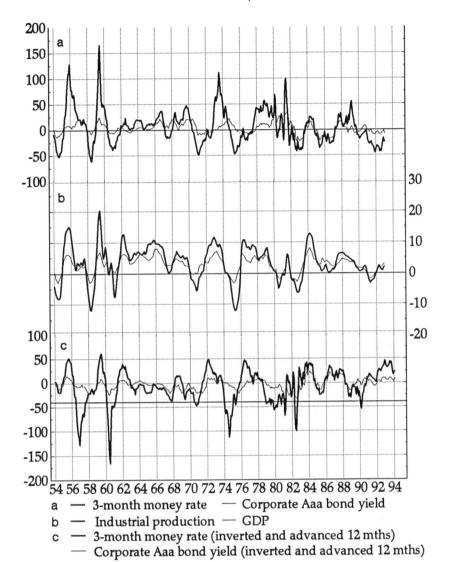

**Figure 1.8** Completing the cycle (12-month rates of change)

is possible to start to put together a behavioral picture of the business cycle, running from changes in the cost of money, through changes in credit and money demand to the real economy.

An important point to note is that there are more cyclical movements than there are actually recorded business cycles. This is not just an interesting footnote, to be recognized and then forgotten, but is absolutely fundamental to understanding the business cycle. What can be observed are the more regular, more frequent behavioral cycles referred to earlier. In order to understand why these cycles move the way they do, and why they are *behavioral*, it is necessary to look at Fig. 1.8.

The chart in Fig. 1.8 reverses the sequence of relationships, thereby completing the circle. The rate of change of interest rates is placed on top, followed by industrial production and finally the rate of change of interest rates again, but this time inverted and advanced 12 months, as in the previous chart. Falling interest rates will stimulate economic growth, after a lag, and the stronger economy will, in turn, put almost immediate upward pressure on interest rates. But then, higher interest rates will cause economic growth to slow down, and so on.

The seeds of a new recovery are sown in the preceding downturn; each recovery contains the conditions for a slowdown in growth, but that does not have to end up as a recession. This is the behavioral interaction that determines cyclical patterns. Each business cycle is born out of the cycle that went before, a real chip off the old block. In effect, each contains common genes. They need not look alike, but they will share certain basic characteristics. The close relationship that exists between series helps to explain why statistical studies find lagged correlations for an individual series, and between series, running in both directions.

As the economy weakens it takes some of the upward pressure off interest rates. Now there is a race between the negative pull on the economy and the regenerative effects of lower interest rates. This is the mid-point along the high wire, *the critical juncture within the cycle*. Any sudden disturbance here can easily knock the economy off and into recession, but such an outcome is not necessary. There are a great many potential influences that come into play, with only a marginal effect on the behavioral cycle, but which may be enough to turn a growth slowdown into a recession. A major determining factor is likely to be the trend of inflation, which extends beyond the normal cycle, and can play a leading role in determining the severity of the downturn. This is a critical point for all investors when evaluating the risk/reward of their portfolio.

Running through the background is a long-wave cycle that is discussed later in Chapter 6. In the up-wave, the recorded cycles are more likely to contain a number of smaller behavioral cycles. In more usual language, the recoveries will be extended, while the recessions will be shallow. On the down-wave, the measured cycles become shorter, and the recessions are deeper and more threatening.

## The stock market and the economy

Market tradition holds that changes in stock prices cause changes in economic activity. This is a widely held view that is also reflected in economic forecasting, since changes in the stock market are an important ingredient in the leading economic indicators published by the Department of Commerce.

Explanations of this leading relationship have been based on the wealth effects resulting from changes in stock prices. As wealth increases, so consumers feel more confident; needing to save less in order to achieve a given wealth target, they increase their spending. At the same time, producers see demand rising, while the increase in stock prices reduces the cost of capital, thereby creating the conditions for increased investment. While there is a certain plausibility in the argument, it vastly exaggerates any wealth effects that do exist. What it does not explain is why stock prices should be bid up in the first place. Surely, the improvement depends on the anticipation of an upturn in the economy and profitability. There seems to be no way of getting around the fact that stock prices anticipate the economy, rather than determine the economy.

The leading relationship is dragged up every time the stock market suffers a significant correction. A classic example was provided by the market crash in October 1987. Following the crash, the consensus immediately became that the world economy was about to follow prices down into recession or worse, depression. As a result, the economy would weaken substantially and stock prices would tumble even further, despite the fact that prices, on average, had already fallen by 35 per cent from their highs. Even accepting the initial premise, that the stock market was forecasting a fall in the economy, it still did not follow that stock prices had to fall further; after all, a recession had already been fully discounted—overnight. In fact, what was being forecast was only the *potential* weakness of the economy. Understanding why that forecast was wrong, and why the stock market is not a reliable leading indicator of the economy, provides important insights into the whole issue of causality—which is a theme that is returned to many times throughout this book.

In an article published in *The Times*, London, November 1987, just weeks after the crash, I challenged this consensus view, arguing for continued economic growth and a recovery in stock prices. The world economy had been heading towards a recession, but that risk was greatly reduced because of the stock market crash, since interest rates would now fall. The following quote draws attention to this reverse causality:

There is a widespread opinion that the crash on Wall Street portends a severe recession in the US.

Before the stock market crash it had seemed to me that the US was heading towards a recession in the middle of 1988. Interest rates were pushing up and the need to correct the trade imbalance suggested that a recession was inevitable. The crash in share prices has, if anything, raised the possibility that the recession will be avoided, as it has allowed interest rates to fall.

The drop in share prices is likely to have some small effect on consumer confidence but it is far from clear how much. It is true that stock prices fall ahead of a recession, but that is a reflection of higher interest rates and a squeeze on credit; it is just that this shows up first in stock prices. This is exactly why these prices play such an important role in leading indicators of the economy. Evidence of a leading relationship is not evidence of causality. At present there is a struggle going on between recession and reflation. If there is a recession in the US it will be because the rest of the world has not stimulated demand, and interest rates are pushed back up eventually to hold the dollar and restrain demand. It will not happen because the Dow has fallen back to where it was this time last year.

The similarity between the change in stock prices and economic activity is quite remarkable. There should be no doubt that these two series are closely related, as shown in Fig. 1.9. Over the post-war period, it is possible to identify a lead of approximately six months from stock prices to the economy. A close relationship also existed prior to the war, but surprisingly, it was coincident: there was no lead. During the war, the linkage was broken, as free markets were suspended and normal economic relationships became distorted.

Changes in stock prices are an important component in the official leading economic indicators but this has, in fact, only worked over the post-war period. The most likely explanation for this leading relationship depends on the improvement in information and understanding. Over time, investors have become better able to anticipate turning points in the economy. Naturally, expectations are not always correct. The attempt by investors to anticipate the economic cycle has resulted in the relationship being not quite as good as it was before, although the cyclical patterns are still remarkably similar. The major example of this over-anticipation came in 1987, when the stock market crashed but the economy kept growing.

To take one example of how expectations work, the initial effect of an improvement in demand is likely, first, to show up in the form of a reduction in inventories. Maybe not even a reduction, but simply a slowdown in the rate of deterioration. Moreover, a decline in interest rates will reduce the cost of holding inventory. For some companies, these developments will set the scene for an improvement in profitability, even before there is any improvement in the economy. It may also be sufficient to generate a sharp increase in stock prices among the cyclical leaders.

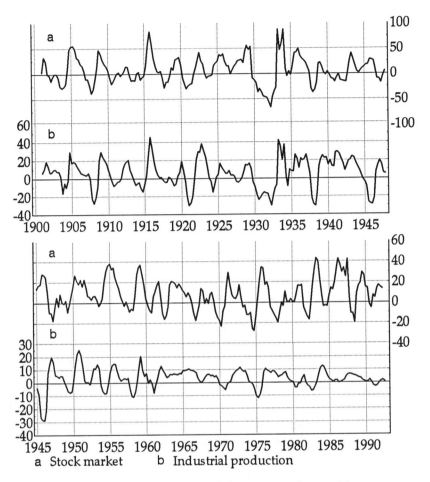

**Figure 1.9** Stock prices and the economy (quarterly)

Towards the lows, most sellers have sold and the market is washed out. There is much apprehension, and potential buying has been postponed; most investors will be neutral. There is, therefore, likely to be considerable pent-up demand, and a small positive in one sector could lead to a significant move in prices, which can quickly spread to other groups. The economy is on the road to recovery, but it takes time to show up in the published numbers. In the meantime the stock market reaction is much quicker.

Weakness in stock prices does anticipate weakness in the economy but not necessarily a recession, as was patently clear in 1987. It has to be remembered that investors are anticipating, consciously or not, the outlook for profits, not the economy *per se* and, as already mentioned, profits vary more widely than economic activity. The famous comment, that the stock market has forecast more recessions than there have been, is misleading and is based on a false interpretation of what the stock market is anticipating. In interpreting the implication of any change in the stock market for the economy, it is important to take account of the circumstances leading up to the change, and the circumstances that follow. If the economy is in recession and stock prices pick up, it is reasonable to assume that a recovery, at least in profits, is not far away, but still not inevitable.

In 1987, for example, the monetary authorities reversed policy, cut interest rates and headed off the recession that had seemed inevitable up to that point. The market was not wrong in its overall concern about future profits, although the reaction was clearly exaggerated. Had policy remained in the direction it was headed, there would have been a recession. However, the violence of the stock market reaction produced a change of course that switched the economy into a new track and, in turn, invalidated the motives for the crash.

The case in favor of causality running from the economy to stock prices, despite the appearance to the opposite, has always seemed obvious. Events in 1987, and the subsequent reactions, have made the case overwhelming. Stock prices are like a highly sensitive antenna, finely tuned on to events in the economy and how these will effect corporate profitability. There are no neon signs flashing warning notices and, in fact, most commentary is bullish as prices start to move lower, and bearish at the bottom of a price slide. The reaction comes in terms of uncertainty and increased caution, rather than positive action—the sort of behavior discussed later in Chapters 8 and 9 on investment strategies and the formation of expectations.

# 2

---

# THE PROBLEMS OF INFLATION
## (what goes up keeps going up)

Investment choices over the past 30 years have been dominated by the fear, and fact, of accelerating inflation. In making the important choice between real and financial assets, the prospect for future inflation is the most important factor to take into account. Mistakes have been made on both sides: expecting too little inflation, and too much. In order to better judge what the future holds in store it is, therefore, essential to consider the pressures which result in inflation; i.e. the reasons, not just the event itself.

It is a subject to be approached with trepidation. Popular explanations have more to do with mythology than fact, and, like myths of the past, contain many-headed monsters which frighten the unwary, even though it is well known that such beasts do not really exist. At times, there is a dark foreboding that smothers rationality, making sense out of nonsense. The reality is not always brightly lit and problem-free, and it is certainly more complex and difficult to deal with than the simple extremes.

One subject it is necessary to deal with is the role of money in the inflationary process. It seems like only yesterday when the only thing that mattered for inflation was the supply of money. But if that is the case, then why worry about a rise in oil prices, for example, at a time when money growth is extremely slow? The reaction to a jump in oil prices has been that this increase is all that matters. Clearly, something is missing.

The truth, as it has a habit of doing, lies somewhere between these extremes. The most important point to remember is that inflation is a symptom of excess demand. Money growth is likely to accompany rapid inflation, without necessarily being the cause of it. Equally, a sharp increase in oil prices may well result in a rise in consumer prices, but at the same time reduce demand for other goods and services. Under these circumstances the key to what inflation will do in the future will depend on what happens to excess demand in the future.

Money, or rather credit, growth is a necessary accompaniment to inflation, but both are really symptoms of more fundamental forces. Money and credit growth will be very similar, at least for broad definitions of money. The distinction being made here is between cause and effect. In order to understand what created the accelerating trend of inflation it is necessary to look below the surface at the underlying forces creating excess demand within the economy. That is, it is necessary to look at both supply and demand. In addition, particular attention is given to the pervasive role of government and the political system in creating and sustaining inflation.

Inflation is itself a natural solution to eliminate excess demand by raising the prices of the things that can be bought, which has the effect of reducing liquidity and raising interest rates. These natural forces have, however, been widely resisted. For a long time, the monetary authorities actually did the opposite; they held the nominal interest rate down below the rate of inflation. The realization that the real cost of money is the important factor has dawned only slowly and is, in fact, still far from universally accepted. As a result, there have been times requiring sudden changes in policy, when the monetary authorities have moved from excessive ease to excessive tightness. The effect on short-term interest rates has been magnified many times, as the effect is transmitted through changing perceptions of liquidity. More gradual adjustment is much preferred.

Understanding what has caused inflation in the past is a necessary step to identifying a return of accelerating inflation in the future. In order to protect from such an eventuality, it is also necessary to understand how inflation will influence different investment choices. In this respect, it makes a difference whether inflation is generally expected or not. Inflation is a major influence on investment choices extending beyond the normal business cycle, and is given special attention in considering the risks and opportunities associated with particular investments.

Many people consider inflation to be the greatest single impediment to economic growth and social stability, confusing and distorting rational investment decision making. This view has an important element of truth, but not in such a simple and straightforward way. Paradoxically, periods of apparent price stability have been even more distortionary. The explanation lies partly in definitions, and partly in the exaggerated claims made against inflation. Inflation created havoc in the 1970s and reversed the normal ordering of investment priorities. However, inflation continued in the 1980s, and yet financial assets came back into favor while gold and commodities generally suffered real declines in prices. If that seems a little confusing, it is because part of the explanation has been missed out. This link is also missing in most discussions of inflation, thereby permitting the continued confusion.

The problem in the 1970s was not that there was inflation, unspecified in type and magnitude. The problem was that inflation was accelerating; i.e. the problem was not that prices were rising, but that they were rising at an increasingly rapid rate. Initially, the acceleration took individuals and markets by surprise. This caused real losses in bond markets and fixed price contracts. Later, expectations adjusted, and in many cases over-adjusted, extrapolating past trends into future hyperinflation. That was about the time the monetary authorities began the long struggle to restore confidence in the value of money. The timing was not accidental. The same fears were afflicting the monetary authorities, and the conclusion was unacceptable.

What really hurt investors were the unanticipated changes in direction. To the extent that the acceleration and deceleration of inflation were fully anticipated, there was no problem. Anyone who did that, and understood the implications for the various markets, would have benefited substantially. It was not inflation that did the damage but the extreme movements, the sharp changes. There was still inflation in the 1980s without depressing investment, investment returns or economic growth. The difference was that it did not change dramatically, and was reasonably expected. This is a very important distinction.

Inflation is still with us but it has remained relatively subdued. Most importantly, low inflation remains at the top of the list of objectives for monetary authorities around the world, and there continue to be efforts to reduce the size of government spending and budget deficits. While there has been only limited success in achieving these objectives, the priorities are important. Inflationary expectations remain high both in the financial markets and in government. This shift in emphasis and concern is more important to the longer-term trend than anything else.

Most supporters of price stability make the point that stable inflation is not possible, and they are right, but that does not mean that price stability is an alternative. True price stability, where prices do not change at all, is just one example of inflation stability, and zero is actually more difficult to maintain than a small positive rate. The attempt to hit zero inflation will mean periods when inflation will be positive and periods when it will be negative. In addition, if inflation in some sectors is positive, then the average will only be kept down to zero if some other sectors have negative inflation. However, negative inflation, deflation, brings even greater dangers which are likely to be even more unacceptable.

Many people seeking a solution to the problem of inflation have recommended a return to a gold standard. Unfortunately, there was inflation even then, accompanied by great economic and price instability. This conflict between history and belief is discussed later in this chapter and in Chapter 16, where the operation of the gold standard is considered in more detail. The nature of inflation has changed over time, with significant implications for investors. The modern alternative is not as bad as generally supposed and, anyway, investors need to deal with the world as it really is and not base decisions on wishful thinking, or nostalgic references to the past.

## Inflation and investing

The art of investment is difficult enough at the best of times, but the problems created by sudden changes in inflation make it considerably more difficult. It is wrong to conclude that the only favorable environment is one of zero inflation. A reasonably stable, reasonably low rate of inflation can easily be built into investor expectations and need not be a problem. Such a situation will provide as many opportunities as risks. What creates major problems are wide, unexpected fluctuations in inflation. It is much less important whether these movements are around an average of zero or 3 per cent, they still have the potential to create havoc with investment decision making. The main effect is to increase greatly the degree of volatility in all markets, and the potential gains and losses can be enormous. In many cases, the game ceases to be about slide-rule decisions to maximize returns for any given risk, and becomes simply a question of survival.

At first, the acceleration of inflation after the Second World War was mild, although there was still considerable concern expressed about inflation levels reaching as high as 3 per cent, as they did in the 1960s, on their way higher. As is often the case, concern preceded the real problem. Prices had risen in the past, and often quite sharply, but this time it was different. This time, there was no subsequent fall in prices as there had been before. This time, the value of money was being continuously eroded. Instead of periods of rising prices followed by falling prices, there were now periods of rising inflation followed by periods of declining inflation; a very different state of affairs. The late 1960s witnessed a speeding up of this inflationary trend, with further acceleration through the 1970s.

This accelerating trend of inflation had very important consequences for investors, which in many cases swamped normal cyclical opportunities. Traditionally safe, low-risk investments, such as government bonds, became highly speculative as inflation created substantial capital losses. On the other hand, gold and commodities, which were more normally thought of as highly speculative, produced substantial long-term gains for those who bought them.

Inflation greatly complicates the investment process. With no inflation, and bond yields around 3 per cent, there is a pre-tax real yield available which is equal to the nominal yield. Under such circumstances, returns on stocks will generally also remain fairly stable. Nothing is constant, there will be temporary disturbances, and the mechanics of the business cycle will continue to operate, producing above average returns for those who understand its mysteries. But at least the rules of the game are well understood and, to a certain extent, investors can choose the amount of risk they are prepared to take in search of desired returns.

All this changes once inflation starts to accelerate. The problems created are particularly acute when inflation is not anticipated. However, problems are still created for investors even if an acceleration of inflation is expected. The economy becomes more unstable as cyclical extremes are exaggerated, government reactions become uncertain and potentially destabilizing, large-scale debts are built up which greatly complicate the process of restoring price stability, all of which leads to increased volatility in the prices of financial assets and commodities.

The general taxation of interest income, except in the case of government exemptions, further complicates the effect of rising inflation. Consequently, at times of inflation, parallel increases in interest rates will not actually provide compensation for the decline in purchasing power. For example, a 4 per cent return with zero inflation and a 50 per cent tax rate produces an actual real return of 2 per cent. Alternatively, a 14 per cent nominal return with 10 per cent inflation, i.e. an apparent 4 per cent in real terms, really produces an actual real return of $-3$ per cent, after 50 per cent tax; the loss of five full points of interest in real terms. The problem arises from the failure of the tax system to recognize that, as interest rates rise with inflation, an increasing proportion of interest paid does not represent a genuine return on investment, but is really just compensation for the loss of capital value. This provides a great incentive to consumption as opposed to saving, and requires even higher interest rates than would otherwise be necessary in order to produce a cut-back on demand.

Investors in the stock market suffer a similar fate, because capital gains are taxed without deducting the effect of inflation. Therefore, if stock prices only rise with inflation, be it 100 per cent, 200 per cent or 1000 per cent, the investor who realizes a gain will end up with an after-tax loss in real terms. This is discussed further in Chapter 13. Such inflationary distortions are not necessary and could be easily avoided by amending the tax code.

In the early years of a new trend, be it inflation or whatever, the majority will not be aware of the change in direction. The few who perceive what is going on will consequently profit handsomely. Some changes will be of minor importance to the majority, and the effects will not reach outside a particular industry or area. Inflation, however, is quite different, as its influence will extend through all aspects of economic life. The initial effects of higher inflation will most probably seem beneficial, as nominal prices and wages increase, providing a spur to economic activity generally. It does not take long, however, for the illusion to die, as higher and higher inflation becomes expected and the realization dawns that there has been little benefit in real terms. In fact, some, perhaps the majority, will actually be worse off, and many who are not will still think they are, under the distorting influence of inflation. The illusion can be kept alive longer if inflation continues to accelerate, but eventually expectations will adjust to that also. Then the perceived benefits of inflation will disappear to be replaced by the opposite view, that inflation is harmful.

The trend to ever-higher rates of inflation becomes increasingly obvious to a wider group the longer it persists, as people learn from experience. Finally, the majority become aware that their traditional view of reality is no longer valid. Such times are characterized by extreme market behavior, as fear takes over as the predominant emotion. This is the type of reaction which occurred in the late 1970s, particularly with gold and silver but also in the financial markets. Losses were experienced by those investing in what were supposed to be safe, secure assets, the haven of widows and orphans, while speculative commodities provided high returns over extended periods.

There are two aspects to living with rising inflation which greatly complicate the investment process. Firstly, investors and businessmen become more short-term oriented, as fortunes can be made or lost in the blink of an eye. Secondly, there is a move away from traditional values, as conservative investments become highly risky, and speculations provide enormous profits. Under these circumstances, long-term investments become viewed as risky, and short-term trading is seen as the road to profits. As speculation increases, so it adds to price volatility. This process can continue to the point where it risks a total breakdown of traditional values—where financial manipulation becomes more important than real productive investment.

However, once inflation has stopped rising, the situation is dramatically reversed. The financial manipulators, who flew high when it was accelerating, come down to earth with a crash, while the dull plodders, who under-performed during inflationary times by sticking with proven values, emerge in a very strong position. This has been the lesson taught by inflation throughout history, and yet each time it still traps the unwary.

## Defining inflation

What is inflation? That might seem to be a simple enough question, but it is surprising the variety of answers that are frequently given. The answer is not as easy as it seems. Inflation is the name given to rising prices. But are all price rises inflation? Inflation is really a condition, a situation of continuously rising prices. All price increases tend to be called inflation, but there are times when a price increase actually reduces inflationary pressure. For example, an increase in indirect tax rates combined with a tight monetary policy would raise prices, but also reduce spending power. The likelihood would, therefore, be that prices of other things would have to fall, or at least rise at a slower pace, and the overall inflation rate will fall back down below where it was before.

The same thing happens in the case of the rise in price of some widely used commodity such as oil. If there is no move in fiscal policy or monetary policy to accommodate a substantial price increase, then total spending on everything else will have to fall. Prices themselves may have to fall, not simply the rate of increase, although the reaction will be complicated by the fact that production costs for many companies will have increased. With spending down, but some prices up, this means there will be some real output declines. The process will not be painless. Whether this is the best response is a subject which is considered later. John Maynard Keynes made this same distinction about inflation, between a continuing process rather than a one-off price increase. He gave the following definition (Keynes, 1919):

> [Inflation occurs] when the aggregate of purchasing power is increasing faster than the available supply of goods.

The actual measure of inflation used will be an aggregation of many different price changes. The prices of different goods will not all be rising at the same rate; some may even be falling. The pattern in the 1980s has been for service sector prices to rise faster than average; in particular, medical and education costs have risen very rapidly, while the price of goods has been rising more slowly. There are many examples of goods prices actually falling, and falling significantly.

Figure 2.1 shows four different dollar-based definitions of inflation, all measured as 12-month rates of change. From the top down these are the GNP deflator, consumer prices, producer prices and *The Economist*'s index of general commodity prices. It will be noticed that the patterns of the top three definitions of inflation are very similar, but that they become more variable as we move down, from GNP to PPI. Moving on to the commodity price index, it can be seen that again the rate at which prices change follows the same broad pattern as in the other indices, but in this case the volatility and scale of movement is very much more pronounced. This may not be immediately obvious, since the scales are adjusted for each series so as to maximize the movement on the chart. When the rate of increase for all these indexes peaked in the 1973–1974 cycle, the commodity price index reached 86 per cent, the PPI reached 20 per cent, CPI managed only 12.5 per cent while the GNP price deflator increased by only 11 per cent at the peak. There is also a noticeable difference in timing. Commodity price inflation demonstrates a clear tendency to change direction ahead of the other series, with the PPI a little ahead of CPI and the GNP deflator.

All of the series are subjected to the same broad cyclical influences, but the speed and magnitude of the response depends critically on the extent to which prices are determined within a free market. To the degree that a market can be cornered, this will prevent prices from moving to reflect the normal competitive forces of a free market. In many countries, trade

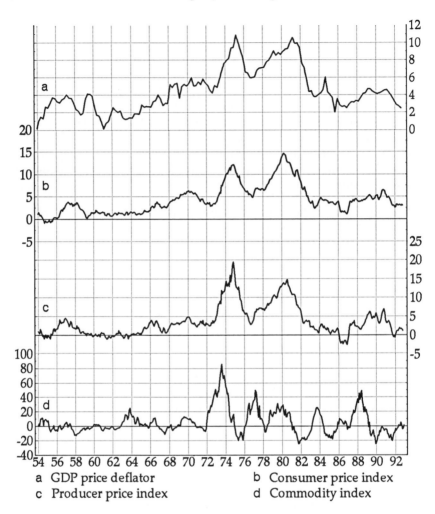

a   GDP price deflator              b   Consumer price index
c   Producer price index            d   Commodity index

**Figure 2.1** Four measures of inflation (12-month rates of change)

unions have succeeded in cornering large sections of the labor market but only with government support for their jobs, at least in the short term. In other countries, pressure groups have effectively cornered certain parts of the economy with the aid of dependent politicians. Through brand names and advertising, many companies have carved out sections of the market, and for extended periods often act as if they did not face significant competition. This type of behavior is particularly noticeable within the government and its agencies. In many, if not most, cases full protection is granted through the conferring of absolute monopoly powers.

As a result of this institutional structure, the prices of manufactured goods and services are set periodically by contract rather than flexibly through the unconstrained operation of free-market forces. The pricing structure is such that it is slow to adapt to changing circumstances, while the cost structure, particularly for labor, is extremely rigid. Workers have typically come to expect continuing increases in real wages, even when economic conditions warrant a significant decline in real wages, if jobs are to be preserved. Wages are often seen as the major cause of inflation. That, however, is rarely true, though it would be wrong to say never. Wages typically follow inflation, and cause inflation to become entrenched, making it difficult to bring down. This is the true significance of wages, and explains why unemployment tends to lag behind the cycle. It is late in the cycle that real wages rise the fastest. Prices start to flatten out or even decline, and final demand falls, but wages are based on expectations derived from the inflationary past, so that profits become squeezed. Commodity prices in the free market react quickly to these pressures, but workers do not. And if prices will not change, then the quantity must, so layoffs increase and unemployment rises.

The net result is that price, or inflation, declines are slowed. This is an expected result of strongly organized trade unions and pressure groups generally. These influences are felt most strongly in the widest index, for GNP, then prices of the products making up the consumer price index, slightly less in the components of the wholesale price index, and least in the commodity price index. It is these structural, institutionalized forces that account for the main difference in timing and volatility between the four series.

## Excess demand and inflation

The real point to note is that inflation is a symptom, not the illness itself. Inflation and balance-of-payments deficits on current account are both symptoms of the same problem—an excess of domestic demand above domestic supply. It is important to recognize that it is not simply increases in demand that cause inflation, but increases in demand relative to supply. Therefore, events or policies that reduce the domestic supply potential can be just as inflationary as events or policies that increase demand. Good policy will be a question of achieving an even balance. Unfortunately, there is frequently extreme uncertainty and disagreement as to how this might be achieved.

Excess demand can have many causes. All that is required is that some group in society demands more of the total economic pie without adding an equal amount to total output. In effect, they are demanding a change in relative prices. The most obvious source of these additional demands is the government, but inflationary pressure can also come from groups of workers or workers in general, certain industries or the corporate sector as a whole, OPEC, or from actions abroad or outside human control—for example, the weather.

The value of looking at inflation this way is that it throws light on the *process* involved. Inflation is not the description of a one-off price increase, but is the systematic, continuing rise of prices over time. The term inflation describes a continuing process not a single event. Rising prices are a symptom of pressures building elsewhere, and provide a *solution* to excess demand, rather like a fever of someone who is ill. Inflation is nature's cure to excess demand. Rising prices will eliminate excess demand—if allowed to, and it is necessary to enquire how it is that excess demands are maintained in the face of persistent inflation.

Consider the case of an increased claim over and above productive potential. One possibility is that this will result in a decline in the relative share of some other sector of society, in which case there is a change in relative prices but no inflation. Alternatively, if all relative shares are protected, the result will be continuing, or even accelerating, inflation. How disruptive any particular claim might be, and the extent to which it is inflationary, will depend on how large the claimant group is relative to the rest of the economy. For example, an exceptionally large claim by a few highly specialized athletes or actors will have a minimal direct effect on inflation. Alternatively, an additional small claim by any group representing 25 per cent, or more, of the economy is likely to have a significant effect.

The initial increased claim on resources could come from the private sector, the public sector or from abroad. There are also competing claims between profits and wages, workers and the unemployed, the young and the old, the healthy and the sick, and there is no easy reconciliation. The claim could be generated by the most noble of sentiments, e.g. a desire to increase the real income of retirees, or to improve medical conditions for the poor and needy. However, if the additional claims are not accepted by the rest of society, inflation will be the result. In a static economy, relative improvements in living standards for retirees would require the loss of real income for some other group. In a growing economy it means passing on some of the production gains in one sector to another sector. Sometimes this is just as difficult to achieve as an actual reduction in income.

## Money and inflation

Inflation is caused by the forces creating excess demand as discussed above. However, these excess demands do need to be financed, and that generally will require an increase in credit. The stock of money, consisting of the main liabilities of the banking system, and often including the liabilities of related institutions, will, to a large extent, reflect this credit expansion. Money, therefore, becomes a measure of potential inflation without necessarily being the direct cause of it. Excess demand will generally be reflected in excess money growth, resulting from the increased credit growth, as explained in Chapter 4, where money is discussed in greater detail. Over the long term it is reasonable to argue that, for inflation to persist, monetary policy must be accommodative. It is less obvious, but equally true, that fiscal policy must also be accommodative.

Monetary policy, as opposed to money itself, is one potential source of inflationary pressure. In a free-market environment this occurs when the real rate of interest is kept too low. During these periods, liquidity ceases to be a scarce resource. The low real interest rates do encourage, and accommodate, expansion which helps to counteract other negative developments, of which rising taxes are the most obvious. However, the benefits are distortionary and are, anyway, only short term and not sustainable. Holding real interest rates too low is a classic way to achieve over-investment in capital intensive plant, pushing returns artificially low. Even a casual look around at the excess capacity that was created in steel, automobiles and heavy industry generally bears eloquent witness to what happened. In terms of group shares, there was a diversion of real interest away from lenders towards borrowers. The former lost out in terms of spendable income after taking account of inflation, to the benefit of the latter.

Easy money policies work as long as inflationary expectations lag behind actual inflation. The evidence, in fact, suggests that the lags are very long, which allows the process to continue for some time. However, once inflationary expectations catch up with inflation, real interest rates will be pushed up, and it gets harder and harder to stimulate the economy through new injections of liquidity. Lags in the formation of inflationary expectations also work in the other direction. Attempts to reduce inflation through tight money policies once inflationary expectations have caught up will result in high real interest rates. This will affect decision making over a long period, adding to the time and cost of reducing inflation.

The relationship between money growth and inflation has changed over time, as can be seen in Fig. 2.2. Money growth was pretty much coincident with inflation until the 1950s, but since then the relationship has changed. Friedman and Schwartz (1963) concluded that money growth determined inflation with a variable lag of approximately two years. The evidence seems to contradict this conclusion. Strangely, the one occasion the relationship seemed to work that way was the period around the time they were writing, and immediately after. Unfortunately, velocity also seems to have become more variable over that time, thereby reducing the extent of the correlation, even with lags. There definitely seems to have been a change

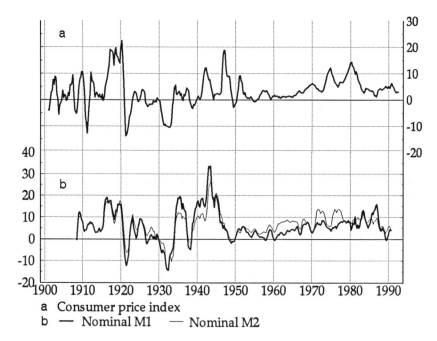

a  Consumer price index
b  —  Nominal M1      —  Nominal M2

**Figure 2.2** Money growth and inflation (four-quarter rates of change)

in the relationship between the growth of money and inflation, and the recent correlations have been extremely unconvincing.

The main macroeconomic change over this period has been the government's increased responsibility for, and intervention in, the economy. The monetary authorities have reacted more quickly to signs of economic overheating by raising interest rates and restraining demand. This direct intervention seems to have radically changed the relationship between money and inflation and, as shown below, between inflation and the economy.

Not so long ago, strictly applied monetary targets were seen as the foundation of any serious attempt to limit inflation. The very existence of monetary policy was inextricably linked with the announcement of restrictive targets for monetary growth, and the subsequent achievement of these objectives. The slightest deviation from this path was viewed with great alarm, and punished in the bond market. Monetary targets still exist, but they have changed a lot since the early 1980s and are now taken much less seriously. Restrictive targets were used to justify the painfully high interest rates required to kill off inflationary expectations. They represented emergency action that was effective in that environment, but less practical under more normal conditions. This subject, and money generally, is discussed at greater length in Chapter 4.

Inflation is usually presented as a monetary phenomenon, which is perfectly true, and by extension to be quite simply the result of an expansion of the money supply. That is rather like saying that limiting the supply of gasoline would reduce the amount of road accidents. Certainly, automobiles need gasoline to go, but that is hardly the cause of the accidents. Such a limitation would be very disruptive, and would result in the development and use of alternative fuels. And so too with the money supply. It is much too simple to suggest that all that needs to be done to stop inflation is stop printing money. Simply, to cut off the supply of money without resolving the underlying causes of the excess demand would be very damaging to the private sector of the economy.

There are times when tight money may be wholly appropriate but, more often, particularly when the private sector is competing against the excessive demands of the public sector, it may be wholly inappropriate and highly destructive—like cutting a toenail with a chainsaw. A consistent policy approach will have more chances of success, not purely in terms of reducing inflation, but of minimizing the cost of reducing inflation, and thereby increasing the chances that such policies can be sustained. Recent inflation has its roots in the political and social system that has developed, and it is pointless suggesting solutions for which the political will does not exist, or where they will quickly cause a violent reaction. More consistent policies require a better understanding of the true causes of inflation.

## The government and inflation

Governments play a major role in the inflationary process in two ways. First, they make their own demands upon resources. They run many services such as fire, police, defense, education and, often, health. In nearly every country, governments directly employ a vast army of workers to staff these services and their own giant administrative bureaucracy. Second, modern governments have a major impact on inflation through their control over the disbursement of money and distribution of income. Governments, at all levels, are major purchasers of goods and services from the private sector. In addition, governments have increasingly attempted to improve health care, pensions, unemployment pay and social welfare, even where the main service is not directly administered by the government. In many cases, these entitlements have become index-linked to compensate for inflation. When growth is low or negative, this makes it increasingly difficult to bring inflation under control, since it means the cuts in living standards must come from somewhere else, which is probably unacceptable to the other groups in society.

The roots of recent excess demand run deep into the democratic, political and social system that has been developing for a long time, feeding on the conflicts and tensions that inevitably exist. There are many aspects to this development, not just the role of politics and politicians. However, it is not surprising that the accelerating trend of inflation was associated with the sustained growth of government, but neither was it a necessary development. It is just that in the process of greater government intervention and expansion into different fields of economic activity, governments have tended to expand demand excessively in response to the conflicting and excessive demands that have been made upon them. The key element for excess demand in this case is that government demands are expanding at a faster rate than the private sector is prepared to accept. This leaves open the possibility, which can be observed in reality, that the level of acceptability will vary in different countries.

The originating pressures may, however, lie elsewhere. It may be that there is a direct attempt to stimulate growth, either through Keynesian demand-management policies, or by an easy money policy, or both. Alternatively, the government may be responding to excess demand pressures from the private sector. There is, in fact, a large degree of interdependence between direct government action, as the government sees it, and private sector behavior. For example, as already pointed out, the demand for a greater share of the cake, whether growing or not, by one sector can only be satisfied if some other sector gives up an equal share. The government, for one, is unlikely to give up its share.

There are many good causes, and claims by different groups. It is not necessary to debate the social, political, moral or economic desirability of these demands in order to recognize that they are potentially extremely inflationary unless the rest of society is prepared to make the required transfer of resources. And for the purposes of the present discussion this is all that matters. Given the varied and wide-ranging objectives of government, politicians have found themselves forced to finance the additional demands of each new group in order to prevent other groups from losing out in the struggle for shares in the national pie.

In a perfectly free market, the swift will prosper and the slow will not. There will be high returns available, but also high risks—risks which are unknown now in the industrialized world, of real and absolute collapse on a mammoth scale, inevitably combined with a large amount of human suffering. In a democracy, human suffering on a large scale is unacceptable, and governments will go to great lengths to avoid it; reducing risk even if this also requires reducing the potential gain. The development of democracy and large-scale government has produced a fundamental change in the inflation equation.

## Oil and inflation

A good example of an external inflationary shock, and the problems facing governments when dealing with it, is provided by a sudden sharp rise in the oil price. The initial effect is a shift in relative prices in favor of oil, and an increased flow of income to oil producers. This is not a humanitarian cause, or a cause that the majority of voters are likely to sympathize with. All they are likely to notice is the fall in real disposable incomes. There is no simple way for the government to respond.

Part of the problem with understanding the effect of sharp increases in oil prices is the way in which the past crises have been interpreted. For example, it is widely, almost exclusively, held that OPEC set alight and fueled the inflation that exploded in the 1970s. While that would be a convenient explanation, it is not true. OPEC, as a large oligopoly, can certainly influence prices to some extent, but it is limited in its actions by the laws of economics, as are all others. Under normal circumstances, OPEC will act as profit maximizers do, reacting to the forces of demand and other sources of supply. In the event of natural catastrophe, or war or revolution, normal economic forces may be suspended for a while and a major disruption created. However, in that respect, oil is no different from any other commodity which might be hit by frost, drought, storm or political disruption. The Middle East, with its concentration of oil, and its political instability, is a special cause for concern which has played a role in the inflationary process, but less than generally supposed.

The oil price held remarkably steady through the 1960s and on into the early 1970s, as did commodity prices in general; this is shown in Fig. 2.3. The first major oil price increase came only in late 1973, but when it did come it was truly dramatic, an increase of 400 per cent in less than six months. The manner and form of the increase did depend on the existence of OPEC, and the increase was all the more disruptive as a result. However, OPEC was not the cause of the troublesome inflation that became endemic during the 1970s. General commodity prices, excluding oil, had risen by more than 100 per cent over 1972 and into 1973, from an index figure of 44.4 at the end of 1971 to over 100 by July 1973, and the price of gold had risen by more than 200 per cent over the same period. During this period the price of gold in terms of oil, shown at the bottom of the chart, rose by nearly the same percentage, representing a major depreciation of the value of OPEC's oil reserves.

It is hard to avoid the conclusion that the oil price was responding to the inflationary excess demand that had already been created. The combination of the OPEC cartel with the low substitutability of other energy sources for oil did magnify the rise in the price of oil when it came. However, as

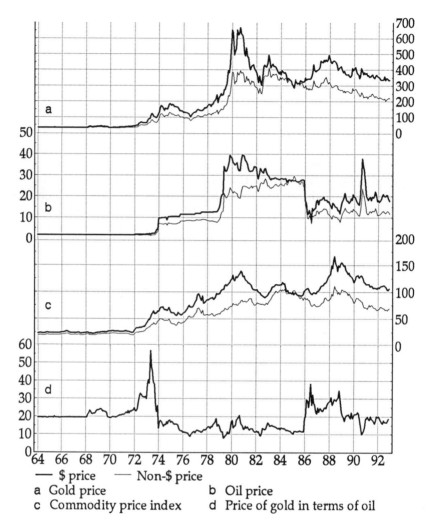

**Figure 2.3** Commodity prices (monthly)

demand conditions stabilized over the next few years so the price of oil stabilized.

At the time of the second oil-price explosion, inflationary pressure was less than during the earlier episode, and the rise in oil prices in 1979 was exaggerated by the political and economic chaos in Iran. However, the basic pattern was the same. The oil price increases lagged behind the general inflationary spiral, but not by nearly as much as in 1973, and the rise was not quite so sharp when it came. The price increase, this time, contained more of a political premium and, therefore, had the potential to fall further. The potential price vulnerability was first reflected in the price of gold and other commodities. There was a slight fall in oil prices in 1981, and even greater downward pressure on oil prices in 1982 and 1983. The price dropped back sharply in 1986, as the countries of OPEC finally capitulated to rising excess supply.

The conclusion must be that oil prices followed inflationary pressure rather than led it, but that the strength of non-market forces was sufficient to put a temporary floor under prices and prevent them from falling, at least as fast as they otherwise would have. The effect is similar to that created by trade unions, who find it easier to justify, and achieve, real increases in wages than real cuts. So, even with the need to halt inflation, it becomes difficult to get real wages to increase more slowly. These forces do not necessarily cause inflation, but they do produce substantial inertia against a decline once the process is under way.

The first two increases in the oil price came at a time of high inflation and substantial excess demand, when the problem was not well understood and inflationary expectations were running wild. The sharp jump in 1990 occurred under very different circumstances, and was not sustained. Military action in the Middle East was a constant that undoubtedly caused concern, but the inflationary environment was completely different. The initial response was partly caused by a false interpretation of the earlier experiences. The panic reactions seemed excessive, even at the time. However, the early ending of hostilities makes it hard to draw any conclusions.

An important feature about oil in this situation is that demand is relatively inelastic in the short term. What that means is that real demand falls only slightly when the price rises a lot, which, in turn, implies that the value of oil sales, and receipts, increase substantially. The increased money spent on energy reduces the amount of disposable income left for the purchase of other goods and services. This decline in spending elsewhere in the economy is unlikely to match the rise in spending on energy, so that overall demand increases.

Remember, what we are talking about here is nominal demand. Real supply, on the other hand, is now faced with higher costs so that supply potential is reduced, assuming no other changes. The net result is an increase in excess demand and higher inflation. That, at least, is the initial effect. There is not much anyone can do about that—it is an external shock which policy makers have no control over. The policy response will affect the next round.

No accommodation at all will result in a reduction in real demand and little inflationary follow-through. The risk in this case is that of creating a recession. Easing monetary policy sufficiently to pay the higher oil prices, in theory, allows the economy to maintain the pre-existing level of output, and return to the previous inflation rate, once the one-off impact of higher oil prices has worked its way through the economy. The difficulty in this case is that it ignores the effect of higher energy prices on inflationary expectations and future wage claims. These reactions will spread out the price increases and put additional downward pressure on supply potential. If the monetary authorities do not respond by easing further, the effect of inflation will be limited, but again at the risk of recession.

What is highly inflationary is if the monetary authorities keep anticipating the potential economic weakness by lowering interest rates or easing fiscal policy. Under those circumstances, inflationary expectations are realized and there is a danger of the situation getting out of control. The monetary authorities have to pick a road in between, and will almost certainly be accused of creating a recession and higher inflation. While there is an element of truth at both ends of the spectrum, the ground at the center provides the safest course—which was essentially the response following the 1990 surge in oil prices. The situation was made easier by the fact that oil supplies were maintained through production increases by Saudi Arabia, and by the ease with which victory was achieved over Saddam Hussein.

## The changing inflation/growth cycle

There have been three major changes to the inflation cycle over the post-war period. The first, between inflation and money growth, has already been dealt with earlier in the chapter. In addition, the relationship between inflation and economic growth has changed. There used to be a close link between economic growth and inflation in the first half of the century, but that no longer works the way it did, as can be seen from Fig. 2.4. If anything, there is now a negative correlation between inflation and economic growth—a major change from how the relationship worked prior to the Second World War.

The reason is related to the increased interventionist policies of government over the post-war period, and the simultaneous attempt to achieve strong growth while limiting the spread of inflation. The reasoning is similar to that used to explain the changing relationship between money growth and inflation earlier. The third change is the most dramatic of all. In the past, inflation would be negative as well as positive. This symmetry is what, in retrospect, is used to justify claims of price stability in earlier times, a subject discussed further in Chapter 16. And here again, increased intervention is the cause.

Mitchell (1941) described the relationship between inflation and output over a typical cycle. The path he outlined followed the dotted diamond

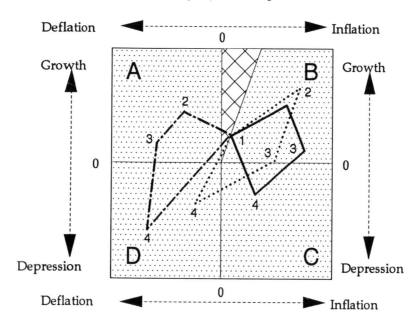

**Figure 2.5** The economic box

fall together, and in the process set up the conditions for an upturn in the economy. The close correlation between growth and inflation during the early part of this century can be seen in Fig. 2.4, when inflation closely followed the growth of industrial production with very little lag.

This close relationship between economic growth and inflation has shifted over the post-war period, with the added complication that now prices no longer fall in the down-phase. Typically the rate of inflation falls, but does not actually turn negative. Wholesale prices have fallen at times in the United States, as in the 1960s, and in other countries, but these have been the exceptions rather than the rule, and consumer prices have hardly fallen at all over the post-war period. In the United States and elsewhere, the normal case has been for prices to continue rising during recessions, but at a slower rate. Also, the extremes of cycles have been smoothed down. Consequently, the cycles have become squarer, following a course similar to that laid out by the continuous line in quadrants B and C.

This change has not happened by accident, but has resulted from the direct intervention of the public sector in the economy. The depression in the 1930s was directly associated with falling prices which made monetary policy ineffective. When prices are falling it is impossible to bring real interest rates down by lowering nominal rates. Nominal rates will always be positive; even in the depths of the depression, bond yields still aver-

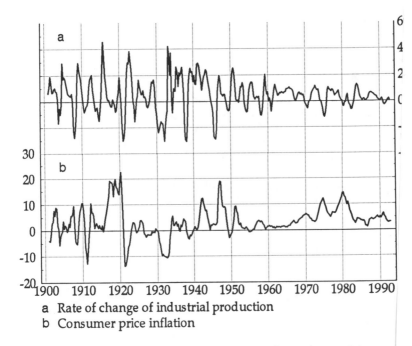

a   Rate of change of industrial production
b   Consumer price inflation

**Figure 2.4** Industrial production and inflation (quarterly)

pattern shown in Fig. 2.5. This chart has been labeled 'The Economic
and shows the bounds of possibility between inflation/deflatior
growth/depression. Upward movement represents a higher  ra
growth, or a slower rate of decline if still below zero. A move to the
reflects a higher rate of inflation, while one to the left of zero refle
increasing rate of decline of prices, i.e. increasing deflation. Quadr
shows the combination of growth and deflation; quadrant B show
combination of growth with inflation; quadrant C, declining outpu
bined with rising prices; while in quadrant D both output and pric
falling.

Starting from recession, economic activity picks up while prices r
subdued, but soon prices move up with output, as shown by the
line. In the second phase of the cycle, business activity accelerates f
but so too do prices, as the added demand uses up capacity and cos
to rise with the introduction of less efficient means of productioi
increase in prices puts pressure on wages which add further to cos
time when interest rates are rising and it is harder to pass on the in
in the form of higher prices. In the next stage, both inflation and
remain positive, but the rates slow down. Finally both prices and

aged over 4 per cent. That means, with falling prices, real interest rates are very high. Such a situation, combined with a weak economy, can create a downward spiral which monetary policy is helpless to do anything about; a situation I have previously referred to as the *time-preference trap*. This is quite different to Keynes' famous *liquidity trap*. The time-preference trap refers to the effect that *real*, as opposed to nominal, interest rates have on demand. The trap refers to times when nominal interest rates are substantially above the expected rate of inflation. This could be because of very high rates of interest or a very low, even negative, rate of inflation. Under such circumstances, there is a strong incentive to postpone as much consumption and investment as possible in order to buy more cheaply in the future.

The liquidity trap proposed by Keynes (1936) was about something else altogether. Keynes argued that liquidity preference, and *not* the consumption/saving decision, determines the rate of interest. The trap comes about when 'liquidity-preference may become virtually absolute in the sense that almost everyone prefers cash to holding a debt which yields so low a rate of interest'. This was seen as more of a theoretical possibility than a practical reality, since Keynes claimed that, 'I know of no example of it hitherto'.

A time-preference trap which, I would argue, existed in the 1930s, has been avoided in subsequent business cycles. Such a situation is completely unacceptable in a democracy, where politicians are under constant pressure to be re-elected. Consequently, there has been a conscious, or unconscious, decision to err on the side of inflation rather than risk the danger of deflation. This is an extremely important change, and one with highly significant implications for investors.

The cycle associated with the 1930s depression is particularly interesting: the path is traced out in Fig. 2.5 by the heavy dashed line. In this case, the cycle went into reverse. The initial recovery phase in 1928 was fairly normal, with inflation quickly responding to the pickup in the economy. However, the inflationary response was very subdued and, before the end of 1928, wholesale prices were already falling. During the second phase of the cycle, growth accelerated but prices fell. As the growth rate slowed in the third stage, the fall in prices accelerated. The final climax came with both output and prices falling sharply.

There are other examples in history when deflation has not been associated with depression, but the experience of the 1930s has left an indelible impression. Inflation is unpopular, and there were concerns in the late 1970s and early 1980s that it would get out of control. There is real fear about the merest hint of deflation, maybe not so much among investors, but certainly by the monetary authorities. As long as that bias continues, the monetary authorities will keep the output/inflation mix in the right half of the *box*, and ideally in the upper section.

Critics of the authorities demand nothing less than zero inflation with rapid growth, while avoiding ever creating a general deflation of prices; that is, to achieve some position along the upper reaches of the center vertical line. What is being asked is, of course, impossible. The whole point of a free market economy is that competition creates opportunities that could not be foreseen through central planning. Another way of saying the same thing is that the exact nature of the economy, its strengths and weaknesses, are not forecastable. So even if the tools of economic management were perfect, they could still not be used with a precision that would keep the economy on such a narrow path. And the tools are far from perfect. Governments made a major policy mistake in the 1960s by believing that they had the power to generate higher rates of growth.

Since what is being demanded cannot be achieved on a sustained basis, there is always disappointment and criticism of policy actions and achievements. While a case can be made for at least trying for perfection, there is a danger in raising expectations too high. If success is interpreted as failure, it becomes difficult to distinguish between a genuine deterioration and an improvement in economic performance. This is not only confusing for policy makers, who are on a hiding to nothing, but also for investors and businessmen, who can easily be left with the impression that the world is going to the dogs when, in fact, conditions are actually improving.

The monetary authorities have generally been aiming to stay in the shaded wedge area. The objective has been strong growth, and some inflation has been acceptable in order to achieve it. However, once inflation starts to accelerate, the authorities have moved in to slow demand and bring inflation back down, but never carrying the restraint to the point of creating deflation—by which is meant a sustained fall in prices that gets out of control. It seems reasonable to expect the bias against deflation to be maintained, and that any movement in this direction will be met with significant monetary easing.

To summarize, there have been important changes in the cyclical relationship between inflation and economic growth. The relationship was much closer in the early part of this century, but has not been very good over the post-war period. Moreover, to the extent that a correlation of some sort does still exist, it is negative instead of positive. The explanation for this lies with the massive growth of government and the general acceptance of government responsibility for *managing* the economy. Depression is closely associated with deflation, and fear of the one implies fear of the other. This has imparted an inflationary bias to monetary and fiscal policies, a bias that is likely to persist in the future. Consequently, it is very unlikely that the United States will actually move into deflation—i.e. an uncontrollable fall in general prices. For those making long-term investment decisions, that is a crucial distinction.

## Zero inflation

When it comes to considering the prospects for inflation in the future it is useful to consider the likelihood of achieving and maintaining zero inflation, i.e. absolute price stability. At the start of the 1990s, Federal Reserve Chairman, Alan Greenspan, claimed that it was possible to reduce inflation to zero over five years, and to do so without creating a recession. What he then went on to prove was that it was possible to have recession without achieving zero inflation. Representative Stephen L. Neal (NC) introduced a resolution in the House at that time directing the Federal Reserve 'to adopt and pursue monetary policies leading to, and then maintaining, zero inflation'. In other countries the same objective has been widely discussed and generally accepted. The advantages flowing from such an achievement seem to be overwhelming. Once inflation has been eliminated there is apparently no reason for it to accelerate again, and economic growth will increase in an environment of stable prices. In addition, since inflation is a major cyclical variable, the business cycle would seem to disappear.

Inflation can be reduced to zero, that never was a problem. The bit about no recession is, however, a little harder to achieve. Once reduced to zero, there is very little chance of inflation staying there; that has never been the case in history, and there is no reason to believe that it would be possible in the future. The proposals for zero inflation seem to assume a static economy; quite different from the dynamic reality. There are no grounds for advocating a policy of deliberately stimulating inflation. Price stability that results naturally from the combination of 'good' policies and favorable circumstances would be very welcome, but there is nothing to be gained by targeting the symptoms while leaving the causes unattended.

John Maynard Keynes argued that inflation 'engages all the hidden forces of economic law on the side of destruction, and does it in a manner which not one man in a million is able to diagnose'. This is quite clearly an exaggeration of reality. His views were no doubt colored by the devastating hyperinflation that Germany suffered in the 1920s, and which he observed first-hand. What is really destructive is sudden, unexpected changes in inflation. A low, relatively stable rate of inflation need be no more disturbing than a relatively stable zero rate, and deflation is certainly more dangerous than inflation. It should be noted that Keynes also had even harsher words to say about deflation. The proposal for achieving stable prices is generally discussed without also considering the question of *economic* stability; stable should be the key word, not zero. Stable prices are an easy choice if there is no cost involved, but not if this implies a less stable economy or a slower growth rate.

Inflation is widely discussed as the major problem facing the United States, and the industrialized countries generally. That is only because there has not been a depression for a long time. A prolonged, and severe, economic downturn would quickly cause a re-ordering of priorities. Inflation may be unpopular, but not as much as high and rising unemployment. Inflation hovered around 4.5 per cent for much of the 1980s, and it is hard to find anyone who suffered too badly from it; employment grew rapidly, the economy was expanding and asset values rose strongly. What is so terrible about that? Particularly when compared with falling output, people being thrown out of work, collapsing stock prices and soaring government spending.

Inflation does complicate decision-making, but then so do taxes, variable exchange rates and many government actions, and they all affect various groups differently. Part of that negative effect results from the fact that not all prices rise at the same rate, but exactly the same distributional effects are likely with zero inflation. This last point is usually overlooked, but is very important when discussing the negative effect of relative price changes. In fact, in those cases when a change in relative prices is desirable, as in the replacement of old industries with new, this will be more easily achieved with mild inflation than a fixed price level.

There are a number of problems in setting up inflation as the main villain. Inflation is anyway a symptom of excess demand and is not the only possible reaction. The symptom should not be ignored, but successful treatment requires the correct diagnosis of the underlying cause. The attraction of a zero inflation target, and inflation baiting generally, to the political community, is that it passes the buck over to the Federal Reserve and attention is directed away from the pork-barrel politics that have played an important role in accelerating inflation.

There are a number of assumptions underlying the objective of a zero inflation target:

1.  Any inflation is bad.
2.  Inflation always accelerates unless brought back to zero, and will eventually turn into hyperinflation.
3.  Hyperinflation inevitably results in a breakdown of democracy and morality.
4.  Economies grow faster when there is no inflation.
5.  Smoothing out the business cycle requires eliminating inflation.
6.  There used to be price stability, so why not now?

This is an impressive list, but it is too often accepted without question. It is, therefore, worth considering how true these assumptions are. And it turns out that is exactly what they are, just assumptions, and not the result of any study or analysis of inflation.

1.  There is no evidence to suggest that low levels of inflation are such a

bad thing. Rapidly accelerating inflation is bad, but low levels of inflation have been associated with steady growth over the post-war period, and at other times. Inflexible tax laws, and contracts, may impose a cost of continuing inflation, but these are not necessary.

2.  Inflation does not have to accelerate out of control. Inflation has remained positive almost continuously throughout the industrialized world since 1945 and has not turned into hyperinflation, and there is no reason why it should. Inflation does not remain constant at any fixed number, and the same would apply to zero. An average of zero over time would require periods when prices were falling. That is a much more dangerous situation than gradually rising prices.

3.  Hyperinflation is definitely not desirable, but the dangers should not be exaggerated. Contemporary views on the dangers of hyperinflation are formed by looking back at the disastrous effects of the German hyperinflation of the 1920s. But there is much more recent, and relevant, evidence available. The events in Latin America in the 1980s have shown that even hyperinflation can be controlled, and also that it can be associated with the development, as opposed to the destruction, of democracy. There are signs of emerging political nationalism in Japan recently that have nothing to do with the effects of hyperinflation.

4.  Japan continues to astound the world with its ability to grow and adapt to changing conditions. Japan has also had low inflation through the 1980s, but then growth has also slowed over this period. The real high-growth days, when the economy was expanding rapidly, e.g. in the 1960s when GNP grew at an average annual rate of over 11 per cent, also saw CPI inflation averaging 5.7 per cent. The real Japanese miracle was played out to the accompaniment of rapid inflation, not low inflation. At the same time, France was the fastest growing European country and it also had one of the highest inflation rates. In the 1980s, the United Kingdom had the fastest growth rate in Europe, and also has the highest inflation rate. The Asian Tigers—South Korea and Hong Kong—have grown much faster than the average, and also have much higher inflation than the average.

I am certainly not suggesting inflation should deliberately be increased in order to stimulate growth, that would be a disaster. But equally, stopping inflation altogether is unlikely to produce the gains in growth that are generally expected. there is no evidence to support such a claim. It is more likely that growth would be slowed by the strenuous efforts to keep inflation at zero.

5.  The business cycle has been flatter over the post-war period than at any other time in history. Keeping inflation at zero would require making some prices fall sharply if others were rising sharply, as is bound to

happen at times. These price declines, if forced by monetary policy, would likely be associated with recessions, at least in some sectors. If anything, it seems likely that the attempt to maintain zero inflation would result in greater cyclicality, not less.

6.   The belief in past price stability is based on the fact that, over a hundred-year span, the price index ended up basically where it had started, i.e. no change in prices. This was not stability, however. In between these dates there had been wide swings in the price level, and even bigger swings in inflation. Inflation accelerated sharply at times, more than over the post-war period, and then plunged—not only falling, but actually becoming significantly negative. There was nothing even remotely resembling stability of inflation, the price level or economic activity. Figure 2.6 shows the pattern of inflation from 1830. The data have been smoothed by a five-year moving average, but still the volatility is very great.

The evidence is so obvious that it hardly seems worth the time to discuss it, except that a popular perception to the contrary has grown. There is often a nostalgic yearning for the good-old-days, but in this case, as in most others, there is nothing desirable about that past experience. Those who complain about present day instability would be shocked by the volatility of those days. Consider what Warren F. Hickernell (1928) had to say on the subject:

> As a result of wars and the inability of governments to discover sound banking systems and the proper way to regulate the monetary standard, the human race during the eighteenth and nineteenth centuries passed through 200 years of disgrace. The extreme fluctuations of prices caused more human tragedy than the mortalities of war.

Whichever way you look at it, prices were anything but stable over the nineteenth century and through the first half of the twentieth century. Perhaps there is some virtue in forcing prices back down to where they had been but, firstly, that is still not stability of prices and, secondly, it is an action that will result in an unstable economy. Stability of prices is a desirable objective, but so too is stability of the economy and the maintenance of conditions that enable continued growth. Governments cannot control growth in the way they once tried to do, and some people still think is possible, but they can slow down the potential by putting obstacles in the way.

Since 1983, when inflation came down to reasonable levels, inflation in the services sector has remained fairly stable at just below 5 per cent, with health costs rising at a much faster rate. At the same time, consumer price inflation has averaged close to 3.8 per cent. In order to achieve that combination it is clear that the prices of other things must have been rising

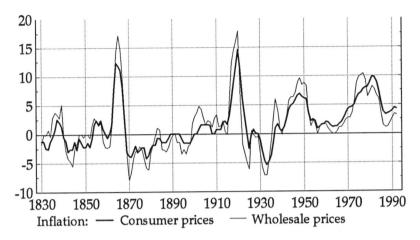

**Figure 2.6** Inflation history (five-year average of annual data)

more slowly. With services representing 55 per cent of the CPI, and with low productivity growth, the task of reducing inflation to zero is likely to bear heavily on the rest of the economy.

The objective of zero inflation means *on average*, so if the price of services continued to rise, goods prices would have to fall. High interest rates, designed to keep inflation out of existence, would raise costs in manufacturing more than in the service sectors, and would depress demand for goods more than services. High interest rates would also tend to raise the exchange rate, thereby depressing external demand and making imports cheaper. Here again the main impact is on manufactured goods and commodities rather than services.

If the prices of goods are already falling on average, someone needs to ask whether these prices should be depressed even further in order to compensate for rising costs of services. These price reductions will not happen automatically or painlessly, but by depressing demand and causing these industries to contract. Such action may be necessary in order to administer a sharp shock to the economy at a time of rapidly rising inflation, and there is a need to stop expectations from accelerating even faster. However, does it make sense as a normal state of affairs? A tight monetary policy designed to bring inflation down to zero would have its greatest impact on the manufacturing sector. But is such an outcome desirable, particularly if that is not where the main inflation is coming from? And what if manufactured goods prices were actually falling, but not enough to offset increase elsewhere?

A zero inflation target, if mandated by law, would be extremely dangerous. No doubt the proposers of such laws envision a benign government that is sensible and honest and working to the same ends as the Federal Reserve. This does not have to be the case. When setting rules, it is necessary to consider all possibilities no matter how remote, and the implications that follow. As long as the government cuts the budget deficit and restrains the growth in expenditure, the objective of a low level of inflation is easily attainable. But what if the government expands expenditures rapidly and runs a substantial budget deficit? Or even that the price of oil shoots up to $100 a barrel? Or adverse weather conditions cause food prices to rise dramatically? Or all these things together? If the Federal Reserve's hands are tied then it would have no alternative but to tighten monetary policy dramatically.

We can all agree that high inflation is bad and low inflation is good, but it is still necessary to ask what the alternative would be. Naturally, there will be some optimal policy, but what if strong government expansion is given and cannot be changed? Under the circumstances of a zero inflation rule, or total rigid monetary control requirements, either a gold standard or self-imposed restrictions, the answer is that interest rates will be pushed up rapidly in order to squeeze private sector output. The pressure will be felt the hardest in the manufacturing sector and by new businesses, where interest rates have their greatest impact. Under these particular circumstances, the government should cut back in order for the private sector to recover, and then expand. However, that relies on the goodwill of the politicians in power. It is quite possible to imagine a set of circumstances under which a rigid monetary system fails to act as a safeguard of private enterprise but becomes, instead, its worst enemy.

Under those circumstances large sections of the population would no longer have to worry about higher prices, since they would have no income with which to pay them anyway. Aggressive attempts to maintain inflation at zero, in the face of sharply rising commodity prices or service costs, will not have their main impact on these sectors, but on the manufacturing sector. There may be some logic in this type of automatic reaction, although certainly less than it might seem, and it is not costless or fair. The incidence of monetary policy is discussed further in Chapter 4.

Reducing inflation is a means to an end, it should not be the end itself. Inflation, like the current account, is really a constraint not an objective. The ultimate objective is a strong private sector that is innovative and prepared to take the risks necessary to make high rewards. What good is a zero rate of inflation if the cost of achieving it has been the decimation of private industry? Always remember that the single-minded pursuit of a single objective can easily be achieved, but the result is likely to be destructive. When the target is not even an objective, there is a need to be even more careful.

The real point is that inflation is a symptom, not the illness itself. The problem of general inflation is excess demand, i.e. demand relative to supply. Either side can affect the final outcome. It is possible to suppress the inflation, as was done for a long time in the Soviet Union, but this does nothing to solve the underlying problem of excess demand. A mandatory target of zero inflation could result in all sorts of inspired index-jigging in order to achieve the right appearance. Anyone doubting that possibility has not been following the history of the Gramm-Rudman deficit-reduction legislation.

Low inflation, and even zero inflation, would be desirable if it were the result of consistent policies. What that means is that the policies should not depend on putting excessive pressure on particular sectors to compensate for others which continue to experience rapid inflation. A target of zero inflation at all costs could indeed be very costly; it is the equivalent of treating high fever with leeches and a little blood letting.

There is one catch in maintaining a low, but positive, rate of inflation: countries with lower inflation will gain international competitiveness. Competition for international markets is one way in which a zero inflation rule can be justified, but the domestic dangers are still very real. What if a country achieves significant deflation, does that mean that other countries should try to achieve even greater declines in prices? What is likely to be successful for a single country, because of the relative gain in competitiveness, could turn into a world-wide depression if everyone tries it. Having tested the democratic limits of rising inflation, there is the possibility that errors will be made on the other side. The inflation cycle has not hit its low point yet, but it seems likely that actual deflation will continue to be resisted by the monetary authorities.

# 3

## THE IMBALANCE OF PAYMENTS
### (external exchanges)

It is impossible to discuss recent economic developments without considering the huge foreign trade imbalances that have been created along the way. What had been small gaps became huge chasms between countries. While it is true that these external deficits and surpluses net out within the world economy, and there are certainly errors on calculation, it is not reasonable to ignore them. Large debts also net out across all savers and borrowers, but that does not make them insignificant. The problems can easily be exaggerated, but persistent deficits can also be a real problem; so can persistent surpluses.

A current account imbalance is exactly the same thing as the net saving or dissaving of a country. It can be compared to the income, consumption and saving behavior of an individual. A current account deficit has to be financed either by borrowing or the sale of assets, thereby increasing claims by foreigners on the domestic economy. However, this does not mean that the wealth of the country is reduced; that would only be true in a static situation. Whether or not there is a problem depends on the level of internal growth.

A current account deficit, like inflation, is usually a symptom of excess demand, although it obviously depends on what other countries are doing as well. Major external deficits usually result from the combination of an overvalued exchange rate and excessive growth in domestic demand. Changes in the exchange rate will be ineffective in the short term, but will have a major long-term effect. In the short term, a decline in the exchange rate can actually worsen the trade account through adverse terms-of-trade effects. The longer-run effects of an overvalued currency work by lowering the growth potential of the economy. An overvalued exchange rate need not show up in the form of a balance-of-payments deficit if slower growth is accepted, but typically that is not the case, and attempts to expand demand in order to stimulate growth will produce external deficits.

An overvalued exchange rate is rarely seen as the problem, as most attention is focused on the symptoms—a trade deficit and slow growth.

Slow growth tends to result in frequent attempts to stimulate the economy, followed by a reversal of policy as the balance of payments worsens. Recession, and rising unemployment, typically brings things to a head, with calls for protection against unfair foreign competition. This is a perverse, and potentially dangerous response, since foreign trade has grown much faster than output over the post-war period, providing an important engine for growth. The chance of a protectionist reaction like this should be taken seriously, and is another reason why trade deficits are important.

Some background numbers will help to illustrate the importance of world trade—a role that continues to expand over time. Table 3.1 shows the percentage of merchandise trade and trade in goods and services in each of the G7 countries in 1960 and again in 1990. In every case, trade has grown in importance. Given the emphasis on Japanese trade surpluses, it is perhaps surprising to find that this is the only country where merchandise trade has not grown as a percentage of GNP; particularly as this is being measured here in terms of exports. Growth has been higher once services are added in, but Japan is much better known for the expansion of merchandise trade. What we find, however, is that this growth has only been in line with the rest of the economy. On this evidence, Japan has hardly taken unfair advantage of international markets. What these figures do not show is the concentration of exports to the United States and, of course, imports have not grown as quickly as exports. Exports from other countries have expanded much more rapidly, and none more so than the United States, as a percentage of GNP. The United States and Germany are in close competition as to which is the largest exporter in the world, but clearly there is a big difference in exports relative to the size of the domestic economy. The slowest growth in goods and services has been in the United Kingdom, despite the fact that over this period the country went from being a net importer of the oil, to a net exporter.

Countries have taken advantage of the opportunities offered by foreign trade, and as a result have become more dependent on events in other

*Table 3.1* External trade of G7 countries, 1960 to 1990: exports as a percentage of GNP

|                | Merchandise trade | | Goods and services | |
|                | 1960 | 1990 | 1960 | 1990 |
|----------------|------|------|------|------|
| Canada         | 14.7 | 22.7 | 17.6 | 26.0 |
| France         | 11.4 | 18.7 | 13.8 | 23.4 |
| Germany        | 15.8 | 26.3 | 20.0 | 35.6 |
| Italy          | 9.8  | 16.5 | 12.1 | 19.4 |
| Japan          | 9.3  | 9.7  | 10.9 | 14.6 |
| United Kingdom | 14.6 | 18.3 | 19.8 | 24.0 |
| United States  | 3.9  | 7.2  | 4.8  | 9.8  |

Table 3.2 Growth of exports, money and prices, 1960–1990

|  | Percentage |
| --- | --- |
| World exports | 2733.1 |
| Exports of industrialized countries | 2833.5 |
| World money | 2489.2 |
| Money of industrialized countries | 1727.5 |
| Consumer prices in industrialized countries | 419.6 |

countries. The market has become larger, and subjected to a wider range of forces, which can be good or bad. Table 3.2 shows the growth of world exports over the period from 1960 to 1990. For industrial countries, exports expanded 29 times, slightly faster than for the world as a whole. This rate of growth is also much faster than the growth of the money supply over this period, particularly in the case of the industrialized countries, which expanded only 18 times. Consumer prices for the industrialized countries, on the other hand, rose only five times.

## The balance of payments

There are thousands of separate financial transactions taking place each day, some lending money, some borrowing, some the counterpart of purchases of goods or financial assets and some the counterpart of sales. In some cases, the flows help to create a financial surplus, while in others they are actually part of the savings flows themselves. The first thing to do is to separate out the financial flows that are the counterpart of real transactions in goods and services, and those that are purely financial transactions or the counterpart of transactions in existing assets. This chapter is concerned with the first of these flows only, the counterpart of real transactions. Financial markets are dealt with in subsequent chapters.

The balance of payments, excluding purely financial transactions, can be measured in a variety of ways. The trade balance can include just goods, or goods and services, depending on the precise definition employed. The merchandise trade balance will also depend on whether the cost of freight and insurance (c.i.f.) are included or not. Some countries publish the figures one way, some another. The United States used to publish monthly figures that included c.i.f. on imports but not exports, but then switched to customs-cleared value for imports when compiling the quarterly numbers for merchandise trade. In 1988, the United States started to publish monthly figures on the same basis as the quarterly.

The balance on current account is a wider measure that includes net transfers in the form of interest, dividends and profits. This definition is also exactly equal to the net saving (surplus) or dissaving (deficit) of a country *vis-à-vis* the rest of the world. The saving of a country can be interpreted in the same way as that of an individual, representing the excess of income over expenditure. What is left over is the surplus or, in the case of excess expenditure, the deficit. The counterpart of a current account surplus is an external financial surplus for the country; the two are equal by definition. The current account shows the position of a country relative to the rest of the world after all income and expenditure flows have been taken into account. A current account surplus is identical to the country's net saving over that period, and a current account deficit is just another way of showing the dissaving of a country.

The relationship is genuine and the potential problems are real enough; these are problems of excess. In life, most problems seem to be ones of excess, be they economic, political, social, dietary or geological, and this is no exception. There is, however, no point in exaggerating the disequilibrium effect. The saving or dissaving applies in only the context of inter-country relations within the world economy. The wealth of a country can still grow through internal saving and investment that does not show up in the external financial flows. The process can be compared to that of a domestic corporation that generates growth from internal cash flow.

In calculating the income of an individual, it is necessary to include the income received from existing wealth, i.e. interest and dividends. The same is true of countries, and the current account includes interest, dividends and profits earned abroad. Countries with strong current account surpluses build up a flow of income from the accumulated assets overseas. These flows work to reinforce the situation by helping to generate surpluses in the future. Fortunately, natural economic forces will provide a solution, since these additional flows will tend to push up the exchange rate and hold down trade competitiveness. In extreme cases, companies in these countries will increasingly set up production facilities in other countries in order to avoid being priced out of the market. Switzerland and the United States have been typical examples, which makes the dramatic deterioration in the US external trade account in the 1980s all the harder to understand. Actually, the deterioration is easy to understand; it is the policies that led to it that are difficult to rationalize. More recently, Japan has moved into this position of generating persistent surpluses, with companies expanding production facilities in the United States, Europe and in the developing economies of Asia.

In the case of a surplus, there are funds that can be lent out or used to buy financial assets or gold, etc. For those countries running deficits, it will be necessary for them to borrow money, or sell assets, to cover their excess expenditures. The typical pattern has been for the old, rich countries to run surpluses (save) which are then lent out to younger, developing countries to finance growth. The United Kingdom, and the other countries of Europe, played that role in the late nineteenth century and early twentieth century. The United Kingdom has since shown that the pattern seems to reverse as the ageing process continues. The United States has now also provided a classic contradiction to this rule by becoming the richest country going into the greatest debt.

Large deficits imply surpluses elsewhere. Small deficits and surpluses are not a problem and should be expected in the normal course of business. Persistent deficits might also be expected in developing countries or resource-rich countries, where investment potential exceeds what can be financed through domestic saving. In general, however, the pattern should be like the domestic economy, with borrowers repaying debts, and not persistently going further into debt. Also, sudden, large swings are potentially destabilizing, and that is true for both surpluses and deficits.

The sudden, huge surpluses earned by the OPEC countries in the mid-1970s, and early 1980s created a major recycling problem, and helped set up the conditions for the Latin-American debt debacle of the 1980s. The huge surpluses in Germany and Japan in the second half of the 1980s were as much signs of extensive disequilibrium as the huge deficits in the United States. They were, ultimately, equally unacceptable and unsustainable, although somewhat easier to deal with. In order to achieve a balance on current account, the United States will have to run a surplus on trade in goods and services, while Japan and Germany will need to end up with deficits. Such adjustments can take a very long time, and will be confused by all sorts of disturbances along the way, but that will be the direction in which market forces will be pushing. Germany has had the spending power of the former East Germans to convert a massive surplus into an instant deficit. Japan started to adjust, but the surplus began rising again in 1991 and on into 1993.

Reducing a trade deficit means that proportionately more must be produced relative to consumption and investment, or less consumed and invested relative to production. In a static economy with no growth, that means lower living standards. With falling output, in a recession, it means sharply falling living standards. The easiest adjustment will be under conditions of strong economic growth, but that is a problem for deficit countries, given the policies required to reduce consumption. Surplus countries can help by stimulating demand at home. With growing world markets, adjustment can take place without depressing living standards in the deficit country. This is the most painless form of adjustment, and explains why governments in deficit countries are always keen for other countries to stimulate demand at home. Normally, the surplus countries are reluctant to do anything to encourage domestic inflation, which is why they have surpluses in the first place, and see no need to stimulate when the economy is working close to capacity—producing all those goods for export. In fact, it is often the case that these countries are operating against capacity constraints that require them to adopt restrictive policies of their own. Like most economic problems, surpluses and deficits are much easier to create than to solve.

Markets provide natural solutions, but they can take a long time. When man-made disequilibriums are created on the scale of the 1980s, the natural adjustment process will extend over many years. It is possible for government policies to speed up, and smooth, the process, but it is also possible that they will make things worse; particularly since they were usually responsible for creating the mess in the first place. Governments undoubtedly have powerful weapons at their disposal, but the evidence suggests that they have not always used them wisely. The greatest danger inherent in government, and elector, impatience is the imposition of some wide-ranging import restriction that will endanger the continuation and expansion of free trade.

The protectionist threat is very real, and carries the potential to disrupt world growth. It is possible to devise a situation in which world trade would continue to expand and be very little affected by political restraints on trade, particularly with the growth of regional trading blocs. However, competition would increasingly be based on political rather than economic considerations, and could become much more antagonistic. The trend towards large-scale trading blocs such as the European Economic Community and the North American Free Trade Area take the logic of free trade to the limits, but restrict the area to which it is applied. Despite the apparent similarities between the European and American free trade areas, there is a major difference that is usually glossed over in the United States. In Europe, the countries making up the European Monetary System are moving towards total economic and monetary integration. Admittedly, progress is slow on certain issues, but this is not simply an extended market for the free trade of goods and services. National labor laws and regulations are being rationalized, there is the free movement of people and contracts are enforceable throughout the community. Europe is moving towards a political and economic structure similar to that of the United States of America. Canada is another possible comparison but only in part. Canada has restrictions on trade between the provinces that do not exist even between the different countries of the EEC. The United States, Canada and Mexico are embarked on a much less ambitious plan. These countries are liberalizing trade, but have no broader political aims; nor do they propose to allow the free movement of labor, at least for the time being. As a result, economic integration will be incomplete.

## Consuming the surplus

Temporary fluctuations in surpluses and deficits are the natural order of things, and are of only minor interest. Persistent and large surpluses and deficits are a very different matter. At the point when a country turns from a position of positive net external wealth to negative net external wealth it becomes more difficult to finance current expenditures, as it does for an individual. Positive external wealth produces an income flow into the country which helps to pay the bills. Negative external wealth, on the other hand, produces an outflow that has to be financed, which is on top of the excess expenditures that were so necessary anyway. As a result, the cutbacks have to be even greater. What was a cushion can easily become a lead weight.

The mathematics of an external deficit carry the same message as they do for the government's internal deficit. For example, external borrowing of 3 per cent of GNP, with real interest rates equal to the real growth rate of the economy, will eventually lead to interest payments of 3 per cent of GNP, i.e. the same size as the original deficit. Under these circumstances the deficit will remain at 3 per cent of GNP only if the original excess expenditure is eliminated, since it will now be made up entirely of interest costs. Clearly, once the position has deteriorated to this point, the task of returning to a zero balance is much more difficult than it would have been when the process was just getting started. Balance on current account will now require a trade surplus equal to 3 per cent of GNP.

As long as confidence is maintained, lenders will be willing to finance the spending—topping up income to equal expenditure, and thereby squaring the circle. When confidence gives way, there is not normally a gradual reduction in the desire to lend, but a complete revulsion. New money stops flowing in on the old terms, and past lenders become reluctant to renew expiring loans. At such times, there is a real possibility that the situation can get out of control, creating a crisis of confidence.

The United States is still struggling to recover level ground, following the dramatic deterioration in its external financial position in the 1980s. What happened then was of a completely different magnitude to anything that had gone before. The cumulative deficits quickly wiped out the surplus that had been accumulated over a long period, and then continued to create a huge, cumulative deficit. The cumulative current account deficit for the United States is shown in Fig. 3.1, starting in 1900, i.e. the accumulated savings of the United States *vis-à-vis* the rest of the world.

This series adds up only the net flow of funds, not the change in net worth, or wealth. Originally, Commerce Department estimates of total external net worth were very similar to the cumulative series, but in 1991 they produced a revised series that increased the value of assets held in

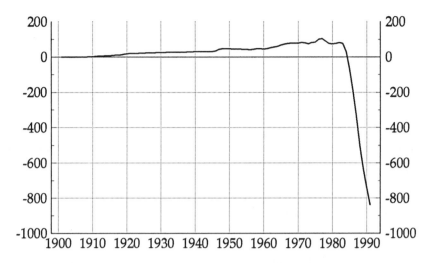

**Figure 3.1** Cumulative current account of the US (in $US billion)

other countries. Previously, the Commerce Department had estimated that the US external net worth turned negative in 1984, around the time of the cumulative current account, but the revised series did not turn negative until 1986 or 1987. Net indebtedness at the end of 1989 was revised from $663.75 billion to $463.96 billion, measuring assets at replacement cost, or $281.44 billion, at market value. The market value of used assets can drop dramatically under adverse conditions, as was demonstrated in the case of many third-world loans, so one is still left with a choice to make about what numbers to use. The cumulative current account is unaffected by valuation changes, and can be related directly back to flow of funds statistics, integrating real and financial flows. This can be helpful, as long as it is always remembered that it is not the same thing as the change in wealth.

Up until the mid-1970s, this series followed an upward trend. There were two upward blips associated with the two wars, and a third in the mid-1970s. Then, in 1976–77, came the first major downturn, which resulted in a crisis of confidence, and a significant decline in the dollar, at least in terms of what was normal in those days. This was followed by a period of belt tightening and a recovery in the current account. In the 1980s, the cumulative series dropped off a cliff.

As long as the dollar was strengthening, there was complacency regarding the deficit. The full extent of the deterioration was not fully appreciated. The external surplus that was built up through this century disappeared virtually overnight. The accumulated surplus was consumed, and the country went into substantial debt in order to keep the spending going; and the debt kept growing. The problem was that the United States was buying far more from other countries than it was selling to them. Excess US demand combined with an extremely overvalued exchange rate, was the perfect recipe for disaster.

Increasing trade surpluses result in a rising flow of funds into a country. Starting from a position of financial equilibrium, where inflows equal outflows, a rising current account surplus should result in a rising exchange rate. Exporters are earning foreign exchange which they will normally switch into the domestic currency, or are paid in domestic currency, which means that the foreign importer has had to obtain currency. There is, consequently, a net additional demand for the currency on top of the flows that existed before. A high currency valuation leads to balance-of-payments deficits, which leads to depreciation of the exchange rate, which leads to balance-of-payments surpluses, and so it goes on. That, in fact, was how floating exchange rates were supposed to work, as described in Chapter 15, on the exchange rate, but reality has not followed theory.

The lags are such that there may often seem, to the casual observer, to be no relationship at all, or even that causality is reversed. What further complicates the whole process are expectations, which are bred by rumor and feed on uncertainty. And there will always be uncertainty. In the case of the United States, the exchange rate continued to rise strongly in the early 1980s despite very high and rising deficits. That had to mean that there were other demands for dollars on the capital account, i.e. for investment purposes, which swamped the selling of dollars by importers or foreign exporters.

One question that has been asked frequently and answered in the affirmative is, has the relationship between the current account and the exchange rate broken down? In fact, that linkage is still very much intact, but it is necessary to take account of the lags involved and these are generally very long. It is a common mistake to expect instant reaction and, when it does not happen, to wander off in search of alternative explanations. In addition, there are other influences on the exchange rate to take into account. One exceptional factor this time was related to the debt crisis of the developing nations that blew up in the summer of 1982. There had been a huge build-up of dollar denominated debts by many countries, and the full extent of the payments problem only became obvious to the banks in 1982, although clear signs had been around for some time before that.

Two things happened as a result. The international banks stopped lending to these countries, and looked around for more secure borrowers. There was a cut in total lending, and an increase in lending to the United States. At the same time the debtor nations had contracted huge dollar liabilities which had to be serviced. These countries became natural demanders of dollars. Money received in other currencies had to be turned into dollars, and dollars received had to be kept as dollars. There could be no diversification into other currencies or gold. The tendency, in fact, had to be in the other direction, to convert existing liquid assets into dollars.

There was also the improvement in inflationary expectations to be taken into account. Confidence in the prospect of future price stability had fallen to a very low level in the late 1970s, when inflation was accelerating strongly and inflationary expectations were rising even faster. At that time, there was a major shift away from the dollar and into the other currencies, gold and other commodities. As it became increasingly apparent that the world was not going to end in an inflationary blow-off of the dollar, the majority of these positions were reversed—not all at once, but as part of a process over time. This lagged readjustment gave the dollar an added boost, and helps to explain the lags involved.

There was another influence on the dollar to be taken into account. That was the high level of real interest rates available in the United States. Here another question is raised. Why, if there was all this additional demand for dollars from abroad, did that not succeed in lowering real interest rates? Answering that will eventually take us back to the major inconsistency in US macro-economic policy. But, first, recognition has to be given to another misconception—that intervention in the foreign exchange markets is always and absolutely wrong. The United States has periodically inter-vened in the foreign exchange markets to stabilize the dollar, but not very often and with seeming reluctance. In the first half of the 1980s, the *laisser-faire* approach to the dollar was followed with ideological fervor. In September 1985, the United States admitted that the value of the dollar was too high. If it was too high in September, after it had already fallen about 25 per cent from its peak against the major currencies, then surely that implies a major policy error in letting it go so high in the first place? US industry would have benefited much more by not travelling on that roller coaster; and could have, had the monetary authorities been prepared to intervene to meet the demand by selling dollars.

The concern may have been that the additional dollars would have pushed interest rates lower and stimulated the economy. However, that was far from being an automatic, or necessary, outcome. It could be that excessive emphasis on the quantity of money outstanding once more muddled the policy reaction. The Federal Reserve clearly had the ability to sell more debt to soak up the extra dollars created through intervention if it seemed that interest rates were likely to fall below the level desired. Intervention complicates the operation of domestic monetary policy, but it does not make it impossible, as sometimes suggested.

Whatever the real motive for not intervening, it is clear that the Federal Reserve felt unable to lower interest rates, and foreign demand had its greatest impact on the dollar rather than the level of interest rates. The Federal Reserve provided sufficient liquidity to meet its objectives for the growth of nominal income after trial and error judgements on changes in the velocity of circulation. The problem for the Federal Reserve was that fiscal policy was creating a lot of additional demand. Reagan was elected in 1980 on a program of large-scale tax cuts and massive increases in military expenditure. These objectives were clearly going to be difficult to achieve at the same time as Reagan's other objective of a balanced budget. In the event, it was the balanced budget that was discarded, and what followed was a huge stimulus to demand. As a result, the economy grew rapidly, and real interest rates remained very high.

In the early stages of recovery, there was the appearance that everything was under control, which encouraged overconfidence. All that had really happened was that the lags had not had a chance to take effect. However, the special circumstances of the time, plus the high real interest rates, were attracting increasing financial flows into dollars. Since there was no change in the quantity of dollars, because of the refusal by the government to intervene, this meant that the price of dollars, the exchange rate, had to rise. Had fiscal policy been more balanced, the disruption to international trade and financial flows would have been far less, US corporations in general would have been in a healthier position and there would have been much less likelihood of extreme swings in the value of the dollar.

## Relative advantage versus competition

Throughout the ages, economists have based the case for international trade on the argument of relative advantage. Absolute advantage provides even stronger support, but is of limited applicability. The beauty of relative advantage is that it applies generally. There is, however, a problem. The beauty of the argument is deceiving, and the argument itself is actually seriously flawed. Trying to justify international trade in terms of a country's relative advantage plays into the hands of the no-change, no-growth ethic. For developed countries, the weakness undercuts the value of the whole argument, giving ammunition to the protectionist forces. In the case of developing countries the argument is even worse, and can be potentially dangerous.

The problem is that the conclusions are based entirely on a static view of the world. That way leads to locking in the habits and patterns of the past, and locking out the innovation and change required to stimulate growth and development. The lesson of the post-war period is that the dynamics of change are crucially important in determining the pattern of international trade. The best justification for free trade is actually the benefits to be gained from competition. Relative advantage is an explanation of why trade may be profitable at a particular moment in time, but also can easily become an argument in favor of restrictive practices. First of all, there is the recommendation to stay with what you can do and not experiment with anything new. Having once made that decision, others of a more competitive nature may come along and try to enter that market; in fact, that is almost certain to happen. Domestic producers will point to the logic of the original argument as they raise the barricades and cry 'protection'.

The benefits of absolute advantage are plain enough. France has an absolute advantage over England in the production of wine, as does California compared with Alaska. Any attempt to compete on equal terms is clearly doomed from the start. These sorts of natural advantages exist in other areas: the Middle East in the production of oil, South African gold production or whisky from Scotland, for example. The case for specialization is most obvious in the case of absolute advantage. It seems only logical that if one country, area or person can produce something cheaper than anyone else, then welfare will be maximized if they specialize in that, and exchange their excess output for the other things they require. Such reasoning provides the origin and essence of international and domestic trade. The trouble is that, even in such an obvious case, there are important qualifications.

On that basis, Saudi Arabia and the neighboring Arab states should be providing a much greater percentage of the world's oil, since they are the lowest cost producers. On the basis of absolute advantage, the North Sea oil fields would never have been developed. But there is a problem that arises once a producer, which can be a country, a company or an individual, is able to control supply conditions, and is thereby able to earn monopoly profits. Accepting the strict logic of absolute advantage may leave other potential but less efficient producers in a situation in which it is difficult, if not impossible, to respond.

There is clearly a strategic aspect to be taken into account, which can become very important. This also shows up in the reaction of Saudi Arabia to the increasing revenues earned. The Saudis are not content simply to import manufactured goods from more efficient producers, but want to set up their own production. But now we are moving into the area of relative advantage, where the case for specialization is even more blurred.

The argument for relative advantage has a certain subtlety about it that is altogether appealing, and at the same time deceptive. The basis is simple and the conclusions not immediately obvious. In a nutshell, what the theory of relative advantage says is that even when one country is the most efficient producer of all goods it still pays to specialize in those things that it can do better than the others, i.e. where it has a relative advantage, and not necessarily the thing it can produce the most of. If each country does that, and exchanges the surplus with the other countries for what it wants, they will all be better off.

As far as it goes, the recommendation is fine, but it advocates maintaining these trade patterns through time, and that is a devastating weakness.

Economic resources cannot be considered fixed in the way assumed by this theory. That seems most obvious in the case of labor, but is even true of land in the sense of natural resources. The changes that can take place, and that need to take place, are clearly demonstrated by the oil sector. Sitting back and accepting the status quo is a recipe for stagnation and loss of competitiveness.

This is no small point. The theory of relative advantage says that you should do what you do best. Behind this is the assumption that resources are fixed, as is their optimal use. The idea that these can be changed does not enter into it. After all, that takes us back into an uncertain world in which the theory has nothing to say. Applying that approach would have kept Japan as a nation of fishermen, while the Koreans would probably be growing rice and making bamboo furniture. And while they may have been very efficient at their respective tasks, these would not have supported the growth and standard of living that has been achieved.

Those examples are so obvious that it is impossible to imagine anything so stupid as to try to preserve existing economic structures that have been inherited, and not to try to break out in new directions. However, that is exactly what the theory of relative advantage prescribes, and it is actually the case that international organizations have advocated just such paths for developing nations. Tinkering with existing methods and patterns of production is something that can be quantified. Tables can be constructed and measures of performance drawn up. Inspectors can go round and see what is being done, and, all in all, it is a regulator's paradise. But it is not the path to dynamic growth that can propel a country out of an inefficient, subsistence-style economy.

The lesson of Japan, and more recently Korea, is very salutary on this point. These countries were not content with the status quo, with the traditional economy, and set out to change it. What were important to them were not the existing skills in fishing or whatever, but the inherent capabilities and ambitions of the people. The approach in this case was to emphasize education and provide the circumstances to encourage risk taking and competition. Through western eyes, Japan often appears as a single large corporation under government control, but the reality is of fierce competition between many individual companies.

Here we come to the true justification and value of international trade. It is so important because it fosters competition, and that is the way to maximize growth and welfare over the long term. Only by constantly challenging the existing state of affairs, and trying to improve products and production methods will progress be made. This is quite the opposite of the prescription provided by relative advantage, which advocates concentrating on what is currently done at the expense of less efficient activities. Clearly, Japan was hopelessly inefficient at making cars at the beginning, but that is, equally clearly, not the case any more.

Competition provides a dynamic that is totally missing from the theory of relative advantage, and the benefits apply equally within the international environment as they do domestically. Accepting that you are the best in a particular area, even relatively, creates complacency. Equally, that mentality finds it hard to accept any challenge to that position. The approach advocates staying in the quiet waters of the river bank watching the rest of the world at the center rush by.

In any competition or race there will be one who comes first, which means that the majority are also-rans. However, taking part is important. In effect, one cannot help but be affected by the economic competition, since everyone will still end up being placed even if they do not take part actively. Through competition one should be capable of doing better than would otherwise be the case. While it is true that someone, or in this case some country, must come last, that does not justify dropping out altogether. Even the slowest person in the race will pass the person who is just standing watching.

Improvements will only be made by trying to improve. And if there is a true relative advantage it will be possible to build on that. There is no doubt that the most that can be lost is by sitting back and doing nothing. The idea of preserving existing conditions is totally deceptive. That only works if everyone is doing the same and there is a return to the stagnation of the Middle Ages. If everyone else is changing, then standing still does not maintain the status quo. The environment changes, perceptions change and competition intensifies. Accepting the existing state of affairs is potentially dangerous.

Relative advantage could be used as an argument against barriers to international trade as with the nineteenth-century Corn Laws in England. However, in retrospect, it is also possible to see the theory as being born out of a mercantilist mentality by English economists who wished to explain why the United Kingdom would maintain the lead it had built up as leader of the Industrial Revolution. Relative advantage in those terms meant that the United Kingdom kept the advantages it had already gained, and the other countries remained doing what they were doing, i.e. they did not compete with UK producers. And all this dressed up in the language of free trade.

Consider how different the mentality is if the starting point is that any country can compete in any product, excepting maybe some cases of absolute advantage. It is then necessary to be striving constantly to introduce new products, to be aware of changes in consumer tastes, always trying to improve productivity and generally to increase competitiveness. No such incentive is provided by the concept of relative advantage.

The alternative argument presented here clearly starts from the position that competition is a good thing—that it will foster growth and improve living standards. Anyone who doubts that should compare living and working in Africa with conditions in the United States or Europe; not living as a foreign transplant, but as an average working citizen. However, there are still those for whom growth is an unnecessary evil. For them, relative advantage is a convenient excuse for their passive views; showing that even the relatively disadvantaged are owed a living by economic theory. Any disruption of that happy state of affairs automatically justifies protection. Within a domestic context this reaction will take the form of strikes, and internationally, as restrictions on trade.

Time and time again, one comes back to the conclusion that the arguments of relative advantage can too easily be used to justify restrictions in trade rather than freedom of trade. Competition, however, offers no such ambiguities. Once one accepts the benefits of competition, then the more the better. To accept the advantages of competition means also to accept the disadvantages, since there must be losers as well as winners; but with the happy conclusion that everyone ends up being better off.

In addition, recognizing the existence of competition in the world raises the question of what the alternatives might be. A country that adopts a static, relative-advantage view of the world will eventually be swamped with imports from everywhere. The alternatives at that point are limited and decidedly unappealing. Ultimately, the only option left is isolationism. That will tend to lower living standards in the country concerned and in other countries; the relative effect depending on how large the country is. The larger and richer the country, the less affected the people will be, and the more affected the rest of the world will be. The main conclusion, however, is that everyone ends up being worse off by restricting the advantages of competition. What that means is that to argue against competition is to argue in favor of a lower standard of living than otherwise would be possible.

For a small country, the difference could be very great indeed. To argue for no competition amounts to a program of de-industrialization, and a relative decline in living standards. For a larger country, the results are less dramatic, but still in the same direction. The difference in policy terms is that in the case of a small country the rest of the world is little affected by the decision made. In the case of a large, rich country, such as the United States, it is very much in the interests of the other countries to keep it within the international competitive pool, which introduces wider political considerations.

The more competition there is, the faster the world will grow. It is quite acceptable within that context for governments to control the rules of the game by limiting damage to the environment, etc. The role of government is to represent the people as a whole. There is nothing strange or illogical about the idea that what is good for the individual person or company is not in the interests of society generally. As a result, there are laws to regulate behavior of various forms, and the environment is clearly a public good. The people affected may well complain about the costs involved but that is only to be expected. The existence of added costs which may slow down growth only increases the need for competition. Once the idea is accepted that there is nothing inconsistent between competition and setting restraints on what is acceptable, within limits, then it should be possible to devise environmental legislation that actually encourages competition. The caveat must be added that this should not be designed to protect inefficient and outmoded industries.

The greatest pressure group will always come from existing, entrenched businesses that may well have passed their useful life. The young and immature have a faint voice which can hardly be heard, and anyway the management of small, new and rapidly growing businesses have better things to do with their time than to go around justifying their existence, and are anyway unlikely to represent a cohesive group. The unborn have no voice at all, and the truth is that no one even knows what form they will take. Unlike the human analogy, mutants are acceptable, and are actually desirable. No planner in the 1950s could possibly have seen the growth and potential of microcomputers. A true policy that favors competition should assume no foreknowledge of what direction the economy will take in the future.

# 4

## MONEY
### (makes the world go round)

Money has received most attention in relation to inflation, with the monetarists claiming that excessive money growth was the sole determinant of inflation. This view was widely accepted in the late 1970s, but has subsequently lost majority support. The reason for this change of heart has been that money has performed rather poorly as an indicator of future inflation. That might be taken as evidence that money, and monetary conditions, do not matter, as the Keynesians had concluded in the 1960s. Nothing could be further from the truth. Money has a crucially important role to play.

Money is the oil that lubricates the economy, ensuring the efficient operation of the economic machine. The existence of a highly liquid asset that is generally accepted as means of payment plays a crucial role as a financial buffer between income and expenditure. The ability to separate these decisions, thereby avoiding direct barter in all trade, has been fundamental in the development of a modern industrialized economy.

For all its importance, the actual stock of money is not the only thing to look at. What is really important is to understand monetary conditions— the credit markets and the price of money, i.e. interest rates. The central role played by interest rates in the business cycle has already been emphasized. It is these credit conditions and, in particular, the price of money, that is most important in explaining inflation. The quantity of money also plays an important role as an indicator of real economic growth.

### Money and markets

Money exists as a medium of exchange, to fill the gap between decisions. Because of time there is uncertainty, and for both these reasons there is money. With no uncertainty, all trade could be conducted as straight swaps. With time, however, outcomes are not known. Money allows the separation of decisions to buy and sell by time and place. Prices will be better, production higher and efficiency greater, since the seller does not have to take whatever the buyer has to offer. Money is neutral, it is generally accepted and can be used for any purpose. For these reasons, money acts as a buffer that allows there to be leads and lags within the economy.

Money actually comes into existence through the creation of new credit by the banks. The monetary authorities can influence this process by changing the supply of reserves and in that way change interest rates. Money, on a narrow definition, will follow changes in interest rates very closely, and there will be little, if any, disequilibrium between demand and supply. Adjustments between demand and supply will take place within broad money definitions, acting as a buffer between decisions made elsewhere. Demand is brought into line with supply by the sequence of events that follow the process of credit creation. As I have written previously (Coghlan, 1981):

> The role of money as a means of payment means that it enters as intermediary in *all* market transactions. For this reason it is the perfect buffer to soak up any disequilibrium in an uncertain, imperfect world. Therefore, any disequilibrium in other markets is likely to be reflected in a disequilibrium in the money market. People will accept money but it would be wrong to suppose that they necessarily wish to retain ownership of it. Money is a means to an end, and only to a relatively minor degree (compared with the transactions it facilitates) is it an end in itself. Money is held but this does not mean that it represents an equilibrium demand for money. Any increase in the supply of money above the equilibrium demand must be followed by an adjustment in the determinants of demand in order to move towards equilibrium. These adjustments can take the form of output or interest rate changes and the actual response is obviously very important.

This description seems obvious, but it is not widely accepted. Some people have denied that there could be any difference between broad money and credit, while others have claimed that demand and supply must be in equilibrium at all times. That has to be an academic view of the world. From a position closer to the markets, it is hard to argue that they are ever in equilibrium. Equilibrium is a condition that is always the point of reference, but never the point. It is a long-run condition that is itself always changing. The important distinction is in the behavior of the individuals involved rather than the published statistics that show up on paper.

Take the example of something as simple as a Keynesian multiplier model. This says, quite rightly, that an initial injection of demand will have secondary repercussion round the economy. People who receive the initial payment in exchange for goods or services will themselves increase their spending, and so on. This process of adjustment takes time, and the buffer that allows this to happen is money or, more realistically, the gap between the supply of and demand for money. The monetary adjustment is a mirror image of the real market adjustment.

The fact that the demand for and supply of money are not always in equilibrium does not mean that individuals and institutions are not behaving rationally. It seems logical that money will be accepted as payment for goods or services, but only as an intermediary in the process of exchange, and need not necessarily represent a position of long-run equilibrium.

> Because of transactions costs, limits to information, and the essential characteristics of money enabling the separation of the two sides of income and expenditure decisions, both temporally and spatially, money will be held without it necessarily being desired for its own sake. (*ibid.*)

One implication of this way of looking at money is that standard attempts to identify stable, statistical relationships for the demand for money, at least on a broad definition, are doomed to failure. Since this forms the basis for the way money is included in most large, and small, scale models of the economy, it creates something of a problem. If the model is flawed then so will be the forecasts that it produces.

An alternative approach is to focus attention on the credit side of financial activities. While it is right to emphasize the banks, it is also necessary to take account of transactions that bypass the banking system. Credit totals from a particular institution, or group of institutions, will never tell the complete story, and that means attention should also be paid to the cost, or price, of credit. These topics are discussed in this and other chapters.

## Money and the economy

Before turning to the credit markets, it is interesting to consider the relationship between money and the economy. The discussion, so far, suggests that there is a close relationship, but that it is not simple. The connections are made in a variety of ways, through the demands for credit, the supply of goods, the price of money, etc. In Chapter 2, it was shown that money growth and inflation are not particularly well correlated. Even more interesting is the fact that the relationship between money and inflation has changed over time. Inflation has been the big exception within the business cycle. The cyclical response of everything else in the economy seems to have stayed the same, only inflation has changed. So what about money? If the money/inflation relationship has shifted, does that mean the relationship between money and real economic activity has also changed?

Figure 4.1 shows the relationship between the rate of growth of industrial production and the growth of real money, M2 and M1. The rate of change of interest rates, inverted, is also shown at the bottom. The two world wars distorted the path, but less than might have been expected and, excluding these, a cyclical connection can be identified. The striking exception to the rule is that real money growth did not fall sharply ahead of the depression

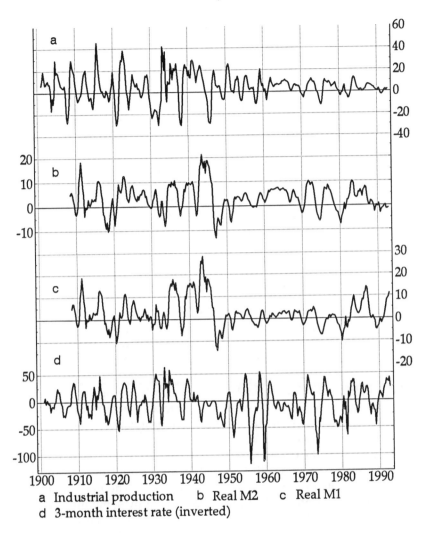

Figure 4.1 Money and the economy (quarterly)

in the 1930s. What did fall sharply, however, was the growth of nominal money. Nominal money growth was slowing down throughout the second half of the 1920s, even as the stock market was soaring, and rising stock prices were requiring more and more money. M1 growth was barely positive from 1926, while M2 growth became negative in 1929. Money growth turned sharply negative in the early years of the 1930s. These growth rates were shown in Fig. 2.2.

The fact that money has its first effect on the real output of the economy is consistent with the timing outlined in a seminal article by Milton Friedman (1968). Over the long run, it may be that excess money growth will be fully reflected in higher prices. However, the run is so long that it really is impossible to say, since all nominal series are basically rising over time. It will be a very long time before the rapid money growth in the 1980s becomes reflected in higher prices, and, before that, maybe low money growth will offset the excess. The relationship between money and inflation has changed, but that between money and the economy seems to have remained intact.

The cost of money is also a key element of the way monetary conditions affect the economy. Changes in interest rates will affect money growth and economic growth. The economic effect comes directly from the effect of the change in interest rates, and via the effect on the demand for credit and money. This relationship is illustrated by the behavior of the rate of change of interest rates.

## The functioning of the credit markets

The credit markets perform two major functions. First, they recycle the surplus funds from individuals, companies or institutions who spend less than they receive and put it in the hands of people who have expenditure plans in excess of their current receipts. Second, the credit markets can inject new finance into the economy, to finance real growth and/or inflation, and it is in this role that the banks are particularly important. The fact that the banks, and the financial system in general, are carrying on both of these functions at the same time confuses interpretations of the data, and confuses many people.

The first role of the credit markets, the recycling of money, is required in order to prevent demand falling and setting up a cumulative decline which eventually results in the collapse of the economy. The majority of credit creation is the counterpart of the act of saving by someone else in the economy. This credit creation is not expansionary, quite the opposite; without it, the level of economic activity would contract. Consider what would happen if all savings took the form of banknotes stuffed under the mattress at home. Individuals would be receiving money in payment for services provided, i.e. the cost of production, and then withdrawing part of that money from circulation. Demand, in the sense of what people want, would be less than supply, and inventory levels would have to take up the slack, with the result that output and/or prices must fall to restore the balance.

The process will continue to the point where there is no more hoarding of cash, for only then will demand be equal to supply, with producers able to sell all of their output. Contraction occurs as long as desired expenditure in aggregate is below actual income. This is why attempts to hoard cash that is not recycled, as happened in the United States in the 1930s as a result of the collapse in the banking system, can have such a devastating effect on the economy. In order to maintain a given level of demand, it is therefore necessary for savers to pass on their surplus to those whose planned expenditure exceeds their revenue. This is a necessary condition just to hold the level of national income and expenditure where it is.

There is a whole complicated array of financial transactions required simply to preserve the status quo. Within a modern industrialized economy this requires a large sophisticated financial system—the same system that will also finance excess demands. And, despite what many people have suggested, it is impossible to distinguish one type of transaction from the other. It is only possible to tell whether credit demands in aggregate are excessive, and even that is often difficult, except in retrospect.

Excessive credit demands will tend to speed up the circulation of the stock of money in existence, thereby providing new credit which is additional to that provided through the banking system and which adds to the money stock. It is also possible for new finance to be supplied through the banking system which does not increase the money supply directly—this is particularly true when considering narrow definitions of money, e.g. M1, which do not reflect the lending behavior of banks.

To summarize the argument so far, it is possible to think in terms of a fixed pool of finance associated with any particular level of economic activity. In a static equilibrium in which economic activity remains constant, finance continues to circulate, being drawn down by those in deficit and paid back into the pool by those in surplus. It should be clear that for this equilibrium to be maintained it is necessary (a) that it is expected to continue, i.e. there is confidence in the economic future, and (b) the credit markets continue to function normally. Any breakdown in these conditions will result in corrections taking place in the economy and in the credit markets.

Money is often referred to as the *lifeblood of the economy*. Accepting that analogy, it then follows that the credit markets, with their two major functions, represent the heart and the bone marrow of the economic body, keeping the circulation going and supplying new blood as necessary. Continued functioning is essential to continued existence. The economy will collapse if the circulation is severely restricted, and growth will be prevented if new credit is not available.

A rise in the level of economic activity, either nominal or real, will generally require the creation of new credit, i.e. a new flow to add to the existing stock. A significant proportion of this new credit will, under normal circumstances, be provided through the banking system, as providers of residual finance to the government and private sector. Because there must be a financial side to market transactions, except in the case of a very limited number of barter swaps, this new credit will reflect what is going on else-where in the economy.

One way of looking at the credit creation of the banks is by calculating something called *domestic credit expansion* (DCE). This, as the name suggests, measures the expansion, or change, in bank credit extended to all domestic sectors of the economy, including the government. Figures 4.2 and 4.3 show the growth of domestic credit in nominal and real terms, along with the growth of money, on the same basis, industrial production and inflation. The main difference between money growth and the growth of domestic credit is accounted for by the outflows or inflows on current account. A large current account deficit will keep money growth below DCE, while a surplus will add to money growth. As the name implies, it is expansion of *domestic* credit. The other way the series may diverge would be if the banks raised significant amounts of capital, i.e. a non-deposit form of raising money to finance lending. One implication of this comparison is that domestic credit creation has been more expansionary over recent years than would be concluded from looking only at money growth. The effect of this growth has, however, been reduced by the external drain on current account.

Many changes to the financial system have taken place in response to the normal competitive forces of the market place, and in order to get around deliberate obstacles that have been erected by governments. A great many market inefficiencies have been created by politicians and bureaucrats, which have made the system more complicated, more costly and more unstable than was necessary. Controls on banks have resulted in the growth of near-banks offering similar if not identical services, domestic restrictions have led to increasing offshore operations, and so it goes on. Not only are these new institutions outside the particular controls, but they are usually outside all existing limitations and supervision. Consequently, it frequently happens that the financial institutions which are growing the fastest are those which are unregulated and about which very little, if any-thing, is known. The risks of an institution becoming over-extended are greatest in this type of environment.

For many years the financial side of the economy was almost totally neglected. Now the pendulum has swung back the other way, so that now the mistakes that are being made are different, and lasting solutions will be impossible until the true underlying causes of inflation are more properly understood. Increasing real demands do need to be financed and this gives the financial system a pivotal role in the process of expansion and inflation. Without easy liquidity, sustained inflation would be impossible, regardless of what happens to any particular arbitrary definition of bank liabilities. But then, with no new finance, growth in one area could only take place at the expense of some other sector or group.

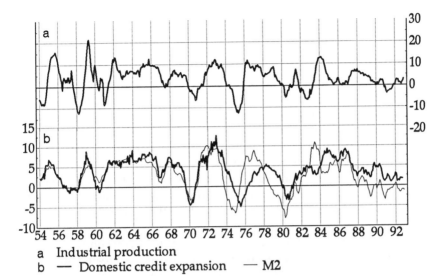

a   Industrial production
b   — Domestic credit expansion    — M2

**Figure 4.2** Industrial production and real DCE
(12-month rate of change of monthly data)

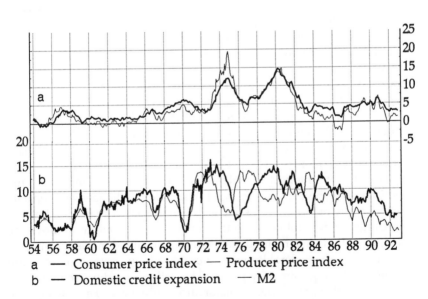

a   — Consumer price index    — Producer price index
b   — Domestic credit expansion    — M2

**Figure 4.3** Inflation and domestic credit expansion
(12-month rate of change of monthly data)

## Monetary policy

Monetary policy can take two forms—market controls and non-market controls. The non-market control mechanism works through the imposition of direct credit controls, including restrictions on competition. This creates massive distortions and inefficiencies, as financial institutions strive to get around the constraints, thereby gradually eroding the short-run effectiveness of such controls, and forcing the continuing expansion of controls. The process can easily be pushed so far that the only alternative to still further controls becomes their total abolition. Having travelled down the first road for much of the post-war period, the monetary authorities in most of the major industrialized countries have, since the 1970s, been in the process of changing direction.

Monetary policy has become so closely identified with control, or lack of it, over the stock of money in recent years that it has created substantial confusion as between the indicators, the objectives and operating instruments of policy. Contrary to popular belief, the money stock is not a tool of monetary policy. Within a competitive market system, central banks operate on the reserves of the banking system and often other financial institutions in order to establish a desired level of reserves, and thereby achieve a particular level of interest rates. Cash reserves, in effect, become the fulcrum on which the central bank operates in order to gain leverage over the level of short-term interest rates. Operations are carried out by buying or selling debt, usually short-term, but not necessarily, from/to the banks or non-bank public. Payment, in the case of a sale, is made by a check drawn on a bank, which will have the effect of reducing its reserve deposits with the central bank. In addition, it is possible for the central bank to buy and sell longer-term debt for/from its own portfolio with the intention of influencing the structure of interest rates. Much has been made of this ability in the past, but it is really much less than used to be thought.

Central banks may also set a discount rate directly by decree. Here again the effectiveness of such acts has been greatly exaggerated; discount rate changes will prove ineffective unless market rates change in line. In the United Kingdom, the Bank of England has abandoned the idea of a separate discretionary discount rate. The same is true in Canada. The Federal Reserve in the United States still clings to the concept, but its failure to move the rate in line with the federal funds rate has often resulted in sharp swings in borrowing from the Federal Reserve, and only administrative controls stop this from frustrating monetary policy. This failure to adjust the discount rate to the market represents a major inconsistency in Federal Reserve operations, and gives a political importance to discount rate changes that is unnecessary. This political aspect does, however, mean that the discount rate should be considered separately as an indicator of policy.

The pivotal role of reserves would seem to suggest that the level of reserves would make an ideal target, or indicator, of monetary policy, and that proposal has a number of supporters. It is, however, misleading to view reserves as an exclusive guide to policy. In the same way that the brake and accelerator are used to regulate the speed of an automobile, reserves can be used to regulate the supply of money. The extent to which each pedal is depressed will give some idea of the speed, but not a lot, since many other considerations will need to be taken into account, e.g. the inclination of any hills, wind speed and direction, etc. Few would think it wise to look only at the accelerator and brake pedals in judging the speed and direction of a vehicle. So it is with reserves and the stock of money. It is also important to pay attention to the level of interest rates. These depend not only on the supply of reserves, but also the demand for bank credit. If loan demand is strong then interest rates may actually be rising while at the same time reserves are being added to the system. Alternatively, with weak or declining loan demand, falling interest rates may still be associated with a declining level of reserves.

The pressure on reserves and interest rates shows up early in the business cycle recovery, as the improvement in economic activity takes up the slack in the system, and companies start to raise loans for expansion. This is a major testing point for monetary policy. Loan demand strengthens while unemployment is still high and there are sufficient signs of potential economic failure to justify a chorus of complaints against higher interest rates. It is likely, under these circumstances, that additional reserves will be pumped into the market, not with the express intention of stimulating the economy, but rather simply to soften the rise in interest rates in order to keep the economy growing. This psychological aspect is important to understanding how inflationary financing can start again. The major inflationary push is actually given when interest rates are rising, but so too is the demand for credit.

Typically, what has happened in the early part of an economic recovery is that sufficient reserves have been added to meet a large part of the increased credit demands, but not sufficient to prevent interest rates from edging up. The monetary authorities, and many outside commentators, have been able to claim that monetary policy was tight, or at least non-accommodative, on the evidence of rising interest rates, when it was actually very easy, in the sense that new credit creation was continuing at too fast a pace to be consistent with future price stability. One implication of this reaction is that nominal interest rates on their own will not be a good guide of monetary policy, and it will be necessary to consider real interest rates and the yield curve.

## Monetary and fiscal policy

The operation of monetary policy is complicated by the stance of fiscal policy, and it is necessary to consider the two together. Printing money to finance a budget deficit can prove to be highly inflationary. However, to fund the deficit by selling bonds may well crowd out the private sector and cause considerable damage to private corporations. Achieving an acceptable balance between monetary and fiscal policies is essential for the smooth operation of the economy and financial markets. There has been increased awareness over recent years of the connection that exists between fiscal policy and monetary policy. Neglect of this relationship in the 1960s and the 1970s can be identified as a major cause for the policy mistakes that fostered the massive acceleration of inflation at that time. The lessons that were supposed to have been learned at such great cost, by those who sat through the lessons, are being forgotten.

There is nearly unanimous agreement that the bigger the budget deficit the more expansionary, or inflationary, it is and vice versa. There is no doubt that a high and rising budget deficit can be inflationary; that was certainly the case in the 1970s, but it is not necessarily true in every case. The potentially inflationary effects of a high budget deficit can be offset by an aggressive funding policy which involves the issue of sufficient bonds to finance the excess expenditures without adding liquidity to the economy.

Budget deficits financed by cash creation, i.e. low short-term interest rates and an extremely positive yield curve, can be highly expansionary. The potency of this combination was realized by economists in the 1930s, as a way to stimulate the economy under the conditions existing at the time. Usually, this corollary to running an expansionary budget deficit is forgotten. Keynesians used to argue that budget deficits were needed to stimulate the economy while at the same time interest rates were pushed ever higher in order to restrain the expansion of demand. Given the logic involved, it is hardly surprising that liquidity creation was substituted for higher interest rates, with the result that inflation accelerated. That was one of the major lessons learned early in the 1980s by investors and central bankers. Around the world, central bankers seem to be forever demanding lower budget deficits as a means of achieving lower interest rates, which is the natural response to establishing a better balance of fiscal and monetary policies.

The distinction has to be made between a high budget deficit at times of full employment and a high deficit at times of recession. In the former case it is necessary to finance the deficit in such a way that reduces private sector demand by an equivalent amount—assuming that inflation control is the objective. In particular, it is important not to increase the level of liquidity in the financial system. The reverse is true in the latter case. When the economy is in recession, the objective should be to increase the level of demand, and this will generally require an increase in liquidity. To the extent that the recession has been caused by an increased desire to save in the form of government bonds, then raising the supply and matching spending will add to overall demand. More normally, in a recession there is a rush for liquidity, so that is where there is the greatest need. However, except in the case where prices are actually falling, i.e. inflation is negative, it will almost always be more efficient to stimulate the economy through an easier monetary policy than by increasing government spending.

The stance of fiscal policy can have an important influence on the behavior of financial markets, and investors need to understand what the current position really is. It is no use depending on the government for an independent assessment, since any opinions expressed, and there are no shortage of these, will be highly political. The Federal Reserve is likely to be more objective in its assessments, but here also politics, of a different sort, can play a considerable role. Investors have to make their own judgement of policy, based on actions rather than words. Politicians are always 'fighting inflation', or 'reducing interest rates', but inflation and interest rates have both been known to rise, sometimes quite sharply, despite such protestations. Unfortunately, accurate interpretation of events is not as straightforward as might be hoped, or as it is often made to appear. There is a maze of misleading signals, false starts and sudden changes in direction which can easily confuse those who are looking for clues. Intentions must be judged by actions not words.

Figure 4.4 follows on from the question of the appropriate combination of fiscal and monetary policies. If fiscal policy is tightened this should allow monetary policy to be easier, i.e. short-term interest rates can be lower. This relationship was brought into sharp focus at the time of the budget debate in 1990, when the Federal Reserve made a reduction in interest rates dependent on an agreement to cut the budget deficit. Fiscal policy in this case is measured by the budget deficit as a percentage of GNP, while monetary policy is approximated by the ratio of short-term interest rates to long-term bond yields, i.e. the yield curve. The argument is frequently made that the deficit should be adjusted for the state of the economy. A 'cyclically adjusted' deficit is certainly a good idea, but there is little agreement on the 'natural' rate of unemployment, or the 'true' growth potential of the economy. The logic suggests that monetary policy should also be adjusted for the business cycle. Both will reflect, and be affected by, the particular stage of the cycle. The danger of preset rules is that they will produce misleading conclusions when conditions change.

There is a sharp contrast between the early years and the later years. The policy mix starts off well but deteriorates over time. In the 1950s, monetary and fiscal policy were in reasonable balance; there were no less than five

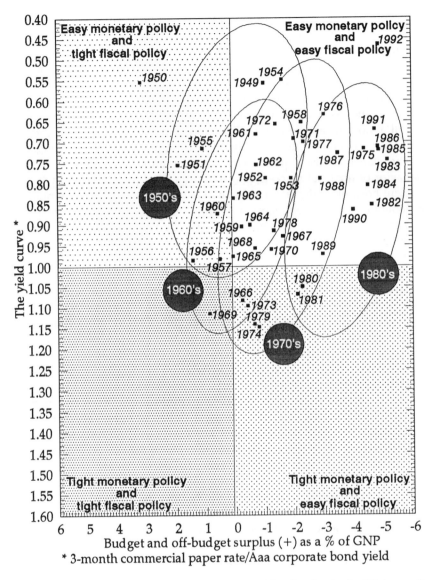

**Figure 4.4** The combination of monetary policy and fiscal policy in the US (annual)

years when a relatively easy monetary policy was combined with tight fiscal policy. The 1960s saw a move towards tighter monetary policies—partly a reflection of the gradual move away from direct controls on interest rates and credit. There were more budget deficits, but these were compensated for by a relatively tighter monetary policy. The year 1969 represented the only one of a budget surplus combined with an inverted yield curve, and the result seems to have frightened policy makers so much that it has never happened again. The response was a distinct rightward shift toward fiscal and monetary ease in the 1970s. There was much discussion in the 1980s about the need to improve the balance and, in particular, reduce the budget deficit, but the rightward shift actually accelerated in the 1980s.

Arriving in the 1990s, we discover that the combination of fiscal and monetary policy in 1991 was very easy. Policy, in fact, was about as easy as it had ever been, with the average for 1991 showing up in the top right-hand corner of Fig. 4.4. In 1992, the combination became even easier, as the yield curve became much more positive than the average for the whole of 1991, and the budget deficit remained extremely high. No wonder the bond market became unsettled by all the talk of additional cuts and expenditure increases.

The position of the combined setting of fiscal and monetary policies at that time can be justified, explained and accepted as a response to the weak economy. It is a way, if you like, of cyclically adjusting the policy combination, rather than just fiscal policy. In terms of Fig. 4.4, the policy combination should be expected to move north-east during a recession, as the budget deficit increases and the yield curve becomes more positive. During times of economic recovery, the budget deficit should fall, possibly even move into surplus, although it is so long since that happened it is hard to imagine, while the yield curve will become less positive, possibly even becoming negative; i.e. the policy combination should move south-west. This is one case where fact follows fancy, and this pattern can actually be observed.

While the short-term responses are perfectly understandable, and justifiable, there has been a long-term trend that is very disturbing, particularly in light of the present political debate. Abstracting from the cyclical pattern of the policy combination, there has been a distinct eastward shift over time. That is, fiscal policy has been getting easier and easier for a given level of monetary policy. In order to illustrate the trend more clearly, ellipses have been drawn on the figure, approximating the cyclical movements in the policy combination over each decade. Once that is done, the sideways progression becomes obvious, and more than a little discouraging.

As at the end of 1991, the 1990s were holding within the pattern that existed in the 1980s, while 1992 actually fell out the bottom end. This was hardly comforting given the widespread demand for fiscal expansion. At this point there is no evidence that the eastward march is over. But over it must be. The ever-increasing tendency for the budget deficits to keep expanding cannot continue forever, and is already stretching the limits of credibility. Politicians should be looking beyond the temporary effects of the recession, and towards some more permanent solution to this problem.

## Supply-side effects

The impact on demand has always been the aspect of monetary policy that has been emphasized. It has been considered a tool of demand management—as was fiscal policy. But that takes much too narrow a view of the way in which monetary policy works. Like fiscal policy, there are supply-side effects which must be taken into account. Unlike fiscal policy these have gone unrecognized.

Not only will companies face a decline in demand for their products, as higher interest rates start to bite, concentrated in those areas where demand is interest sensitive, they will also be faced with a substantial increase in costs. The cost of investing in new plant and equipment will be raised, as will the cost of holding inventories—which may themselves be increasing. All existing borrowing at variable interest rates will go up in cost, not only new borrowing, and this can quite easily make the difference between profit and loss. Investment will be held back, bankruptcies will increase and small companies—the main innovators and the big companies of the future—in particular will find it hard to raise money to survive. The increase in costs combined with the fall in demand provide the two arms of a pincer which is capable of squeezing the private sector to death. Moreover, the effect is immediate.

An argument that has frequently been made is that the use of monetary policy to control inflation is at least fair, in the sense that the pain is evenly distributed and, therefore, does not require the government to make value judgements. This argument gains superficial appeal when compared with the alternative of direct controls over the supply of credit. However, a tight monetary policy, operating through the free-market movement of interest rates, will not be unbiased. To begin with, the purpose of raising interest rates is to squeeze the credit demands of the private sector. The point to emphasize here is that it is the private sector, not the public sector, which bears the brunt of a tight monetary policy. In fact, it is far more likely that the public sector's financial demands will increase as the policy has its effect and the economy moves into recession.

In addition, the incidence of policy is not evenly distributed within the private sector. The sectors that will suffer most will be those which sell their output on credit, which hold large inventories that have to be financed, where production is relatively capital intensive, and small companies which typically do not have strong financial backing. A tight monetary policy will also affect the domestic economy through its influence on the exchange rate. A substantially overvalued exchange rate raises the cost to foreign buyers, and/or reduce margins to the exporters. Foreign producers will also gain from relatively lower interest rates. The external impact can be quite significant. A major problem has been the failure to recognize these supply-side consequences of monetary policy, despite the fact that they can be highly destructive.

Monetary policy poses a very real threat to the existence of the free-market economy if applied blindly, irrespective of what else is going on. For example, massive expansion by the public sector which added greatly to excess demand, combined with tight monetary policies which attempted to offset the inflationary pressures, would be capable of effectively destroying large parts of the private sector—in particular, the manufacturing sector. In a very real sense, the proper use of monetary policy requires the goodwill and good judgement of the politicians in power; it is misleading, and potentially dangerous, to assume that the use of monetary policy frees economists and politicians from the need to make value judgements. Contrary to what is normally claimed, monetary policy is not neutral in its effects. That is not even true in the rarified atmosphere of the abstract theory of a perfectly competitive economy, and far less so in the real world.

The incidence of monetary policy is also affected by the use of taxes, subsidies and other measures which penalize or favor certain sectors of the economy. There is, therefore, a direct way in which fiscal policies influence monetary policy. The main beneficiary is typically the public sector itself; what is the point of monopoly power if you do not use it? Certain private sector groups typically receive special financial advantages as well, such as house buyers, agriculture and, more recently, small businesses. Powerful arguments can be made at different times to favor different areas, but it is very difficult to take away any special advantages once granted. The question should always be asked, 'at what expense are these benefits granted?'. In a world in which finance and true liquidity are scarce resources, it is essential to recognize that subsidies to one group can only be made at the expense of other groups in society. Frequently, it has been the corporate sector which has suffered, whereas this sector should really be encouraged as the driving force behind economic innovation, growth and ultimately the rise in general living standards.

Make no mistake about it, the immediate objective of a tight money policy has got to be to reduce the demands of the private sector by encouraging saving and, more particularly, by reducing borrowing. The more that particular groups are protected, the greater the effect must be on the unprotected. From what has already been said, it should be clear that it is the manufacturing and construction sectors that will be hurt the most by the cutting edge of monetary policy, and which suffer most from the negative supply-side effects.

## Control versus support

The mechanics of control are further complicated when, as is the case in the United States, the banks are required to hold different reserve ratios for different categories of deposit, with the highest reserve ratios being required for the most liquid deposits, and the percentage required declining as the term is extended. In such a case, the reserves available to the banks for expansion will vary as the composition of their deposits vary. Under such circumstances, the central bank has little choice but to provide reserves as demanded by the banking system, since different reserve totals can be associated with the same money stock, i.e. there is no unique relationship between reserves and money. But then central banks will always respond to any conflict between monetary control and the potential bankruptcy of the banking system by supplying reserves in whatever quantity needed.

It often seems to be the case that central banks are in business solely to control the stock of money, at whatever cost. But this ignores the fact that it was not simply for this reason that central banks were created. There has always been a control function, but greater emphasis has traditionally been placed on the task of supporting the banking system. Although recent emphasis has been directed towards the other function, the support role has actually gained in importance. As democracy has developed over the past 50 years, governments have offered, and society has come to expect, increased economic stability and an improving standard of living. A depression, such as that experienced during the 1930s, has become unacceptable and will be avoided at all costs. Moreover, it is now widely recognized that in order to avoid such a collapse requires continued confidence in the banking system. Central banks are agents of the government and, within a democracy, that must always be where ultimate responsibility lies; despite the attempts by politicians in power to disassociate themselves from tight money policies, and claims for independence by some outside observers. Central bankers possess a natural tendency to support the banking system for which they have responsibility, but even if that were not the case there is a clear need to preserve stability for political reasons.

At times of crisis, the control and support functions may seem to be in conflict, although that is much less true than it appears, and under more normal circumstances the complementarity of these roles is becoming increasingly obvious. The first step in creating a crisis is to allow the economy to expand too fast, so that borrowers become over-extended, and debt burdens become unsustainable unless growth and accelerating inflation are continued. The crisis actually arrives after interest rates have been pushed up high enough in real terms to create a recession, threatening to bring down the whole fragile financial structure and the economy with it. In the third stage of the process, as creditors become nervous, and less concerned about their return than the preservation of their capital, the central bank will typically pump in liquidity upon demand in order to prevent a panic.

It may seem that this expansion of reserves runs counter to the control function, but that is not really so. Two things are happening. First, there is an increased demand for short-term assets relative to longer-term assets, i.e. an increase in the demand for money relative to income and wealth, resulting in a decline in the velocity of money. In this case, the added money is going not to stimulate economic demand, but to satisfy changed portfolio preferences. Secondly, there is likely to be an increased demand for government debt, as the most secure, and in meeting that demand the monetary authorities may actually cause a drain of reserves, and this has to be replaced. However, it must be emphasized that this expansion of liquidity should be seen as an emergency operation. There is a danger that the easy stance will continue beyond what is necessary, leading to excessive ease as confidence and the economy starts to pick up, thereby establishing the base for a renewed inflationary surge.

Lack of control at this stage will set the scene for a future crisis. Stricter control under more normal economic conditions will actually help to maintain the stability of the financial system, if it avoids establishing the conditions for a crisis. The control and support functions can, therefore, be seen to depend on each other to an important extent. It is unreasonable to expect rigid control at times of crisis, and the support role will always dominate under such conditions. It would be economic and political suicide to do anything else.

Further support for a more cautious approach also comes from the existence of lags in the system. There are lags between interest rate changes and changes in the monetary aggregates; between interest rates and money and economic activity and inflation; there are also lags in the availability of information, the analysis of that data and the implementation of policy actions. All of which help to contribute to the cyclicality of the economy, and the instability of the financial system. It is difficult for politicians and public officials to appreciate the full implications of their actions in the future, particularly when they are under intense pressure to react immediately to each separate event. Moreover, because of the lags involved in the formation of inflationary expectations it should be clear that the costs of achieving an average level of inflation of, say, 2 per cent, are likely to be lower if the rate remains close to 2 per cent at all times, rather than if it is allowed to accelerate first over a significant period and then has to be brought down.

There can be no doubt that to expand cautiously when faced with a myriad of urgent competing demands is not easy, but it is necessary to move away from the modern desire for instant gratification. What is needed is a longer-term perspective, and recognition of the potentially destabilizing effect of present actions on future events. The debate on monetary policy, and inflation control in general, should be turned towards ways of preventing inflation from accelerating in the first place.

## Practical monetarism

The 1970s were the age of monetarism. At the start of the decade the Keynesian troops still held the intellectual high ground, and were safely barricaded inside the corridors of power. Friedman led a small band of dissidents whose constant sniping at the old guard seemed to be nothing more than a minor irritation. Standard textbooks devoted little if any space to such exotics as money. By the end of the decade all this had changed; the monetarists had gained the high ground and were stampeding through the corridors.

With the fading of the Keynesian star, politicians searched around for another banner to follow which would lead them out of the mess they found themselves in. What they found was a ready-made alternative. Milton Friedman, and the monetarists, had for many years been criticizing Keynesian economics for its neglect of money, and its assumptions about the power of demand management policies. So much of what the monetarists were saying seemed intuitively reasonable, and they did indeed seem to be able to explain the inflationary mess which had come to dominate political debate. The apparent evidence in favor of the monetarists' view helped to make it more easily acceptable to politicians, but without them necessarily understanding the full implications.

Ultimately, the reason monetarism gained acceptance was not due to the infallibility of the theory, or the eloquence of the arguments, but to the persistent acceleration of inflation. Non-market controls were given a try in many countries, but this went against the trend towards increased internationalization and liberalization, quite apart from the fact that they did not work and created major distortions. The politicians wanted a solution, and it had to be easy to understand. Monetarism was the natural successor; the problem that monetarism set out to solve was inflation, whereas Keynesian economics was devoted to unemployment and growth; it was already an established theory; money growth had accelerated ahead of inflation; and, above all, the basic principles were simple to understand.

It is hard to believe now, but money, monetary policy and interest rates, had virtually no role to play in the Keynesian models of the economy in the 1960s and early 1970s. The Keynesian revolution cast a shadow which obliterated money as an important economic variable. Keynesian economics emphasized the importance of income and expenditure flows, and seemed to show that governments had complete control over the economic destiny of the countries they governed, within a relatively free-market environment. This conclusion has now been seen to be nothing more than an assumption, and invalid at that. The myth was exploded as rapidly rising inflation, combined with low or even negative growth, replaced the growth of the 1950s and 1960s. Some attempts were made, and still are, to capture monetary influences, but within the existing Keynesian framework. This was rather like trying to graft a third leg onto a man. The approach has been unnatural, *ad hoc*, and not particularly successful, adding further confusion to an already confusing subject.

It was not that the economics of Keynes had nothing to say. Keynes, after all, had been a monetary economist, and had maintained an important role for money in *The General Theory* (Keynes, 1936), and afterwards. For some reason the post-war Keynesians that came to dominate policy either neglected, or rejected, any role for money at all. Quite a remarkable situation really. Friedman has said that inflation is a monetary phenomenon, which is both true and at the same time not particularly helpful. It is much more important to recognize that nominal GNP is a monetary phenomenon— which means that macroeconomics is a monetary subject. Macroeconomics and monetary economics are generally seen as separate branches of economics, but they are not. In the 1970s they were seen as almost totally exclusive, now overlapping areas are recognized, but really they are the same; money is not independent, but actually an integral part of the dynamics of the economy. Earlier chapters have shown how interest rates play a crucial role in the movement of the business cycle, while money is the buffer between actions and reactions within the real economy.

Central bankers are really more interested in financial conditions in general and the health of the banking system and industry in particular, than in the money supply. The persistence of inflation, and the monetarist onslaught, forced them to pay attention to the growth of money. However, they did not accept the arguments in total. What developed has been termed practical monetarism and that was a very good name; it was more practical than monetarist. Understanding this helps explain why the policy worked and why it has subsequently been more or less abandoned.

Practical monetarism took the form of announced targets for some definition of the money supply. In the United States the main focus was on M1, in the UK it was on a broad measure—sterling M3, while in Germany they devised a reserve measure called, appropriately, central bank money. The fact that different definitions were used, that they all seemed to work, and that all have subsequently failed, is an important clue to the mystery. It is interesting to note that while much less attention is now paid to monetary aggregates, the emphasis in the United Kingdom has shifted to a very narrow definition of money, really monetary base, while the Federal Reserve and the Bundesbank have focused attention on broader measures of money.

Policy took the form of announcing a range for the growth of the chosen money target, and then varying interest rates in order to get inside these targets. There was no attempt to reduce inflation 'at a stroke', although that was demanded in some quarters. The central bankers recognized the dangers of any attempt at sudden solutions, and sensibly resisted the dramatic gesture in favor of a gradual approach. The targets were meant to be restrictive after taking account of current expectations for economic growth, inflation and the behavior of velocity. The degree of approximation and wishful thinking involved in such estimates meant that there was a strong element of trial and error involved, and allowance for this should have been, but generally was not, allowed for in judging policy performance. There is always a tendency to assume much greater knowledge than actually exists, or ever will exist. Even in the controlled experiments at modern laboratories mistakes happen, and erroneous conclusions are drawn. Real-world economic experiments, which the introduction of monetary targets amounted to, are a long way from that.

At the time when inflation was still accelerating, and for some time afterwards, the financial markets became obsessed with the published figures for money growth. Attention focused on each monthly, or weekly figure, and deviations from target, or from expectations, were capable of generating a substantial reaction in the bond markets. After years of underestimating inflation, which resulted in negative real interest rates, it was only natural that investors should be nervous and suspicious of the authorities' resolve to carry through with their intention of stopping inflation. Inflation accelerated the trend towards shorter and shorter-term investment horizons. Since the monetary authorities were still looking at trends over a quarter or longer, the potential for substantial misunderstanding was created, and fully exploited.

Practical monetarism did not work without its problems, and without many doubts about its eventual success, but it did work. By holding to some restrictive target for money growth, regardless of definition, inflation was finally brought down to very low levels again, and actually became negative in some countries. For the monetarists, however, the moment of victory also brought defeat.

As inflation came down, so the growth of money was accelerating. In the United States in 1983 the growth of M1 was running at a rate of over 13 per cent. This was way above the target range at the time, and was very high even without such comparison. It was, after all, substantially higher than the peak growth rates in 1973 and 1978 which had caused so much concern. Friedman went public with a forecast that inflation would rocket in 1984, and condemned the monetary authorities for allowing this to happen. Inflation did not explode, but continued to trend down. In 1985, the growth of M1 started to accelerate again, and again there were predictions of dire consequences for 1986. As before, inflation failed to rise, and, in fact, fell even more sharply under the weight of crashing oil prices. What is more, the growth of M1 continued to expand so that by the end of that year yet another new record had been set.

A similar pattern of events was being experienced in the United Kingdom, but in this case the delinquent target was sterling M3, a broad measure of money. In 1983 this measure of money was growing at a rate little short of 15 per cent, accompanied by warnings of dire consequences, only to be followed by further declines in inflation. The growth of money in 1986 was even more extreme, reaching nearly 20 per cent. This time there was an economic boom, leading to an acceleration of inflation and a substantial deterioration of the balance of payments, but the warning signs were missed because attention was, by then, concentrated on the monetary base.

Targets have been kept, but emphasis has shifted. In the United States, the importance of M1 has been downgraded, with more attention being given to the broader measures. The official justification for this change seems to be that M2 and M3 have been better behaved and, therefore, it is possible to produce the appearance of control. This, it should be clear, is very poor reasoning, even though it might have resulted in the right decision. The monetary emphasis in the United Kingdom has shifted in the opposite direction, but largely for the same reason. The search for a reasonably well-behaved series has forced the monetary authorities to create a new series M0, which is essentially the monetary base, and not money at all. This became the official target of monetary policy in the second half of the 1980s.

The selection of M0 in the United Kingdom has demonstrated the dangers of adopting such a cynical approach to monetary policy. The growth of M0 remained reasonably under control in the late 1980s, while at the same time the growth of broad and narrow money growth accelerated strongly. Even when inflation again soared into double digits, M0 remained reasonably under control. Common sense suggests that a measure of the monetary base that is unrelated to the growth of money, and is not interest sensitive is a complete sham and totally useless.

Any explanation of the success of monetary targets has also to be consistent with their subsequent failure. The monetary authorities always had the capability of raising interest rates sufficiently to kill off private sector demand, create a recession and bring down inflation. There has been extensive debate about the efficacy of monetary policy etc., but this has confused capability with policy as it existed. It is also important to recognize that the monetary authorities were not simply following a set of well-known, tried-and-tested rules, for all the faith of the monetarists. A more apt characterization shows them groping in the dark.

Monetary policy in the 1970s represented a process of gradual tightening, as the authorities stumbled towards regaining control over inflation. It was not that they were being deliberately expansionary but they did under-estimate, first, the extent of the demand being created by the highly expansionary fiscal policies, and, then the effect that rising inflation had on real interest rates, which thereby made even high nominal interest rates expansionary fiscal policies, and then the effect that rising inflation had on authorities finally reached a point where it started to bite. By that time con-fidence had deteriorated so much that real interest rates had to rise very high to be effective.

The effort can be compared with the attempt to stop a runaway truck on an icy hill. Once control has been lost then reasonable pressure on the brakes can be potentially dangerous. However, as the speed picks up that becomes the greater danger, and eventually it is necessary to do whatever you can to stop. Moving down the gears would help, but if that is com-pared with fiscal policy, then these were stuck in overdrive for most of the 1970s. Once your only concern is to stop, regardless of the consequences, you will be prepared to scrape the sides of the truck and to run off the road if it will help. As long as the situation has not become desperate such extreme action will be avoided, but that was the equivalent situation reached by the end of the 1970s.

The important contribution of the monetarists was in reminding every-one of the role of money and monetary policy in determining inflation, when almost all had forgotten. But they went too far; they claimed too much for monetary policy by neglecting the different pressures leading to inflation, and the detailed mechanism through which monetary policy had its effect.

The monetarists' argument which dominated the political debate, main-tained the extreme position that the stock of money was/is all that the monetary authorities can and should control. Moreover, and this is where the real problem lies, it does not make any difference what else is going on in the world. Budget deficits become irrelevant, OPEC price hikes are inconsequential, union power only penalizes the workers, so they can be ignored. However, ignoring the political and social pressures that lead to inflation in this way is a crippling weakness of the whole philosophy, and has unbalanced policy in the other direction. Narrowly focusing on money without paying due regard to the underlying financial conditions, and the means through which control is achieved, is a recipe for disaster.

Desperate situations result in desperate solutions, but that does not mean the same actions will be acceptable under different circumstances. Tight monetary targets will always work to slow the economy. There really is no problem in stopping inflation if that is wanted badly enough. The more difficult task is balancing the different objectives of growth and low inflation, particularly when faced with contradictory fiscal policy. Under these circumstances, rigid monetary targets are capable of being extremely destructive to the private sector of the economy; as would have been proved had they been vigorously applied over the 1980s. Fortunately, the practical side of monetarism took precedence over ideological rigor.

# 5

## DEBT MOUNTAINS
### (and the danger of avalanches)

Deficits and debts are generally viewed with the same inevitability as death and taxes, and with about as much pleasure. Deficits, and the resulting debts, always seem too high. On the few occasions there has been an improvement, the gains have not seemed to last very long. Because of the effect on interest rates, corporate gearing and questions of credit quality, changes in debts and deficits have effects that extend into all other financial, goods and commodities markets. The sheer volume of borrowing, and the absolute size of the bond markets, makes such considerations essential for the actual or potential investor.

Debt levels are invariably discussed without mention of asset levels. Stories about dangerous debt levels are easy to write, partly because debt is a four letter word that alliterates so nicely with descriptions of unpleasant outcomes, such as death, destruction, defeat, despair and debacle. The poetic attraction seems to be irresistible to writers on the subject, and usually is gratefully accepted. The literary result is an exciting description of dreadful possibilities not necessarily based on analysis to support the conclusions. Including assets would only confuse the issue and qualify the conclusions. Assets, unfortunately, do not have the same alliterative potential.

High levels of debt are blamed for everything from the weakness of the economy to the potential for a depression. Clearly, there are problems, but does that mean that all debt is bad and should be abolished? That often seems to be the case put forward. Accepting that view, however, could lead to greater confusion and danger in the future, and in the process would slow the growth potential of the economy. The truth is that debt is not only useful, it is an essential component of a capitalistic economic system. The issue must then be, not the existence of debt itself, but the level of the debt. That leads to the idea that there must be some critical level, but what is it? The real problem is not the existence of debt, but the stupidity of the decisions that brought some of it into being. Saying that debt is the problem is the equivalent of blaming the messenger for bringing bad news, and avoids questioning the real villains. Market reactions are more dangerous than the delinquent debt itself.

One point to bear in mind when contemplating the size of the national debt—the United States has a lot of it, while the old Soviet Union had hardly any at all. The simple view that less debt is better, and least debt is best, leads to the inevitable conclusion that the Soviet economy ought to have been in much better shape than the US economy. That was patently not the case. It is, therefore, necessary to accept that other things are even more important, and so they are.

The level of debt has increased over recent years, but when is high too high? There were widespread complaints and warnings about excessive debt levels 20 years ago and again 10 years ago. Evidence of past exaggeration does not mean that the warnings this time are not justified. They do, however, show that it is not easy to identify the level at which problems get out of control. There are problems, and they are being dealt with; these are already well known and should be fully reflected in financial markets. The real danger is that the reliquification process gets out of control—that confidence in the survival of the financial system collapses. History shows that once confidence collapses the economy will follow, and the pre-existing debt levels do not seem to be relevant; it is really a question of liquidity, and that can easily dry up and disappear altogether. The major change, and cause for hope, is in the attitude of governments, which have abandoned the free-fall approach adopted in the 1930s.

There are times when there is a lot of debt about which cannot be serviced, and that is most definitely a problem for the creditors. It would, however, be a serious mistake to look at the existence of this debt as the problem, concluding that less debt is the answer. Less debt will generally mean less saving, and less saving will mean less investment and slower growth. These are not the objectives most people consider desirable. It is necessary to look at the process that brought the debt into existence. That is where the real problem lies.

The debt that remains in existence is the result of decisions that were made in the past, based on forecasts of the future. These forecasts, however, were often no more than assumptions, hopes or just wishful thinking. In some cases, mistakes were made, bad decisions resulted and insufficient cash flow has been generated to cover interest payments. Bad decisions of this kind result in bankruptcy and default, that is the risk involved. There has to be risk. The bad debt that remains behind, stands as a monument to the follies of the past. Those mistakes are only compounded in the present and the future if the conclusion is drawn that all debt is bad and to be avoided at all costs.

Sometimes, the assumptions are just plain wrong, and the debt could never be paid off. Maybe borrowers and lenders are over-optimistic, or maybe just plain stupid; in some cases the motive is fraud, with no intention ever to repay. More usually, conditions simply do not turn out as expected. A debt that floats easily if prices rise at 20 per cent per year, may easily become a ten-ton weight if prices only rise by 5 per cent, or less. Debts that are small, as long as incomes are rising, become huge if incomes fall, or even stop rising as fast as expected. If there is a problem it is that, too often, borrowers and lenders transact on the basis of the most optimistic expectations, whereas they should base the decision on a less favorable case. Health warnings should be attached to loans: *conditions will change.*

Rising inflation was the scourge of the 1970s, and was replaced by debt in the 1980s and 1990s. This was not just bad luck. To a large degree, one led to the other. As long as inflation was expected to continue at a high level, and even accelerate further, the prudent thing to do was borrow as much as possible at a fixed rate of interest. Accelerating inflation reduced the real cost of the interest rate payments, and also the real value of the principal repayments. For years, lenders lost out because inflation really did accelerate, but slowly they adjusted their expectations and demanded higher rates of return to compensate them for further deterioration. This more cautionary attitude by creditors has continued to be evident in the form of high real interest rates, despite the substantial decline in inflation.

The success in reducing inflation left behind towering mountains of debt. It would seem that inflation came down too quickly in the United States, without the underlying excess demands that fueled the inflation being corrected first. A number of sectors of the economy, and certain countries, suffered through the 1980s from excessively high debt levels. In each case, it was in areas that benefited substantially from accelerating inflation, and the assumption had clearly been made that more of the same was to be expected. That assumption was wrong, and these areas suffered a severe readjustment. The expectation of continuing inflation was not the only explanation leading to excessive debt levels at that time. The United States government embarked upon a reckless desire to pack guns with butter, with predictably messy results. In addition, low equity values at the start of the 1980s offered extremely high real returns to those prepared to leverage up the assets. Eventually, that too was overdone.

## Debt, saving and capital

There is virtually unanimous agreement that there is much too much debt. Wherever you look there are towering mountains of debt to be seen. To be sure, this is all very worrying. The fact that there is such a consensus on the question is also a matter for concern. By the time something gets placed under the microscope, with the world crowding round to take a look, it usually means that the worst has already been realized.

The concern is that the debt mountains will collapse, crushing the financial system and the economy. The implications of such an event are so dramatic that the possibility, no matter how remote, has to be taken seriously and considered carefully. However, never to go into a building because of the possibility of fire, or never to cross the road because of the danger of being hit by a car, is totally unrealistic, unproductive and positively harmful in itself. The same can be said of never investing in the financial markets because of the possibility of catastrophe, no matter how remote. The existence of risk and uncertainty is essential to the operation of a capitalistic economy and cannot be, nor should be, wished away. These, however, need to be placed in the right context. It is destructive to long-term wealth creation to let their existence dominate investment thinking at all times.

The importance of large debts is in the implications they have on future behavior. Debt results from the act of borrowing, and there must come a point when the limit of desired indebtedness is reached. This will vary with the type of debt, individual taste, general income level and the perceived security of employment or profitability. The impression is sometimes given that all debt is bad debt, and there should not be any. That is an extreme view which is totally unrealistic, and not even desirable. Once the existence of debt is accepted as inevitable and desirable, the question then becomes what is too much; and that is much harder to answer. What might be too little in the expansion phase will become too much during a contraction. The economy is dynamic, and that will always pose a problem for logical minds in search of static stability. However, it is this variability that provides the vitality and growth that has been the strength of market economies.

There is no doubting that, at the start of the 1990s, there was a lot of debt outstanding. At what point does the level of debt move from being acceptable to excessive? Considered on its own, the nominal level of debt is meaningless. A debt of $1 million has very different implications if income is only $100 000 than if income is $100 million. Equally, the level of wealth will be important. Normally, income and wealth will be related, but, regardless of income, any particular debt level will be less significant the greater the level of wealth. Having said that, there are plenty of examples through history, where a shortage of cash flow has resulted in a debt crisis.

The level of debt is important only in relation to other nominal values; the number of zeros at the end of the big figure is not important on its own. However, the relationship also changes as economic conditions change. It is impossible to anticipate all eventualities, and operate in such a way that seems to avoid all risk. Such a cautious approach raises the danger that a company will be driven out of business or taken over by more aggressive competitors. There is no way of eliminating risk. Attempts to do so will only result in some unexpected consequence. The Soviet Union tried to eliminate risk in production, only to see the whole economy fall apart and the political system disappear. There was hardly any market debt, but that was no protection from inefficiency, incompetence and irrationality.

Debt is also an asset to someone else and, therefore, a collapse of the debt market will wipe out the assets of the unsuspecting. These dangers are real enough and there are defaults all the time; that is why investors should put great emphasis on diversification. The real concern is that a whole group of debtors will collapse at the same time, so that diversification offers no protection. Over recent years, prime candidates have been the LDCs, the farmers, real estate in several areas, S&Ls over a wide area, junk bonds, various cities and even the government itself.

The concerns have been real enough in most cases, but a little exaggerated as far as the government is concerned. The farmers have suffered badly and the S&Ls have been devastated. In each case there has been some personal hardship for those most closely involved, but there have been no general repercussions for the economy as a whole. The reason for the lack of follow-through has largely been due to government intervention. Departments stepped in and replaced private debt with government guarantees. The fact that this happened, and that it can be relied on to happen again under similar circumstances, is a crucial change in approach from the 1930s which is even more important than the *facts* involved.

In the case of the LDCs, the banks have had to bear a major part of the cost. The countries involved have not declared bankruptcy but have failed to meet their obligations; the difference is slight. The process has taken place over time and with support from the US Treasury and international organizations such as the IMF and World Bank. Here again, the risk has been spread while those nearest to the accident have been hurt. There is no doubting the disincentive effect involved as far as the banks are concerned, and also the international lending agencies.

Much of the criticism of the debt situation is not specific, but simply concerns the sheer weight of debt that is out there. But then, as already pointed out, the debt represents someone else's savings. If there is too much borrowing then does that mean there is too much lending? If there is too much lending, is the problem that people are saving too much?—a strange criticism. Or is it that the distribution of that saving should be more into equity? Well, that may be true, and the outstanding equity had been falling due to all of the takeover activity. But that can only be a small part of any major debt/savings problem. If all the money went into stocks rather than debt where would equity prices be now?

Since debt represents the result of someone else's saving, it makes up part of the assets for other people. That is not a problem, being on the high side. What is a potential problem is the distribution of the debt. Problems of illiquidity generally follow dramatic expansion in a particular sector, based on unrealistic and unrealized assumptions. That, for example, is what happened in the case of the farmers, who leveraged themselves up on the back of rising commodity prices and land prices in the 1970s. The LDCs were encouraged to borrow at low real interest rates. Sometimes, the money was just wasted on conspicuous spending, or syphoned off into private bank accounts, but was anyway employed inefficiently. These sectors went too far, and the distribution of debt was badly skewed. That was the real problem, not just the existence of high levels of debt.

Debt is what is left behind as the result of borrowing and lending. The capitalist system is built on the principle that individuals will save money, which will be invested in a form that will increase output and productivity in the future—capital. However, the people who save are not necessarily, or usually, the best people to invest the money efficiently. Simply to save by hoarding money is actually counterproductive and will lead to a cumulative reduction in output.

Money can be shifted from savers to investors, by gifts, loans or equity investment. Those, at least, are all the voluntary ways. In general business terms, companies wishing to invest have two external sources of finance, beyond internally generated funds, and those are borrowing or equity participation. Even in the absence of money, people borrowed seed grain, farm implements, etc., and paid interest in similar form, such as grain or labor. The existence of money simplifies arrangements and greatly widens the potential.

Borrowing and lending, and general financial intermediation, increase with economic development. To begin with, economic development depends on the existence of such financial markets. As the process gets underway financial intermediation tends to grow even faster, as the methods become increasingly sophisticated. Consequently, we should expect to observe rising debt levels as incomes grow and saving and investment increase. That is, rising not only in absolute terms, but also relatively.

## Debt reduction or destruction

There are four basic ways to bring excessive debt down to more acceptable levels.

1.  The most dramatic way to reduce debt levels, and the one that attracts the most attention, particularly at times of recession, is through default. Mass default is actually no solution, and should be avoided at all cost. The same is not true in the case of individual debtors. Within a dynamic, free-market economy, defaults are an inevitable part of life. Default is never pleasant but may, under certain circumstances, release

resources that lead to increased growth, and is a general benefit. The danger with default is that it spreads, bringing down other financial institutions and corporations. Default not only reduces the outstanding level of debt but also the assets of the lenders. This can then spread through other sectors of the economy. It is, however, not inevitable that the disease has to spread to the stronger parts of the economy. This is what happened in the 1930s, with the encouragement of the monetary authorities. That unfortunate lesson has been learnt.

2.  Another solution to the debt mountains that is often heard is that it is necessary to save more. For an indebted individual, or country, that means reducing outstanding debts, and is exactly what we are talking about. For a single individual it does not matter how this is achieved but, in aggregate, it makes a lot of difference whether it is through spending less out of current income or by spending the same with increased income.

    A general increase in the desire to save will not result in a reduction in debt totals unless it is through default. A general increase in the desire to save means less spending, which in turn means less income to those providing goods and services. In order to try and maintain the velocity of circulation, interest rates will fall. If this was instantly matched by increased borrowing then the income flow would be maintained, but the quantity of debt in existence would be increasing not decreasing. This is also dependent on confidence being maintained. Moreover, it is very unlikely that borrowing would pick up immediately, and it is more likely that there would be some decline in income, in order to reduce the amount being saved to equal the amount being invested. This then makes it more difficult for the existing borrowers to meet their servicing costs, raising the possibility of default. Consequently, exhortations to save more are likely to prove counter-productive as a means of reducing the debt overhang.

3.  An effective way to eliminate fixed income debt is through inflation. This works as long as the full extent of the inflation is not foreseen, and is not reflected in interest rates already, i.e. as long as the future rate of inflation is greater than the current rate of interest. Once expectations catch up, resulting in high real interest rates, then the process starts to work in reverse. New debts are being taken out at a high real cost, which means they are an additional burden and, therefore, much harder to service. Many of the inflation beneficiaries in the 1970s continued borrowing into the 1980s at very high real interest rates, not realizing that the trend had changed.

    The outstanding government debt in the United Kingdom has been deflated successfully through means of high inflation, but that did not immunize the economy from a severe recession in 1990/92. A return to rapid inflation at this point would be counter-productive since it would only confirm all the worst fears of both borrowers and lenders; the desire to borrow would increase while the desire to lend would decrease, with the result that real interest rates would be pushed up very high. There would be small short-term gains for prior debtors, but only at the expense of greatly increasing problems for the future. Alternatively, to go to the other extreme, deflation, risks a severe economic downturn with monetary policy out of control.

4.  The most positive way to reduce excessive debt levels is through real economic growth. This is what happens in the growth phase of the business cycle. Growth enables debt to be paid down but, typically, also leads to new debt being taken on for expansion purposes. Economic weakness has the opposite effect of making the debt situation worse, but also reduces the demand for credit.

It should be clear that economic expansion is not aided by defaults, by attempts to save more without a corresponding decision to invest more, or by a loss of confidence in the financial system. This is an important lesson that seems to have been learnt already. The combination of recession and high debt levels is potentially dangerous, and there is no simple cure-all. It is like the man who, having fallen into a tiger pit, asks what he should do. The best advice is not to fall in the pit in the first place. Those who look for statesmanlike leadership, which will resolve all the conflicts that exist, are dreaming of the impossible. Not only is such a solution impossible, it is not at all clear that it would be desirable. There is no single guilty party, and everyone would suffer if the system were allowed to fall apart. The pain of adjustment has to be apportioned somehow, and the market place is still the most efficient arbitrator, for all its imperfections. History shows that solutions imposed from above are usually nothing of the kind, and only lead to deeper divisions and greater problems later on.

What is not a solution to high debt levels is an economic recession. Tightening monetary policy and slowing the economy will only make the situation worse. Under these circumstances the debt/income ratio is likely to increase, even as defaults are reducing the level of debt. This is the way to turn a difficult situation into a dangerous one.

## Debt deflation and depression

At the start of the 1990s, there was widespread fear within the United States that the debt mountain was about to turn into an avalanche that would splinter and smash the financial system and all productive effort. Comparisons with the 1930s were easily made and frequently referred to. This was not the first time such comparisons had been made; similar arguments were made in each post-war recession. The fear, in each case, was that the debt had risen to extreme levels, threatening the destruction of the financial system and the economy. The final nail in the coffin was the perception that there was nothing the Federal Reserve or the Administration could do about it.

Considering the fact that this argument has been made many times before, and no doubt will be again at times of economic weakness, it is necessary to ask the question as to what is excessive, and whether that level has been reached. The same argument has been associated with many different, and lower, debt levels. Interestingly, the evidence does not support the argument that the depression in the 1930s was brought on by the economy collapsing under the weight of debt, as generally assumed. Moreover, there is still quite a lot the monetary authorities can do to improve the economy, and avoid a crisis of confidence, at least under current conditions.

The terms debt deflation and depression are frequently thrown together with no further explanation—as if the connection from one to the other is so obvious and well understood that no more needs to be said. But what does it mean? What is a debt deflation? Why does that lead to a depression? A deflation of debt presumably means that the value of outstanding debt falls, but that leaves more questions than it answers. Does it matter how the debt is deflated? How far does the process have to go before it creates a depression? No answers have been provided. The argument is simply that excessive debt will result in defaults, disaster and depression. Why?

Figure 5.1 shows the dramatic increase in debt that has taken place over the past 75 years. The early periods became insignificant as the later years dominate the chart. This is another example of how appearances can be deceiving. There is a problem in looking at nominal series over time on an arithmetic scale, as pointed out in the introduction. A constant growth rate will show up as an exponential curve, as the base keeps being raised. Add in the effect of inflation and the increase will become explosive, but without any implication that conditions are out of control.

Figure 5.2 puts the rise in debt into better perspective by dividing it by GDP. Even on this basis, there has been a sharp increase since 1981. Looking back over history there is an ominous similarity with an earlier period that is clearly associated with the depression. This observation, more than anything else, is used to highlight the potential for another depression. A closer inspection shows that the earlier bulge in the debt/GDP ratio is not only *associated* with the depression, it *is* the depression. The sharp run up in the debt ratio is during the 1930s, peaking in 1933, and not *prior* to the downturn in the economy. The debt ratio was reasonably stable during the 1920s, and was actually lower in 1929 than in 1921 and 1922.

On the basis of this evidence, it is hard to justify the argument that

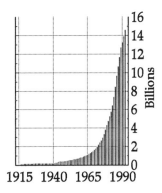

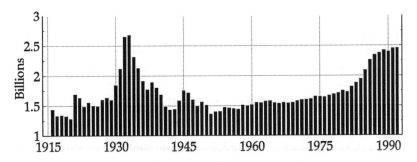

**Figure 5.1** US total debt (annual)

**Figure 5.2** Debt/GNP ratio in the US (annual)

excessive debt creation caused the depression. Equally, it is even harder to make the case that the depression was the result of a *deflation* of the debt. Falling output and declining prices actually raised the real value of the debt. Nominal GDP fell practically in half over the four years from 1929 to 1933. Instead of being deflated down, which might well have helped, the value of debt outstanding declined more slowly, making it an increasing burden on an already fragile economy.

Contrary to the generally accepted view that the depression was caused by a massive debt deflation, there has to be a suspicion that the problem was quite the opposite: excessive attention to the preservation of debt values. Maybe income and production could have been held up better if debts had been written off more quickly. The obsession with price stability at all cost, and the gold standard, were an expression of such a bias. Income preservation was less important than wealth preservation. That relative ordering has been reversed since then, which removes an important trip-rope in the path towards recession—a trip-rope that can turn recession into depression.

Even if the depression in the 1930s was not caused by a massive liquidation of debt built up in the 1920s, there is still the large build-up of debt in the 1980s to contend with. Maybe this time the mountain of debt is high enough to bring down the financial sector and the economy. Before jumping to that conclusion it will help to look more closely at the numbers.

The first point to note is that while the ratio is high, it is not as high as it was in 1933. Even more noteworthy is the fact that this was the year when the economy hit bottom and started a strong economic recovery, it was *not* a prelude to the depression. The recent increase has been dramatic, but much of this rise is accounted for by the huge increase in the budget deficit over the 1980s, and the related current account deficits. The government borrowing needs are a continuing problem, but the federal government is not expected to go bankrupt just yet.

Before concluding that the rise in debt levels is excessive, it is necessary to consider what has been happening to incomes and asset levels. People and companies will tend to borrow more the greater is their income and their assets. In particular, lenders will see them as good risks if they want to borrow in order to take advantage of favorable opportunities. These will be most favorable when asset prices and incomes are rising, and least attractive when asset prices and incomes are falling.

What this means is that debt will tend to rise faster during times of strong economic growth. To the extent that the borrowing goes into new production, either directly or indirectly, this will stimulate production further and create a virtuous circle. A typical reaction to an extended period of strong growth and rising incomes is that lenders will lower their standards for granting new loans just at the time when borrowers have already exhausted the best opportunities. It is very likely, under these conditions, that borrowing will continue beyond the edge of prudence towards the height of folly.

When conditions change, the whole psychology will reverse. Incomes will slide, borrowing will be curtailed, as borrowers cut back and some repay early, while lenders raise the qualifying standards for new credits back to where they had been before. Now there is a vicious circle. Creditors are chasing the debtors with their hands out. New projects are canceled or put on hold, and the economy slows down.

Given these natural tendencies it is hardly surprising that debts rise during periods of strong growth. In general, assets and liabilities will increase together, since most borrowing and lending takes place within the country; sometimes within the same sector and sometimes across sectors. After all, one person's debt must be another person's asset, and existing asset values are also likely to be rising in this environment. Debts may well be rising strongly, but then assets may also be rising by the same amount, or even more.

Taking a closer look at the household sector, debts did rise faster than assets over the 1980s, but not fast enough to prevent net worth rising as well. The pattern was similar to the 1950s and the first half of the 1960s, when liabilities also rose faster than assets. There was then very little change until the early 1980s. Relatively high debt growth has been associated with economic growth, and the flatter trend through the second half of the 1960s and 1970s was associated with weak growth, rapid inflation and poor stock market performance. These relationships say nothing about causality, but rapid debt growth is certainly not always bad, and subdued debt growth is not always good.

The ratio of household liabilities and assets to personal disposable income is shown in Fig. 5.3. The trends fluctuate around, and liabilities have risen slowly over time, but the movement hardly seems extreme. As a percentage of assets, liabilities have risen to around 17 per cent, but even that may not reflect a true valuation of assets.

On the corporate side, the dramatic increase in debt financing is well known. However, even with the dramatic expansion of leveraged buy-outs, and the growth of the junk bond market, liabilities as a percentage of assets are only fractionally above where they were in the early 1970s. Through the late 1970s, and into the 1980s, this percentage dropped to a very low level. This was more like the debt deflation associated with a long-wave downturn—the timing was just right. That created room for an expansion of debt financing in the 1980s. A further boost was provided by the low valuation placed on many companies in the equity market.

An additional feature to note about the rise in borrowing by the corporate

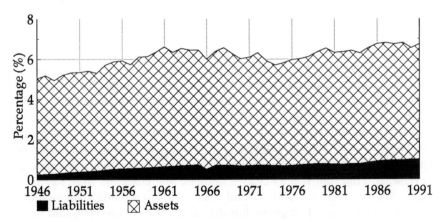

**Figure 5.3** Household assets and liabilities, as a percentage of personal disposable income (annual)

sector in the 1980s is that it was concentrated in particular sectors. Roach (1991) points out that the main borrowers were in those areas most able to service the debt, 'the cash flow—stable sectors of nondurable manufacturing, public utilities, and services'. The greatest danger is in terms of debts taken on by highly cyclical industries, but the fact is that the debt–service ratios, i.e. net interest divided by cash flow, has remained reasonably stable through the 1970s and 1980s. The exception to this rule has been the LBO binge in the retail industry, particularly department stores. Here was an example of insanity at work, but the widely reported problems of that sector should not be assumed to apply to the whole corporate sector.

Undoubtedly, mistakes were made and many bad loans resulted. These will need to be resolved over time through a combination of default, restructuring or work outs. Creditors stand to lose money on some of these deals, but this does not have to extend to all creditors or to the economy in general. In fact, making sure that this does not happen has to be the number one priority of the monetary authorities. Under present conditions, there is no reason why they should not be successful.


## Freedom to fail

There are problems with the S&Ls, the banks, junk bonds, real estate generally and LDC governments. These sound terrible, and they are, but there is also a lot of double counting involved. Real estate debt and junk bonds are the major cause of recent concerns with the S&Ls and the banks; solve one and you automatically solve the other. The size of the government's debt is also generally considered to be too high, but the possibility of default is, so far, not a cause for concern. There is, however, some anxiety over the finances of the states and cities, but that has more to do with the inability to control current spending and revenue totals than with out-standing debt levels.

There was a time, not so long ago, when there were widespread worries that the whole agricultural sector would end up in default. Huge debts had been taken on during and after the sharp acceleration of commodity prices in the 1970s, in anticipation of more of the same. What in fact happened was that commodity prices fell and real interest rates went up and stayed up. Here we have a classic example of how rising inflation distorted decision making and resulted in a huge debt problem. The equation started working in reverse, and the sum was a negative number. Many farmers were squeezed badly. As they tried to bail out, land prices fell. For a while it seemed that the end of the world had come, but the situation has improved, and farm-land prices began rising again in the latter part of the 1980s.

Farmers experienced sharply rising incomes in the 1970s, and saw land prices soaring. Substantial profits were made by buying additional land, both in terms of cash flow and asset values. This was no abstract theory; they could see it happening. Farm land was going up in value, so the banks saw it as secure collateral and were happy to lend against it. In some cases, they positively encouraged such borrowing. The farmers and bankers were forecasting that the future would see similar price rises as the past. Their forecasts were very wrong, and the future punished such errors severely.

The problems were measured in terms of the debt outstanding, but the real cause of the financial difficulties was the decisions that were made earlier. There is still a lot of outstanding farm debt, but the assumptions underlying it are now more realistic. Conditions have improved, and the weak holders have already been taken out of the game. In the mid 1980s, there had been too much debt, now these farm debt levels seem to be manageable.

Bad decisions, based on incorrect forecasts of the future, will always be punished by market forces. That is an essential element of a free-market economy. The potential to succeed, to reward risk taking, which provides the engine for growth, has to be accompanied by the freedom to fail. There has to be a discipline imposed on the system. On the other hand, governments have learned the importance of maintaining confidence, and that requires protecting other people from the snowball effect of bad decisions made elsewhere.

Both elements, the punishment of bad decisions and the effort to maintain confidence in the financial system, are apparent in the S&L crisis. The problems, in this case, originated way back in the past; back to the 1930s. Lending was at fixed rates while the borrowing to finance it was at floating rates, with a cap. It is hard to imagine anything so potentially dangerous. Strangely, very little is heard about the origins of the S&L mess. As inflation accelerated in the 1970s so the level of interest rates rose. Even in the times when the yield curve remained positive, the rise in the level of interest rates meant that old mortgages were being carried at a loss. When short rates rose above long-term yields the problem was made even worse.

Slowly, step by step, the chains that bound S&L policy loosened, but that still left them struggling to come to terms with the hand that history had dealt. Also, each step along the way was hesitant, and for a very long time left major obstacles in the way of free choice. Finally, most restraints were removed, and S&Ls were allowed to put money into a variety of other instruments, including junk bonds, about which they knew nothing. There was even positive encouragement to take such risks in an effort to compensate for some of the low-yielding mortgages.

The rest, as they say, is history. The financial system in the US has suffered badly from overregulation and undersupervision. Less of the one and more of the other could have avoided the S&L debacle, and the pain and suffering of the banks.

Banks, like S&Ls, were for a long time faced with a maximum interest that they could pay on deposits. This encouraged the Eurodollar and commercial paper markets. The banks also faced increasing competition from the S&Ls, as the regulators pushed them into the same areas. Some S&Ls bid aggressively for deposits, paying the high cost by buying high-yield, and therefore high-risk, bonds. Increased competition also came from overseas banks—partly resulting from restraints on banks, and partly from government policy that generated huge current account deficits in the 1980s. The countries with the external surpluses saw money flow in, and the domestic banks had a major role to play in recycling this back to other countries. This trend was particularly noticeable with the Japanese banks, which were anyway trying to expand aggressively.

The American banks did not want to be left behind, but in order to grow they had to search out new and more profitable lending areas. Real estate lending was the hot topic in the late 1980s, but it could not last. Real estate has always been the most cyclical of industries. The longer the market continued to expand the more a correction became likely. What happened instead was that the lending terms became even finer; quite the opposite of what was necessary, particularly since more marginal projects were being attempted.

It is a fact of life that the longer a trend continues, the more people come to expect it to continue. Such extrapolation may not be expressed in that way, but it is clear that decisions are made on that assumption. At the early stages of the real estate upswing there were good projects that had been planned well in advance, waiting to be implemented. The approach was cautious and the projects well financed. By the end, haphazard, hasty decisions were being made on projects that were marginal at best. Often decisions were based on past performance with other projects rather than the merits of the particular case under consideration.

The same sort of deterioration in quality of decision-making and projects was apparent in the leveraged buy-out arena. Spectacular returns were available at the end of the previous bear market, and it took a long time for values to be realized, but eventually the market caught up. By the end of the 1980s, there was very little extra value left to be squeezed out, but the amount of financing had increased dramatically. Early on, when values were good, no one wanted to lend on such high-risk activities. By the end, when values had disappeared and risks were very high, money was freely available in what had become a highly competitive business.

There was a glut of retailers that had prospered through the high consumption of the Reagan years. The market was saturated, and the trend could not continue, particularly since the trade deficit had to be corrected soon, which meant consumption would need to be constrained. Yet there was a rush to pay astronomical prices to buy department stores, and a rush to lend money on such deals. The gods really do make crazy those whom they intend to destroy.

Bad lending practices combined with bad projects left behind debts without value. The debts then become a problem, that is true, but the real problem was the lending procedure of the banks and other creditors, and the incompetence of the borrowers. Future stability requires that these bad decisions are punished, if only to discourage the same mistakes being made again. The freedom to fail has to exist to discipline the process of expansion—to restrain enthusiasm and the unscrupulous.

## Cash flow and confidence

While individuals should pay the penalty for their mistakes, there is no obvious benefit in making other people, and society in general, suffer for the stupidity of a few greedy or disillusioned people. It is much more important to maintain confidence and incomes than to attempt the preservation of some monument to historical misjudgement, an attempt that ultimately will be doomed to failure anyway, but with devastating costs.

There is a high psychological component in all financial markets. Liquidity is not a real thing that can be touched or seen, but is a belief built on confidence. Take away the confidence and the belief collapses, and liquidity dries up in the instant. Confidence requires maintaining two things: (a) the security of capital, and (b) the security of employment and markets.

The key becomes the maintenance of economic growth, avoiding a steep slide in incomes. This was not fully appreciated in the 1930s, but is much better understood today. In the 1930s, there was more concern with preserving the value of the wealth than jobs and incomes, without realizing that the task was impossible *unless* incomes were preserved. Bad decisions have to be punished, otherwise people will keep making the same mistake. At the same time, it is essential that the rest of the financial system is not contaminated by a general loss of confidence. This is a lesson that the monetary authorities seem to have learnt. Getting the right balance between support and punishment is still difficult, and is not always achieved, but the free-fall approach adopted in the 1930s is not about to make a reappearance.

Borrowers do not match the maturity of their borrowing and the use of the funds. That is true of banks, but also of credit agencies, companies generally and many individuals. A company may borrow to finance inventory or continuing operations, which may seem to be short-term in nature. But, in reality, the only way to repay the money without re-borrowing would be to go out of business. At that point the assets may be worth less than they were, and possibly will not cover the liabilities. A classic catch-22.

Maintain cash flow and confidence and the cycle of payments continues. If either drops sharply there will be problems. In the game of pass the parcel, the person holding the debt loses under these conditions. One thing that seems certain is that the monetary authorities will do anything to maintain cash flows and confidence, but they also have to maintain an air of uncertainty. A world of apparent certainty, where everyone is complacent, is extremely dangerous. Caution is justified, panic is not. It makes sense to insure a house against the possibility of fire, but it makes no sense to run screaming from a house just because it might one day catch on fire. The same sense of proportion is required when considering debt and its likely effect on financial markets.

The importance of maintaining confidence is absolutely crucial. In August 1982, confidence in Mexico's ability to repay its debts collapsed overnight. Demands for repayment, by refusing to renew short-term credits, threatened to bring about exactly the catastrophe that was feared. The important point to note is that Mexico was not alone in being unable to meet its short-term liabilities upon demand. Virtually every major corporation, major bank and country is in the same position. Morgan Guarantee cannot pay off all of its depositors upon demand, nor can General Motors pay off its short-term paper. Even the United States government cannot run the printing presses fast enough to meet even a fraction of the short-term claims against the Treasury.

This need for continued confidence is nothing new, and has been a necessary ingredient whenever a credit-based economy has existed. The industrial revolution required and encouraged a massive extension of the use of credit as a necessary counterpart to the rising level of investment. In the early stages, the markets were largely unregulated, which encouraged experimentation and also led to severe abuses, which in turn resulted in periodic financial crises and collapse. These financial repercussions greatly exaggerated the business cycle.

In the up-phase, optimistic expectations are met, which improves confidence further. During periods of expansion, when credit is cheap, confidence first improves, then reaches a high level and, if continued, usually turns into overconfidence. This last state is characterized by the belief that the formula for perpetual motion has been discovered; that scarce resources no longer provide a limit to human achievement; and that growth and prosperity will continue to accelerate far into the distant future. People, including usually conservative bankers, see no risks ahead and are happy to commit extensive funds under the most optimistic assumptions.

Then comes the collapse, and confidence evaporates like dew on a summer's morning; optimism turns into pessimism, and confidence to caution. People will no longer roll-over existing credits and will not extend new loans. Firms, therefore, go bankrupt, eliminating debts and surpluses simultaneously, and spreading the financial squeeze to other firms and individuals. A financial version of multipliers and accelerators working in reverse: a divider and decelerator. Individuals try to save, but all they succeed in doing is reducing incomes and savings in aggregate. Without financial support, the process must run its natural course, until the system stabilizes at a lower level of income, savings, debts and surpluses. From that point confidence can slowly build again.

The government cannot afford to threaten the liquidity of the financial system. In the 1930s, the monetary authorities allowed confidence in the system to evaporate, and with it went the liquidity. That, more than anything else, accounted for the severity of the depression. Confidence in any single institution can be allowed to collapse, but every effort must be made to support the system.

Most short-term money is borrowed in the belief that only a small fraction will ever be demanded under the terms of the loan; and that, on average, this will be replaced by a new flow of money. Under normal conditions this is so, and it allows financial intermediaries, which collect deposits from a wide variety of sources, to lend a large part of that money out over longer terms than the average maturity of the deposits. Moreover, the final borrowers will generally use the funds for longer-term requirements than the period of the loan, since experience has shown that the loans typically can be rolled over, or financed elsewhere.

It is not necessary to continue along this chain; the point should be clear. If the majority want their money back, they cannot have it—the liquidity will disappear as quickly as a mirage in the desert. That is what happened in the 1930s, but is avoided in the typical recession. In a recession, liquidity dries up but it does not disappear. As a result, borrowers run into trouble but, in general, conditions are manageable. There are very few borrowers that can prepay upon demand.

Liquidity represents the immediate spendability of one's assets, but there is a difference in how this is perceived by the owners of the assets and the reality of the situation. Liquidity is in essence something which exists only in the mind. If liquidity is thought to exist then it truly does exist, since the majority will be content to leave their money with the bank, S&Ls, etc., where it will continue to circulate, and the system will not be tested. However, if liquidity is thought not to exist then it just as surely does not. Attempts by the majority to liquidate their holdings by converting them to cash would be impossible. Instant repayment of all short-term debts cannot be achieved, and the attempt to demand it will only destroy all liquidity by bringing the financial superstructure crashing down, and the economy with it. The scramble for liquidity is like chasing a ghost, with potentially frightening consequences.

# 6

BEYOND THE CYCLE
(*a long look back*)

The crash of 1929 and the subsequent depression extending through 1933 administered a huge jolt, and the shock waves are still being felt. The impression of that time still haunts the stock market in the United States. Like all ghostly apparitions, it can be seen more clearly by some people than others. There have been a number of frights, and the clanking of falling prices has been heard many times. It is a brave investor indeed who can smile at the thought of living through a similar experience.

The super-cycle has a bad reputation because it has become associated with impending depression—always impending. There is an enduring belief that a market crash and depression lie just around the corner. This view has been used to scare investors through much of the 1970s and the 1980s, and still in the 1990s. There is no doubt that doom and disaster sell well, even when it unbalances investors and points them in the wrong direction. A problem with these constant warnings is that it weakens resistance, like drug addiction, requiring heavier and heavier doses to have any effect. Like the boy who cried wolf, there is the danger that the real warning when it finally comes will be ignored.

To many, it seems as if the end of the world always lies just around the corner, popularly summarized in the Kondratieff long-wave cycle. Kondratieff still reaches out from his grave and lays his cold hand on their hearts. The name Kondratieff has become closely associated with impending doom; it always seems that the economy is about to turn down into the final down-wave of the cycle. The scare stories that have been told, forgotten and told again, are generally based on superficial comparisons with the past. Facts are never really that, and the evidence is open to different interpretations, particularly when used selectively. How many times is it necessary to be wrong before it is concluded that the view is wrong? and is it just about the one time that, like a stopped clock, it is about to be right?

Holding such bearish views through the 1980s cost dearly—it meant missing one of the great bull markets of history. It is, therefore, crucial to understand how real the threat of collapse is, and the extent to which the fears are exaggerated. Contrary to conventional thinking, the existence of a Kondratieff long cycle does not necessarily mean that it is about to come crashing down into our lives like a destructive hurricane. An alternative reading of the economic entrails strongly suggests that the down-wave has actually been completed, and that the economy and stock market are already embarked on a major upswing.

The whole concept of a long wave has been used to justify the threat of a crash and depression. But there is the other side to this idea, the up-wave, the exciting potential for growth and development. That has received hardly any attention, despite the fact that the theories used to justify a long wave are very much based on innovation and growth. Listening to some of the strongly worded views frequently expressed, one could easily get the impression that there was no such thing as a long-wave cycle, only a long down-wave. However, it is really the up-wave that is the most interesting aspect of the cycle. What is required is an unbiased analysis of the cycle that will anticipate the potential major downturn, but which will also allow investors to take advantage of the great potential that exists during the upturn.

The idea that a depression lies just around the corner seems to have been popular ever since the last one in the 1930s. A massive shock to the system takes time to get over. The bigger the shock, and the greater the surprise, the longer it takes. I argued many times through the 1980s, that the stock market made a long-term low in August 1982 and is now already well into the long up-wave. The economy is in a similar up-wave of a long cycle, driven by a revolution in information, communications and computer technology. The argument is spelt out below. Some of the evidence is in terms of a reinterpretation of the published facts and figures, but other important considerations are in the attitudes of individuals and institutions. These are less easy to measure, but the effects are still very real.

## Identifying the long wave

In setting out in search of the long wave the first thing to do is to identify it in general terms—to prove that it actually exists. If that can be done it is then necessary to get closer, and locate where we are now within that extended cycle. Since the most interesting conclusion to be drawn here is in answer to this second question, it should come as no surprise that a long wave has been spotted moving close by. The surprise comes in the conclusion that the long wave has turned up, and is not about to drop into a climactic free fall as most students of such phenomena expect.

The idea of a long wave, or cycle, predates the formal study of economics or the existence of stock markets by thousands of years. Its origins can be found in the effects of cycles of the moon, or planetary movements, on agriculture. The modern version of this ancient phenomenon has its roots in the work of one Nicholas Alexandrovich Kondratieff, a Russian economist who, in the 1920s, showed that while capitalistic economies were subject to wide cycles they were inherently stable; i.e. every downturn was followed by an upturn. What Kondratieff identified was a cycle of approximately 55 years in prices and basic economic activity. For such heresy he was sent to Siberia.

Karl Marx had also been a student of the economic cycle, which was seen as an unavoidable feature of the capitalist system. He argued that the cycles were deteriorating and there would be no reversal. The cause was underconsumption, i.e. a shortage of demand, which resulted in the paradox of the coexistence of idle manpower and idle capital. The underconsumption resulted from an extreme unequal distribution of wealth. However, that was not the main cause of the great depression, and now the distribution of wealth has become much more even. John Maynard Keynes was also of the opinion that underconsumption had become a constant feature of the economy, which was why governments had to step in to pump up demand. Some have subsequently argued that the distribution has become too even, and the problem is now a shortage of savings, i.e. overconsumption. Whatever the reason, it is hard to imagine that people have run out of things to spend their money on. One may question the necessity of much of this expenditure, but not that there is demand.

There are two main branches to the present-day interest in the long wave. The self-interest of each group has resulted in a common front, but the approaches and conclusions are really very different. Firstly, there is the serious study of economic phenomena and the possibility of long cycles of technological innovation as defined by Schumpeter. This group is populated by academics who are more interested in the details of the process than anything else, but are still capable of producing scary forecasts of crashes and depression. They focus on the economy rather than the financial markets. The other group reverses this emphasis, focusing on the financial markets. Chaos in the economy is an integral part of the process, but that is not their main concern. Their concern is with the possibilities of mass defaults and a rout in the stock market.

One objective of this chapter is to present a comprehensive overview, considering the economy and the markets together, but it is not the main one. More importantly, it challenges the generally held view that we are still in the down-phase of the long wave, with the crash and depression still to come. In order to develop the argument it is necessary to look briefly at Kondratieff's model, how it has been developed, and how things have changed. Along the way we shall use historical charts to signpost the way, and provide important pegs on which to hang the arguments.

What this study shows is that there is an alternative way to look at the evidence, but that invariably a single view has dominated. The reason for this is not the overwhelming weight of the evidence, but simply that in the minds of most people nothing dramatic, or catastrophic enough, has happened to mark the end of a long wave. This is a major problem living through history; the major events are seldom recognized as such except in retrospect. In this case, the desire to see history repeat itself has blinded the vision of people who would otherwise see clearly.

## The Kondratieff cycle

Kondratieff was born into the autocratic Czarist regime, and worked and died within an equally autocratic communist regime. He looked at the capitalist system from the outside, and came to the fatal (for him) conclusion that the system could survive; that it did have regenerative properties. His analysis, while fruitful and provocative, was narrow in focus and short on facts. That is not a criticism. Considering the limitations of data at that time it was a remarkable piece of work.

Historical data on production were available only for such items as pig-iron in countries like England and France, along with commodity prices, and these formed the basis of his analysis. Kondratieff carefully smoothed his data, and then discussed deviations around the trend. Despite the fact that Kondratieff was mainly concerned.with explaining production trends, the standard presentation over the post-war period was in terms of the price level, as shown in Fig. 6.1. There was an obvious reason for the emphasis on prices: the trend showed up beautifully in prices but was not at all obvious for industrial production or GNP. The stock market cycle, or the long economic cycle, do not fit in well with the cycles of prices at all.

On the basis of the price chart of the Kondratieff wave, many forecasters predicted that prices would start to fall somewhere around 1970, that a severe depression would settle over the economy, and stock prices would crash. Hopes ran high in 1970, and then again in 1974, that the time had arrived, but the economy recovered and stock prices ran up. But that was not the end of the wishful thinking, and the bookshelves filled up with warnings of financial and economic collapse. These were extended into the 1980s although the numbers declined a little. And still the forecasts are being made.

For a long time, certainly through the 1970s and into the 1980s, the stylized chart shown here was reproduced, showing prices still going up. Initially, the argument was that the fall could not be put off much longer, and that the fall, when it came, would be even greater. Well, the chart has been updated to the end of 1990, and it has obliterated the stylized Kondratieff cycle. While the link was never very strong between prices and

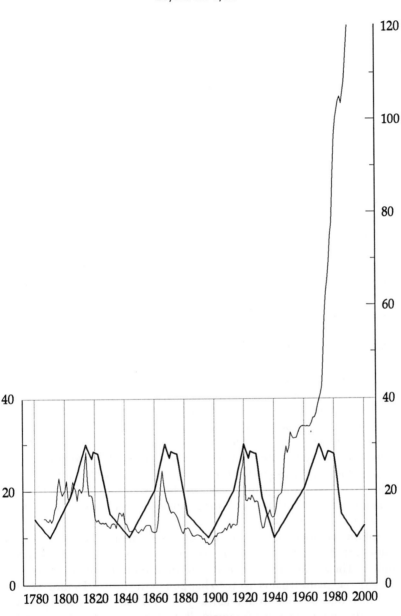

— Idealized cycle†     — Wholesale price index
† Idealized Kondratieff Wave as originally drawn by The Media
  General Financial Weekly, June 3, 1974

**Figure 6.1** Wholesale prices and the idealized Kondratieff wave (annual)

the economy and the stock market, this chart formed the basis of a great many predictions of imminent collapse. The conclusion, however, need not be that the long cycle has ceased to exist. What happened to the price level was the result of the changing role of government within a developing democracy. There is still evidence of a long cycle, but the downturn phase has already come and gone.

## Government, democracy and post-war recovery

The rapid growth of government in the post-war period can best be understood in terms of the dramatic events that preceded it—notably the depression in the 1930s and the traumatic war that followed. As explained in the previous chapter, the contrast between government action and inaction, and economic depression and boom, was too obvious to be missed. Democracy demanded action and history provided the instruction book. All the pieces fell into place, and the result would forever change the composition of the economy and would dramatically influence the next super-cycle downturn.

There are many aspects to this growth of government, and a number of these have resulted in major changes in the structure of the economy. First, the exaggerated confidence that governments could control growth led to an overexpansion of demand in the 1960s and 1970s when the long-term trend growth rate was slowing down. A second aspect has been the attempt to support declining industries. This contributed to the inflationary bias of the economy, and also extended the period of adjustment to the structural changes taking place. Old industries have been kept going longer in the face of falling demand, increased competition from abroad and the development of alternative products. One implication of declining sectors is that relative prices fall for the output of that sector. By attempting to hold up demand, and by means of direct price supports, a bias was given to inflation, since the easiest way for relative prices to adjust was through increases in prices for the output of the growing sectors.

Attention has focused on the role of government in causing the past inflation, but not enough attention has been given to the motives that lay behind it. These motives are more important than the inflation itself, for they help to explain what is likely to happen in the future. Democratic governments reduced inflation dramatically in the 1980s, just when it seemed that events might get out of control. But no one is advocating pushing prices back down to where they were at the start of the 1970s or even the 1940s. Politicians and economists are much more scared of deflation than they are of inflation. And, in a way, the 1980s confirmed that bias. In the 1930s the economy went out of control and unemployment rose dramatically. There is now no way in which a political party could survive in power after presiding over such a debacle. Inflation in the 1980s on the other hand has been brought under control at great cost, but it has not been so sudden, dramatic or noticeable. In a democracy, jobs, and maintaining incomes, are more important than returning to any particular price level.

The Second World War created a great demand for American goods, and permitted a massive expansion of the economy. When it was over, the job of reconstruction following the mass devastation that had taken place propelled the world economy, and maintained a strong demand for US goods, commodities and finance. There were continued cycles but they were subdued. Credit was claimed for the Keynesian demand management policies which most Western governments adopted, but a large role was, in fact, played by the replacement needs of a generation, and the tremendous advances in technology that were taking place.

Technology had not advanced into private industry, or into consumer products, because of the demands made by war. At the same time, war had actually speeded up technological development in a number of important areas, including aeronautics and electronics. There was, therefore, a pent-up supply-side force which peace released onto an unsuspecting world.

On the other side of the equation there was also considerable pent-up demand. The war had provided full employment and rising incomes, but reduced the supply of consumer goods, as resources were diverted to the war effort. One possible result would have been massive inflation, but a combination of rationing and saving held down the price increases. Thus, when the war ended, individuals were highly liquid and bank lending was at exceptionally low levels. The banks were keen to lend, and reduce the weight of government debt in their portfolios, and individuals were willing to borrow, increasingly so as confidence returned. On top of all this, governments were willing to pump up demand so as to avoid a post-war recession such as had developed in 1921.

The adjustment following the war probably took far longer, and was more important, than has generally been allowed for in the refined world of economic model building. The importance of new inventions and innovations in explaining economic growth has been badly neglected by economists, politicians and most others. It is reasonable to suppose that one reason for this was the emphasis on the demand side of the economy. Inaccurate explanations of the past are a poor guide to the future.

The post-war period of prosperity was accompanied by other secular trends; large scale redistribution of income and the increasing importance of government in all areas of economic and social existence. For a time, the increasing role of the government gave a further impetus to the economy, creating the belief that the economic equivalent of the philosopher's stone had been found.

As the motive force of the war recovery finally gave way, government and electorate alike were by this time addicted to growth, and this became the measuring rod of the government's performance. Political success or failure became inextricably linked with economic growth. Political parties boasted of their ability to sustain growth, and even that they could accelerate the process. This was the lever-pulling mentality of high-Keynesianism which came to full bloom in the 1960s and early 1970s.

But the economy was a far more delicate flower than anyone realized at the time. The original high expectations turned to hope and then to wishful thinking, as western governments sought the key to growth by pumping up demand. Economic growth could not be sustained through such crude demand-led measures. The recoveries became shorter and the recessions deeper, and all the time the underlying trend of inflation continued to accelerate.

To a significant degree, the acceleration of inflation was due to the declining momentum of the economy associated with the terminal stages of the super-cycle. Declining industries implied structural unemployment, and a temporary fall in aggregate demand, before the new growth sectors caught up and the economy adjusted to the new opportunities created. The problem was complicated by the fact that no one recognized what was happening, and attributed the problems to a deficiency in final demand. The result was massive excess demand, since demand was being pumped up while at the same time the supply potential of the economy was reduced.

In Chapter 2 it was shown that the rise of democracy changed the character of the business cycle. Instead of capital preservation being the main economic objective of governments, democracy has shifted the emphasis towards the preservation of income and employment. The emphasis now is towards creating new wealth instead of necessarily preserving the value of existing wealth. As wealth ownership increases so this becomes more important. However, in a system where each vote has equal weight, democracy means that policy will tend to be aimed at influencing the votes of the majority. The changes to the character of the business cycle carry over to the long-term cycle, changing its character also. That might seem obvious, but it has been lost on those expecting a repeat of the 1930s.

## The new revolution

In terms of interpreting, and identifying, the long wave there are two important implications of this large-scale intervention by government. Firstly, it has slowed down and smoothed out the transition from one economic structure to another. Secondly, it has changed the standard Kondratieff price cycle forever.

Taking the structural change first. Dramatic events are taking place. In historical terms, these are happening overnight, and it is only the lack of perspective which has kept this from being properly recognized. The industrial sector is contracting, providing no more than 25 per cent of all new jobs, and facing increasing international competition. Service industries are growing rapidly, and a lot of this growth revolves around computers, communications and information. This same revolution is also transforming the way in which goods are produced and industry is operated, with rapidly expanded use of robots in production and computers in the management of inventories, and in carrying out many white-collar jobs.

These changes are affecting all sectors of the economy. New office buildings are being constructed to take advantage of the communications and technological possibilities that exist, and are being made flexible enough to incorporate new developments. These are the so-called intelligent buildings; and there is already talk about creating intelligent cities. It is no longer enough simply to incorporate the latest state of the art. Change is now so rapid that the next progression has to be anticipated in order to avoid instant obsolescence. This is not a sign of a stagnant economy that has run out of ideas at the end of a long up-wave. What is more, this dynamic environment exists everywhere, not only in the United States.

Everybody is aware of changes taking place. However, these are not just interesting developments, but add up to a true revolution. There is no one place in time to which one can point to mark the start of this revolution, but it has been going for some time and is maturing rapidly. It is certainly a dramatic enough event to justify qualifying as a wave of new innovation in Schumpeterian terms. By the time this information and technology revolution is fully recognized as such, it is likely that the cycle will have fully matured and will be nearer a downturn than an upturn.

Joseph Schumpeter (1926) talked about waves of innovation which drive the economy higher. The new technology will have been developed over a period of time, but suddenly there is a rush to bring it into operation. The new leadership does not generally come from the old industries, which are slow to change, but from new entrepreneurs, so that the new industries or methods of production are created side by side with the old. The new then takes over dominance through the normal operation of market forces. Examples would be the revolution in agriculture in the eighteenth century; the industrial revolution in the late eighteenth and early nineteenth centuries; the rise of light industry and electricity in the late nineteenth century; then came the spread of automation and industrial organization in the early twentieth century leading into high-tech industries.

There are no sudden breaks when one technology takes over from the other, but a gradual process of change. The new replace the old only after a long period of coexistence. The identification of revolutionary change comes later and usually only with the benefit of hindsight. The information/

communication/technology revolution is now well underway. What is important from a cyclical point of view is that it is now moving towards a position of dominance within the economy, despite the smoothing and slowing effect of government support for the old and outdated.

Christopher Freeman (1977) drew attention to this revolution in the electronics industry. The character of the industry has expanded and developed, greatly expanding the applications of computers and electronics generally. This process has accelerated dramatically since Freeman made his observations. Even then, however, he anticipated great growth in this area, having a revolutionary effect on production methods. He conclude that 'the competitive substitution pressure in a wide range of industries and services will become intense in the last quarter of this century'.

What is happening within the production and services industries is not the only evidence of dramatic change, there is also what might be called the re-urbanization revolution. This second change is characterized by the transformation of old warehouses, docks and many other ugly manifestations from the era of heavy industry, into attractive living and recreation areas. In this way, the environment is being adapted to the changing needs of the population, reflecting the needs and desires of service and light industry workers. The social unrest that came to a head in the 1960s, and the attack on censorship, were all part of the general upheaval taking place, marking a transitional phase in the economy and society generally.

Figure 6.2 shows the long-run pattern of the growth of industrial production. It can be seen that the long-run cycles do not show up clearly at all, in the way they do for inflation and interest rates and, therefore, require much more careful interpretation. The smoother growth over the post-war period is noticeable—quite the opposite of what is nearly always claimed. Also the weak average growth rate over the 1970s and early 1980s is noteworthy. What is more, this coincided with a significant decline in real wages. Even without taking into account the changed role of government, these conditions look much more like the down-wave itself than the boom that is supposed to precede a crash.

While most discussion of the super-cycle concentrates on the doom impending, there have been studies that support the case that it is already over. However, even then there is a reluctance to make strong statements to that effect. J. J. van Duijn, who is Professor of Economics at the Graduate School of Management in Delft, Holland, has continued the work of Schumpeter in basing the cycle on the clustered occurrence of major, basic, innovations. In 1980, he published the table shown here as Table 6.1.

Following on the chronology in the table, the fourth Kondratieff would be completed by a depression phase, 1973–1982, and a recovery between 1982–1992. Since each phase is approximately ten years it is possible to project out further, to the timing of what, under this definition, would be

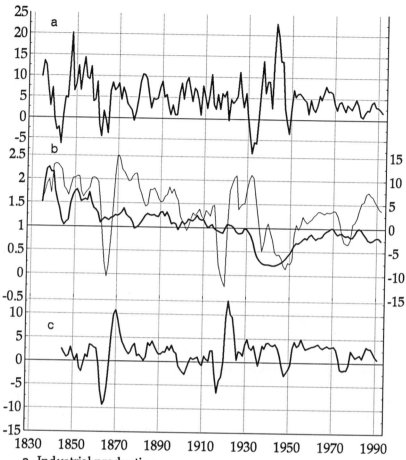

a  Industrial production
b  Interest rates
        — Yield spread (short-term - long-term) (left scale)
        — Real interest rate (short-term - WPI) (right scale)
c  Real wages (deflated by wholesale prices)

**Figure 6.2** Industrial production, real interest rates and real wages (five-year average of annual data)

*Table 6.1* A long-wave chronology

| 1st Kondratiev | 2nd Kondratiev | 3rd Kondratiev | 4th Kondratiev |
|---|---|---|---|
| Prosperity 1782–1792 | Prosperity 1845–1857 | Prosperity 1892–1903 | Prosperity 1948–1957 |
| Prosperity 1792–1802 (War 1802–1815) | Prosperity 1857–1866 | Prosperity 1903–1913 (War 1913–1920) | Prosperity 1957–1966 |
| Recession 1815–1825 | Recession 1866–1873 | Recession 1920–1929 | Recession 1966–1973 |
| Depression 1825–1836 | Depression 1873–1883 | Depression 1929–1937 | |
| Recovery 1836–1845 | Recovery 1883–1892 | Recovery 1937–1948 | |

Source: J. J. van Duijn, Chapter 20, in S. K. Kuipers and G. J. Landjouw (eds) (1980), *Prospects of Economic Growth* Amsterdam, North-Holland, pp. 223–233.

the fifth Kondratieff; prosperity 1992–2002, prosperity 2002–2012, recession 2012–2022, depression 2022–2032 and recovery 2032–2042.

I would emphasize that even the staunchest supporters of the long-wave would not expect this extrapolation to be followed exactly, and there will be shorter-term cycles within these broader trends. In van Duijn's model, wars disrupt the cycle, interrupting the invention/innovation relationship. Other interpretations have tried to incorporate wars into the general theory of the super-cycle. The main reason for extending the cycle pattern in this way is to emphasize the support it gives for the view that the low point has almost certainly passed on any reasonable reading of history. In fact, the timing is truly remarkable. Once one gathers together the rest of the evidence contained here, it should be clear that the down-wave ended in 1982. The timing fits in exactly with van Duijn's table, and yet the evidence here was compiled quite independently of that study.

## The changing nature of inflation

The point has already been made that it is unrealistic to look for a collapse in the price level, as suggested by a simple interpretation of Kondratieff. However, that is not to say that a cycle does not exist—only that people are looking at the wrong indicators. There is nothing to be gained by pushing price levels down to some arbitrary level that existed in the past. Absolute price levels are completely irrelevant, the only things that matter are the rates of change, i.e. inflation, and relative prices. Accelerating inflation can cause distortions to relative price levels, but this is really a problem of adjustment, and will only be increased if prices then fall.

There is a common confusion between inflation and price levels. It is one thing to stop prices rising rapidly and quite another to let them fall, or force them down—there is no political constituency in favor of the sort of policies required to achieve deflation. In the past, these distinctions were much less well understood. Government by landowners, for the benefit of landowners, was much more concerned with maintaining price levels. Not that prices were at all stable, it is just that price falls offset price increases, but only over long periods of time.

Figure 6.1 showed the typical presentation of the Kondratieff cycle in terms of the price level, and it is perfectly clear that prices have failed to follow the cycle, but instead have continued to rise in quite dramatic fashion. Some people have claimed that this is evidence the crisis is still to come that will turn these prices down. Nothing could be further from the truth. The argument has already been made that the cycle has changed, prices will not fall. In this respect it is interesting to recast the Kondratieff chart in terms of the rate of change of prices, i.e. inflation; this is shown in Fig. 6.3, using a five-year moving average. Suddenly the inexplicable becomes explained. There still is a cycle, imperfect to be sure, but at least it does not fly off like the price level.

In this new environment it is necessary to look for the long cycle in inflation rather than the price level. Table 6.2 shows the peaks and troughs of inflation over the past 170 years.

The inflation evidence is consistent with the existence of a cycle, but inconclusive as far as the timing is concerned. Two dates are shown for the trough of inflation. Since in both cases in the past, inflation was significantly negative at the low point, i.e. prices were falling. The second date, therefore, shows the approximate point at which the longer-term trend started to become positive again. In the changed circumstances of the present it is reasonable to assume that a repeat of this same problem would be consistent with the low point coming later on, since prices are not expected to fall on a sustained basis. The last time inflation peaked was in 1920, and the economic downturn did not occur until the 1930s. However, there were exceptional circumstances affecting the timing; the First World War in the earlier period and oil price rises this time, which have affected the turning points. Also, world consumer inflation peaked in 1974, which is really the more realistic timing of the peak inflationary pressure. The conclusion remains that inflation provides evidence of a cycle but is inconclusive in terms of timing.

Table 6.2 Peaks and troughs of inflation (consumer prices)

| Peak | Peak to peak | Trough | Peak to trough |
|------|--------------|--------|----------------|
| 1865 | 52 | 1878/1901 | 13/36 |
| 1920 | 55 | 1933/1937 | 13/17 |
| 1980(74) | 60(54) | (1993)/(2003) | (13)/(23) |

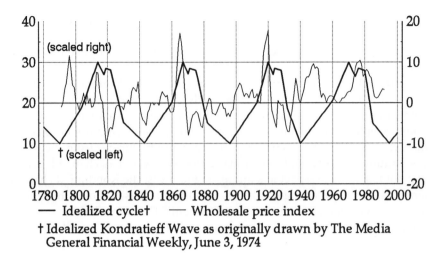

— Idealized cycle†      — Wholesale price index

† Idealized Kondratieff Wave as originally drawn by The Media
General Financial Weekly, June 3, 1974

**Figure 6.3** Wholesale price inflation and the idealized Kondratieff wave (five-year
average of annual percentage)

## Interest rates

Bond prices have followed inflation in the past, and are continuing to do
so. The shorter-term cyclical movements can be seen in the behavior of the
yield curve. The longer-term trends in bond yields are summarized in
Table 6.3.

Here again a remarkable regularity shows up, similar to that revealed by
inflation but with quite a long lag between these peaks and troughs and
those for inflation. In this context we are referring to time in a relative
sense. The present tendency is to shorten time horizons to the point where
the distance between breakfast and dinner is a long time. Within that context,
a few years is not *quite long*, it is well outside the bounds of reason. Bond
yields are related to the rate of inflation, since that affects the real return
available to lenders or the real cost to borrowers. The evidence clearly
favors the existence of a cycle, and supports the view that the down-phase
is already over.

When we turn to look at real interest rates, shown in Fig. 6.2, the evidence
is even more encouraging to the view that the worst is already over. Real
interest rates had one peak in 1925, after the peak in bond yields, and then
peaked again in 1933, marking the end of the downturn in the economy.
Real yields peaked at the start of the 1970s and then rose very high in the
1980s. This second peak marked a significant turning point in the operation of

*Table 6.3* Peaks and troughs of bond yields

| Peak | Peak to peak | Trough | Peak to trough |
|------|--------------|--------|----------------|
| 1818 |              | 1827   | 9              |
| 1874 | 56           | 1902   | 28             |
| 1924 | 50           | 1947   | 23             |
| 1981 | 57           | (2006) | (25)           |

monetary policy. Policy had been tightened steadily, at first reluctantly, and then with conviction born of desperation, until inflation was finally brought down. Only then was the yield curve allowed to unwind, and real interest rates were to remain high for a long time. Had real interest rates continued rising at that point the chances of a depression would have been very high. But that is not what happened.

A long-wave upturn should start with real interest rates very high. That is because real returns on all assets are very high. Another similarity between the two periods is that shortly after real yields peaked, the yield spread between short- and long-term rates fell to historical lows. This is not the type of behavior typical of the sorts of excess that are supposed to precede a collapse in the economy. It is the form of behavior more likely to be seen at the bottom of a recession and early stages of recovery.

In the 1930s, nominal interest rates had been reduced to the lowest levels possible, but real rates were pushed higher by the fall in prices—negative inflation. At such times, monetary policy becomes useless. All the central bank can do is increase liquidity in order to reduce short-term interest rates in nominal terms. At the point where these have fallen as low as possible, but prices are falling rapidly, the central bank loses control. This situation of low nominal yields and high real yields, when monetary policy is effectively out of control, is the set of circumstances described earlier, in Chapter 2, as the time-preference trap. That is not the situation that existed through the 1980s.

It is not necessarily true that falling prices and high real yields will be accompanied by a depression. There are plenty of examples in history when this has not been the case. The problem in the 1930s was that the economy was already overheated and ready for a correction, so that it was more vulnerable to a change in the real price of money. Also, expectations had run even further ahead, as reflected in soaring stock prices, setting the system up for a rapid fall in wealth. The collapse of the banks fed expectations that were already highly negative. Profits were eliminated, jobs were lost, but real wages continued to climb, despite falls in nominal wages. This helped to create a downward spiral. The events of that time are discussed in more detail in Chapter 7, 'Crashes and Crises'. What we find is that there was not a single cause which made the depression inevitable, but a series of major policy blunders that made a bad situation worse, and prevented the natural recovery process from working.

Real interest rates in the United States were very low in the 1970s, when bond holders failed to fully compensate for the future level of inflation. Even with this added incentive, investment never picked up very much, and the fact that so much money flowed into speculative, as opposed to real, investments is more suggestive of a low point in the long-wave cycle than the high point. At the time, there was extensive speculation in gold, silver and commodities, where the objective was simply to benefit from rising inflation. The productive potential of the economy was of secondary importance, or seen as non-existent. The speculative excesses, and the lack of real investment, even with extremely low real interest rates, are very clear signs of a low point in the super-cycle.

Additional confirmation that the bottom of a long cycle has already come and gone is provided by the behavior of the relationship between high and low quality bonds. The historical quality spread, extending back to 1920, is shown in Chapter 12, on the bond market. The striking similarity is in the peak difference between Baa rated bonds and Aaa rated bonds. There was a pronounced peak in this series in 1932 and again in 1982, although at a lower level, fitting in exactly with what seems to be the most likely timing of both low points.

## The stock market

A number of examples of looking in the wrong direction for clues about the position of the long wave have already been discussed. Nowhere is this more patent, and the results more misleading, than in the case of the stock market. Every sustained strong market over the past 20 years or so has been tipped as the boom before the bust. One of the most widely used arguments in favor of a correction is that stock prices have run up so high that a massive correction is inevitable. Well, there is no doubt that stock prices have gone up.

By the first half of 1991 the Dow Jones Industrial Average had risen to more than three times the value it was at the start of the 1980s. And the rise came despite these arguments of impending disaster, which were around at the start and all through the period. The market would have to fall by two-thirds in order to reduce prices to the level they were in 1979. That risk is still perceived as real by some people. What is less well understood is that those who followed such negative advice have seen their wealth reduced by that amount, at least compared to what it would have been had they become fully invested.

There was a major recession and drop in stock prices in 1974. This steep drop was the result of a combination of bad economic management, prior excesses and OPEC intransigence. At the time, there were plenty of doom and gloom stories around, particularly at the bottom, but history has not made this a long-cycle correction, presumably because stock prices and the economy recovered and the result was not bad enough. All that bad news did was whet the appetite of the bears who sat down to dine on the fragmentary remains of the economy and financial markets that were expected to result, but never did. In fact, the stock market did continue to fall, at least in real terms, which is what matters, but the bears paid no attention to this—it was not bad enough, there was not enough obvious pain. Nothing less than a repeat of the 1930s would satisfy those blood-thirsty, but rather short-sighted, animals. They failed to recognize that their natural habitat had changed. The crash in 1987 raised hopes once more, but turned out to be just another example of bear-baiting.

But that was the past; what about now? Since then, stock prices have risen a long way. Maybe the pessimists were not wrong, only too early. At these higher levels maybe the risks are now much greater. This is the Newtonian theory of markets; that what goes up must come down. There is plenty of evidence of price falls following substantial increases in prices, but this only reflects the natural cyclicality of the market. Rising markets will be followed by a correction, and falling markets will be followed by a recovery. That is the easy part. The difficulty is in knowing how high is too high, and how low is too low? It is at this point that the picture becomes a lot less clear.

The stock market is an excellent indicator of underlying profitability, or at least expected profitability and therefore the economy, once allowance is made for changes in the rate at which these prospects are discounted. Under normal conditions, the relationship will be very close. However, the formation of expectations is never perfect, mistakes are made. Not often, but every now and again, market prices reflect overly optimistic or pessimistic expectations. Such times provide great opportunity or great danger. The second half of the 1920s is a classic example of how expectations can get out of control. Stock prices rose rapidly in nominal terms during that period, but more importantly they also grew rapidly in real terms—and that is what really counts.

Under normal circumstances, stock prices will reflect rising prices, since the prices charged by companies and, therefore, profits should rise along with the general price level. An important implication of this linkage between stock prices and inflation is that nominal prices have very little information value. That is particularly true when making comparisons over long periods of time, or across countries. To be told that Brazilian stock prices are up 500 per cent is not particularly meaningful unless you also know the rate of inflation. If inflation is 600 per cent, then stocks have actually done very badly. In this extreme case, everyone will agree that it is obvious, but then fail to carry the logic over to the US market when making historical comparisons. It really makes no sense to compare the behavior of nominal stock prices over recent years with the behavior over the 1920s and 1930s. In the 1930s consumer prices were falling rapidly, in the 1970s inflation accelerated rapidly, and it continued at a slower pace in the 1980s.

In real terms, after deflating nominal stock prices by the consumer price index, there was a massive *contraction* in stock prices starting in 1968, as measured by the S&P or NYSE, and extending all the way into 1982. The decline, extending over 14 years, was a bear market unparalleled in history, and yet most people still claim it was part of a bull market. In the case of the Dow Industrial index, the real peak came in 1966, so the bear market was even longer. The Dow in real terms is still well below the peak reached in the 1960s, and not much above the level achieved in 1929.

Real stock price performance over each decade of this century is shown in Table 6.4. Also, Fig. 13.4 on page 339 shows nominal and real stock prices over this century—as measured by the Dow—together with real and nominal GNP for comparison. How one interprets the behavior of the stock market depends on whether it is considered in real or nominal terms. A striking conclusion is that the real decline during the 1970s was significantly greater than the real decline during the 1930s; 44 per cent versus 25.6 per cent. Not the sort of excess that is supposed to precede a crash.

Whichever way you look at it the 1970s did not have the appearance of the excesses that are supposed to precede a crash. In fact, the opposite argument, that this actually was the crash, looks a lot more plausible. On this view the stock market made a long-term low in August 1982. At that point, real values were extremely depressed, and even by the end of the 1980s stock prices, in real terms, were still below their 1968 highs. The evidence provided by the stock market is usually one of the strongest arguments in support of the case for an impending crash, but it is, in fact, nothing more than a distortion of the facts. Correctly interpreted, the

*Table 6.4* Stock market price index, percentage change

| 10 Years ending | Nominal | Real |
| --- | --- | --- |
| 1909 | +49.9 | +18.5 |
| 1919 | +47.5 | −22.0 |
| 1929 | +131.7 | +155.6 |
| 1939 | −39.5 | −25.6 |
| 1949 | +33.2 | −21.4 |
| 1959 | +290.2 | +213.9 |
| 1969 | +58.1 | +23.2 |
| 1979 | +20.2 | −44.0 |
| 1989 | +334.1 | +203.4 |

movement in stock prices argues very strongly against the down-and-out case. The evidence, once the veil of inflation is stripped away, is overwhelmingly in favor of the alternative view, that a new long-wave recovery began in 1982.

The end of the long wave is typically marked by excesses in other markets. That criterion has been satisfied by the antics of gold and silver prices. Precious metal prices exploded in the 1970s which, in retrospect, looks very like the mania preceding a crash. The price of gold subsequently lost 66 per cent of its value from the high, while silver lost well over 90 per cent of its value, as discussed further in Chapter 16. These manias and panics fit better into the story about a past turning point than one that lies in the future.

The emphasis during the 1980s was quite different than the 1970s. Precious metals were among the very worst of investments, while commodities followed the business cycle, but without the inflationary trend that had set the 1970s alight. The great attraction for that decade was in equities, in the productive potential of the economy. The outstanding evidence of this change in perspective can be seen in the huge interest in takeovers that developed. A few high rollers recognized the tremendous potential value in good basic industries and were prepared to pay very high interest rates in order to buy control of these companies. In other cases, it was the management of the company that understood the unrealized potential. In the early stages of the recovery, these actions were seen to be extremely speculative, with very high risk. As time went by and the values were proved, so even conservative pension funds stepped in to claim a piece of the action.

Companies borrowed to invest, to take over other companies, another way to invest in productive assets, and buy back their own stock. The borrowing was not defensive, as in financing rising inventory levels in a recession, but represented a vote on the future. Some of this was purely financial, in the sense of realizing existing value that had not been recognized in the market. And the fact that such values could be found is a problem for those who argue that the market always values equities fully. Like all good things, this one was pushed too far, taken to excess. But that should not be allowed to hide the fact that many investors made huge profits in the early days by unlocking the hidden values of underpriced companies.

Assets were significantly undervalued at the start of the 1980s. No sophisticated analysis is required to conclude that assets should be extremely overvalued at the end of a major secular up-wave. Undervalued assets are more the sign that the corrective phase is over. That argument still leaves open the possibility that assets may have been cheap at the start of the 1980s, but that they were expensive by the end. Possibly that is true, but it is very unlikely. America, and the world, has made tremendous progress since the late 1960s. Real assets have risen dramatically in value, and production has increased steadily. And yet it remains true that, in real terms, stock prices are still below where they were in 1968—the time of the last peak. This latest long up-wave should end with prices significantly above that level, not below.

## World revolution

The world is in the midst of a political revolution which complements the economic revolution that is taking place; both are extremely positive. The countries of western Europe are coming together, and democracy is taking root throughout the east, as the old communist regimes fall apart. Developments that have resisted the sword and the tank are taking place relatively peacefully. The countries of western Europe are forming an economic and political union. Governments are giving up sovereignty over parts of their economy, legal system and social structure. Most unifications in history have been welded together by force, and Europe has had its share of such attempts. The continent has been torn apart over centuries, as individual fiefdoms, and then countries, fought for supremacy. Here is an attempt to bring the countries together peacefully; through discussion and agreement.

Even more remarkable is the internal disintegration of the communist theology. The crumbling edifice has revealed a grey picture of decay and corruption. Here is proof, if any were needed, that economic controls are no substitute for the operation of competitive markets. That is not to say that an unrestrained free-for-all is desirable, but it is the case that free markets allow efficient allocation decisions to be made. Central controls are totally inefficient, and are almost certain to lead to corruption. Here again there is a relatively peaceful transition to democracy, from a regime that was born in blood and sustained through terror. The system has been brought down by its own logical inconsistencies. Under communism, living standards had improved only slowly, while the people, restrained like prisoners within the borders, became increasingly aware of the improvements taking place outside. The main exception is the war in what was Yugoslavia.

The changes in east and west are not independent of each other, nor of the economic revolution. Economic integration emphasized the size and wealth of the European markets, and the potential which that created. This was in sharp contrast to the impoverished state of affairs existing across the borders in the east and highlighted the need for change. At the same time, the unraveling of the communist web of controls and restrictions accelerated the movement towards unifying the markets of western Europe.

More and more countries of the world are finally accepting free markets as the only way to break out of subsistence-level economies. For years, the people have been held back by central government planning, official corruption and hopeless inefficiency. The command economy survived a long time but has, at last, been exposed as a failed experiment. The implications of this change are dramatic. Up to that point, the majority of the world's population had not been part of the free-market economy. Billions of people have been living a subsistence existence, watching the rising living standards in the industrialized countries, but never experiencing it for themselves. All that is in the process of changing. The impoverishment of so many people through blind ideology, or deliberate corruption, of their leaders is in the process of ending.

There is a new world being created. It will not always be easy, and there are bound to be problems along the way, some of which may be severe. However, in the end, these people will make a positive contribution to world demand and production. They will succeed in raising their own living standards, and in the process will raise living standards elsewhere. This seems to be very much the type of development that should be expected on the positive side of the long-wave cycle, not the down-side.

The revolution in computer technology, information and communication has played a crucial role, both in facilitating growth and allowing, even forcing, other countries to watch. One effect has been to break down geographical barriers. The EEC responded to the pressures and incentives being created by removing increasingly obsolete physical restraints. High living standards grew even higher during the 1980s, with the prospect of going much higher in the future. At the same time it became harder and harder for the communist regimes to conceal the truth from their repressed populations.

These events are consistent with an improving secular trend, and fit uneasily into the impending doom scenario. Mistakes will almost certainly be made given the amazing transitions taking place, but there is nothing new or original about that. These, however, are hurdles along the path towards tremendous improvements, not a set of earth-shattering disasters. This is not a time for emphasizing the negative aspects.

## Wheeler's climate cycles

Additional support for this positive interpretation of the long cycle is provided by the work of Raymond H. Wheeler. This work was no small undertaking, involving the analysis of over 3000 reference sources by a team of several hundred researchers over a period of more than 20 years. His work (Wheeler, 1983) looks for relationships between human activity, including the economy, and changes in the climate. In particular, he identified four distinct phases of temperature and rainfall: warm–wet, warm–dry, cold–wet and cold–dry. These followed cycles of 1000 years, 500 years and 100 years. It is the 100-year cycle that is of interest here. Whether, and in what ways, the climate determines the economy we shall leave as an open question for now, but the conclusions drawn are still interesting, if only because Wheeler's work has, more usually, been used to justify the end of a long wave.

Wheeler made a number of provocative forecasts about business trends in 1950. He said that a serious economic downturn would start in the mid-1960s which would last for approximately 20 years. This was equivalent to a Kondratieff down-wave. However, instead of a simple repeating cycle, Wheeler puts a new twist on the old story. According to his framework, there were two cycles of approximately 50 years within each 100-year cycle. The first cycle occurred during warm weather and the second during a relatively colder period. The 100-year cycle started with a recovery (warm–wet), then came the downturn (warm–dry). The second cycle within the 100 years would be cold–wet followed by cold–dry. The first recovery (warm–wet) was supposed to be the most vigorous and prosperous of the two recoveries, while the downturn phase was shorter but more intense than the second one.

Michael Zahorchak (in Wheeler, 1983) left open the question of when the long-term low would occur, but it was quite clear that 1982 was consistent with Wheeler's forecast. Experience through the 1980s provides incontestable confirmation that that indeed was the case. Zahorchak identified a number of possibilities consistent with Wheeler's forecast, but even in the most pessimistic case the worst would be over by 1985.

This description, and forecast, fits the interpretation provided here almost exactly. The stock market made very little progress from 1968 to 1982, and once the effect of inflation is taken out, stock prices fell heavily over that period. There was a very clear and dramatic bear market that lasted for 14 years or more. At the same time, the economy was operating below par for the whole of this period. The recoveries were anaemic and the recessions were severe. When these factors were added together, the performance was decidedly poor. Also, a significant change occurred in 1982 when the economy shifted into high gear following the take-off of stock prices.

The evidence is not proof that Wheeler's theories are correct, but it is one further piece in the jigsaw showing the down-phase as already ended, never mind begun. This is particularly interesting when it is realized that Wheeler's forecasts have, at times, been used to justify the opposite view; that a depression lies just around the next corner. The analysis by Zahorchak provides no support for that view, but instead fits easily into the *more optimistic* timing suggested here.

## Expansion *not* contraction

The evidence is not 100 per cent in favor of the long wave having already turned, but if it were there would be no novelty in this story. Evidence on such matters never is so unanimous anyway, but the overwhelming weight of evidence favors the view that the economy has already turned the corner.

There are many, it seems, who are still waiting for some cataclysmic event to proclaim the end of the secular up-wave. That, however, is much too obvious and not at all necessary. It is a view that fails to recognize the changes that have taken place: the growth of government, the development of democracy, the increase in wealth and the revolution in technology and competition. The outstanding debts that have been built up are cause for concern, but when considered against any realistic value of the wealth outstanding there is no reason why they should not be manageable—at least for now.

What is more, the problem of these debts has not suddenly exploded on the scene but has been around for some time. Farming has been in trouble for a long time, and the excesses of the developing countries, etc., have been known for most of the 1980s; they are not about to shock an unsuspecting world. There are bound to be some defaults and write-offs, but the majority should survive. These were debts taken on in the belief that inflation would continue to accelerate, and are part of the extended adjustment process that has been caused by the changes that have taken place. They are a large part of what differentiates this cycle from the last one, not part of the similarity.

In the same way that the previous cycle was different from the one before, this one is different from the last. But this time the difference is very great. The cycle is still there, but it has been smoothed by intervention and the prop of large-scale government spending. Under the circumstances, it seems highly logical that the down-phase should have been accompanied by inflation, a new relationship also to be found in recent business cycles, quite different from the past.

Trends are seldom obvious when you are living through them, and there will always be some gainers and some losers—it is really only a question of emphasis. It is misleading to look for overwhelming movement in one direction. Part of the misconception is the belief that there is a visible upsurge in economic growth in the up-phase of the long wave. That is not really so, according to common sense and Fig. 6.2. There have been temporary surges, but these have been more associated with special events rather than the long wave. The difference between the up-wave and the down-wave is in the trend, or average rate of growth; it is this that accelerates and decelerates. This can take time to show up, and it is not so obvious to the casual observer. Those who are looking ahead for the final long-cycle downturn are looking in the wrong direction. It is often difficult to accept a new orientation on an old idea but, once accepted, this suggestion will be seen to fit the evidence much better than the more widely held alternatives.

Negative news always has more impact than good news, as is reaffirmed every day, and there will still be crises to get concerned about. A rising trend does not mean that the path is necessarily smooth. History shows us that this may still include the odd war or two, or other major disruption. It is just that the rate of innovation and of change has speeded up, and the trend rate of growth should improve along with general living standards. Oh yes, and rising real stock prices.

# Section 2

## *INVESTMENT BACKGROUND*

There is not one but many ways to approach the markets. The path to follow will depend ultimately on each individual's particular preferences and circumstances at the time, and, in particular, on his or her willingness to accept risk. Within that framework, rational decisions require that investors are fully aware of the potential returns and risks involved. Too often, such crucial judgements are made on the basis of inaccurate or fragmentary information.

A key requirement for all investors is to have confidence that they will not suffer substantial losses over their whole portfolio. The greatest fear concerns a 1930s type meltdown. The normal cyclical downturns would be easier to bear if there could be confidence that it would not turn into something worse. The ideal situation would be to avoid the downturns altogether. This section shows how to do just that, and also to reduce risk generally.

Chapter 7 in this section looks at some of the great crashes of all times; those that captured the imagination and fears of a generation. We shall look for common characteristics so that it will be easier to identify the likelihood of a repeat performance, and equally importantly, not to be spooked by shadows on the wall.

With this background, and with the benefit of the discussion of the business cycle, it is possible to consider consistent investment strategies (Chapter 8). An important aspect of these is taking advantage of the cyclical nature of the markets. That is something everyone can benefit from, but it is not the only requirement. Strategic investors and tactical traders are playing a very different game, and while it is possible for the one to learn from the other, it is crucial to recognize the differences when deciding the rules to follow. Investors are not all the same, and a major difference is their perception of risk. Each investor should identify a low risk portfolio which will serve as the basis for judging performance.

Chapter 9 forms a discussion of the formation of expectations, how these affect market prices, and how both interact with news. In a world in which everyone is trying to out-anticipate everyone else, the news is usually cold even before it is served up. This is an important aspect of group behavior, and has implications for the economy as well as the financial markets. The way expectations shift around turning points has important implications for anticipating changes in expectations by the majority. What you end up with is something like contrary expectations. Not contrary just for the sake of it, but as a measured approach to staying ahead of majority opinion, and not behind. In that context, uncertainty is a benefit not a negative.

Chapter 10 deals with technical analysis; the use of trend-following techniques to forecast the future. This tends to be treated as a series of straightforward, technical, rules, but successful use of chart patterns for investment is more of an art than a science. The problems of interpretation have increased as more and more investors follow technical rules. A conclusion that may come as a surprise to many people is that many of the technical indicators that have been added over the years, such as on-balance volume, are actually more economic than technical.

Finally, the use of sophisticated statistical techniques is discussed in Chapter 11. The degree of sophistication is so great that there is a tendency to treat the answers produced as gospel. The truth is that most models have a very poor track record when it comes to forecasting the future. A major problem, apart from the fact that the future is unknown, is that the data that go into the machine are badly flawed, and the conditions for use are not met. There is a discussion of the approaches used in this book, and presentation of some leading indicators of economic activity for use as inputs into models of financial market behavior.

# 7

## CRASHES AND CRISES
### (what goes down keeps going down)

Every now and again market prices deviate from their normal cyclical pattern; instead of just weakening they crash. Such action is generally associated with the idea of a long wave, or Kondratieff cycle. While that is often the case, it is not always the way; there have been major market crashes that have not been followed by an economic collapse. There have been a number of famous crashes which have captured the imagination of historians and investors through the ages. They also capture more than just the imagination at the time. But then anyone whose wealth is confiscated by a market collapse is bound to express their views in powerful terms. That alone does not give it historical importance.

Investors and businessmen can deal with average-sized risks, after all, these have to be faced every day. One does not have to be a pessimist to realize that not all stock prices go up, even in a bull market, and that not every decision to invest, or produce, will be a winner. For the majority, however, it is still possible to believe that the situation is under control. However, somewhere in the subconscious, deep or shallow, lurks the fear that circumstances may get out of control, and a deep dark hole will open up to swallow all those who have dared to tempt fate.

There are some for whom these fears loom very large at all times, but these are a small minority. During good times, the majority will concentrate on the prospects of gain, and fears of collapse and total loss will become submerged. However, at less prosperous times, when prices are falling, the fears will re-emerge. Not everyone will be running scared, and there will always be some who are short the markets, who smiling, rub their hands together and proclaim that, 'these bear markets really are terrible'.

It is in such bear markets that the greatest opportunities are created. There have been a great many investors, in real or financial assets, who have stayed reasonably liquid during the downturn in prices, planning to take advantage of the *bargains*, who have been panicked out of their remaining positions right at the bottom, and then had to buy back at higher prices. In order to take advantage of the cyclical opportunities that are created through falling prices, it is necessary to have confidence that there will in fact be a cyclical recovery. Cycles are always different in some way, but only in exceptional circumstances do prices just keep going down. Any market downturn is a painful experience if it has not been anticipated, particularly for those who have bought near the top. However, for those who are prepared for it, such bear markets create fabulous buying opportunities.

The main concern expressed by investors is that the stock market will repeat the catastrophic collapse of the 1930s, as this remains the most indelible impression. It is not surprising that those events should have made such a lasting impression, but what has been forgotten is that the social, economic and political conditions of that time no longer exist. Fear of a repeat of the 1930s has been the largest single factor behind decisions by investors not to invest in stocks. That is a shame, for substantial profits could have been earned over long periods of time. It is clearly important to determine just how real is the risk.

The 1929 crash cast a long shadow that has darkened the outlook for many years. The potential for such a crash happening again was one of the arguments used at the end of the 1970s and early 1980s for buying precious metals after prices had already run up a long way. And yet it was exactly these investments that suffered losses of 1930s proportions. Moreover, there is no yield on precious metals to offset the capital losses and, even worse, these came at a time of record real returns on financial assets. Consequently, investors suffered the devastation caused by such losses and also missed the opportunities that were created.

What really are the possibilities of another crash? It would be foolish to claim that such an event could never happen again, but it is not sufficient to argue that a crash will occur simply because that is what happened 54, or 55, or 56, or 57, etc. years ago: the dates keep being pushed forward as the dread event fails to materialize. As should be clear from the experience of gold and silver, it is not only the stock market that suffers from crashes. Starting from that point, it is necessary to look for common features regardless of the particular market. The main similarity in all crashes, running through the tulip crash of 1636, the Mississippi scheme and South Sea Bubble in 1720, the stock market crash of 1929 and the gold/silver crash of the 1980s, is the speculative mania which precedes them. These leading examples are discussed below in a little more detail in order to further illustrate this important common element.

## Crash characteristics

To justify being called a crash, in the historical sense, prices must fall dramatically, and a long way, in a market that is large enough to attract a lot of attention. There are many cases of an individual company or commodity suffering an almighty crash, but without any record ever getting into the history books. The other key element is a dramatic and extended run-up in price ahead of the crash. It is the sustained and substantial increase in prices, inevitably accompanied by high speculative fever, that turns market weakness into a *crash*. The increase in prices creates a higher level from which to fall. An important element of this increase is that it attracts a lot of media attention. First, the market is made mighty, and then it is brought down.

In the rising phase, as attention becomes increasingly focused on the market, so more and more speculators are drawn in. Longer-term investors are likely to already have positions in the markets. Some of these will now gear up but, more significantly, a new breed of speculators will join the hunt. These late arrivals are only looking for a quick profit, a sure thing. Some will make spectacular profits, and as news of this spreads, so others will be encouraged to take part.

What happens is that more and more marginal players take a hand, and more are prepared to borrow and more prepared to lend against positions. Success is rationalized in retrospect, in terms of superior skill and judgement. Speculative positions are greater, and more people are involved. In summary, the potential for pain is increased. As enthusiasm increases, this is at the expense of natural caution, and diversification is considered unnecessary. Continued success in terms of exceptional profits is a necessary requirement to increase the numbers involved and reduce caution. Only in that way can sufficient pain be created to qualify the subsequent price collapse as a crash.

It is one of the great paradoxes that complacency takes over just when the risks have become the greatest. At the start of any great run-up in prices there will be genuine value. Assets are undervalued, but that is not widely recognized. At this point, there are tremendous profits to be made. Realization of these profits brings more and more people in. By the time the majority are ready to commit themselves, most of the profits will already have been earned and risks will, therefore, have already increased significantly. Yet this is the time when confidence builds, and prices are pushed up far beyond what is reasonable.

The turn, when it comes, is always a surprise, and there are always plenty of excuses to be found. Initially, excuses and explanations are produced to justify what is happening. However, reality impinges sharply on the marginal speculator, and it is not long before the crowd psychology snaps and panic sets in. The greater the euphoria, the greater the panic. A great crash requires a great speculation ahead of it. The great crashes of history are just as much the great manias of history. They are a pair, a matched set.

The super-cycle and stock market crashes have been inextricably linked for a long time—at least since the 1930s. However, the general conclusion is based on that specific example. There have been a number of stock market crashes, not always associated with the super-cycle. In addition, there have been major crashes in other markets as well. It is easy to see that major stock market weakness might accompany a significant long-term down-turn in the economy. The conditions are there for prices to be overvalued following an extended period of growth and prosperity. But the over-valuation does not have to be at the extreme level of 1929. Indeed, the stock market suffered a major super-cycle downturn through the 1970s. The true significance of this event was, however, obscured by inflation and government support—two not unrelated factors; and most people, even in retrospect, have trouble accepting what really happened.

## Tulip mania

Nothing perhaps illustrates the capricious change in tastes and fortunes more than the tulip mania of the seventeenth century. Tulips are a popular flower even today, but who can imagine that a single tulip bulb would rep-resent the most valuable asset in the portfolio? A situation in which a single bulb would be worth a King's ransom; or a Trump tower.

Tulips were introduced into western Europe around the middle of the sixteenth century. To begin with, their popularity was concentrated in Holland and Germany, and it was not until 1600 that the first bulbs were planted in England. Through this time, and up until 1636, the tulip continued to gain in reputation and price. Tulips not only cost a fortune, they also became the measure of it—the ultimate in conspicuous consumption. Prices were bid up to astronomical levels.

The Dutch led the field of speculators, and they became devoted to this fragile flower. To begin with, novelty and rarity produced high prices, but these were swamped once the habit spread. In the early years, only the wealthy indulged in the habit of owning and cultivating the tulips. As time passed, demand spread through other sections of society. Very soon the speculation began to accelerate, as more and more people jumped aboard the fast-moving bandwagon. As the speculative crowd grew, so there was a demand for tulips through the whole spectrum—the good and the not so good. This provided a base from which prices were pushed to ever higher levels. It seems that this progression proceeded fairly smoothly up into the 1630s, at which point the speculative mania reached fever level, thereby creating one precondition for a crash.

Mackay (1932) continues the story:

> In 1634, the rage among the Dutch to possess them was so great that the ordinary industry of the country was neglected, and population, even its

lowest dregs, embarked in the tulip trade. As the mania increased, prices augmented, until, in the year 1635, many persons were known to invest a fortune of 100 000 florins in the purchase of forty roots.

At this point the tulips were graded by species (quality) and sold by weight, 'the most precious of all, a *Semper Augustur*, weighing 200 perits was thought very cheap at 5500 florins' (*ibid*). Kindleberger (1984) claims that the highest price paid for a single bulb was an Admiral von Enckhuizen, for which the florin equivalent of £20 000 was paid. That undoubtedly was a great deal of money 360 years ago.

For all their great value, the store of wealth chosen was not particularly durable. More than that, it was not even recognizable as valuable to anyone not party to the manic demand for these little bulbs. They looked remarkably like any old bulb, or worst of all like an onion. As a result, it is hardly surprising that mistakes were made, and a number of anecdotes have been told about events at the time. Whether these are sad or funny depends totally on whether you were directly involved or not.

There is the story of the sailor who picked up an old onion lying on the side which he then ate as an accompaniment to his breakfast. Only then was he appraised of his error by the outraged, and undoubtedly distressed, merchant who had been the owner of this bulb valued at 3000 florins. Through the ensuing months in prison the sailor had time to reflect on what was probably the most expensive meal of all time:

> The price of that breakfast would have regaled a whole ship's crew for twelvemonths; or, as the plundered merchant his self expressed it, 'might have sumptuously feasted the Prince of Orange and the whole court of the Stadtholder'. (Mackay, *ibid.*)

Then there is the story of an amateur botanist from England who was on a tour of Holland. He discovered what he thought was an onion in the conservatory of the Dutchman he was visiting, and promptly set about dissecting it. When asked what he was doing by his incredulous host, he answered that he was 'Peeling a most extraordinary onion'. He was none the wiser upon being informed that it was an Admiral Van der Eyck. He was also given time in his majesty's jails to ponder his actions, and raise the 4000 florins for his dissected 'onion'.

The speculation reached its peak in 1636, when activity became frenzied. Prices were pushed ever higher. Special tulip markets were set up. Fortunes were made overnight. Tulip exchanges were also established in London and Paris with some success, but never on the scale of those in Holland. Suddenly, it seemed that some new truths had been discovered, that tulip prices must continue rising forever—another precondition for a spectacular crash. It was also a clear warning signal that reality was about to serve a nasty blow to the speculators' perfect world. But few saw the signs until afterwards, and fewer still left the party in order to listen to such pessimistic warnings.

At this point, tulips came to dominate trade and commerce. Tulips were no longer bought for their own sake, but in order to sell to somebody else at a higher price. This was the point at which the *greater fool* theory came to the forefront; the stage at which everyone admits that prices are too high, but that there will always be someone else to buy them at a higher price. This might also be called the *cleverer than thou*, or *omnipotent* period. Sometime the cycle had to be broken, and then the trades would unwind with prices spiraling downwards.

The euphoria was followed by the realization that prices could not keep rising for ever, and that when the buying dried up someone would be left holding the bulbs. When confidence broke it did so suddenly, and with the dramatic force of water bursting through a dam. Prices collapsed.

Suddenly, in November 1636, buyers were replaced by sellers. Overnight, prices collapsed from 4000 florins to 400 florins. People who had contracted to buy at the higher prices, defaulted on their agreements. The road to riches turned to clay, as the pot of gold turned to ashes just when it seemed to be in reach.

> The cry of distress resounded everywhere, and each man accused his neighbor. The few who had contrived to enrich themselves hid their wealth from the knowledge of their follow citizens, and invested it in the English or other funds. Many who, for a brief season, had emerged from the humbler walks of life, were cast back into their original obscurity; substantial merchants were reduced almost to begging, and many a representative of a noble line saw the fortunes of his house ruined beyond redemption. (Mackay, *ibid.*)

The government spent many months in deliberation, but failed to come up with any solution which was satisfactory to both parties of transactions. The courts refused to enforce the contracts on the grounds that such gambling was outside the law. It was like some giant game of pass the parcel. When the music stopped the tulips belonged to those in possession, and the money to those who hung on to it. The consequences extended way beyond tulips, destroying credit and credibility, and it was many years before economic activity recovered from the shock. And tulip prices have never regained the spectacular levels they achieved during those few hectic years.

## The Mississippi scheme

Mississippi gave its name to one of the great financial debacles of all time, but the setting was Paris, and the central actor was a Scotsman named John

Law. From such improbable beginnings developed an even more improbable story, proving once again that truth is stranger than fiction. The tale actually concerns one of the first experiments with fiat money, and the fall-out was more devastating than the early experiments with nuclear fission.

John Law was born in Edinburgh, Scotland, in 1671. He was a good mathematician and a skilful gambler. At one stage, he was forced to leave England in a hurry after killing a certain Mr Wilson in a duel over a lady, his other great passion. He travelled through the mainland of Europe studying finance and trade, and gambling; not an obvious connection, but one that at least seems to have sustained the young Scotsman. In 1700, at the age of 29, he returned to Edinburgh and published his *Proposals and Reasons for Constituting a Council of Trade*. Shortly afterwards he also published proposals to set up a Land-Bank. The trade council idea was a non-starter, but the Land-Bank received a good deal of attention, and was discussed in Scottish Parliament.

The idea behind the Land-Bank was for the bank to issue notes, with the amount outstanding limited by the value of the lands of the state. Owners of the land, such as John Law, stood to benefit handsomely from such a scheme. The apparent stability created was false, since a financial squeeze would lower land prices, thereby contracting the note issue, causing defaults and extending the squeeze still further. It would be possible to get into a situation of extreme instability under these circumstances. However, such objections were brushed aside. Contrary to what might be thought from a modern-day perspective, the intention was to expand the supply of money, not contract it.

Law's interest in establishing an expanded paper currency was hardly unique. The existing financial system was creaking under the strain of trying to accommodate the expanding financing needs of the industrial revolution. Metallic coins could not meet the rapidly expanding needs of industry, and the rudimentary banking system could not increase the velocity of circulation sufficiently. Moreover, there was an insistent demand from the new breed of entrepreneurs for a stable currency which was not consistently being depreciated by monarchs in their attempt to raise finance. It is sometimes forgotten that the financial system has at times been a major restraint on economic progress and expansion. Such blockages can only be removed by the innovation of new ideas, and these have not always been proposed with society's best interests at heart. Great changes were taking place in the economy, and in society, and these were matched in the financial system. Not surprisingly, there was extensive debate about what changes were needed. It was uncharted territory for everyone, and Law was not alone in attempting to take advantage of the situation.

Law spent the next few years continuing his travels through Europe, dividing his time between his studies and the gaming houses. It is perhaps only just, that his most fruitful contacts were made in these latter places. In one such place, in Paris in 1708, he made the acquaintance of the Duke of Orleans, and succeeded in making a very favorable impression. This was a fateful meeting that was to have dramatic consequences. In 1715 Louis died, leaving behind complete financial chaos and an infant king only seven years old. The Duke of Orleans was appointed regent, and he desperately needed help. John Law returned to Paris, as if he knew his moment had come.

The French government was desperate. The political and military stability of the country was in danger, as a result of the huge debts run up by Louis XIV. The government was totally corrupt, and the national debt stood at 3 billion livres. Taxes brought in 145 million while ordinary expenses were 142 million. That left only 3 million to pay the interest on the debt, which at 4 per cent would have amounted to 120 million. Paper currency had swamped the market and circulated at a huge discount.

Right from the beginning, Law set out an ambitious plan for a company to manage foreign trade, collect taxes and issue paper money. The government was desperate, but cautious. In May 1716, it gave Law the right to set up a small bank with capital of 6 million livres, three-quarters of which could be paid in devalued government paper. Law made the notes issued by his bank payable at sight, and in the coin current at the time they were issued. This latter provision has been considered the masterstroke of his plan, for it made his notes more valuable than the coins themselves, since these were frequently being depreciated.

The note issue quickly rose to 60 million livres, or ten times the original capital, and in April 1717 these notes were made acceptable for the payment of taxes, and redeemable upon request into gold or silver. As a measure of financial stability was restored, so the economy began to improve and trade expanded. It was not long before the notes issued by the General Bank, as the institution was known, were trading at a 15 per cent premium over the government's own currency, while the government's notes were at a discount of 78.5 per cent. Nothing succeeds like success, particularly with a government that has no alternative to offer.

In August 1717, the Louisiana Company was incorporated, with exclusive rights to trade with the North American lands watered by the Mississippi. The capital for this company consisted of 200 000 shares valued at 500 livres each, but payable with the devalued notes issued by Louis XIV. Demand was ensured by the promise to redeem the shares at face value, thus guaranteeing an instant profit. The regent gave the General Bank a monopoly over the sale of tobacco and the sole right of refining gold and silver. The next step was to convert the bank to the Royal Bank of France, with Law as the general manager. To celebrate the change, the regent authorized the note issue raised to 1000 million livres.

Early in 1719 the monopoly powers of the company were extended to trade with the East and Africa, and the name was changed to Company of the Indies. To finance this expansion the company created 50 000 new shares, and Law guaranteed redemption. Demand for stock had been increasing for some time, but this is the time that the speculative mania started in earnest. There were 300 000 applications for the new issue, and the share price quickly rose 1000 livres. Law's house was besieged by people from all walks of life, from the highest to the lowest, all in search of a quick profit, clamoring to be allowed to buy stock. The government took the opportunity to pay off the national debt, and, during the first half of the year, 300 000 new shares were issued at a price of 5000 livres each. Even that did not satisfy demand, and in November 1719 the stock price rose to 10 000 livres.

Law accumulated massive wealth and bought 14 large estates, with titles. Because advancement was restricted by his religion, Law became a Catholic, and in January 1720, he was made Controller-General of Finances. At this time he was the most influential person in France. He was mobbed wherever he went. But this was also the beginning of the end. The inflation of the currency, and the associated speculative fever, created a great expansion of trade and prices. Over 300 000 people moved to Paris. Wages quickly increased four-fold, and many working people made fortunes by being in the right place at the right time. The price of shares sometimes rose by 10 per cent or 20 per cent over a few hours. For a while it seemed that there were riches enough for all.

Not everyone shared that view, however. Certain beneficiaries of this easy money converted their profits to hard metal and jewels, and smuggled it out of the country. It has been estimated that 500 million livres in gold and silver were exported in this way. The Royal Bank was severely weakened by this depletion of its reserves, which was in sharp contrast to the vast expansion in notes that had been issued by this time, amounting to 2.5 billion livres. As this realization dawned, so the speculators tried to liquidate positions, with the result that prices crashed. The government made numerous attempts to legislate calm and restore order, but they were all useless in preventing the collapse of the share price, the currency and ultimately the Royal Bank.

To begin with, edicts were issued depreciating the value of the currency, and payments by the bank were restricted to 100 livres in gold and 10 livres in silver. But that did nothing to improve the attractiveness of the paper. At around the same time it was prohibited to use gold and silver as money, and private individuals were forbidden to hold more than 500 livres in metallic money. Between the end of January and the end of May, notes to the value of 1500 million livres were printed. This attempt to float away the problem on a sea of paper money was doomed to failure. Whatever it did for prices generally it did nothing for the price of Mississippi stock, as it was more generally known.

In March, another edict was issued, fixing the stock price at 9000 livres, with the bank making a market at that price. The plan had completely the opposite effect to that intended. Most people would gladly have sold their shares at a lower price, any price, were it not for the set minimum. The conclusion drawn was that if the shares were not worth 9000 livres, then the currency being paid out was not worth its face value. By this time there were 2.5 billion livres in circulation, and there was a mass attempt to unload the paper money, which depreciated significantly against the specie.

By the end of May, the point had been reached at which the notes were worthless, and merchants refused them as form of payment. On 27 May 1720 the bank completely suspended payment in specie, and two days later John Law resigned. There was no lender of last resort, and even if there had been it is hard to know what could have been done after such an orgy of expansionism. The correct action would have been to prevent ever building such an explosive situation. By the summer of 1720 the explosion had already occurred, and the damage was done. All that could be done was to clean up the mess as best possible. The great mass of bank notes were converted back into government debt, equal in value to that existing prior to the creation of the General Bank, and with the interest rate reduced by one half.

These moves restored stability to the finances of France, but at great cost and loss of liquidity. The development of banking was set back a generation, and a period of stagnation followed. The experience was a prime example of *too much of a good thing*. The Duke of Orleans, in particular, was so impressed with the early success of John Law's scheme that he believed that more could only mean better. That is a costly mistake for controllers of the money supply to make. All those who counselled caution, and opposed the grandiose plans, were overridden or dismissed. The safe-guards of democracy were absent.

John Law believed in his system and invested all his great wealth in property in France. So when he fled Paris he had only a single diamond worth £5000 to show for his endeavors. The French government over-ruled previous guarantees, and confiscated all his lands and properties. Law died practically destitute in Venice in 1729, after living some years in England.

## The South Sea Bubble

While financial fireworks were exploding in France, the blue touch-paper was also being set alight across the channel in England. Whereas the Mississippi scheme was born of naivety and stupidity, the South Sea

Bubble was pumped up deliberately and fraudulently. The fact that the outcome was less disastrous was mainly because the currency was not inflated and the integrity of the financial system was maintained. This also meant that the inflation was predominantly restricted to the price of the South Sea Company stock, and did not spread to general commodities. There was not the surge of economic activity as in France, but neither was there the disruption which followed.

The South Sea Bubble had its origins in the political rivalry between the two major parties, the Whigs and the Tories. The Bank of England had been established in 1694 when the Whigs were in power. The success of this venture, which had proved very profitable for the investors in the bank's stock, was the cause of much envy by the Tories. Consequently, when the Tories took over the reins of power in 1710 it was perhaps only to be expected that the men of commerce in the Tory party should seek to use the political system to gain some commercial advantage. They did not waste much time in putting such plans into operation.

The South Sea Company was formed in 1711 with the declared intention of improving government finances. The company subscribed to government debt amounting to £10 million, in exchange for which they received 6 per cent interest and a monopoly of trade with South America and the Pacific Islands. Over the next few years, the South Sea Company grew in reputation despite the fact that there was no appreciable growth in south sea trade. The Company was really more of a monetary institution in competition with the Bank of England. In 1720, the South Sea Company sought to build on this position, and proposed a grandiose plan whereby the Company would take the £31 million of government debt in exchange for shares in the South Sea Company, at a reduced rate of interest of 5 per cent, reducing to 4 per cent after 1727. The Bank of England offered a counter proposal to take on the debt, with both companies offering the government large sums of money for the privilege. In the end it was the South Sea Company that offered the most, over £7.5 million, and, as it was discovered afterwards, substantial amounts of illegally created stock to certain influential members of the government. For these favors they won the right to take on the debt.

London, at this time, was already caught up in the speculative fever which had swept across the channel from Paris. The directors of the South Sea Company made extravagant claims for future dividends of as much as 50 per cent, even though it was inconceivable where such profits would come from. In January 1720, the price of the stock was £128 10s., but once Parliament approved the plan in April the directors were asking £300 for a new issue of £1 million nominal value. Demand was very great, and far exceeded the amount on offer. Payment was to be made by five payments of £60. Within a few days, the shares had already risen sufficiently for the initial subscribers to double their initial outlay. Later the same month a second issue was authorized at £400, and was oversubscribed within a few hours.

Speculative fever was running at a high level by this time, and Exchange Alley was crammed with people from all walks of life. Innumerable stock-companies were started up—given the popular nickname of *bubbles*. Mackay (*ibid.*) comments that:

> The populace are often most happy in the nicknames they employ. None could be more apt than that of Bubbles. Some of them lasted for a week or a fortnight, and were no more heard of, while others could not even last for that short span of existence. Every morning produced new schemes, and every evening projects.

Some companies were based on basically good ideas, some were simply ludicrous. All seemed only to have the objective of parting gullible speculators from their money. One company came to market, 'For a wheel for perpetual motion', while another, displaying uncharacteristic frankness, 'For carrying on an undertaking of great advantage, nobody to know what it is'. Even more remarkable was the fact that people actually lined up to throw their money away on such bubbles.

The price of the South Sea Company continued to advance. Stock was fed on to the market at ever higher prices, with the directors, and inter-ested parties, going to extreme lengths to spread favorable stories, etc. Stock was sold in large amounts at £530 in May and £890 in June. When the price hit its peak in July 1720, £5 million nominal were unloaded.

Liquidity had been increased as a result of the influx of gold and silver being smuggled out of France, in anticipation of the Mississippi crash. However, the note issue was not increased, which put a limit on how far the speculation could continue. The goldsmiths/bankers did make loans on the basis of the inflated prices of South Sea stock. When prices crashed, many of these eminent gentlemen retired, very suddenly, to the country or abroad.

It has been recorded that Isaac Newton sold his stock in April at a sub-stantial profit, commenting that 'I can calculate the motions of heavenly bodies, but not the madness of people'. He might also have observed the power of gravity to bring all things back down to earth. Unfortunately, he forgot his own advice, buying back in a few months later, and emerging from the experience £20 000 poorer.

Credibility was being stretched to the limit, and it could only last so long. In July the Lords Justices, rather like the Supreme Court, ordered most of the new *bubbles* to be illegal. In August, the biggest bubble of all finally burst. The price fell through the whole month of August, and was down to £700 at the beginning of September. In September, there was an abortive attempt to enlist the support of the Bank of England, which tem-porarily rallied the stock price. But it continued to plummet, as it quickly became clear that no agreement had been reached. By the end of September, the price had fallen to £175, and in November it reached £135.

There were no laws to govern much of what had gone on, so Parliament made up the crimes and penalties as they went along. Politicians were disgraced, but few suffered detention, and then only temporarily. The directors had their estates confiscated, and were permitted to retain only a small allowance. Parliament judged the situation (Mackay, *ibid.*) as follows:

> And thus were seen, in the space of eight months, the rise, progress, and fall of that mighty fabric, which being wound up by mysterious springs to a wonderful height, had fixed the eyes and expectations of all Europe, but whose foundation, being fraud, illusion, credulity and infatuation, fell to the ground as soon as the artful management of its directors was discovered.

And Mackay makes an interesting observation:

> Nobody seemed to imagine that the nation itself was as culpable as the South Sea Company. Nobody blamed the credulity and avarice of the people—the degrading lust of gain, which had swallowed up every nobler quality in the national character, or the infatuation which made the multitude run their heads with such frantic eagerness into the net held out for them by scheming projectors. These things were never mentioned. The people were a simple, honest, hard-working people, ruined by a game of robbers, who were to be hanged, drawn, and quartered without mercy.

## The next 200 years

Over the period from the Mississippi scandal and the South Sea Bubble in 1720 to the present, the financial markets have developed and become much more organized. Those earlier experiences were part of the troubles that always seem to occur when major new trends first get under way. The process of developing new forms of financial organization, along with the changing political and social environment, has been accompanied by a great number of temporary failures, or crises.

These crises were dramatic for those who lived through them, but they failed to capture the collective imagination in quite the way the early examples had succeeded in doing. Kindleberger (1978) lists financial crises over the 200 years from the 1720s to 1920s in 1763, 1772, 1793, 1797, 1799, 1810, 1816, 1819, 1825, 1828, 1836, 1837, 1838, 1847, 1848, 1857, 1864, 1866, 1873, 1882, 1890, 1893, 1907 and 1921. Each crisis was preceded by speculation in a variety of assets—commodities of various types, housing, canals, railways, securities, mines, land, gold and silver—a wide enough list to encompass virtually any story of human greed, excess and panic. In some cases, the extremes were associated with wars, or the aftermath, or new discoveries.

This list contains a combination of normal business cycle downturns and real financial crises. Cyclical recessions tended to be much worse in those days than they are today. That may seem surprising considering the language that is generally used to describe any downturn in the economy, or in stock prices. In the eighteenth and nineteenth centuries there was no safety net, and those who fell, fell hard. The unemployed were often completely destitute, while unsuccessful businessmen would find themselves in debtors' prison.

Most attention was given to those who lost their money, and much less to those who lost their jobs, livelihood or even lives. Economic downturns were extreme, and financial markets were illiquid and highly volatile. With a much more fragile financial system in place, each economic downturn threatened a collapse of the banks or other financial institutions. The crises were real enough, and each was preceded by some form of speculation, excess or mania. What followed was the panic. Some brief examples will have to suffice as illustration.

Andrew Jackson viewed the 1836/7 financial crisis as an 'overwhelming catastrophe', following the redundancy of paper money and other facilities of credit and a 'spirit of speculation'. Homer (1963) called this one of the country's four great economic catastrophes. In this instance there had been speculation in cotton and land, financed through wildcat banking and silver imports. Crop failures in England in 1835 and 1837 caused financial problems there, then came a fall in the price of cotton. The main problem, however, resulted from government mismanagement, and a failure to understand the importance of the credit markets. The government reversed its land policy and demanded immediate payment for public lands in hard money instead of state bank loans. The inevitable result was that security prices declined and banks suspended payments of specie. Banks failed, some states defaulted and commodity prices fell; specie payments were not resumed until 1939.

The collapse of the New York branch of the Ohio Life and Trust Company on 24 August 1857 triggered what has been referred to as the first worldwide crisis. The California gold strikes in 1848 fueled speculation in railroads and public land. During the Crimean War, grain shipments from Russia had ceased and this had pushed up grain prices and stimulated railroad building. When the war ended, grain prices fell and the previous optimism was seen to have been excessive. Security prices fell sharply and 14 railroads were forced into bankruptcy, as money became tight and banks again suspended specie payments. The crisis spread to Europe, South America and South Africa.

The Civil War, 1861–1865, marked a major dislocation in the economy. Over the first 60 years of the century, the population of the United States had risen eightfold: from 4 million in 1800 to 32 million. The opening up of the west was the dominant feature stimulating the economy. The secular trend was the dominant feature, but this only served to exaggerate the cycles of boom and bust. So much was new, and there were very few controls. Recession following the war was brief, and railroad construction resumed, quickly restoring boom conditions that lasted until 1873. There then followed another major international crisis and depression. Once again the lack of financial supports was a major contributing factor to the depth of depression, but some downtrend had become inevitable due to the widespread speculation and fraud that been allowed to proceed unchecked. The free-market system will finally correct imbalances, but a better game will be played if some basic ground rules are applied.

Austria, Germany, Italy, Holland, the United States, England, France and Russia were all caught up in this financial crisis. In the United States, the Northern Pacific Railroad failed, and that brought down Jay Cook & Co., the institution that had financed the Civil War. Once more banks suspended specie payments and security prices dropped; the New York Stock Exchange was closed for 10 days. Financial scandals shook confidence, and 20 per cent of the existing railroad mileage was sold under foreclosure. Crop failure in Europe eventually helped to get the recovery moving, which shows that bad news in one part of the world can have beneficial effects elsewhere.

There continued to be periodic crises, but nothing really serious hit the scene until 1893. There was the Baring crisis in England in 1890, but that failed to carry over into a full-blown panic thanks to the early intervention of the Bank of England, which led a group of banks in providing financial support. Slowly the evidence was accumulating that a rupture in the line of credit was accompanied by a financial and economic crisis, and that supporting the financial system could head off the worst of the problems. The worst was a collapse of confidence in the system so that no one wanted to lend any money, a time when hoarding took over. The lessons were learnt only slowly, and the Barings support was still an exception. More often than not, the actions of the authorities actually led to a reduction in the liquidity of the system.

The New York panic in 1893 resulted in the collapse of the stock market and 600 bank failures. The preceding speculation had been in gold and silver. Less important crises occurred over the early years of the twentieth century, often related to commodities. Then came the reaction following the end of the First World War. This was a classic example of the confused objective of returning things to normal. In 1920, reserve bank credit fell from $3.5 billion to $1.5 billion, commodity prices declined almost 50 per cent and, not surprisingly, industrial production dropped by a third.

## The German inflation

The post-war disruption in the United States was dramatic, and totally unnecessary, but it pales in comparison to the catastrophic events in Germany. Economic recovery was crushed under the sheer weight of inflation. Domestic prices of internally produced goods rose significantly during the war. From 1913 to 1918, domestic prices increased by close to 150 per cent, while the quantity of money rose nearly 350 per cent. The dollar exchange rate at this time only rose by approximately 50 per cent. These were pretty standard features of a war-time economy that could be found everywhere. However, this time, the process did not stop with the ending of hostilities. From October 1918 to July 1919, the dollar caught up, rising over 120 per cent, while domestic prices rose by 40 per cent; and still the quantity of money rose faster. From July 1919 to February 1920 the the mark's value accelerated sharply, the dollar rising to 236 times its former parity. As a result, imported prices rose even more dramatically, leaving domestic prices to lag behind.

There then followed a period of relative stability up to May 1921, but it was not to last. Soon the dollar, inflation, money and debt were all rising strongly again. Through 1922 and 1923 the situation went totally out of control, until the process was ended on 23 November 1923. National finances lay in complete disarray, there was no control over the deficit or the currency circulation. In index terms, between 1913 and the end of October 1923, currency in circulation had gone from 1 to 413 million; the dollar exchange rate from 1 to 17.3 trillion; and wholesale prices from 1 to 18.7 trillion. Anyone who doubts that exchange rates are affected by movements in relative prices should consider this example.

The economic consequences were equally dramatic. In those few years, huge industrial concentrations were built up by those who understood the strange workings of hyperinflation, and with the help of the government. The government also contributed to the fall in unemployment, at least down into 1922. The sharp and continued depreciation of the mark played a crucial role in preserving jobs. Each time the mark rallied, unemployment increased. The statistics (Bresciani-Turrone, 1937) show a very clear relationship. In 1923, consumption and production fell sharply, but that was the time of the occupation of the Ruhr by the French in demand of reparation payments, and passive resistance by the Germans.

Prices in the shops were fixed against the dollar exchange rate, just as was happening in Argentina in the early part of 1990. By the end, prices in domestic currency terms were rising so fast that money had to be exchanged for goods immediately, since it could lose over 50 per cent of its value by the afternoon. At such times, the system of production breaks down, and that was what was happening when the government finally stepped in to restore order. Unemployment was following the same pattern as inflation. On 1 September 1923 there were 249 192 unemployed in the unoccupied territory. By 15 December, the number had risen to 1 485 014. To be added to this number were nearly 2 million on short-time working, and another 2 million unemployed in the occupied territory.

Share prices rose along with inflation, but did not always keep up. The fall in *real* terms, when prices were moving so violently, could be quite dramatic. This was shown in the valuation of Daimler, the maker of Mercedes-Benz automobiles, which at one point in late 1922, was worth the equivalent of only 327 of the cars the company made. This did not last for long, but it shows how values can get out of line under extreme conditions. The extreme economic conditions were not the result of what was happening in the stock market. Stock prices were forever trying to anticipate changes in the economy and inflation, and not always making a good job of it. In effect, the same was true of the depression in the United States in the 1930s. The relationship between inflation and stock prices in Germany at the time of the hyperinflation is discussed further in Chapter 13.

The inflation cannot be separated from the whole problem that Germany faced in adjusting from the war. The reparations demanded, in combination with the huge war debts incurred, made the return to normalcy virtually impossible. Recognizing this, John Maynard Keynes had resigned from the British Treasury on this issue and written his bitter condemnation (Keynes, 1919) of the allies' unrealistic demands, which became an immediate best-seller.

This was a very different experience to most of the manias and crashes that have occurred in history, but it contained the same elements. There was intense speculation and panic enough for anyone. And government folly played its part in full. Financial speculation in new areas played little part, except as in the experiment to inflate out of the debt and reparations pit into which Germany found itself. Wars are generally disruptive, and this one was devastating to the financial condition of the country.

## The crash of 1929

The story has now been brought up to the stock market crash which began in October 1929. The extent of the collapse in stock prices, and the associated economic depression, have created a lingering fear in investors, businessmen, politicians and workers generally, which still exercises an important influence over present-day actions. The crash is seen as a special event, but also a repeatable event. There are even some fervent believers in the long wave who expect a repeat simply because of the passage of time, regardless of what else is happening. However, this crash did not occur without the prior mania, and was made much worse by the perverse actions of the monetary authorities.

The events of the 1929 crash, and the subsequent depression and collapse in asset values, has been well documented. Consequently, only a brief outline is required here. The period from October 1929 through 1932 has become part of the folklore of the market. Sometimes it takes on so much importance that it seems to be the whole folklore, as if nothing else that has ever happened was of any consequence at all. The facts of what happened way back then are often obscured by the web of myth and mystery that has been woven around the events of that time.

The traumatic decline in the stock market is generally considered in isolation, but really needs to be placed in a wider context. The events leading up to and following that period are relevant. In addition, changes in the price level affected the real return available, while price movements in other markets offered the potential to reduce risk through diversification.

This was still in the early days of popular investing—the first time the general public had really had the opportunity to play the market. In the heady atmosphere of the 1920s, as the United States strode to the center of the world stage, it was hardly surprising that investors were beguiled by the seemingly unlimited potential. During the First World War, and after, Europe turned to the United States to provide money, capital goods and consumer goods. Gold and foreign exchange flowed to the United States both in payment for goods and to invest, as it became realized that a major shift in the balance of power was under way. Under the circumstances, it is hardly surprising that confidence should have grown: professional investors were joined by the general public in pushing share values higher, and they were joined by another group of professionals with the objective of separating the public from their money regardless of whether there was any value in what they were selling. Fast markets attract fast types, which helps to destroy confidence totally when it becomes vulnerable.

There certainly was potential. Stock prices on average rose by over 300 per cent between the end of 1920 and September 1929, and this was only part of the story. There were spectacular advances in some of the newer high growth companies. RCA, for example, went from 25 when it was issued in 1925 to 420 in 1928. In 1928 alone, the price rose from 85 to 420. It was a new age, with new technology and new industries, and America was at the forefront. These were exciting times, and much of the optimism was justified. Unfortunately, as the optimistic expectations were borne out by events so optimism became exuberance, and then moved on to something far more extreme.

There was good justification for buying stocks in the early years of the 1920s. Values were high and there was tremendous potential for growth. As prices rose, so a large part of this potential was used up. Prices moved to discount the future, and the future lived up to expectations. Eventually, prices moved to over-discount the future and then there had to be a correction. That is what took place in 1929. If all that had happened was that the market overpriced the future then prices would surely have recovered again fairly quickly. But that was not all that had happened. The financial system was over extended, and suffered from a combination of poor loan policies and fraud. Cracks appeared in the system and nothing was done to hold it together.

As the financial infrastructure started to disintegrate, people ran for cover. Under the circumstances this meant a rush for liquidity, which disappeared even quicker. Liquidity is something that only exists as long as it is not needed. If everyone demands liquidity it dries right up and disappears. A comparison can be made with the doors in a crowded building. These may be perfectly adequate for people to enter and leave under normal circumstances, but in the case of a panic it is likely that no one at all will get out. The financial system had been allowed to get out of control. Everyone knows that banks went bust by the bucket-load in the depression, but more than 5500 had actually failed over the nine boom years up to 1929.

There was a major problem with the level of real interest rates which because of falling prices were very high, regardless of low nominal rates, since it paid people to postpone expenditure decisions. An even bigger problem was the lack of institutional support from the Federal Reserve or the government. There is no series that can be plotted and looked at, but the effects in destroying confidence, and therefore demand, were real enough. The supply of money fell, but this was more because of the collapse of confidence in the financial system than restraint on the supply of reserves.

The economy fell apart. The crash of 1929 played a part in triggering the depression that ensued, but the events that followed were not inevitable, and were entirely avoidable. There were, in fact, only 1.5 million individuals with active brokerage accounts at the height of the market. That compares with 48 million at the end of the 1980s. Approximately 10 per cent of the population owned stocks and there was not the widespread indirect ownership, through pension funds, insurance companies and mutual funds, that there is today. With the effect so concentrated, there is no reason why the wealth effects of the decline in stock prices should have had such a devastating effect on the economy. Stock prices actually rallied from the initial decline and it took some monumental stupidity and bad management to bring the economy to its knees, and stock prices fell in sympathy.

Some companies went bankrupt but more did not, and share prices tumbled. This was bad news for investors, but not as bad as it was for those people thrown out of work. Dividends continued to be paid during this

*Table 7.1* Comparative yields

|      | Dividends | 3 Month Tbills |
|------|-----------|----------------|
| 1930 | 4.26%     | 1.48%          |
| 1931 | 5.58%     | 2.41%          |
| 1932 | 6.69%     | 0.04%          |
| 1933 | 4.05%     | 0.29%          |

period, and these were worth more because of the fall in prices. Anyone who maintained an income in those early years of the 1930s did very well. Dividend yields from 1930 to 1934 are shown in Table 7.1 together with the interest rates available.

When the crash hit, the Federal Reserve dropped interest rates sharply. The rediscount rate had been raised four times between January 1928 and August 1929, from 3.5 per cent to 6 per cent. Call money over this period rose from 3.5 per cent to 20 per cent. Corporate bond yields hit a five-year high of 4.59 per cent in September 1929. These increases in interest rates were not insignificant in determining what happened next. Following the crash, the rediscount rate fell to 3 per cent by mid-1930 and 1.5 per cent by mid-1931. Call money rates collapsed to a low of 1 per cent in 1931. Bond yields came down more slowly, falling to 3.99 per cent in May of 1931.

Stock prices tried to stabilize in the first half of 1930, and by April had practically returned to the levels of a year earlier. Then the downward momentum of the economy took over and dragged the stock market down. The government had missed its first chance to stabilize the situation. In 1931, the market again started to recover but from a much lower level, only to be hit by a series of foreign crises, accompanied by widespread currency devaluations and the collapse of the banking system. Following the forced appreciation of the dollar, there was then a loss of confidence, which resulted in the export of gold. Even more surprising under the circumstances was that the Federal Reserve responded in the traditional way by raising interest rates. There is nothing like hitting a market when it is down. This became the straw that broke the back of the economy and the stock market. The bond market also turned sharply lower. When faced with such irrational action there was little else to do. Conditions were now set for the final convulsive down-move in the stock market. Corporate bond yields jumped back up to 4.83 per cent by June 1932. The reaction did not last long, and yields quickly fell back down, the economy started to recover and the stock prices raced ahead. June marked the low in the market.

There were wide currency fluctuations over the inter-war period, and the pound is an illustration of general trends. Between the end of 1918 and

1920 the dollar rose by 36 per cent against the pound. Two years later the pound had rallied back 32 per cent. The currency markets then remained fairly stable through 1930. The dollar again rose from the end of 1930, when it was $4.85, to a high of $3.28 in late 1932; a gain of 48 per cent. The timing was disastrous for US stocks and the economy, as companies had the added problem of lost international competitiveness to contend with, just at the time when demand was collapsing at home.

The log jam was finally broken in late 1932 when the United States devalued the dollar against gold, and the other currencies. The dollar quickly went to $5.15 against sterling at its low, a 57 per cent drop in less than a year. This played an important role in helping the economy to recover, and raised the value of foreign assets held in portfolios. The stock market hit its low in June 1932, and by the end of December 1933 had rebounded over 100 per cent. By March 1937, the market was up 280 per cent, and exceeded the 1929 peak. Such point to point comparisons are misleading since the market then eased back, but it makes as much sense as comparing the drop from peak to trough. The recovery was as dramatic as the decline, but that never seems to be mentioned. Somehow it was a disaster from which investors never fully recovered.

The crash was not a happy time for investors, but for those who maintained a disciplined approach to their investments there was at least as much opportunity as destruction. The real losers were the highly leveraged speculators, who had no one to blame but themselves, and the millions of people who were thrown out of work—victims of an unfortunate set of circumstances, and extremely poor judgement by the authorities. Moreover, it was not the result of any single event, but a combination of things—many of them avoidable.

There was not one single cause of the crash of 1929 and the subsequent depression, despite the fact that the two events have been inextricably linked in the descriptions of that time, and in the minds of investors. The depression was not caused by the stock market crash, although the reduction in asset values clearly did not help. In reality, both the stock market crash and the depression were affected by the same things, the collapse of the financial system. Prior excess meant that some readjustment was required. This started in 1929, but then got out of control. If the banking system had not collapsed the market would quickly have recovered, but the system did collapse. As a result, confidence evaporated, demand shriveled up, and the fundamentals underpinning the stock market turned negative. It is a story of mismanagement and confusion, and there was no inevitability about the chain of events. Even so, the use of cyclical indicators, of the type discussed here, would have enabled investors to avoid the worst of the decline.

## A post-war postscript

The time has come to put the stock market crash of 1929 into perspective. What happened in 1929 was directly related to the attempt by the monetary authorities to cool down the excessive speculation that had taken hold. The correction was bound to be painful for some, given the heights that had been reached, the leveraging of positions and the extent of the fraud that had taken place. The effects need not have been long-lasting, however, had confidence in the financial system been maintained. The tendency to see the 1929 crash, the depression and the stock market decline into 1932 as a single, inevitable event is extremely misleading. Now, every time the market falls, the comparisons with that period are dragged up once more. The history can be fascinating, but the inevitable conclusion proves to be more of a hindrance than a help.

The stories were repeated, with graphic illustration, in 1987 when the market crashed once again. In that case, the one day drop was the largest on record, exceeding even the worst that 1929 had to offer. The popular view was that the market, and the economy, was dangling in space; hanging by a thread, badly frayed by years of excess, and about to give way. The alternative view, that the safety harness was holding, and that recovery was imminent, got very little air play. The year 1929 was supposed to be so terrible because of the collapse in stock prices that occurred, particularly on Tuesday, 29 October. Books and articles have been written in their thousands, movies and documentaries have been made and stories told, all about that experience—many concerned with the crash itself, and others including the events surrounding it. What follows are just four examples, with references to what happened in October 1929. Perhaps the best known reference is that by Galbraith (1954). This is a good description of events, which also considers the implications for the economic structure and society. Galbraith comments that:

> Tuesday, October 29, was the most devastating day in the history of the New York stock market, and it may have been the most devastating day in the history of markets. It combined all the bad features of all the bad days before.

Rodgers (1971) wrote about the events of Thursday, 24 October. This was not the worst day, but it was the most dramatic. As prices crashed the banks stepped in to provide support, and lifted prices in the afternoon. The belief that the worst was over, and that a recovery had started, did not last long. The author takes a typical historical view of the events at that time:

> In 1776, America had fired the shot heard round the world, and in October 1929 it produced the crash felt round the world. Forever after, the word *crash* was to mean 1929, and the year itself would stand as a symbol of something special to the nation and the world, as do 1492, 1620 and 1914.

Brooks (1969), takes a broader look at the period and personalities of the time. Less attention is given to the details of the crash, but he does comment that:

> October 29, the day things got so far out of hand that whole basketfuls of orders to sell stock were simply forgotten in the confusion and stood unexecuted on the trading floor.

The most exciting description of the events at that time is given by Thomas and Morgan-Wills (1979). The day featured in the title of their book is 29 October, and the story is told through the lives of those who lived through it. The authors note that:

> The Wall Street Crash of 1929 was the most climactic financial disaster in history. It still affects our lives today. Eventually, the total lost in the financial pandemic would be put at a staggering $50 billion—all stemming from a virus that proved fatal on October 29, 1929: the day the bubble burst.

Inevitably, the 1987 crash brought out comparisons with 1929. On 19 October 1987 (October is definitely a popular month to run out of confidence), the Dow Jones Industrial Average fell 508 points, valued at $500 billion, on volume of 600 million shares. In absolute terms, that was far and away the largest hit the market had ever taken, but that is a misleading comparison. In percentage terms, the fall was still huge, amounting to 22.6 per cent. The worst day in 1929, Black Tuesday, 29 October, the market dropped *only* 12.8 per cent, worth $30 billion.

The Dow hit its high at 2722.42 on 25 August 1987, and by the time the market closed on 19 October 55 days later, it had fallen 36.1 per cent. By 29 October 1929 the market had fallen 39.6 per cent; that was 56 days after making its all-time high. There can be no doubt that the events themselves were very similar, but the implications were not. Only if the crash in 1929 *caused* the depression in the 1930s would one have followed from the other. The argument presented here has been that this connection is false, and the fact that the economy did not drop off a cliff following the 1987 fall is further evidence in support of that case.

Other collapses have also taken place which have not been associated with a depression. Gold and silver prices suffered a crash through the 1980s that ranks along with the 1929–32 experience. Gold prices fell from a peak of $850 in January 1980 to a low of $285 in February 1985, a drop of 66 per cent. Even in 1992 the price was still only $330. The fall in the price of silver was even more dramatic, from a high of over $50 in January 1980 to a low of $3.67 in December 1992, a decline of 93 per cent. A decline the extent and duration of which makes the 1930s look like the good old days. At least in the case of the stock market there was a high dividend yield to provide some compensation to investors, but gold and silver carry no yield at all; in fact, more usually, there is a cost of storage.

Other examples include the 50 per cent drop in Hong Kong share prices in October 1987, a shock for investors that was made worse by the fact that the stock market was closed for a week. The Taiwanese market, with a capitalization of over $300 billion, fell by 80 per cent in 1990. The markets, economies and investors in general survived these calamitous events. The year 1929 was special because of when it happened; as the general public first took an interest in the stock market, and because of the events that followed. The total of these events helped accelerate the form of democratic capitalism as it has subsequently developed. It forms a watershed between a cheap-labor, *laisser-faire* economic structure, with its bias towards the preservation of wealth, and a high-wage, welfare society with its emphasis on the preservation of incomes and employment.

The period from 1929 to 1932 was unique. There will be stock market crashes in the future, and there will be recessions, there may even be a depression sometime in the future, but only when all the options have been tried and failed. The special combination of mistakes that contributed to that sequence of events are very, very unlikely to be repeated. The popular comparisons with that time are often persuasive but are also spurious. These are comparisons of shadows not of substance.

# 8

INVESTMENT STRATEGIES
*(planning for the future)*

Investment is subjected to as many fads and fancies as the fashion business. Depending on which star is in the ascendancy at the time, it seems that there is only one way to make money. In fact, there are many ways, and one does not necessarily preclude the others. It is possible to emphasize stocks, or bonds or commodities, including gold; domestic markets versus foreign markets; income versus capital gains; high risk or low risk; an investor may like small companies or low P/Es or virtually any specific element, country or condition. These differences can be important matters of principle, or minor points of emphasis; and attitudes may be fixed or flexible. Many have prospered and many have managed to lose money doing exactly the same things.

There is no single way to make money in the markets, but many. There are even more ways to lose money. Many people who make money when the trend is with them lose it all when the trend turns. Hard work, knowledge and some spark of originality are the most likely combinations to ensure persistent success. The greatest potential for failure comes from slavishly following trends, acting on hot tips, taking large positions based on little knowledge or understanding, and a lack of diversification. These actions are the result of complacency and over-confidence, of expecting something for nothing and accepting easy answers.

When it comes to setting out a basic approach to markets, it is possible to make money as a short-term trader or a long-term investor. Trading is not as easy as it is generally made out to be, and requires a very special talent and temperament. The emphasis here is on a long-term investment approach, but the topics under discussion should also help to clarify the context within which short-term trading decisions have to be made. The most important single input into the decision-making process, short-term or long-term, is some forecast of where the business cycle is headed.

Understanding improves investment decisions. Information alone is not enough, since the interpretation given is often very misleading. In making judgements about the future based on current events it is crucially important to distinguish between simple explanations, of which there are usually no shortage, and true causes. There is a tendency to simplify events by reducing everything that happens to a cute phrase or saying—rather in the way politicians employ *news bites* to attract attention. Simplicity has its virtues, and certainly grabs the headlines, but one should never forget that the world is a complex place.

There is little profit, and much danger, in following simple rules that assume the markets will follow precise patterns. The future cannot be explained in terms of such simple maps. Any investment decision requires a forecast about the future, and it is well recognized how difficult that is. Investment decisions can take many forms, and require forecasts of many different aspects—interest rates, corporate demand, wage costs, exchange rates, etc. There is no end to the potential influences once you get started. The main focus in this book is at the macro level, i.e. how the overall markets will move, since this should improve decision making at all levels and nearly all markets.

Uncertainty is a basic element in a market economy; it is no good ignoring it or wishing it away. Most investors, and speculators, go through a stage where they act as if they had complete knowledge. Some never get out of the habit, they just grow poorer. Commentary on the markets often encourages the belief that the impossible is possible. The only rational approach is to recognize the lack of perfect knowledge, and build that into a consistent decision-making process.

Investing is not like building a bridge or laying a road. Investment decisions require a view about the future, and the future is unknown. The investor is not dealing with an identifiable, known terrain. The future cannot be seen or felt. We cannot even be sure that it is there. There is only the present— the link between the future and the past. This is the ground we all inhabit, where expectations are transformed by events into experience.

A key conclusion that results from this inevitable uncertainty is the need for diversification. For investors, there is no alternative to taking bets on the future, but it is crucial to control the risk involved. The existence of the business cycle is an absolutely fundamental consideration. Not all sectors are moving at the same speed, or are in the same stage of the cycle; some lead and some lag. In addition, while the different countries are linked through improved communications, widening foreign trade links and increasingly competitive financial markets, they do not always move together, thereby creating a range of investment opportunities and means of diversifying portfolios in order to improve return and reduce risk.

The objective is to avoid the big risks while taking advantage of genuine investment opportunities. The intention is to get to the right platform before the train pulls out, and to avoid chasing after trends that are already well established. This latter approach works when strong trends are in place but will, more often than not, result in a violent whipsaw, and losses. Chasing trends, like a dog chasing cars, can be injurious to the health if you are not careful. Individuals need to adopt an open approach—open eyes, open ears and open mind. There is much to be learned and there is no advantage in ignorance. Watch, listen, and above all try to avoid prejudice and pre-formed views.

Everyone responds to incentives. Each investor needs to identify which category he or she comes in, and also where the people they deal with fit in. There are some who will love risk, and others who will do anything to avoid risk. Each group will react to a good rumor in different ways, and there are all the shades in between. An individual is much more likely to be successful if he or she stays in character. Just because someone else has been successful in a particular way does not automatically mean that you will have the same success trying to copy that approach. And if you are acting out of character it will be hard to know how to react when things go wrong. At such times it will be easy to panic and do the wrong thing.

Investing is a job like any other, and the technical skills can be learnt. Unlike other jobs, excellent technical skills can still result in a disastrous performance; efficient maybe, just not very good. Efficient losses are still losses. What makes a good investor—what makes a good tennis player, or surgeon etc.? Hard work and dedication will be crucial but, more than that, there is something else that cannot be learnt. Some instinct, some feel for the situation that others do not have. There is strength in diversity. Investors need to understand the markets, and how they interact with each other and the economy, but also take advantage of their own individual strengths.

## Maintaining confidence

The psychological effect of a major reversal can be traumatic, and it generally takes a long time to regroup and reform. Confidence is crushed just at the time when courage is most needed, when all around are feeling pain and recommending capitulation to the inevitable. That usually means selling at the bottom. What is needed, if it really is the low point, is the confidence to stand against the tide and bet on the turn, but this is exactly when confidence is in short supply. This is why it is so important to anticipate the cyclical movements in the markets. If the downturn was explicable before the event then it will be easier to believe in the forecast of an upturn. Afterwards everything becomes obvious, but by then it is too late.

The more that confidence has been dented, the longer it takes to recover. The extent of any reversal can be measured in terms of the loss of capital suffered. Capital preservation is important not only in itself, but also in opening up opportunities when prices are down. This can play a crucial role in building wealth in the future.

The general perception is that small investors have short-term horizons while institutional investors are long-term. Like so much received wisdom on the markets, this is not necessarily so. Many individuals become locked in by the tax system, both by profits and losses. In addition, stocks and bonds are often bought with long-term objectives in mind, e.g. children's education, retirement, etc., then put away and not looked at again. Institutional investors on the other hand usually have monthly reporting requirements. Theirs is a highly competitive business, and there is constant pressure to perform—both between institutions and within. Each opportunity to beat the market has to be taken. To fall too far adrift of the pack will create a gap that becomes increasingly difficult to close. As a result, institutional fund managers will be forced to jump aboard every fast-moving trend if they missed it at the station. In fast-moving markets, professional fund managers are likely to be moving fast as well.

The acceleration of inflation in the 1970s also played a role in shortening time horizons and emphasizing trading activity. Rapid inflation increases uncertainty. It confuses returns by emphasizing nominal yields rather than real value, it shortens time horizons and turns everyone into a trader. This trading mentality, and loss of confidence in the financial system, took years to develop. And, like most developments of this kind, it came after the event. As one stable door clangs shut behind the bolting horses, so another door swings open. The time to become more short-term orientated, and to look beyond traditional investments, was when the trend of inflation was accelerating through the 1970s. However, only as the process was coming to an end did people recognize that bonds had not provided the security expected. Bonds lost their reputation as safe havens for conservative investors, and people began to talk about gold and diamonds as secure, risk-free investments, just as the other stable door was swinging shut.

Like any job, the more you know the better you will do it. Listen, read, learn, but most of all think. Do not take the obvious at face value. There is a lot of free advice around and most of it is worth every cent. Most of this advice comes after the event, and after prices have already moved. Those who anticipated it will be in a position to benefit, those who did not will have to chase after, only to find that price adjustments can be very, very fast.

There are usually a great many opinions, some may be right and some will certainly be wrong. After the event it will be easy to see which is which, but it is not so easy beforehand. Consistency is the greatest asset. A forecaster who is always wrong will be invaluable, whereas one who is half right will be useless. Beware of the obvious. If something is well known then the conclusion is already reflected in market prices. That will be true of fundamental forces, although these are always changing, and even more so of simple technical rules. When it comes to making money, uncertainty is an advantage. If it is too simple then everyone will do it, and there will be no value left. The obvious never happens, it will already have happened. *Everything is obvious after the event, but never before.*

Simplicity has its virtues but also its trip wires. H.L. Menken once said:

> To every complex problem there is a solution which is neat, plausible and wrong.

Financial markets reflect human behavior. There is a logic to behavior, but it is not the mechanical repetitiveness often suggested. There are cycles in nature, and these are often imposed on financial markets. Nothing so simple could possibly be observed. As soon as it was recognized, people would act on it, thereby changing the pattern. This feed-back mechanism is missing in machines or nature. Life is multi-dimensional, and the markets are an extension of life—they also are multi-dimensional.

What has happened, and there is probably nothing new about it, is that people look for simple trends and then use complex investment techniques. There are so many techniques for investing that hardly anyone really understands. There are defensive hedging strategies which only work when they are not needed. As soon as the market falls sharply they fail to provide full protection. When they are used, but not needed, they can increase costs dramatically.

There are options, which can be shown to produce tremendous gains under certain extreme conditions, but the chances of hitting that right rank somewhere below winning the lottery. This can be a major problem with the markets, or at least those that inhabit them. There are many unscrupulous or naïve salesmen who will tempt you with the possibility of spectacular gains. If you succumb to these temptations you are gambling with your wealth. You will get better odds in a casino, and probably more fun. The net result is likely to be the same. Unfortunately, even among the legitimate alternatives it is the high-return, high-risk choices that tend to receive the most attention. Over 2500 years ago, the Chinese philosopher, Lao Tsu, noted the dangers of trying to get too fancy:

> In making furniture, the more you carve the wood the weaker it gets.

The complexity should be in the analysis. That is the time for hard work and looking for differences, the time for study and analysis, not when prices have already moved significantly against you. If the approach work has been done thoroughly that allows the execution to be done simply. Buy real value, buy real claims on the future, let others play on the periphery. Derivative products can have real value in hedging existing positions. But even then, getting the timing right is a lot more difficult than is usually made out. In many cases, time is working against you in a very costly way. Some derivatives do allow investors to execute simple strategies: using futures to establish positions, or index instruments to reflect market behavior. The problems start with complex combinations, and when time premiums become an important consideration.

There is no doubt that, in very many cases, complexity in execution is seen as sophistication in investment. Work put in understanding these complex investments is seen as research, deserving of reward. For the professionals specializing in these instruments and devising new ones, this is true, but for the amateur investor, and for most professionals, this is not true. The odds are heavily weighted against the outsider. Nothing will repay greater dividends than an understanding of the macro environment.

## Traders and trading

One of the most obvious distinctions in the approach to markets is that between a tactical view and a strategic view. A tactical approach covers all short-term decision making; what might also be called speculation or trading activity. A strategic approach, on the other hand, means taking a longer-term view, the type of horizon normally associated with investing. Investment, in a production sense, means putting long-lasting assets in place, and the same is true in the case of financial assets. The difference is that financial investments will generally be more liquid, in the sense that the time horizon can be shortened dramatically if desired. Also, financial investments offer the ability to diversify more easily than is the case for a company investing in its productive process. For investors these are important distinctions.

The emphasis in this book is on the investment side of the market, and in particular on investment over the business cycle. That means concentrating on the character of the markets themselves rather than the individual parts. This emphasis should prove useful to traders as well, who need to be aware of the general environment within which they are operating. Equally, investors need to be aware of the short-term noise in the markets. Even on the calmest of days attention can easily be distracted by the lapping of waves, so that it becomes hard to focus on the underlying tide. When the seas grow stormy, and the waves are running high, immediate events are even harder to ignore. It is well in all cases to remember the underlying pull.

There may be traders who totally cut themselves off from the rest of the world, from all news reports and any consideration of economic developments, but that is very hard to do. It is certainly not how most traders talk about the markets. The chances of success are going to be better if you are trading in the same direction as the main trend rather than against it. Determining the true position in the business cycle, and the individual market cycles, can provide an invaluable background for traders in all types of markets.

The foundation of modern financing is that there are liquid markets. Even long-term positions are not forever, and people like to be able to change their minds. This means that an individual investor can get his or her money out with reasonable ease and low cost, although if everyone acts together they will not be so privileged. Equally important, it means that a company in need of funds is able to tap the pockets of a wide number of individuals. It is crucially important that both sides of the market are able to diversify.

Liquidity is an essential ingredient, but it is not provided by long-term investors. Traders, prepared to take speculative positions against the trend, play a crucial role in providing this liquidity. Without them, there would likely be greater consensus and greater volatility in prices. Traders are often blamed for the increased volatility in the markets, but under normal circumstances quite the opposite is true. In the United States, the short-term speculation permitted by the rise in the use of derivative products, index options, futures, etc., was widely blamed for the 23 per cent fall in stock prices on 19 October 1987. However, stock prices fell even more in Germany, not a country known for its speculative tendencies and where such derivative products did not even exist. A wider vision, taking in events in other countries, would have made it hard to accept such a simple conclusion.

The fact that speculators are willing to bet on the unexpected allows conservative investors, institutions, farmers and businessmen to hedge their positions—in effect, to take out insurance. In this way, the extreme price movements that are being insured against can generally be avoided. As long as this speculation is peripheral to the main markets, there is no problem. Normally this is the case but there are times, generally associated with sharp increases in uncertainty, when speculation takes over as the major force in the market. This is not necessarily due to added activity by traders but to the fact that people who had taken a long-term view now shorten their horizons dramatically. Moreover, the traumatic effect on prices does not depend on the existence of derivative products.

Under these conditions, the normal adjustment mechanisms break down and prices become extremely volatile. It is the difference between a well-oiled machine, and one that is flooded with oil. It is one thing to reduce friction, and quite another to make contact totally insensitive. This happens less often than generally thought, but it is a danger that has been recognized through history. John Maynard Keynes (1936) remarked that:

> Speculators may do no harm as bubbles on a steady steam of enterprise. But the position is serious when enterprise becomes the bubble in a whirlpool of

speculation. When the capital development of a country becomes a by-product
of the activities of casino, the job is likely to be ill-done.

Trading involves a high level of nervous tension and quick reactions.
For professional traders each day is a battle against the odds. Such people
live on the edge of their seats, driven by enthusiasm and living on high-
octane adrenaline. To suddenly find yourself on the wrong side of the market
is to feel like General Custer when he found himself on the wrong side of
the battle. Only the most astute survive long enough to become experienced
traders. The successful trader has much in common with the successful
gambler, and it is at this level that the fundamentals have the least relevance.
Reading the markets is like reading the cards, and the skill is in cutting
losses early and letting profits run—which is a lot more difficult than it
sounds. Even so, improved information about the environment, the direction
of the economy, inflation, interest rates, etc. is bound to result in better
decision making.

Most people are not cut out for the high nervous tension required to be
a successful trader, never mind the other skills required. Those who do satisfy
that criterion would never be happy sitting with positions through highly
volatile markets. Temperamentally and physically most people are better
suited to take a longer-term view of the investment process. Speculation
may seem more glamorous, but the personal costs are high. There are people
who thrive in such an environment, and the job is best left to these few.
Mark Twain once said:

> There are two times in a man's life when he should not under any circum-
> stances speculate—the first time is when he can't afford to, and the second is
> when he can.

The dangers of speculation are aptly summarized in the financial mis-
fortunes of the Hunt brothers. The Hunts speculated in commodities
and attempted to corner the market for silver. The net result was that the
brothers went from reported wealth of nearly $6 billion at the end of the
1970s into bankruptcy in 1988. They would have done well to have heeded
the words of Mark Twain. They had no need for high-risk ventures.
Unfortunately, there seems to be a human preference to take risks in the
hope of making substantial gains. What else can explain the habit that people
have of making frequent, and often large, donations to lotteries, casinos
and bookmakers?

## Investment strategy

For those who wish to take a longer-term perspective, investment rather
than speculation, and what might be called a strategic approach, it is necessary
to adopt different procedures. In this case, much greater emphasis has to

be placed on the fundamentals. The emphasis here is on the macro scene, the cyclical movements in interest rates, inflation, commodity prices, exchange rates, stock prices and economic activity. This adds up to an important investment approach in itself. In addition, it provides an essential background for investors, or traders, operating within this environment.

Each droplet of information is life and death to the trader, which is not true for the true investor. The investor should be accumulating information, trying to build a composite picture. It is a more deliberate, considered approach. Each piece of information on its own will generally be insignificant. Only when put together will the complex jigsaw start to fall into place. The picture will never be completed, since it will change long before all the pieces become available. The gaps have to be filled by forecasts, or left blank.

A strategic approach requires planning ahead and trying to avoid Dunkirk situations. It is necessary to consider carefully the potential risk as well as potential reward of each position and the overall portfolio. What this demands is a consistent approach with diversification across individual assets, sectors, asset types, countries and time. The basis for asset selection should be an informed view of the business cycle, ideally not only in a single country but within all the major economies. An example of the sorts of considerations that are crucial to rational asset allocation are the expected direction of interest rates, including movements in the yield curve, where exchange rates are headed and the direction of economic activity and corporate profitability; i.e. the relative position within the business cycle in the future. The present will have already been discounted.

Investors should try to avoid being taken by surprise. It is always preferable to make an orderly withdrawal from positions wherever possible, and avoid being caught in a rout. To sell while on the run, and in a state of panic, rarely results in good decisions, and is the way to maximize losses not gains. There will be times when some unpredictable event will shock the markets. Traders will respond to this and try to make money by being the first to act. The way they hope to make money is by then off-loading their positions to those who get the news later, or who take time to react. The professional traders start with the best hand, and the amateurs or longer-term investors who try to beat them at their own game are likely to end up paying for the pleasure.

This is where the importance of consistency comes in. If the news of an unpredictable event does not change the underlying fundamentals, the investor should be able to take advantage of sudden, rapid price changes. Examples would include the fall in stock prices when President Kennedy was shot. Another example was the effect of the rapid increase in oil prices in the second half of 1990 in depressing bond prices. In both cases, prices went sharply against the main trend. A trader caught on the wrong side of such a move will almost always have to sell, and an investor on the other hand should be in a position to buy. The collapse of stock prices in 1987 was different. There was definitely great opportunity to buy cheaply but the fall itself need not have been unexpected, as made clear in Chapter 13.

Typically, a trader will take large, leveraged positions looking for relatively small price moves. Obviously, large price moves in the right direction will be highly appreciated, but there will be very little ability to tolerate large moves against the position. As a result, stop-loss orders are an essential discipline for traders. This is the only way that a trader can achieve diversification. When you are operating with leverage, it is possible for a single bad position to wipe out all of your capital. People have suggested using such trading disciplines within a longer-term investment approach. However, while discipline is required whatever the time horizon, it is dangerous to apply such rules to investment behavior. The basis for decision making is very different, and stop-loss orders consistently applied could well achieve exactly the opposite result to that desired.

In a strong bull market, setting stops may not matter as long as the price rises fast enough, although if you keep raising the stop there is no doubt it will be hit. Setting a stop 10 per cent to 20 per cent below the price on a stock almost guarantees being sold out of the position. Practically every stock during every year will at some point fall by that sort of percentage. Whether you are stopped out will depend on exactly when the position was purchased, and will have nothing to do with the fundamentals or your own analysis of the company. There were a number of stocks in 1990 and 1991 that would have hit stops like this four or five times during the year, and yet still closed the year with substantial gains.

Setting stops in an investment portfolio means replacing logic and analysis with plain luck. The rules of gambling should be applied to gambling activities, there is no doubt about that, but such rules do not necessarily apply to long-run investment behavior. Peter Lynch, who was extremely successful managing the Magellan fund for many years, makes the same point (Lynch, 1989):

> I have always detested stop orders . . . With the volatility in today's market, a stock almost always hits the stop . . . The investor has turned losing into a foregone conclusion.

The same logic, or lack of it, applies to bonds. Selling out after bond prices have fallen sharply guarantees large losses, and makes no sense at all if the decision is based solely on the fact that the price has fallen; which is not to say that price weakness should be ignored, or that it is never right to sell on weakness. The order to sell should, however, be based on a conscious decision and not an automatic rule of thumb. The fact that the price has already fallen is not a good reason. A good reason is the expectation that the price will fall in the future.

Portfolio allocation decisions should be based on a long-term view, but they should also be constantly monitored for changes in the economy, and the markets, to determine whether events are consistent with expectations and whether there are any developments that might cause expectations to change. Investors should always strive for consistency but never become complacent. If conditions change, then so will expectations and the structure of the portfolio. An example was provided by the sharp acceleration in the trend rate of inflation in the 1970s. One possibility was to place stops on bond positions and then go to sleep until the stops were hit. A more sensible approach would have been to observe the fast growth in government spending, low real interest rates and rapid money growth, and reach the conclusion that inflation was heating up. Under those conditions, bonds were not a great investment. This conclusion should have been reached long before crisis hit the Middle East, sending oil prices soaring.

There are surprises in the world, but not nearly as many as those who are taken by surprise would have you believe. Times like these may require emergency action, but even then this should be within a rational overall framework. A lot of potential problems can be not just avoided, but taken advantage of, through careful monitoring of the business cycle.

## Base-building

A certain amount of discipline is necessary when it comes to deciding on a strategy and carrying it out. Institutional fund managers will establish internal procedures to decide policy and rules to ensure that individual managers conform to the guidelines. The need to ensure a consistent approach is easy to understand in the case of a large institution, but individual investors will also benefit by doing the same. It is all too easy to ignore warning signs. These may cause an individual to become more suspicious about the market, or a particular security, but without triggering an actual response until it is too late and the price has already moved. And if a reaction is required, what should it be?

Part of the potential confusion is created by the fact that many decisions are made for bad reasons; tips, rumors, a whim of the moment. Even where investments are based on specific forecasts of the future, it is very hard to take the degree of risk into account. One way to do this, at least to some extent, is to establish a base index. This is a difficult idea to get across, but I believe it can play an important role in helping to control risk. Setting objectives such as a 25 per cent gain with no risk is fine, but is totally unrealistic. It will certainly be possible to achieve 25 per cent returns under certain conditions, and possibly much more, but it is not very helpful to pretend that there is no risk involved. What would be helpful, when setting off in search of those high returns, is some idea of what each investor would consider to be a low-risk portfolio.

An investor should sit down and spend some considerable time trying to identify what a low-risk portfolio would look like. What may look like low risk to one person may well be thought high risk by another. Investment managers should do the same thing with their clients, and institutions should decide on their own low-risk portfolio. It is not necessary for this base index to be set in stone, but it should change only slowly in response to new circumstances. Some individuals pay little attention to the structure of their portfolio, being more inclined to jump in or out of particular areas with scant regard for the risks involved. A base portfolio would help to bring such inconvenient thoughts to the foreground and, in this case, might be changed fairly frequently. Investment managers on the other hand would probably change the client's base view more slowly.

The line of least resistance for institutions is some published index. A US domestic stock fund will compare with the New York Stock Exchange, or some other relevant index. Similar indices exist for bonds, short and long and for a wide variety of different sub-indices. For international managers, there are published indices for stocks and bonds which provide the typical standards of comparison. These are often convenient, but not necessarily the most representative of the perceived risks or objectives of the client or institutions. Individuals often compare their theoretical portfolio against the stock market index, at least when prices are rising, even when the actual portfolio looks nothing like it.

Setting up a base index requires taking account of risk as well as return, at least in a long-run or structural sense. The base index should reflect the investor's basic, underlying attitude toward risk and reward, weighted by the anticipated economic and financial trends, and take account of the particular strengths or weakness of the investor. Shorter term, and more specific, risks and opportunities would then be dealt with in terms of deviations from the base.

A realistic base allows investors to deal with risk in a more consistent way; it should also lead to more consistent decision making. Unrealistic comparisons make it harder to make rational decisions, can be confusing and make interpretation difficult. Making judgements on the future is never easy, and the task is made much more difficult when even the base weightings are not representative of the individual's, or institution's, real attitude towards risk. To take an example from the international world: if an investor is worried about a collapse in Japanese stock prices, an index-weighted portfolio in which Japan has a very high weighting would hardly be perceived as low risk. Under those circumstances, a conservative fund manager might never consider holding a full market weighting in Japan, so why compare performance as if that were a logical base index? One possible solution might be to use GNP weights instead of market weights, as discussed in more detail in Chapter 14, or even to assign a completely different set of weights which would be more representative of the perceived risk.

A natural response for individuals might be to suggest that the low-risk portfolio would almost always consist of 100 per cent cash. But that ignores the income risk. The volatile conditions of the 1970s and 1980s have made people very aware of capital risk—the possibility of capital loss. However, there is also an income risk that seems to have been forgotten about. Individuals who require a certain income to live on, and insurance and pension companies charged with the responsibility of providing such incomes, are at risk if interest rates fall very low. High real bond yields have existed for a long time now, and there has been a certain amount of complacency that these will continue to be on offer for long into the future.

Bonds typically do not offer such high, or apparently obvious, real rates of return; that makes investing too easy. Conditions are bound to change and, and when they do, people with fixed commitments in the future and a lot of cash will have a painful reminder about income risk. In the present context, the point is that a low-risk portfolio may not consist entirely of cash. It is necessary to balance the different risks, and some risks can be offset against each other.

The base portfolio against which performance will be measured should also be the low-risk portfolio. The base index is where an investor, or investment manager, cuts back to at times of uncertainty. If that is not a position the investor or client is happy with, then there is something wrong with the base, and risks are higher than they ought to be. Anyone can make money, and feel good, in a bull market, but few feel comfortable when conditions are less favorable. A good part of the reason for this distinction is that the risks involved tend to be ignored when times are good. A particular solution would be to stay in touch with reality by paying more attention to what the underlying base portfolio would look like. Such an approach would prove beneficial in other areas. Had banks and S&Ls applied a discipline of this sort to their lending activities, they could have avoided the extreme pain created when conditions changed.

## Controlling risk

The only certainty about the future is that it is unknown. There are trends that can be exploited but the timing may be off. Sectors follow different paths, companies within industries are not all the same, each country has its own particular environment and, in the background, there is the possibility of a coordinated downturn in all the stock markets. There are, therefore, different levels of risk that have to be taken into account, but also great potential; the glass is also half full. The different risks, and how to deal with them, is something that has to be given careful consideration. The conclusion is that most risks—what we shall call micro risks—can be avoided through appropriate diversification. The macro-risk, of a coordinated collapse, is more difficult but here again diversification helps, by diversifying over different classes of asset and over time. In addition, risks can be contained through careful analysis of the business cycle and the longer-term cycles. There is evidence that such an approach can be successful and extremely rewarding. In this way it is possible to develop a coherent, long-term investment strategy. Without that, investment decisions are likely to be determined in an *ad hoc*, piecemeal way, and the portfolio has no form or shape. There may be times when such an approach will yield high returns, but it will prove impossible to control risk—a potentially fatal flaw.

Micro-risk covers the possibility of loss associated with a single investment; stock in a single company, a certain bond, etc. This risk may be just of relative underperformance, real losses or actual default. In a world of perfect knowledge everyone would only buy the winners. On the other hand, how could there be any losers under those conditions? The point is, there is no perfect knowledge, and all decisions have to be made under conditions of uncertainty. The company that you buy may turn out to be a dog. The more research you do, the better you understand the company, the industry and the business cycle, the more likely you are to pick a winner. But it is impossible to be an expert in all areas, and mistakes happen.

Investors remain vulnerable to complete price collapse in a particular market in which they are over-exposed, even when they are diversified. This is what I have called the macro-risk. The most dangerous variant comes from a coordinated decline in all stock markets, since this will affect almost everyone directly or indirectly. The most memorable occasion was the period from 1929 to 1932 in the United States, when stock prices fell by 83 per cent. More recent, but less devastating, examples occurred in 1974 and 1987. At such times, holding a broadly diversified portfolio of stocks across companies and industries will offer some protection, but the risks that remain are still very great. Diversification across counties will help as long as country markets are not all knocked down in the same way. In addition, diversification across different assets, particularly bonds, will significantly reduce the risk of a sudden, sharp drop in stock prices.

Market declines are never exactly the same across all countries, so that cross-border diversification will reduce risk to some extent. All markets fell in 1987, but some certainly did better than others. For example, the Japanese market, with the highest market capitalization in the world at the time, confounded expectations by holding up relatively well. Even in the inter-war depression, country diversification would have reduced losses in the short term and improved returns over the medium term. This is such a key episode, if only because it is constantly being trotted out as an example of all the bad things that can happen, that a section has been included below to show exactly what would have happened to a diversified portfolio held over the inter-war period.

## A question of value

The first rule to follow in order to reduce risk to manageable proportions is careful buying. When you first buy a stock, bond or any other asset, there is no way of knowing under what conditions you will have to sell it. It is fine to be optimistic, but one should never be complacent. There is a need to be aware that even the best-laid plans can go wrong, and good management can turn bad. When you come to sell, it could be under very different conditions from those expected when you bought. Most people have trouble selling anyway. When a stock is up they do not want to sell the winners, and when it is down they do not want to take a loss. Since the practical and psychological difficulties in selling are so great, this should be recognized at the time the position is first taken on.

Everyone knows the importance of buying low and selling high, and we are certainly not going to attempt to change that by advocating the opposite. But what is high, and what is low? A $1 stock is just as likely to fall to 50 cents as a $100 stock will fall to $50; possibly more so. There is no protection in cheapness. Equally a rise from $50 to $100 is as likely as a move from 50 cents to $1. Confusion over the absolute price level is a common mistake. Double the amount of shares and the price will halve, and vice versa. Nothing of significance has changed. If positions represent the same proportions in the portfolio, then relative price is unlikely to be a relevant factor. What matters is the price relative to future prospects: in the case of bonds, the outlook for inflation, the new supply of debt and the creditworthiness of the issuer; for stocks, the prospects for the growth of profits.

The answer is to buy value. Well, everyone does that! Who wants to buy something without value? But actually that often happens. People buy because someone else said it would go up, or they buy because the price has gone up and they anticipate it going up further, when they can sell it to someone else at a higher price—the greater fool theory. Eliminating such emotional procedures is crucial, but it still leaves open the question of what is value. Oscar Wilde claimed that 'a cynic is someone who knows the price of everything and the value of nothing'. Maybe there are others to whom that adage more aptly applies in today's rush for speculative profits.

The price of an asset will be determined by the interaction of the forces of supply and demand, but what gives it value? Value in the case of stocks will depend on the skills of management and the labor force, the quality of the product, position in the market, development of new products, demand for the product, etc. There are a great many variables involved in fixing value, and the net result is existing profitability and the prospects for future profits. Value can also reside in asset value: real estate etc. or, more recently, brand names. The emphasis changes but, in all cases, investors will be interested in the earning power and the cost structure of the company or institution. On the positive side, there is the possibility of earnings growth. The reverse position is the possibility of declining earnings, or worse, actual losses, or worst, bankruptcy and default. The best is always wanted, but the worst should always be avoided.

In the case of bonds, value will depend on the income flow relative to present and future inflation, i.e. the real yield available, and the prospect for future supply. In addition, the quality of the issuer is important. The United States government is now considered the risk-free benchmark against which all other bonds are measured. That was not always the case. There was a time when the government was considered a high default risk. Homer (1963) reveals that: 'Government credit sank so low that by 1787 certified interest-bearing claims against it were worth less than fifteen cents in the dollar'. For much of the nineteenth century the federal government had a worse credit rating than the old New England states; this is certainly not the case in the 1990s.

There are also the worlds of commodities and precious metals to be considered. Excessive speculation in these areas can easily result in large losses, without any producers having to go into default. Witness, for example, the dire straits to which the Hunts were reduced through their speculation in the silver market. Losing billions is excessive in anyone's vocabulary. Value in these instances is much harder to define, and depends only on what someone will pay when the time comes to sell. Food production is subject to the vagaries of the weather, while base metals are closely related to the business cycle. Precious metals are to some extent linked to inflation and the value of the dollar, and are sometimes seen as a safe haven when the international financial system seems to be in danger of collapse. Demand is much more psychological in this case, and value resides more in the mind than in reality. As a result, risks are generally very high. These can be reduced by investing in the producers rather than the commodities themselves. Then other forces come into play, like the skill of management, etc.

## Diversify or die

No one gets it right all the time, no system is perfect. The future is shrouded in darkness, covered with a dense mist, behind a brick wall. Investors should invest with the confidence that they are right, while at the same time recognizing that they will not be. Individuals who put all of their money into a single company may do spectacularly well or spectacularly badly. Some people may behave in this way, but for the individual trying to build wealth and security over time it makes no sense. So while they should follow the cycle indicators discussed here, combined with careful selection of particular assets and companies, investors should still pay attention to the individual risks involved by diversifying over companies, assets, time and countries.

Commodity traders avoid risk by setting stops on their positions. This is essential when leverage is high. Under those circumstances, what starts out as a small commitment of capital could become so great as to clean out the vault. For speculators trading on margin, stop limits are therefore necessary in order to achieve a form of diversification. Dealing in stocks on margin also requires a similar discipline, and involves a very short-term view of the world. What we are proposing here is a longer-term perspective, holding a diversified portfolio over a wide range of companies, industries and countries.

Diversification means more than simply buying a group of different companies. The spread of companies should not be determined randomly, but should be planned. A large part of the benefits of diversification are lost if the majority of the companies held are all in the same sector, or closely related sectors. Active management of a portfolio will result in shifting emphasis between different sectors, but there is still a need to maintain a balance through diversification. The availability of alternatives is now so wide that it is very easy to combine a strong view of market trends together with wide diversification.

Diversification reduces the exposure to default by any single company and to the underperformance of a single company or even sector. In addition to providing insurance against catastrophic loss, diversification provides a more stable performance. Individual stock prices fluctuate fairly widely, responding to news and rumor. Combining different stocks together reduces this variability, as usually measured by the standard deviation. Standard deviation is simply what it says, fluctuations around the average price or, more sensibly, the trend of prices, standardized to give a single measurement which is independent of the actual price level.

The standard deviation is often used as a measure of risk, but all it really measures is volatility. The volatility measure is the same regardless of whether the price trend is up or down, yet the *risk* is entirely different. A lower standard deviation is a worthwhile achievement in itself, but the default risk, or risk of underperforming, is something else again. Still, the standard deviation is likely to remain the popular measure if only because no one has yet found anything convenient to take its place.

Even under the most extreme circumstances, diversification still helps in the sense that the ultimate risk of default is reduced. More importantly, a properly diversified portfolio would include some bonds, and these will usually rally strongly under the conditions of a major collapse in stock prices—what is called macro risk. At that point, the economy is falling into a recession and is expected to continue heading lower. Credit demand drops and bonds become attractive.

So far, we have been concerned with investment within the domestic markets, in this case the United States. However, investment opportunities can be increased by extending the horizons to include the rest of the world, or at least the industrialized part. The developing world contains some of the greatest potential, but the risks are also hard to quantify and can be very great. The different environments provide additional opportunities to diversify the company and sector risks that were discussed above, while opening up the door to new opportunities. In addition, it allows investors to diversify the risks of being invested in a single country.

Investors can avoid the extreme risk of sudden major weakness in a single country by spreading investments across a number of countries. Most of the time, countries move in a line, but there are always subtle differences and occasionally there can be dramatic changes. Governments change, tax laws change, interest rates vary, natural disasters may occur, countries may be in different stages of development, with different natural resources and skills. The subject of international diversification is considered in Chapter 14.

When it comes to getting invested, risks will be reduced if the full amount of money is not placed in the market at the same time. If that happens to be the low point in prices then the full potential will be missed by not becoming fully invested there and then. However, if prices turn out to be at a peak, or just an early point along the way down, then the full potential loss will be avoided. The greatest damage in a bear market is caused to those investors who have bought at the top of the market. Diversifying over time is one certain way to avoid such an extreme. This takes us back to the earlier discussion of the need for careful buying. Such an approach is only possible if investors look beyond the very short term, and have a view of economic conditions and prospects ahead.

Exactly how investors will carry out such diversification is a matter of individual taste and temperament. Some may feel happier adding to a position at higher prices, but not if prices fall, while others will have a natural inclination to do the opposite. There are plenty of people ready with advice such as 'never add to a losing position', but these are usually related to trading activity. Just taking a look at what has happened in the past shows evidence to justify almost any advice—as long as it is used selectively. There are plenty of instances when it has paid to add to positions as prices rose over time; certainly that was true for the vast majority of stocks over the post-war period. Equally, it has also paid to buy the same stocks when their prices have fallen, and at times these price drops have been quite severe.

Part of the judgement depends on the time horizon under consideration. In the case of a true investor the time horizon ought to be long enough to allow for both approaches to pay off. It would be foolish to keep adding to positions if the outlook for the company, say, deteriorates significantly. None of this is to suggest blindly buying stocks or other assets, while ignoring developments that may change the outlook for prices in the future. The assumption here is that the original prospects have either not changed, or have improved.

Diversification over time can be an important way to reduce risks associated with individual stocks or bonds, or other assets. Such diversification also has a role to play in reducing macro-risks, i.e. the risk of a whole market suddenly collapsing. If the whole portfolio is invested at a particular point in time, the potential risks can be horrendous. At least by spreading asset purchases out over time, the worst case is avoided. Here again, timing should not be random or left to chance. The message of this book is that the business cycle is predictable to some extent, and such information should be used in market timing.

## Cycle timing

In a bear market, virtually all prices will fall together. This will be true for stocks, bonds or precious metals, etc. Not all stock prices will fall to the same extent, and some will recover before others. Equally with bonds, a bear market will drag down Treasuries, corporates and convertibles, but not all to the same degree. Typically, there will be a widening out of the quality spread between high and low quality bond yields. In general, the lower the quality the higher the yield and the greater the risk. A similar pattern can be observed in the stock market, where the fastest growing stocks will often fall the furthest when conditions deteriorate.

The risks in these cases are of the macro variety, and are related to the business cycle. Secular declines, as associated with the depression of the 1930s, are different in degree rather than anything else. They start out as a business cycle downturn and get carried to extremes. The prospects for a more severe depression of this type are typically associated with a deteriorating secular trend. That is certainly something worth considering, and was analysed in Chapter 6. The conclusion about the present status of the long wave is quite different, however, from the more popular view.

There is a widespread belief that it is not possible to predict business cycle-related movements in markets. Mutual funds offer a wide variety of different portfolios for people to invest in, each concentrating on a particular market or segment of the market. The market selection, and timing, is left to the individual. The approach is sold as a way to maximize individual choice, and as such has been extremely successful. What it means, however, is that the macro risk is left to the individual. All the individual has to do is pick the right market to be in and the right time to invest, and then the mutual fund will allocate the funds in an efficient way. There is no doubt that small investors can benefit in this way, but they also have the hardest choice to make.

Many fund managers operate in the same way, but there are still some who offer clients the possibility of fully diversified portfolios, managed in such a way as to take account of changing market conditions. However, even these are becoming a declining breed, as more and more portfolios become indexed to a particular market. The increase in indexation is partly a reflection of the widespread scepticism that it is possible to anticipate cyclical changes in asset prices, and partly of complacency following an extended bull market. In a bull market, investors consider it to be their right to receive the full potential of any increase in market indices. However, these same investors will not appreciate the full extent of market losses in a bear market.

Much work has been done on efficient market allocation, which generally supports the case for indexation within a particular market or market segment. This may or may not be the case; there have been striking examples of certain managers beating the averages on a consistent basis, while on the other hand, the vast majority have failed to do so. Market timing and selection has not been subjected to the same rigorous analysis, but what evidence there is has tended to support the agnostic view. The argument is that market prices at any time incorporate all known information and there is, therefore, no way to benefit from what is generally known. Oddly, this is exactly the same assumption made by technical analysts, who conclude that, *therefore*, prices themselves have the power to forecast; but more about that in Chapter 10.

Majority opinion will be fully reflected in market prices, but that does not exclude the possibility that certain individuals may have a different interpretation of known events. To be of any advantage, it is essential that the majority do not have access to the same information, or at least interpret it differently, otherwise it will have already been discounted. One point to make about market timing and selection is that this can still be associated with indexation within the individual markets. That really involves a separate set of decisions.

A cycle watch is essential if investors are to avoid major market downturns, and it also has a key role to play in getting investors in the market when conditions turn favorable. By remaining cautious and underinvested during a bull market, investors can suffer an opportunity loss as great as if they got caught in a crash. Such missed opportunities are not as painful as real out-of-pocket losses, but they raise the possibility that patience will run out at the wrong time, so that exposure is increased just before the end.

Other chapters include evidence that it has been possible to anticipate major cyclical turning points in different financial markets and different economies on a consistent basis. In particular, the stock market crash in October 1987 was *preceded* by a published warning of an impending 'crisis' in the stock market. By anticipating such high-risk periods, investors are better able to protect their existing wealth and to take advantage of the situation in order to build wealth in the future.

A good example of how much difference cycle timing can make to long-term performance has been provided by Shilling (1991). Taking the period from January 1946 to June 1991, Gary Shilling computes the annual average return on the Dow Jones Industrial Average to be 11.4 per cent, compounded quarterly and including dividends. Treasury bills over this period provided a return of 4.2 per cent. However, if an investor was able to anticipate the business cycle well enough to be out of the market during the 50 weakest months, while remaining fully invested the rest of the time, the compounded annual return jumped to 19.9 per cent. Such are the wonders of compounding that the investor ended the period with a gain that was three times that provided by a buy-and-hold strategy. In money terms, that converted $1000 into over $3 million.

This improvement is achieved without shorting the market, i.e. selling stock you do not own, or adopting any other form of high-risk approach. Missing out on some of the strong months will lower the potential gain but not produce a loss. In the example used here, it was also shown that even if the investor was out of the market for the 50 strongest months, as well as the 50 weakest, the annual return would still have been 12.1 per cent, again exceeding the buy-and-hold strategy. Perfect timing is therefore not required in order to beat the market, and the potential rewards make it well worth the effort. The indicators included here show that it has been possible to anticipate the major market downturns and recoveries on a consistent basis. What is even more important is the fact that these were not the result of wisdom after the event, when all things are known, but were actual published forecasts produced ahead of time.

## Active asset allocation

There is body of thought that proposes a set menu of portfolios depending on the particular stage of the cycle. For example, in the early stage of recovery the choice might be 5 per cent cash, 45 per cent bonds and 50 per cent equities. These percentages would then be adjusted as the cycle progresses according to some predetermined formula: raising cash levels as the economy starts to turn down, and reducing equities when it appears the economy is about to go into recession. Such a proposal might seem to fit in with what is being suggested here, since a strong case has already been made for varying asset allocation according to the particular stage of the business cycle. There is, however, an important distinction to be made. It is a mistake to try and allocate assets in a fixed, predetermined, way.

Here is yet another auto-pilot approach to portfolio management. An auto-pilot may work reasonably well at high altitudes in calm weather. The nearest comparison in the investment world is the indexed fund, which amounts to a buy-and-hold strategy. However, it makes no sense to fly on regardless of direction or ultimate destination. Active asset allocation over the business cycle requires frequent landing and taking off, and flying at different altitudes with frequent changes in direction. To rely on an auto-pilot to do the job for you is asking for trouble. The appeal of such a simple approach is easy to understand. It is a substitute for thought and hard decisions. Why not choose the easy way out? The reason is that in practice it is a road that runs right to the edge of a cliff. To follow simple rules without thought risks falling off the edge. The advantages of diversification will provide a safety net and prevent a real disaster, but the full potential will not be realized.

In many cases, the amount of variation is very limited regardless of the theoretical ranges that are established. In practice, cash varies from 5 per cent to 20 per cent, bonds vary from 20 per cent to 40 per cent and equities vary from 40 per cent to 70 per cent. Changes on the scale often proposed are generally inadequate to reflect the real risks or opportunities of the cycle. Even more importantly, the recommended changes are only made after the stage of the cycle has become obvious to even the most casual observer; when it is too late to do any good. A fixed set of asset allocation rules is inappropriate both because investor preferences are different, and because the business cycle is not always the same; it is, in fact, more accurate to say that the business cycle always differs from the one before. Mechanical rules do not work for the business cycle, and they are inappropriate for making important investment decisions.

In the case of a single investor, or homogeneous group of investors, it will always be possible to define a particular portfolio allocation depending on the forecast of economic conditions. Emphasis should be put on the fact that the portfolio will depend not on current economic conditions, which will already be discounted in market prices, but the expected direction of the economy. The situation becomes much more complicated once other investors, with different preferences and concerns, are included. Some investors like to take high risks in search of high gains, others are prepared to sacrifice above average returns in exchange for greater security. There are investors who will invest primarily in bonds, others who will emphasize stocks, conservative or aggressive, those who will invest in precious metals and commodities, and those who will invest in foreign securities, bonds or stocks or both, and still others who will hold a high level of cash. There is no single portfolio allocation that can possibly apply in all situations.

The task becomes even more complicated when recommending portfolio allocations for investors using different base currencies. In this case, each portfolio normally will emphasize assets denominated in the base currency. However, even in this there are important exceptions. A large pension fund, for example, will typically allocate funds to different managers. A single manager may, therefore, be responsible for an international bond fund that invests in all countries except the base country, and yet performance will be measured in terms of the base currency. In that case, performance will typically be measured against a base index of bonds, weighted by the size of the market.

Portfolio decisions for such funds can benefit substantially from the sort of cyclical indicators presented here, but it will be no use recommending a 50 per cent equity weighting, or investments in the base country. A Swiss pension fund will hold a very high weighting in bonds and property, and a very low weighting in equities. US pension funds will be rather more adventurous, although some still only invest in the domestic markets. International diversification has been increasing in the United States, as elsewhere, but exposure still varies widely.

It should be clear from this brief survey that there is no single portfolio that will apply to all investors. Attempting to provide a range of portfolios to cover all tastes would prove extremely complicated and confusing. What is more, even that degree of complexity would still not justify a set menu of choices that could be relied on over each successive cycle. There are also the differences in the cycles to be taken into account.

In this book I have discussed the particular nature of each market, each with its own indicators. Such detail would be superfluous if there were a fixed set of portfolio choices depending on the particular stage of the business cycle. Set portfolios means set markets. If stage one in the cycle means 40 per cent bonds and 60 per cent equities, while stage two means 60 per cent bonds and 40 per cent equities, the outlook for those markets has been decided; there is nothing more to be said about it. Not only are the markets related, which must be true, but they are tied together in a completely rigid and inflexible way. The real world is not like that.

A major distinction between cycles is the behavior of inflation. Inflation does vary across the cycle, but the relationship has changed over time, as shown in Chapter 2. In addition, there has been a longer-term trend to inflation that has extended beyond the normal business cycle. Inflation continued to rise through the 1970s despite two recessions. The trend reversed in the 1980s, and the trend of inflation turned down through the 1980s and into the 1990s, despite an extended recovery. The bond market reflected this pattern, with yields trending higher through the 1970s, and trending down in the latter period. The business cycle did affect bond allocation decisions throughout this period, but the emphasis was very different. The underlying trend of inflation also affected the relative attractiveness of different stocks, and of the stock market overall.

Another major influence on asset allocation decisions is the exchange rate, or exchange rates generally. Here again, there are forces that extend beyond any particular business cycle. Exchange rates are influenced by what is happening in different countries, and that will necessarily complicate investment decisions. The US dollar rose dramatically from 1982 to early in 1985, and then fell equally dramatically down to the end of 1990—all within what has been classified as a single business cycle. The implications of such wide currency swings are highly significant. There is the direct effect of exchange rate changes on domestic returns that comes from exchanging foreign currency income or values into the domestic currency. Exchange rate changes also affect the financial markets themselves. Such effects can come through improved competitiveness of domestic corporations from a decline in the exchange rate. Alternatively, the monetary authorities may change policy in response to a change in the exchange rate, and the bond market may react to this, or in anticipation of such a move.

Taken together, the lack of uniformity in successive business cycles and in investor preferences makes it inappropriate to try to squeeze the variety of possible portfolio choices into a small box with a limited set of fixed compartments. It is misleading, and potentially dangerous, to apply a pre-determined formula to portfolio allocation decisions. Knowing where the economy is in the business cycle, and having a good forecast of where it is headed, is not enough to decide the appropriate portfolio allocation for all individuals or institutions, nor even for a single individual or institution. The real world is much more sophisticated and interesting than that.

## Diversification in the inter-war period

The stock market crash of 1929 and the subsequent market mayhem have exercised a fatal fascination for investors. The wealth-destroying effects of those dramatic events have left an indelible impression, making the stock market seem far more risky than it really is. There are risks, but rational decision making is not made easier by blowing them up out of proportion. Doing anything involves some risk, but this can be kept under control through diversification and respect for the business cycle. Certainly investors lost money between 1929 and 1932, but the pain and suffering of investors has been exaggerated by the habit of concentrating on a few well-chosen examples.

When investors sit around the camp fire and tell stories, there will always be someone who will turn the blood cold with a chilling tale about the losses that resulted in the depression. The full effect is achieved by comparing the stock market peak in 1929 with the lowest point reached in 1932. An investor who managed to achieve that perfect timing would have to be a genius, perhaps not in the way one normally thinks of as desirable, but certainly possessing an extraordinary talent. The truth is that probably no one achieved that unfortunate distinction. Even so, books on that period retell the horror stories of how individuals were wiped out when stock prices crashed.

The hard-luck stories are real enough, but they are usually taken out of perspective. These tales describe the poor unfortunates who lost everything when they bought at or near the top, using margin to leverage up their positions. It is hard to understand the message conveyed in these stories; are we supposed to feel sorry for such crude examples of speculative stupidity and naked greed? These were, anyway, the exceptions not the rule. The foolhardy recklessness of these few should hardly be used as the benchmark to measure rational behavior of the majority. Every market downturn, even a minor one, throws up more examples of people who were heavily leveraged on the wrong side of the market, and who consequently were wiped out. The inter-war period does not hold a monopoly on such foolishness.

Fears associated with a repeat performance of the 1929–32 period continue to intrude on normal rational thought about the stock market, particularly in the United States. The history of that period was discussed in the previous chapter, where an attempt was made to put the episode into perspective. What we want to show here is that diversification would have substantially reduced the risks involved. Anyone who had been buying all the way up, so that they were diversified over time, and had also bought some bonds and some equities abroad, e.g. in the United Kingdom, were not wiped out—in fact quite the opposite. The cautious investor who did not panic out of the market at the bottom, actually did very well, taking the 1920s and 1930s together. In addition, it should have been possible to anticipate the business cycle downturn, particularly considering the excesses that led up to this period. It is relatively easy to show how this could have worked, but then all things are easy to see in retrospect; the true test is always in the future. As a result, this comparison deals only with the advantages of diversification.

The decline in stock prices over the 1930s was partly offset by the dividends that were earned. If these are included, the total return index still ended the decade a little lower than it was at the beginning. To the modern way of thinking, this would seem even worse, because of the effect of inflation reducing purchasing power. However, it is necessary to adjust the thought process to allow for a different era; a time when prices actually fell, i.e. inflation was negative. As a result of this adjustment, the total return in real terms was actually positive over the 1930s.

The difference between adjusted and non-adjusted returns is considerable. Figure 8.1 shows the cumulative returns available on the three different assumptions, together with the return from simply holding cash over the whole period. The value of stock prices is the same as the cumulative return based solely on changes in stock prices, i.e. a price index. This is what is normally used to show how bad the period was. The other market returns show the cumulative returns achieved when dividends are included and, in addition, when inflation is taken into account. Total returns were not great, but they were hardly disastrous either, and this was without allowing for diversification over a longer period.

Diversification over time would have produced a more favorable outcome. Purchases made through the 1920s, particularly in the earlier years, would have greatly reduced the average cost of the portfolio. The same would be true of purchases made during the steep decline in prices in 1931 and 1932. Further protection was provided by wider diversification over a range of assets and markets.

The first and most obvious form of diversification was provided by taking positions in cash and bonds. When an economy moves into recession, interest rates typically fall and bonds rally. Much has been made about how poorly bonds performed over this period. That was not because of an inherent weakness in bonds, but because of the strange monetary policy followed at the time, as discussed in Chapter 7. Even so, government bonds and high grade corporates still provided a steady, reliable return through this

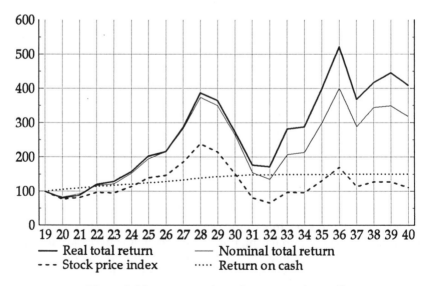

**Figure 8.1** Interwar stock market returns (annual)

period; the total return was negative only in one year, and that was 1932. The returns earned on bonds and stocks are shown in Fig. 8.2. Bonds provided a more stable return over the inter-war period, outperforming stocks in the 1930s, but lagging behind for the whole period.

The potential for diversification is increased by including investments in foreign markets. The main overseas market at that time was in the United Kingdom. The equally weighted portfolio shown in the chart assumes that a US investor had a diversified portfolio consisting of 25 per cent US stocks, 25 per cent US bonds, 25 per cent UK stocks and 25 per cent UK bonds. The ratios are assumed to be re-established at the start of each year. Part of the return in this case will be determined by changes in the exchange rate, which were quite violent over this period. The returns are shown in dollar terms, before taking into account the effect of inflation.

The results are encouraging. The diversified portfolio did better than US stocks over the whole period and with considerably less volatility. Investors did better in US stocks up until the crash, but then lost out. The whole point about diversification is that it requires foregoing the best returns available in any single market or sector in order to avoid the very worst results. It is a compromise. The best market of all was actually in UK stocks, particularly in dollar terms. However, volatility and risks were high. Bonds offered greater stability, but far less potential. The compromise offered more stability than could be had in the most volatile markets and a higher

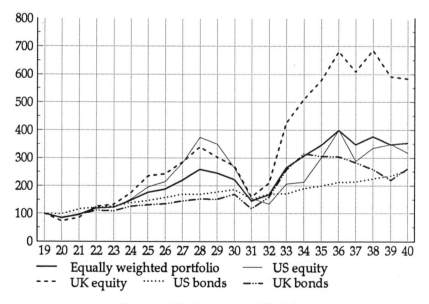

**Figure 8.2** Total returns in US dollars

return than that available in the most stable markets. The important message of this example is that risks and volatility were reduced through diversification, even during the most dangerous time in the history of the stock market. Studies of diversification usually concentrate on recent history, which leaves open the question of whether the principles would still apply in a period like the 1930s. The answer is that they do.

The results obtained here are based on the assumption that investors remained fully invested over the whole period. The use of cyclical indicators of the type discussed here should have enabled investors to avoid the worst of the decline in stock prices and, therefore, experience far greater returns than those shown. The results are a strong vindication for investing in the stock market as long as this is within a diversified portfolio. Such an approach, when combined with a careful watch of the business cycle, provides tremendous potential to build wealth over time.

# 9

---

# *EXPECTATIONS AND NEWS*
## *(the past, the present and the future)*

Investment decisions depend not only on what is actually happening at ground level, as it were, but also what investors perceive to be happening, and what they expect to happen in the future. In the short term, there are many influences at work, and facts, to the extent they are known, will be colored by human emotion. It is rational and in the nature of the human condition to try to anticipate events. That is the way to maximize profits, but it also opens up the possibility of mistakes. Expectations are the link between the present and the future, and are based on the experience of the past.

One approach is to know everything about the future, or at least something perfectly, so that investment decisions can be made with absolute certainty about the outcome. Nice work if you can get it. For the rest of us, the mere mortals, it is necessary to be a little more circumspect about our positions, recognizing that the future is always going to be uncertain. For this group, the greatest danger is complacency.

All rational decisions involving time are based on expectations about the future. Time is an essential part of the investment process and, therefore, of a modern industrial economy. And with time comes uncertainty—the duo are inseparable. There would be no place for such emotions as optimism or pessimism, or expectations, which is what they really are, in a world of certainty—where the future is known. Expectations embody our best guess about an uncertain future. And the opinion expressed in the market, or by the market, will be no help. If the market goes up, optimism rises; if prices fall, there is a distinct increase in pessimism. Market opinion follows the market, just as consumer confidence follows the economy. Investors looking for a guide to where the market is headed in the future need something else that is independent of market opinion.

Many investors fear uncertainty and wait for calmer times when they can feel more confident about the future. That will generally mean waiting until everyone is more confident; when newspaper articles talk about rising profits and the prospect of even higher profits in the future, and do not talk of falling profits and the weakness of the economy; when there is near certainty of falling inflation and rising bond prices, rather than the opposite. Unfortunately, that is the time of highest risk, when the majority will have already bought. By the time the positive aspects of the economy are widely recognized it is time to start looking for flaws in the argument, and considering the alternatives. *Far from being a negative, uncertainty is a desirable condition.*

Uncertainty is absolutely fundamental to the functioning of a capitalistic economy. Time is required between the decision to invest and the sale of the production that results. Over that period, conditions can well change, and usually do. Within a free market, individuals are free to make decisions even if these are stupid. The freedom to lose money is inseparable from the freedom to make money. An unknown future and imperfect information about the past and the present make life difficult for those making decisions. But decisions still have to be made, if only to do nothing, and these have to be based on the best guess possible. It is no good to say 'forecasters are always wrong, shoot the forecaster'. The very person who might say that will almost certainly be guilty of that very crime.

All forecasts can be seen as an attempt to try to reduce uncertainty about the future; there is no way of predicting what will happen with total accuracy. By deliberately setting out to forecast the economy, stock prices, food prices or any other of the possible variables, one of the major objectives, hopefully, is to identify any obvious pitfalls. It is amazing how often existing problems only become obvious when someone else points them out, and when it is already too late. Beyond that, there should be an attempt at identifying the major trends in markets, society, demographics, etc., that are slow-changing and might be expected to continue. Further discussion of forecasting methods, and some of the difficulties involved, is contained in Chapter 11—where there can also be found a discussion of the approach employed here, together with cycle forecasts.

Expectations of the future are so all-pervading, so much a part of everyday life, that frequently their role in the decision-making process goes completely unrecognized. They come in many different forms, and travel in a variety of disguises. Assumptions, guesses, hunches, intuition are just some of the different names given to the same thing. Then, under different circumstances, and perhaps with the title of forecasts or predictions, they are catapulted into the spotlight.

Recognizing these alternative names also draws attention to the different degrees of precision attached to expectations. Sometimes they are vague and general, sometimes they are very specific, but in one form or another they are always there. Buying on known information, such as the announcement of increased profits, still implies making a forecast about the future—in this case, that the future will be just like the past. A straight line extrapolation is the least interesting of all. There may be times when such simplicity is proved correct, but the probabilities are heavily weighted against it.

The increased availability of information, and the widespread analysis of the data, have helped to make financial markets increasingly volatile. Communications have improved dramatically over recent years, while more and more information has become available, along with the ability to crunch numbers and extract conclusions. Improved knowledge might be supposed to smooth out market fluctuations and reduce volatility. In fact, quite the opposite has happened. There is great competition to be the first to identify any turning point, but all investors can do is interpret the past while the future remains uncertain. Increasing attempts to outguess an uncertain future adds to price volatility when everyone is looking at the same information in the same way, and trying to anticipate the future earlier and earlier.

There is a constant interaction between news and views. Expectations are formed about future events on the basis of what is known at the time, and decisions are made. Subsequently, the news of these events will be reported and investors will react, depending on how close the report is to the expectation. A wide error will generally result in a violent response. Sometime in the future, the reports may be revised. It will be too late to affect the decisions made when the news first came out, but there is likely to be some effect on expectations for the future. The forecast itself may be changed or just the degree of uncertainty associated with it.

## The importance of expectations

Why play with expectations that could be wrong? Why take the risk? Why not wait for results to be published and base decisions only on what is known? The answer is that what is known is already past, and by the time it is known it will already be discounted in market prices. It is even hard to discuss decisions to buy or sell without introducing expectations about the future. After all, what makes something an attractive purchase, and when is the right time to buy or sell?

Take the example of a company that is expected to report rapid growth. If that is a widespread forecast, then it will become reflected in the price long before the results are published. In fact, there is a good chance that the price of the stock will actually fall once the news comes out. To buy on the news is to buy known value. The meal is over, and only a few crumbs are left for the late-comers, and they may well end up washing the dishes. If the price is to continue rising, it will have to be on the expectation that the growth rate will continue, and possibly even accelerate further. True value can only be obtained by anticipating the future. Past performance is no guarantee that it will continue, although certain characteristics can provide a useful guide. The point is, no matter how good performance was in the past, the value of an investment made now will depend only on what the company does in the future.

The same is true when it comes to such macroeconomic phenomena as inflation. People in the early 1980s, who expected a renewed acceleration of inflation based on the experience of the 1970s, and therefore sold bonds, made a very big mistake. The value of bonds in the 1980s depended on the future performance of inflation, not what had happened before. In an earlier time, investors who bought bonds in the early 1970s on the basis of the historic inflation performance suffered potentially huge losses.

The decision to invest in plant and equipment, or in the stock market, assumes an optimistic view about the future. In the same way, the decision not to invest in this way will also be based on implicit, or explicit, expectations about the future, whether this is recognized or not. Many of these forecasts are not very sophisticated, and may have more to do with a natural optimistic or pessimistic nature than anything else. These instinctive 'reactions' have a 50/50 chance of being right.

The way in which expectations are formed is discussed below, but for now it is sufficient to recognize that an extended period of rising prices and output creates the expectation that these conditions will continue. As these expectations prove successful, so they are reinforced further, and the majority increases. In a major bull market the country is quickly filled with geniuses. When circumstances change and the bull market stops, the disappointment can be very great. It is at these times that a proper understanding of the forces at work will increase in importance. For individuals, it is easy to go from euphoria to despair, as one extreme takes over from the other.

News is discounted in market prices almost instantly; there is no time for reaction or thought. The sudden revelation of lower than expected earnings may produce a dramatic response: a 20 per cent or 30 per cent drop in price in minutes. Surprises are also possible on the upside. When the news is good and people feel like buying, prices are likely to have risen, and/or be rising, strongly. As a result, everyone will try to anticipate the news, so that they can benefit from the announcement and not be left behind. The reaction gets pushed back in time, as investors react to the forecasts that are made. Price movements will tend to be smoothed out, at least temporarily. By the time the news finally breaks there may be little if any impact left to move prices. In fact, they may well move in the opposite direction. There are innumerable examples that could be used to illustrate this pattern of behavior. The following one was a classic.

Emperor Hirohito of Japan fell ill on 19 September 1988, and informed opinion concluded that the market would shut down when he died and then prices would fall sharply as a sign of mourning. This expectation undermined the market for months, and clearly became discounted. Had the Emperor died in those early weeks, stock prices probably would have fallen as anticipated. However, by the end of the year the Nikkei Dow had risen to a record high, and news of the death of the Emperor on 6 January 1989 was actually followed by the strongest price rise for over a year, on high volume and with a strong advance/decline. Suddenly, the argument became that it was the birth of a new age, but this explanation followed events rather than preceded them. The news of the Emperor's death had been fully discounted in the price and, as often happens, had been overdiscounted.

Another piece of evidence to consider is that provided by the rush for freedom in East Germany, and the tearing down of the Berlin Wall and all the old barriers to intra-German cooperation. The dismantling of communism in the rest of eastern Europe had received a muted reception in the markets, not because events were less dramatic, but because the immediate beneficiaries were hard to identify. However, in the case of East Germany, a more direct and immediate link with West German companies was easy to see, and quantify.

As a result, stock prices and the exchange rate were bid up sharply by eager investors. Net foreign investment into West Germany jumped to DM16.5 billion in October 1989, and DM15.5 billion in November, compared with a monthly average of only DM3.7 billion in the first nine months of the year. There was no waiting around for the first published profits from such new ventures—clearly that would be much too late. There is also the danger of being too early, and enthusiasm died down dramatically in 1990–91. Questions of timing like this all involve expectations about the future.

The final example goes back in time to 1688, and illustrates that human nature has not fundamentally changed over the last 300, or so, years. Joseph de la Vega, when talking about the Amsterdam exchange in *Confusion de Confusiones*, states that:

> The expectation of an event creates a much deeper impression upon the exchange than the event itself. When large dividends or rich imports are expected, shares will rise in price; but if the expectation becomes a reality, the shares often fall; for the joy over the favorable development and the jubilation over a lucky chance have abated in the meantime.

How quickly prices respond to new information depends on how widely known the information is. If only one or two people realize what is going on then it is unlikely to make much difference to market prices. A quick reaction is most likely when expectations are strongly affected by some dramatic news, rather than the gradual development of expectations based on imperfect and incomplete information. In the case of widely known information, such as the opening up of East Germany, the only delaying factor is the speed of reaction. The result is a very rapid discounting of the information and possibly overshooting.

## Forecast or following

Whatever happens is always explained immediately. There are always rumors or news of one sort or another, and there is always someone around who is prepared to draw obvious conclusions from one to the other. Every day, each movement in prices is *explained* by something that happened, something someone said, a recommendation, a report, etc. It has always been thus, but it seems to have become more so. The growth of communications has led to instant analysis. It is like a drug. More and more news, instant explanations, instant quotes in remote farmhouses, opinions, explanations; the world is dominated by the moment and anyone can be a trader. Technology and society have accentuated the short-term trading aspect of the markets.

One day the stock market will go down because the exchange rate was weak. Next it might go up because the exchange rate was weak. In trying to understand the market it is necessary to read through the hype and see the underlying trend. This is helpful even if you are a short-term trader, where fact and fiction are merged, and truth becomes less important—only the instant market reaction counts.

Most *explanations* are convenient, just that. Anything slightly out of the ordinary will typically be seized upon as *the reason*. Rationality, evidence of cause and effect, or even any relationship at all do not seem to be important criteria. The legal equivalent would be that anyone in the immediate vicinity of a murder would be arrested, convicted and executed without a trial. No motive would have to be proved, no weapon found nor any other consideration taken into account. However, someone really did commit the crime, and beyond this instant analysis there are underlying trends which are important.

The daily fluctuations add up to distinct cyclical trends, yet this underlying cycle is never mentioned as part of the explanation. There are good reasons why that would be—after all, most people are not focusing on that horizon, and the same old explanation every day would become extremely boring very quickly. However, these cyclical forces clearly determine the dominant trend in the markets and, therefore, should not be ignored by investors. Recognizing this is a key distinction between forecasters and followers.

Followers are those who wait for the evidence to accumulate before taking positions. This evidence could be fundamental, that is economic in nature, i.e. rising profits, signs that inflation has peaked, that the economy is recovering, etc. The evidence could also be technical in nature, i.e. crossing a moving average or two, or a trend line, completing a head and shoulders pattern, etc. Inevitably, market prices will have moved a long way by the time such confirmations are available. Not only will prices reflect what has happened so far, but will very quickly incorporate the confirmations themselves. To the extent that they are interpreted as meaning that the trend will be continued, so prices will move to discount that. The markets may not be perfect, but they are usually extremely efficient.

There is no hard proof of some event or trend that still has value in itself, since this will already be embodied fully in market prices. Reacting to such news means following, not forecasting. To the extent that such decisions make money it will be because the trends are continued. In which case, the evidence provided good forecasts of the future. There will undoubtedly be times when that is the case, but the success rate is likely to be less than 50/50; that is, a better choice would be made on the flip of a coin.

Also, there is a feedback mechanism that works against repeated use of simple trend-following techniques. For example, money and inflation accelerated strongly twice in the 1970s. That environment provided exceptional opportunities in commodities and precious metals. Then, during the 1980s the early signs of a repeat performance were identified frequently, resulting in numerous predictions of hyperinflation and soaring gold prices, only to find that the appearance of the same trend was just an apparition. The environment had changed. People, including the monetary authorities, had learned an important lesson from the previous experiences.

## Controlling emotions

Uncertainty is the fertile breeding ground in which the seeds of optimism and pessimism flower into overblown greed and fear. The ship has run aground and the occupants are panicking. They know the boat is sinking, but because it is totally dark they are unable to know where they are. The fear is that they are about to sink to the bottom of the ocean like the *Titanic*. What they do not yet realize is that they are in the shallows and close to shore. There are still risks, but they are clearly manageable.

The unknown creates shadows and images that distort facts and confuse thinking. At extremes, these circumstances can make rational beings do irrational things, like selling at the bottom or buying at the top. In retrospect, when the future has become the past, these actions will seem inexplicable, but then circumstances will have changed. To understand the difference, walk through a deep forest on your own, miles from anywhere, on a dark and windy night, and then try it again on a bright, sunlit day. Same place, different emotion.

Greed and fear are the key emotions which have to be kept under control, and it is a thin line which keeps them apart. In fair proportions, these forces will promote rational decision making. When out of balance, they can easily be destabilizing, setting up an emotional roller-coaster, as each hiatus is followed by another. Worst of all is the fact that destabilizing behavior is most likely just at the point when the markets themselves are becoming extremely volatile, thereby piling up the risks on top of each other. Just at the point when a clear head and a steady hand are needed in order to steer a path through stormy seas, the brain seizes up and the hand starts to shake.

Excessive optimism will obscure the risks involved, leading to high-risk investments which, at the time, are not recognized as such. Later, if expectations are not realized, and losses replace the anticipated gains, one extreme will be followed by another, with excessive pessimism replacing the optimism; in this case greatly exaggerating the risks involved. In such an environment, prices can temporarily be carried down below what would otherwise be justified, thereby actually maximizing losses.

Too much uncertainty may be a negative, but so is too little. Risks are at their highest following an extended move, when the great majority have already made their commitments. This is when uncertainty is at its lowest, and complacency at its greatest. What is at issue here is partly the individual perceptions of the investor, but usually such situations are also characterized by unrealistic expectations of future economic developments, or the belief that the link between particular market prices and the economy has been broken. At such times the possibility of sudden, sharp changes of direction is greatly increased—when only small shifts in demand will cause dramatic price movements. An improved understanding of how the economy works, and the interrelationships between the economy and different markets, is a critical factor in helping to avoid such extremes of emotion and improve decision making.

Investing means forecasting which means uncertainty. The two are inseparable, and help shape the psychology of the markets. When prices suddenly change direction there is a tendency to think that the majority of people have identified something very important; and there is usually no limit on the supply of possibilities being put forward. More usually, the truth is quite the opposite, with the attitude of the majority characterized by extreme uncertainty and total confusion. An investor trying to understand the cyclical movement of market prices needs to be aware of the way in which expectations change, particularly around turning points.

## Informed uncertainty

There is great competition to be the first to identify any turning point, with everyone using the same or similar forms of analysis. Not surprisingly, they arrive at the same or similar conclusions. This similarity is more important than whether the conclusion is actually correct, at least in the near term. The increasing attempt to outguess an uncertain future using established techniques is adding to price volatility. Stocks that have good growth potential will quickly be pushed to levels that discount the future growth of earnings. Similarly, if a dip in earnings becomes clear, the price of the stock will drop like a stone to discount it. Any new information that affects the outlook is immediately incorporated into market prices. The increased availability of information and the widespread analysis of the data have helped to make financial markets increasingly volatile, not less.

The more similar the analysis, the greater the consensus, the bigger the majority and the greater the price changes will become, since there will be fewer people on the other side of the transaction. For example, if there are only bids in the market and no offers, prices will have to rise until some offers are made and/or the bids dry up. The more that investment managers come to think alike, and the more evenly information is distributed, the easier it becomes to create a substantial majority, correct or incorrect, and the more volatile market prices become.

There is a fairly general consensus on the economic conditions required to create a bull or bear market in bonds or equities, or exchange rates or gold. Each new piece of information is instantly fastened upon and the obvious implications extracted. On occasion, this can result in almost a unanimous market expectation, and consequently very sharp price movements. The more efficient markets have become at digesting the latest piece of information, the more short-term orientated they have had to become. Not a very comforting conclusion, and not one normally discussed by supporters of efficient markets.

A classic example was provided by the crash on 19 October 1987. The Dow Jones average dropped 23 per cent in a single day, as the expectation took hold that the economy was headed into recession. There was no gradual adjustment, no pause, just instant discounting. The assumption had been right, but the crash actually aborted the process. Prices did not immediately adjust back up, because this was outside the consensus model. In this case, hard experience was required in order to force a change in expectations.

There will always be uncertainty; the future will never be known. That is not all bad. It is also the case that without uncertainty there would be no opportunity. Uncertainty cannot be, nor should be, wished away, but it does need to be controlled. Decisions will be improved, and the decision maker will sleep easier, if they are based on tried and tested procedures. Expectations that are based on the simple repetition of past events are likely to prove unreliable and potentially dangerous. Confidence will be increased if expectations are based on proper understanding of the behavior that resulted in the observed outcomes.

This is the only way to control uncertainty. Disaster lies around every corner when uncertainty controls the investor. Then, every dark shadow portends an impending storm, and every chink of light, the dawn of a new beginning. Under these conditions, the decision-making processes contain all the rationality of a dog chasing its own tail. The investor will be constantly buying and selling in response to changes in news and market values, and get terribly whipsawed in return.

## Forming expectations

Given the obvious importance of expectations in investment decisions, it is clearly of interest to understand how these are formed. What we are discussing here is the behavior of groups. As far as any single individual is concerned it is impossible to say how he or she will react to a given set of circumstances. Some people are pessimists, some optimists, some react instinctively while some like to think things through, some are stubborn and some are easily led. In talking about how individuals will react we are necessarily referring to the average, and marginal changes around the average. The only time it is easy to forecast the future is when nothing is happening, but then that is exactly when it is least interesting. Forecasts are most useful when they deviate from the average, from the consensus and, of course, when the consensus is wrong.

Unfortunately, there are much greater risks to reputation from not running with the pack if you are wrong, and the danger that no one will believe you anyway if you turn out to be right. John Maynard Keynes (1936) recognized this bias:

> Worldly wisdom teaches that it is better for reputation to fail conventionally than to succeed unconventionally.

The future is unknown and unknowable, but the past provides some clues which can be used to piece together a picture based on expectations. This will never be a perfect likeness, but the objective is to make it as complete as possible. Forecasts are not made in a vacuum, divorced from what else is happening in the world. The raw material that is used to make any forecast will be based on the record of what has already happened. It is quite clear that news, rumor and other people's views will have an effect on the formation of expectations. The receptor for this information will not always be neutral, but will also be subject to certain biases. Expectations are formed within the human mind, with all its preconceptions, phobias, optimism, pessimism and overall fear and greed. All of this affects the way any news or views will be interpreted.

From what has been said so far, it might be supposed that market prices will have already discounted all the news, so when the news comes out there is no market reaction. That would be the case if the news actually lived up to expectations, but that is not always so. In fact, market prices often react very violently when it turns out that expectations were wrong. At one level, news is the basis of all forecasts and, to the extent that the news is unexpected, it is capable of having a major impact on prices. When it comes to interpreting any new piece of information it is necessary to know what the prior expectation was. Many is the time when appalling news has been followed by rising prices. Maybe the news was bad, but better than expected, maybe there was the market equivalent of a sigh of relief that the bad news was now out of the way.

The adjustment process works the same way at the macro level as for individual companies. The constant stream of information on retail sales, industrial production, inventories, orders, consumer prices, etc., is gathered, processed and wrapped in reams of paper to disseminate the conclusions to a waiting world. Most of the time, expectations adjust gradually to what is happening, but every now and again there is some major break from trend that has a catalytic effect and causes a sudden change in direction, or a speeding up of the adjustment.

Essentially, market prices move in response to news, but it has to be new and not just the announcement of something that is already known or anticipated. What is expected is based on the constant flow of news, either in the form of facts and figures or statements made by others. When the news is close to expectations there is little effect on prices, and expectations adjust gradually. Large differences result in more violent reactions to prices and expectations.

Ultimately, the reality of the situation will dominate the final outcome, but in the short term it is quite possible for the same news to result in the market going up one time, but down on another occasion. There is a learning process, and expectations will gradually adjust to a persistent trend in the news despite the original biases. The same place may be reached in the end, but via alternative routes. There is always some prejudice to contend with, and it is necessary to keep this under control, retaining as open a mind as possible. If you have a tendency towards optimism or pessimism, it is well to recognize it and take that into account when it comes to making decisions. Joseph de la Vega (1688) had something to say on this subject of human emotion as well:

> The bulls are like the giraffe which is scared of nothing, or like the magician of the Elector of Cologne, who in his mirror made the ladies appear more beautiful than they were in reality . . . the bears, on the contrary, are completely ruled by fear, trepidation, and nervousness. Rabbits become elephants, brawls in a tavern become rebellions, faint shadows appear to them as signs of chaos.

Information is available to help form opinions about the future, and investors should try to make maximum use of this. Frequently, strong views are expressed on the basis of extremely limited information, often a single piece of news. If the news is important enough, this may be justified, but that is not always the case. This reaction seems particularly noticeable when it concerns macroeconomic events. One month's figures on inflation or the balance of payments can easily be interpreted as the start of a new trend.

Not only should investors use as much of the available information as possible, they should also try to approach the same problem from as many different directions as possible. Technicians who claim that 'the market tells everything and that is all one needs to know', are deliberately weighing the odds against themselves. The same can be said for the fundamentalists who, as a matter of principle, will never look at a chart.

The future does not stand still and wait for the present to catch up; it is constantly changing. Imagine a one million piece jigsaw puzzle of a picture of smoke. Each item of news, each price change, is a piece in the jigsaw; each piece of information improves understanding. Sometimes more of the picture will be visible, and sometimes very little. The task is complicated by the fact that the picture keeps changing. Just when it seems that some recognizable image has been achieved, the smoke swirls and it is time to start on the whole process over again.

Clearly, if sense is to be made out of the mass of information that is churned out each day, it is necessary to have some systematic way of interpreting it. Moreover, any old system will not do. There is only any benefit if the interpretation is correct, and yet it is easy to misinterpret the past and so build up the wrong picture. Here we come to the advantages of the sorts of indicators presented in Chapter 11. These function as totally neutral receptors. There is always room for interpretation, since no forecast of the future will ever be perfect. However, this is a way to obtain a consistent interpretation of what has happened, and thereby produce forecasts of future changes in market prices.

## Rational or adaptive expectations

Quite clearly people try to anticipate events and economic trends, and on balance most markets discount information very efficiently. Inflation is passed through to interest rates and the prices of precious metals, and interest rates certainly have an effect on stock prices. These sorts of relationships are understood to some extent from looking at what has happened in the past. As that reaction becomes accepted so the expectations become reflected in market prices. In order for investors to make money from current developments it is necessary to anticipate these reactions by moving further back along the chain to form expectations about inflation and interest rates.

The task of anticipating the future is made more difficult for the individual because market prices will react before there are any clear signs of what is happening, and before most people are aware of any change. No one needs to *know* that inflation is about to pick up for interest rates to start rising in advance, that is the beauty of how the theory of group behavior works. All that has to happen is that there is an increase in uncertainty about inflation. At any time, there will be so many pessimists and so many optimists, and others who are uncertain. Now if some of the optimists become uncertain and reduce demand, that is all that is needed for yields to start rising.

The degree of uncertainty, and speed of reaction, will to a large extent depend on what has happened in the recent past. In the example of inflation, investors underestimated price increases in the 1970s because inflation had not continued to accelerate in the previous decade. As a result, real yields were very low and investors lost out to higher inflation. Experience in the 1980s was quite the opposite. Investors then demanded exceptionally high nominal yields on bonds in order to compensate for the possibility of accelerating inflation, but it never came, and real yields maintained very high levels.

What happened in this example, and most others, is that people learned from their mistakes. There is nothing new or original about that: Oscar Wilde pointed out that, 'Experience is the name everyone gives to their mistakes'. What is more, everyone is trying to correct their mistakes based on this experience, which is another way of saying that they are fighting yesterday's battles and solving yesterday's problems. To quote Keynes (1936):

> The process of revision of short-term expectations is a gradual and continuous one, carried on largely in the light of realized results ... the most recent results usually play a predominant role in determining what these expectations are.

This process works well, eventually, as long as the same trends remain in place—like inflation in the 1970s—but will tend to leave investors facing in the wrong direction if conditions change suddenly. The attempt to be first, to anticipate market trends before they change, means that people become increasingly dependent of forecasts further and further down the economic chain. This means understanding the relationship that exists between different events.

People learn from experience. They learn important lessons, but normally after the event—and that creates opportunities for those who recognize what is going on beforehand. For example, the stock market crash in October 1987 made investors extremely cautious. This meant that stock prices were able to recover only gradually, although a 40 per cent appreciation over two years is not a bad return, particularly when dividends are added to it. What it did mean was that it was virtually impossible for prices to fall. Everyone was so nervous, so shell-shocked, so terrified of a repeat performance, that the worst that could happen was considerably overdiscounted. And when the worst did not happen, there was only one way for prices to go.

The attempt to model the process of expansion and contraction opens up the possibility of changing the relationships themselves. For example, if it is assumed that rapid money growth leads to inflation which will, in turn, result in higher bond yields, then investors will not wait for inflation to increase. Investors will sell bonds as soon as money growth starts to rise, which will continue to a sufficient degree to slow the economy and prevent inflation accelerating. Economists have given the name *rational expectations* to this type of reaction. The point is that what was expected to happen did not happen. Bond yields went up without inflation rising. So now the relationship is between interest rates and money growth. Now it will be necessary to anticipate the growth of money. When carried to extremes this type of reaction can lead to absurd conclusions. Falling bond yields are one possible explanation of faster money growth. As a result, it is necessary to conclude that lower bond yields will mean higher bond yields, and yields never fall unless money growth changes for some other reason.

One problem is that there are always plenty of other reasons. The explanatory model is typically not very good. In 1985 and 1986 narrow money growth in the United States increased rapidly, going to record levels. Bond yields did not go up in response to this dramatic acceleration in money growth, but then neither did inflation. Market participants, it turned out, were smarter than the models in this case.

Clearly, there is an important element of truth to rational expectations. Markets will reflect expectations of what is going to happen, thereby anticipating events, and seeming to reverse causality. The classic example is the behavior of stock prices. Also, as illustrated by the quotes above, this element of human behavior is not new. To the extent that it is possible to develop an accurate model of market behavior, and this becomes widely known, the conclusions will be incorporated into market prices immediately. However, as already discussed, this will change the pattern of behavior. For example, if falling stock prices are interpreted as implying an impending recession, interest rates will fall, and this may well be sufficient to stimulate demand sufficiently to prevent the recession that would have taken place otherwise. If this happens enough times, people will stop thinking that falling stock prices mean recession, interest rates will not come down and a recession will occur.

There is a catch-22 at work. If there is a well defined, proven and known model of the world, this would clearly influence behavior. However, the reactions would invalidate the assumptions of the model and change it, so that there would no longer be a well defined and proven model. The conclusion is the same for a technical model of market behavior as for an economic model. The more we know the less we know. But this only applies in the aggregate. There is great advantage in knowing something that the majority do not know, and little advantage in knowing what everyone else knows. For this reason, the indicators presented here will require some work to fully understand. The answers are provided, but not with paint-by-numbers simplicity. Everyone can benefit by understanding the cyclical interrelationships better, but no one will benefit if everyone employs exactly the same forecasting model.

## Majority at the margin

In order to take advantage of the business cycle it is necessary to understand what happens to supply and demand over the cycle, and particularly around major turning points. At turning points, prices rise or fall because of the actions of a few, not the majority. The majority are by then committed, and are waiting for their optimistic or pessimistic expectations to be realized. The key to successful investing is to buy when the majority are buying, or, ideally, a little before, but not when the majority has already bought. Bullish sentiment will be greatest at the latter point, and that is the time to take contrary positions.

In any broad market there will always be both buyers and sellers. When prices are unchanged it does not mean there is no activity, only that there is an even match between buyers and sellers. Every day, new buyers and sellers will turn up, each with their own motives. Some will have strong conviction about where prices are headed, but others may have no idea and no interest. This latter group may be simply raising liquidity for some other purpose, e.g. to buy a house or selling an inheritance. The price determined will be the result of an equilibrium between supply and demand.

Markets are anything but static. A market equilibrium is not like a block of wood, but more like a jar of flies. The flies may not end up going anywhere, but there will be a lot of buzzing and frantic activity. There is a flow of money and securities etc., which is based on other expectations than simply where the market might be headed. Companies go bankrupt, estates are split up and sold, new savings flow into the institutions, people need money to meet unforeseen circumstances, and so on. Transactions motivated by such disparate motives will provide a minimum level of activity at turning points—the action against which to get a reaction—the Hegelian law of market reversals. The new flows into the market will very often accentuate the effects of marginal decisions. Some days will see more selling and on others there will be more buying, for no special reason at all.

The relative strength of emotions can only be detected from a longer-term trend. Even on days when there are violent price movements there will still have to be someone on the other side of the transactions.

As prices fall, some people will increase their demand, but others will reduce theirs if it creates the expectation of still lower prices. Equally, selling pressure will change; some people will become more reluctant to sell, while others will be more willing. The fact that any decline, or increase, in prices is limited is evidence that, despite the scepticism often expressed, price changes do, in fact, produce an equilibrium. The more unbalanced the forces, and the more expectations feed on what is happening, the greater the price change will have to be. But eventually prices will change sufficiently to match supply with demand, and thereby stabilize the market.

An upturn in markets generally occurs not because demand has picked up, although that is what everyone looks for but cannot find. The pickup in demand comes later. At turning points, uncertainty is typically still the main emotion but the selling, or buying, dries up. The first thing that happens when prices turn higher is that there is very little selling, as those who want to sell finally exhaust their holdings, leaving a rough equilibrium between supply and demand. From a situation in which buyers and sellers are evenly matched, a reduction in selling will be enough to send prices higher, often quickly.

Expectations on average will have improved, not because anyone has become more positive, but only because some are now less negative. The improvement in prices will then affect the expectations of others, bringing them into the market. There are certainly ways in which expectations feed on the market itself, in addition to the well-recognized route of technical analysis. The formation of expectations is very largely extrapolative—that is, they build on recent history. Market prices themselves will be part of that process, but there are many other expectations that play an even greater role, and these include expectations about interest rates, inflation, corporate profits, the economy, the balance of payments, etc.

There are a great many theories about what determines stock prices, bond prices, the price of gold, exchange rates and whatever else, but the popularity of trend-following techniques bears witness to the failure of any to prove convincing. No one individual has so far been able to supply a conclusive answer, but still the collective wisdom, or ignorance, of the market does get it right. As already pointed out, it is not necessarily or usually the case that buying picks up in the initial phase but, rather, selling declines. The starting point is, therefore, to identify the forces behind these changes in behavior in order to create indicators that will actually forecast turning points.

At the bottom of the business cycle, optimism is a scarce commodity, and at the top, optimism is boundless and pessimism has all but disappeared.

What happens when prices turn up is not an increase in optimism but a reduction in pessimism, in a sea of uncertainty. Confidence in the future remains low, but the change, small as it is, can have a significant impact on market prices. As the economy and the markets start to hold up, signaling that they just might not fall apart, so others will become more confident. To be told that everyone is bearish is not necessarily bearish. At some point, all those bearish people will have sold out their positions. Once they are out of the market they may remain bearish and be surprised to see prices going up. Here is the basis for a contrarian approach to investing.

## Contrary opinions

From what has been said so far it should be clear that the greatest profit, and least risk, is obtained by anticipating what the majority will eventually do, but currently do not; that is, by taking a contrary opinion. Waiting for the majority to act means having your decisions made for you. There may be a greater feeling of confidence at such times, but it is misleading. Risks are much higher under these circumstances.

The contrarian approach has a lot of emotional appeal, but it is not always clear how it is supposed to work. Taking the opposite tack to everyone else just for the sake of it must inevitably lead to disaster. To sell just because prices are rising hardly amounts to a coherent approach. Clearly, in order to make money in the markets it is necessary to buy in anticipation of prices rising and sell before they start falling. That means that the time to buy is when there are still more people waiting to buy than to sell, and to sell when there are still more potential sellers than buyers.

At the bottom, there will be many more pessimists than optimists, but the great majority of these will have already done their selling. What counts is change at the margin, the change in *effective* buying and selling. A comparison might be made with a rate of change that is hugely negative which then becomes slightly less negative. The sign has not changed, but the direction has. Like that rate of change, the measure of confidence improves as pessimism or fear is reduced, even though it may only be less negative, rather than increasingly positive. To repeat the central point, it is not the *level* of confidence that is important to the direction of market prices, but the *change at the margin*.

Once an individual has changed his or her mind and acted on it, this ceases to have any influence except to the extent that the action itself may encourage or discourage someone else. To take an extreme example, once everyone is bearish, the only place left for prices to go is up. But then that is too extreme, since it should be clear that if everyone is bearish there can be no buyers and prices must be zero. The principle is clear enough, however—*the more potential sellers who have sold, the less there will be to sell in the future.* It also implies that a number of speculators will be short the market and will have to cover in the face of any sustained rally.

What we have, therefore, is a mass of uncertainty with generally small changes in conviction at the margin. Boundless optimism or extreme despair are not likely to result in substantial price changes; by that time, the price will have already adjusted. It is the change in sentiment, expectations, leading up to these extremes that has the most influence on the market. In truth, uncertainty is a much more positive emotion to support rising prices than high optimism, as has been proved in markets over and over again. This makes sense of the apparently contradictory saying that in a bull market 'stock prices climb a wall of worry'. That is not the exception but the general rule. Once the conditions that underlie the price increase become obvious it is too late to expect very much—by that time the vast majority of decisions to buy will have already been made.

Widespread uncertainty enables large price movements as the result of the actions of only a small group of investors. In a bear market the vast majority will sit on their securities, but the lack of buyers enables a small group of concerned individuals to push prices down a long way. The action can just as easily work in reverse in a bull market. The real decisions are made at the margin, but the majority prefer company. It often seems that investing is a herd activity; people like company when they are buying or selling. Maybe this provides psychological reinforcement that their decision is right. That impression is certainly reinforced by the increased use of trend-following techniques.

When prices are rising, there will certainly be more buying than selling, that follows by definition. In a sense, this is the action of the majority, but it is only the majority of those who are active in the market; it is not the majority of all potential investors. The majority opinion will seem to be bearish at the bottom and bullish at the top, and that will truly be the majority opinion. At the point where the majority of the potential sellers have sold, the atmosphere will be extremely bearish. They would not have sold without the expectation of further falls in the future. The same relationship applies, except in reverse, at the tops of market moves.

The majority, in this sense, is the cumulative total, when most people have sold or bought—not at a point in time but over a period of time. That is when it pays to adopt a contrary opinion. There is still a problem with deciding how high the majority has to be. There are many times when prices rise even though the general view is bullish, which opens up the question of when enough is enough. There is no doubt that gold was extremely overvalued during 1979, but that did not stop the price rising. And the higher the price went, the more people became convinced that it would continue going up. What was happening, although it was not visible at the time, was that more and more potential buyers became actual buyers. As a result, the number of people who had bought became large, and the potential buyers that remained became fewer and fewer in number. In addition, more than a few of the buyers were not true believers, but were short-term speculators taking advantage of the emotional state of the market to make a turn by selling on at a higher price. It would not take much of a price fall to flush out these non-believers.

On a fundamental view, enough was enough well before the peak was reached, but the price continued to rise. Some people probably made a killing in that final surge, when all the gold experts were forecasting astronomical prices just around the corner, but more got killed. The answer has to be that investors should keep an open mind. Keep with the majority as long as that view is justified, but remain sceptical. To object to an opinion just because it is popular is hardly logical, but it is also important to question the accepted wisdom, consider the assumptions, focus on the conclusions and look for the flaws in the argument. To simply follow the majority will lead into all sorts of traps and one-way streets. That is why technical rules, which anyone can understand, are particularly dangerous. If something is simple enough for everyone to understand, then you can be sure that enough people do understand it so that it loses any predictive value it may once have had.

# 10

## THE ARTFUL SCIENCE OF
## TECHNICAL ANALYSIS
### (drawing conclusions)

Technical analysis has become increasingly popular over recent years as an approach to forecasting market behavior. The technical approach, known as chartism in the United Kingdom, is presented by its proponents as distinct from, and superior to, fundamental analysis. It is also true that there are a great many technical systems that are as different from each other as from a fundamental approach. Moreover, it will no doubt come as a surprise to discover that a lot of modern technical analysis is really a form of market economics.

Justification for attempting to gain some insight into future price movements by looking at what prices have done and are doing is provided by the effect of uncertainty on price behavior. Earlier in the book, there was discussion of the fact that prices can quite easily, and usually, change direction not because of a strong conviction on the part of buyers and sellers, but because of an increase in uncertainty. Prices could, for example, rise significantly without there being any strong support for such a move. The explanation need not be that the number of buyers has increased, only that the number of sellers has decreased. Watching actual price movements provides a possible solution to the absence of any obvious warning signals. Another possibility is to look for fundamental clues to changes in behavior, even though they are not obvious. That is the subject matter of the rest of this book, and also happens to be what many technical analysts are doing as well.

Technical analysis is based on the assumption that past patterns will repeat in the future. For example, if a certain type of price behavior was followed by a strong up-move or down-move, then a similar pattern of price movement is assumed to be followed by the same type of price action. One distinguishing characteristic that has helped to popularize this approach is that the techniques, at least in terms of trend lines and price action, can be applied to any market. The same patterns are looked for, and found, in all markets. Many different measures of market action have been calculated in addition to price movements which are specific to particular markets, and further complicate the analysis. Charts show past trends, and it is nearly always possible to identify interesting price patterns. The obviousness is deceiving. All things are obvious in retrospect, this is just a pictorial representation of that fact. The key in every case has got to be the prior forecast, not the retrospective—that is always right.

The name *technical analysis* carries the connotation of something of a mechanical nature. It is easy to picture a *technician* hunched over some laboratory apparatus, making the precise calculations that will unlock the secrets of the future. This is also the image that some practitioners try to encourage. Others recognize the reality of their endeavors by emphasizing that interpreting the charts is an art rather than a science. Charts can be helpful, but generally not in the obvious ways. Simple rules are exactly that. There is little profit in doing the obvious, and following the majority.

## Price patterns

The most basic form of technical analysis involves the identification of patterns in price movements. There is much discussion of tops and bottoms, heads and shoulders, wedges, gaps, etc. One will, therefore, find mention of 'an attractive head and shoulders', or 'a good-looking bottom'. These patterns imply that prices will follow a particular course in the days, weeks or months ahead.

A head-and-shoulders pattern is represented by three rallies above a neckline, and subsequent fall back to the neckline, with the second rally going the furthest; an example is shown in Figs 10.1 and 10.2. These demonstrate some of the more common price patterns that are referred to by technical analysts, and are accompanied by a brief commentary. No attempt has been made to provide an exhaustive list. Time is given in units, representing numbers of days. These are actual series rather than special lines drawn just to illustrate a type of pattern. Further details on the series are provided at the end.

Behind the chart patterns shown in Figs 10.1 and 10.2, there is a psychological explanation of what is happening. In the case of a head and shoulders, a typical explanation would be that there was some investor enthusiasm, which then died down leaving the stock virtually unchanged. Next there was a second bout of enthusiasm which carried the price to a new high, but this also died away leaving no real gain at the end. This in itself would have to be taken as a bad sign, and there will be times when the price breaks down from this point. In that case, it may be necessary to rely on a trend-line violation to provide the explanation. The final shoulder is formed when the next rally carries the price up from what has become the neck-

**A**

The chart demonstrates a good example of how many changes in direction develop. The price moves into a step decline, trapped within the down-trending tramlines and remaining below its moving average. Then the price breaks out of the tramlines on the upside, but the price trend remains down but at a more gradual pace. This *consolidation* sets up the base for the major break out on the upside, when the price breaks conclusively above the moving average.

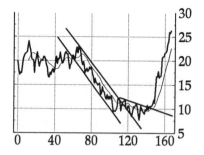

**B**

Here the price follows a slight downtrend, with movement remaining within a fairly narrow band. The price holds on the lower trend-line and then breaks out on the upside, holding above the moving average and establishing a new uptrend. When this uptrend is broken the price moves down sharply before establishing a new base. It is clearly important to emphasize *conclusive* breaks in trend, since there are many minor fluctuations that need to be ignored.

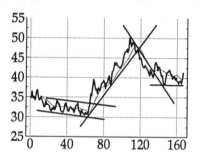

**C**

Very often a downtrend will accelerate on the downside before finally hitting bottom and turning around. That pattern can be seen clearly in this chart. The price trends down, tries to stabilize, and then drops even more sharply. Once this steep downtrend is broken the price rebounds strongly. This is typically explained in terms of a sudden loss of confidence that forces the final weak holders to sell, thereby setting the scene for a dramatic recovery.

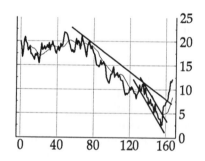

**D**

The price starts off moving sideways, but with a slight uptrend. The pattern is very positive, suggesting underlying strength that is eventually realized when the price breaks out from a rising wedge. The rise starts strong and then starts to slow and roll over. That sort of loss of *momentum* is typical of many price moves. As in this case, the price moves into a holding pattern that may be a base for further increases, *consolidation*, or a top preceding a fall, *distribution*.

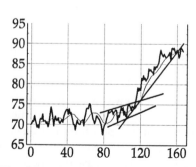

**Breaking Trends**

**Figure 10.1** Technical indicators: breaking trends

**E**

The early price action is extremely negative, at least in retrospect. The price clearly runs into *resistance* when it tries to go up. A wedge is formed by the pattern of rising lows, which could be positive if the price could break out on the upside. In the event the price breaks down. Having fallen below 34, the price starts to build a base, which, in this case, takes the form of an inverse *head-and-shoulders* bottom, with the *neckline* at around 38.

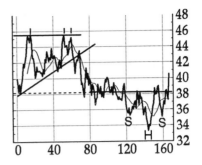

**F**

The price is in a steady downtrend that eventually finds support. Here again the base takes the form of an inverse head-and-shoulders pattern. In the process, the downtrend is broken, and the moving average starts to turn up. The conclusive evidence of a change in direction is, however, provided by the head and shoulders. Other attempts to stabilize on the way down, and find a base, had not been able to set up such a convincing pattern.

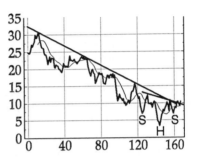

**G**

In this case the price falls in two stages, trying to stabilize around 10, but then falling down to try again. The second attempt looks a lot more successful, succeeding in breaking the downtrend, and making a clear *double bottom*. In the process, the price does something that is very typical, by rallying back to the old low and re-bounding off resistance at that point. Having established resistance and *support* at the lower level, it now becomes important which way the price breaks out.

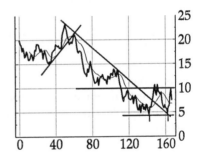

**H**

The *double top* at 58 is a clear warning that the uptrend is running out of steam. When the price breaks the uptrend it then also falls below the last higher low, therefore breaking the positive sequence that had existed up until then. This point then becomes an important resistance level when the prices tries to rally back later on. Again, this is a very typical type of price action.

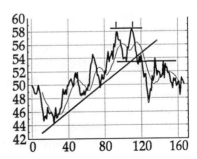

**Top & Bottoms**

**Figure 10.2** Technical indicators: tops and bottoms

line, but fails to reach the old highs before falling back to where it started from.

Now the head-and-shoulders pattern has been completed and the technical reading is that the price will now fall. Even the extent of the decline can be forecast from the chart; the fall from the neckline should equal the height of the head above the neckline. That is unless the price goes up. If the head-and-shoulders pattern fails, i.e. the price does not fall, then the price is expected to rise, possibly strongly. An alternative possibility always exists. There are certainly examples of the completion of perfect head-and-shoulder-patterns, and very impressive they look. However, they are also quite rare. There are many, many more occasions when it looks as if a head-and-shoulders pattern is developing, but then it does not. Still, observing such a pattern develop can be quite helpful in timing decisions, particularly when interpreted in the light of forecasts from alternative sources.

Accumulation or consolidation, after a strong up-move, describes what happens when investors build up positions, or distribution, as investors in the know get out of the asset in question. These represent sideways price movement. The difference is that a consolidation is followed by an up-move and a distribution by a down-move. A sceptic might ask, who are the people who know whether to accumulate or distribute? Clearly, they are not using any trend-following systems, since those will not be triggered until the price has broken down or up. Such break-outs are supposed to be followed by a strong move one way or the other, but false break-outs are also possible. A false signal is then usually followed by a sharp move in the other direction.

The best-known technical tools are moving average cross-overs, and trend-line violations. These can involve the cross-over of the actual price and some moving average of the price, or trend line, or the cross-over of two or more different moving averages. In Japan the cross-over of the 5 day and the 25 day moving averages is known as a *golden cross*. Adding to the variety, and complexity, of possibilities is the use of exponentially weighted moving averages, i.e. a moving average that gives a greater weight to the latest price and less weight to prices further away in time. And a wide variety of weights are possible. A number of examples of trend-line violations are included in Figs 10.1 and 10.2.

In addition to signals being given by the price crossing over the moving average, it is also possible to interpret wide divergences between the price and moving average as indicating the possible limit of a move, that the price has perhaps moved too far, too quickly, and that prices are about to reverse direction. This is similar to an extreme rate of change in the price, as shown below.

Moving average cross-overs received a lot of attention in the 1970s and early 1980s, when these techniques were used to show how investors could have benefited from the huge price moves in precious metals and commodities, and then the dollar from 1982 to 1985. Fundamental analysis failed to provide adequate explanations at the time, and most forecasters missed the moves. That, however, was not necessary, since the massive inflation followed huge monetary and budgetary excess and, therefore, should have been forecastable. The point was that most forecasters were not looking at these developments until it was too late, and this left the door open for the technicians to walk through—an opportunity that was not missed.

It goes without saying that trend-following techniques will work well when prices follow pronounced trends. Signals will come late, but the argument can be justified that the first 10 per cent to 20 per cent of the move and the last 10 per cent to 20 per cent can easily be given up if it means capturing the main 60 per cent to 80 per cent. It can be justified, that is, as long as prices are moving in a strong trend. Being late will, however, prove disastrous if there is no main trend and prices are simply moving up and down across a relatively flat moving average. This can result in frequent whipsaws and a series of serious losses.

## Complicating the picture

In order to try to filter out the false signals, technicians have tried to refine the analysis by taking other influences into account. The simplest of these, which keeps attention focused on prices, is the rate of change of prices, usually called momentum. The rate of change is seldom used on its own, but normally in conjunction with a moving average rule. Persistent trends will show up in the rate of change, and it will be very similar to a moving average cross-over. However, there will be slight differences, so this gives a second filter to interpret the trend. This is not a different approach or a new angle, only another way of looking at the same information. It adds breadth but not depth. Figure 10.3 shows a price series with its moving average, the same series as example H in Fig. 10.2 and shows the rate of change underneath, together with the deviation of the price from its moving average.

The rate of change should change direction ahead of the price series itself. For the quantitatively inclined, the rate of change will change direction at an inflexion point, i.e. at the point at which the rate of ascent or descent slows down, while continuing in the same direction. If the movement of prices can be compared with a speeding car, then the car has to slow down before it can change direction. The rate of change of the speed will reverse direction before the car changes direction. This relationship will prove very helpful as long as the price follows a smooth path and does not suddenly

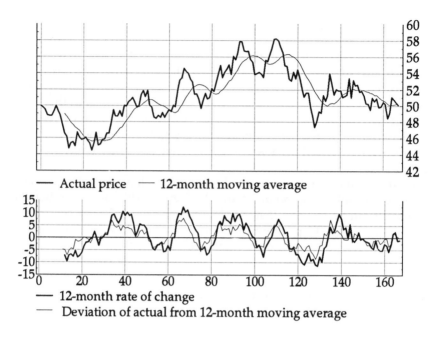

**Figure 10.3** Momentum and moving average

reverse; or as long as it does not slow down and then speed up again without changing direction.

There are some very sophisticated trend-following techniques available,
called time series analysis, or ARIMA (integrated auto-regressive moving-
average process) models. These are computer-based programs that analyse
the price series to identify any trend in the data. The idea is to fit a statistical
relationship to the series that results in only random errors between the
fitted and actual series—what is called white noise. This is really nothing
more than a highly complex filtering system used by a number of large
institutions to trade the markets. These models are designed to operate at
the trading end of the market. Each small price change is fed into the
computers to produce an instant conclusion.

It is traders that make greatest use of technical analysis. It does seem
possible to look at the way prices move during the day and get a feel for
the emotion that lies below the surface. Prices will test resistance and support
levels, break through, charge ahead or pull back, and very often there does
seem to be a technical basis for the move. At that level, over the very short
term, there is little else to work with. The markets will react to breaking
news, and the movement will be tested within technically set parameters.

However, practically all traders now employ a technical system of some sort, which can mean that the more obvious signals become misleading.

A trending market will inevitably give off the correct signal, but this will become disguised if too many people are watching the same thing. Either the price will have to move extremely fast, so that the risk of a reversal is established almost immediately, thereby limiting the number who are prepared to jump on board; or volatility will be increased dramatically, so that it becomes possible to get the trend right but still lose money. As a result, traders end up having to out-guess each other in anticipating which way prices will move.

Wide use is made of trend lines, moving-average cross-overs and new highs and lows to establish stop-loss orders or trigger buy or sell orders. There are fairly well-established rules, particularly for stop limits, related to these sort of price movements. The trouble is that these are widely known, so that some of the large trading houses will deliberately *run the stops* as a way of forcing an extreme price movement, up or down, of which they will then be able to take advantage. This type of behavior introduces a feedback mechanism which changes the technical signals that could be expected, and requires a reinterpretation of the charts. One person looking at a particular chart in a particular way may make money from it, but if a large number of people base their decisions on it, they are more likely to lose money. Their group action opens the door for a contrarian view.

Pring (1991) makes the point that technical analysis is an *art* rather than a science. Everyone may end up looking at the same charts, but the interpretations can be very different. Past trends are always obvious with the benefit of a retrospective perspective but the key, and the skill, is in identifying these at an early stage, while at the same time filtering out the false signals. To do this most analysts make use of a wide range of additional indicators typically categorized as technical, but really economic in nature. Trees grow the way they do, and presumably do not think about it. But investors are not robots; there is a feedback mechanism that adjusts behavior.

## Supply and demand

For a long time, other aspects of the market have been added to the technical armory; such as advance/decline lines, on-balance volume, etc. More recent additions are measures of market sentiment, including the ratio of bullishness to bearishness of traders, evidence of insider trading, etc. The wider use of these indicators is taking practitioners away from chartism, as narrowly defined. There has also been the development of highly sophisticated mathematical modelling techniques, which are more closely associated with rocket scientists than with chart lines. These approaches attempt to filter out as much information as possible from a time series, e.g. stock prices, measured over a period of time. That is what a technician or chartist tries to do, in a much simpler way, by looking at different moving averages, momentum and trend lines.

In the pure sense of only looking at market prices, technical analysis is quite different from a fundamental approach, which is not to say that both may not come to the same conclusion. As other pieces are added to the technical picture, so the approach becomes a part of market economics, although the practitioners would generally disclaim such glory—and in fact deny it vehemently as, I am sure, would most economists. But think what market economics is about. First, it is about behavior—how people react to a given set of stimuli. Measuring sentiment is a way of trying to understand the behavior. Second, adjustment to any disequilibrium invariably takes time. One of the classic technicians of the past was W. D. Gann, who always saw adjustment in terms of both price and time; see, for example, Gann (1942).

Third, one of the most basic charts in first-year economics is that show- ing the relationship between price and quantity, or volume, determined by the intersection of supply and demand. By studying advance/declines and volume traded etc., technicians are including a measure of quantity along with price, in order to help understand what is going on. That really only applies in the case of stocks. There is some attempt to try to use volume in the futures market, but that is only a fraction of the whole market for bonds or currencies, for example. Whether a market is rising or falling on high or low volume is generally considered important. Normally, analysts like to see high volume as prices rise and low volume as prices fall, but other interpretations can be found.

The advance/decline (A/D) line of the stock market is a popular indicator. This simply takes the number of advances less the number of declines and adds this to the total already reached. The cumulative series that results measures the breadth of the market. If the Dow is moving higher but the A/D line is falling, that is supposed to tell you that the overall market is not very healthy. What it may only be saying is that high capitalization, blue chips are doing better than smaller companies. That may, or may not, be ominous. There are likely to be times, and there have been, when small, low caps have done better than the Dow, and times when the reverse was true. Whether that was good or bad depended entirely on which group of stocks you owned. To be meaningful, the A/D line should be viewed rela- tive to the whole index, in this case, the NYSE. In that case, like is being compared with like. Comparing the Dow with the advance/decline of the NYSE is close to meaningless, and yet that is often done.

Granville (1976) developed a novel indicator based on this approach. The indicator, known as on-balance volume, adds or subtracts the net volume of the day depending on whether the market is up or down. The intention is to measure investor sentiment by combining the movements of price and volume. That is not a new idea but has strong foundations in basic economic theory. Joseph Granville would no doubt protest violently at being called an economist, as someone taking a fundamentalist approach, but he is carrying out a very basic form of economic analysis: trying to identify shifts in supply and demand. What he succeeded in doing was taking price and volume, two main dimensions of any market, and relating these to time, the third key dimension.

Market economics is about behavior, about how individuals, acting in a group, make choices subject to the constraint of their budget. The subject matter, therefore, encompasses anything that might move either the demand or supply curve. Economists have long realized that it will never be possible to identify all the possible influences. A major complication in the attempt to identify at least some influences is the difficulty in knowing whether any given change in price and quantity is due to a shift in supply or demand. Like economists, that is what many, if not most, technical analysts are trying to do.

A market price will rise because either there are less sellers, i.e. the supply curve has shifted in, or because there is greater demand. Just knowing that a price has changed does not tell you very much. That is a common problem faced by economists, market analysts, investors and anyone interested in price movements in any market. One way to try to identify what is actually going on is to look at what happens to volume or quantity. An expansion of volume when a price increases should be associated with an increase in demand, and a reduction should mean that supply has fallen. When seen in this light, Joe Granville created an interesting economic indicator.

Most of the technical indicators can be interpreted in the same way—as attempts to measure the underlying supply-and-demand relationship. The sorts of things that are looked at are the behavior of the market in the last hour of trading; new highs versus new lows; margin requirements; margin debt; short interest; insider buying and selling; odd-lot buying and selling; large block trading; trading sentiment indicators; the tick; the trin and quite a few others. Some of these are already more economic than technical, e.g. margin requirements, but even the technical indicators are measures of sentiment or expectations and are, therefore, examples of the same influences that interest economists.

## Attitudes and expectations

Many technical analysts place emphasis on the human emotion that results in buying and selling decisions. The change in attitudes and expectations in response to events in the real world produces price patterns that, hopefully, repeat and can be used to forecast future movements. The future will follow the past in a predictable way only if the behavior *and* the events follow the same path as before.

The emphasis on the psychological aspects of price movements is often used to distinguish technical analysis from other forms of decision-making tools, in particular fundamental analysis. However, that distinction is totally without justification. The idea that behavior is rational and consistent is absolutely basic to economic analysis. Without that, it would be impossible to explain market behavior at all; all forms of planning would be impossible and anarchy would rule. Explaining and understanding is not the same thing as being able to forecast the future. It would seem that technical analysts, at least to some extent, are using basic economic relationships to try and forecast market prices. In many ways, what they are doing is not very different from what economists, or market analysts, do. They look for developing trends to follow and try to identify turning points.

Sometimes the argument is made that market prices exist in a vacuum, independent of economic forces, and are only influenced by investor psychology. Suddenly we are back in the real world. Investor intentions are not formed in abstract, but are determined by what is going on in the economy. Investors take account of inflation, growth, job prospects, etc. in deciding whether to buy or sell. With their consumer caps on, these same people will make other buying and selling decisions that will provide the justification for movements in asset prices.

Financial, and other asset, markets are an integral part of the overall economy. There is no magical separation that allows asset prices to follow a life of their own. If that seems to be happening then it is only because there are limits to what is known, and there is a gap in that knowledge. This is where technical analysis can prove helpful. For example, the price of a particular stock may start rising for no obvious reason. Later it will become clear that orders were piling in and that earnings were likely to expand rapidly. The majority would not know this, but could observe strong *relative* action in the price of the stock, reflecting the actions of better informed investors. Such timely information can make technical analysis a useful investment tool, but it is no reason to throw out everything else you may know about that stock or economic conditions generally when it comes to making a decision. After all, those early investors, the ones who created the bullish technical pattern in the first place, they were basing their actions on fundamentals. It is just that they were probably closer to the situation and were better informed. They could, also, turn out to be wrong. Strong trends sometimes break down violently when the underlying assumptions are suddenly shown to be false. In that case, trend followers will find that they have been led into a trap.

A potentially interesting approach would be to apply technical analysis to those parts of the price movement that cannot be explained by what is known about the market. For example, in a situation in which inflation is trending higher, it should not be too surprising to see bond yields also moving up. Or, in the case of the exchange rate, to see a decline at a time when relative interest rates are low and inflation is high. What would be interesting is the price movement that is left over after taking out these known influences. The strength of technical analysis should be in filling the gaps in what is known, but it does not mean investors should ignore relevant information.

The example in Fig. 10.4 is intended only as an illustration of the type of approach that could be used, it is not intended to be a complete analysis. What it shows is the difference between the Deutschemark/sterling exchange rate and an index of purchasing power parity. Figure 10.5 shows the exchange rate on its own. It does seem that the deviation chart could have been helpful in identifying periods of relative strength for sterling. A more complete analysis might take the influence of relative interest rates out as well and consider the residual price movement, the objective being to use technical analysis to explain what the fundamentals do not; i.e. emphasize its relative strength.

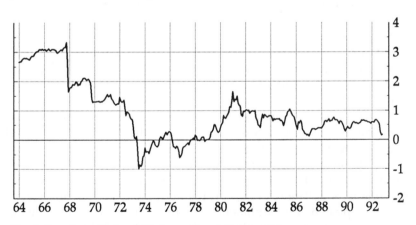

Deviation from Index of International Competitiveness

**Figure 10.4** Deutschemark/sterling exchange rate (deviation from Index of International Competitiveness)

**Figure 10.5** Deutschemark/sterling exchange rate

The sophisticated statistical techniques referred to earlier can be used in this way. One form of ARIMA models will first identify fundamental influences, and then use auto-regressive procedures to extract any trend remaining in the unexplained residuals. This combines a fundamental view with a sophisticated form of technical analysis adapted to take advantage of the power of high-speed computers. This approach will only be helpful to the extent that the model explanation is valid, i.e. the specification is correct, and the trend continues. Most technicians also talk about budget deficits, debt levels, consumer confidence and much more besides, thereby bringing in major economic influences. The suggestion here is simply that these forces be incorporated into the analysis in a more rigorous way.

When trying to make difficult decisions about the future it would be foolish to deliberately ignore information from other sources. Commodity traders who pay no attention to agricultural news or weather reports are likely to get left behind. If you have good information that inflation will accelerate, it would seem foolish to buy bonds no matter how bullish the technical picture. It is necessary to question the inflation forecast but, if that is accepted, then why go against it?

In addition to trying to eliminate certain fundamental influences, there is the need to consider price movements in the right form. For example, over the long term, inflation will distort the movement of stock prices. If stock prices are plotted on an arithmetic scale they will look very different than if they are plotted on a logarithmic scale. Not only will the two series look different, but trend lines and price patterns will show up differently. An even more realistic way to look at stock price trends over time is in real terms, after taking out the effect of inflation. In that case the price trends

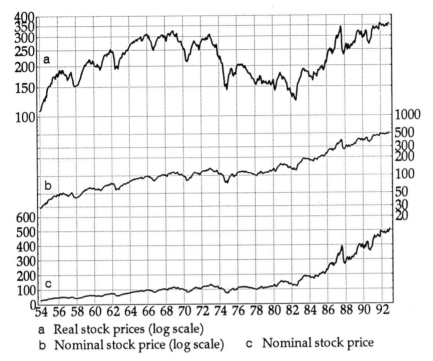

a   Real stock prices (log scale)
b   Nominal stock price (log scale)      c   Nominal stock price

**Figure 10.6** Real and nominal stock prices—S&P 400

are even more different, and provide alternative implications for the future. Figure 10.6 shows nominal stock prices on an arithmetic scale and nominal and real stock prices on a logarithmic scale. Practically all analysis is done on the bottom line, but the more relevant series is that measured in real terms, as argued in earlier chapters; and the implications are quite different. Even the nominal series measured in logarithmic terms implies quite different trend lines.

When making price comparisons it is also essential to compare like with like. This point cannot be over-emphasized, since misleading comparisons are being offered up for consideration all the time. An example would be a direct comparison between the price of gold and the price of bonds, normally shown as one divided by the other. Such a comparison makes no sense, because gold has no yield while bonds offer a significant yield. Changes in the price of gold represent the total return, or loss, on holding that asset, but that is not true for bonds. And the higher the yield the less true it is.

When just looking at bonds alone, a different story will be told depending on whether it is in terms of absolute price or a total return index, as discussed

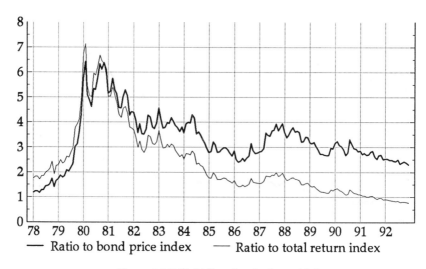

— Ratio to bond price index        — Ratio to total return index

**Figure 10.7** Gold/bond ratio (monthly)

in Chapter 12. It is perfectly possible that price movements on their own
will look bearish but that the yield is high enough to make bonds an attractive
investment. Figure 10.7 shows the price of gold divided by an index of
bond prices and by a total return index. Gold has appeared stronger
overall, and more recently, on the basis of comparisons with an index of
bond prices. Gold looks relatively less attractive when compared to an
index of the total return on bonds. There is certainly a case for making
direct comparisons between different investments, but care should be
taken to do so on a consistent basis.

It is always worth remembering that technical conditions will look
favorable right up until the moment they stop looking good. Sometimes
there is a period of sideways price movement, *distribution*, that sets up a
change in direction. But quite often that sideways movement is just a
pause, *consolidation*, before going still higher. Sometimes there is a broad
top, or bottom, another time a price will break down sharply after just
making a new all-time high; basically, anything goes.

The rules of technical analysis are made to be broken. There are many
different signals and many different interpretations, which is why
technicians are no more unanimous than any other group of forecasters.
Charts provide an invaluable map of the past, but there is real skill in project-
ing that into a future path. The emphasis on mechanical, technical rules has
given the appearance that this is something anyone can use to make
money. This has had the advantage of popularizing the approach, but at
the cost of devaluing the skill involved. Technical analysis is an art. Brilliant

traders, who understood market behavior well enough to profit consistently from price movements, have not been able to pass that knowledge along to others. They have written books and distributed charts, but these all lacked the personal insights which only they possessed.

It follows from what has been said that technical analysis will be most valuable when there is least other information available on which to base a decision. Technical analysis will have its greatest advantage when it comes to short-term trading. Breaking news will affect prices in the short-term, sometimes violently, but there are many more times when there is no real news. Even then, prices will move about, reflecting rumors, emotions and a million and one different influences that seem to have no bearing on the rest of the economy. In that volatile environment, a reading of price movements will make the difference between profit and loss.

Over the longer term, the method in this madness will become clear. Short-term volatility will be seen to be moving in a trend determined by the underlying fundamentals. Inflation will be a dominant influence on bonds, and stock prices will tend to rise the fastest for companies where earnings are growing the fastest. Within these trends there will be major short-term deviations which the trader can ignore only at great cost.

There is another problem when moving away from the very short term, which has to do with the scale of the price movements. Short-term charts develop price patterns over a very narrow price range, often fractions of a dollar, which allows traders to control risk. Similar patterns will be observed in monthly data, but the price scale will be very much wider. Using long-term charts necessarily requires taking much more risk. In the short term, using daily, or even hourly data, a reasonable stop may be $1 or $2 away from the entry price. Once the time-frame has been extended to using monthly data, a price reversal may require a move of $10, or over 10 per cent of the price, and often more; on gold, for example, it has been as high as 20 per cent. Given this added risk, and the fact that there is a lot more information available as time is extended, so chart patterns lose many of the advantages they have in a very short-term trading environment.

## Perfect repetition

Included within technical analysis is a group that assumes mechanical repetitiveness of markets, despite overwhelming evidence to the contrary, and is in sharp contrast to the attempt to explain human psychology from market prices. These are simply rules to follow if your brain stops functioning. A good example of this approach is the so-called *January effect*. This can take various forms: that the stock market will go in the same direction through the year as it did in January, or that the market will follow the direction of prices in the first week of the year. A similar rule has been

proposed for the dollar as well. To the extent that there seems to be a correlation in the case of stocks it is simply because there is a long-term
upward trend; the majority of cases are of rising prices. In some cases the
January change accounts for practically the whole change for the year as
well. Take out that influence and the evidence is inconclusive. In fact, other
months have been shown to have an even closer correlation with the year
outcome, but that knowledge is no help.

Within this category should be included repetitive cycles. One that has
received a lot of attention in recent years has been the 10-year cycle in
stock prices. Would not that be wonderful, just put your money in the market
at the right time, sit back and enjoy the rising prices, then, when the automatic timer switches off, take it all out again before prices drop. Figure 10.8
splits the post-war period into 10-year periods and plots one above the
other. Looking at this chart, I am hard pressed to identify a repeating cycle
that I would want to put money on. There is a tendency for prices to rise
over time, which gives an upward bias to the lines. Partly, that trend is
explained by rising productivity over time, and partly by inflation, at least
over the post-war period. However, it is hard to identify a cyclical pattern
that repeats with any degree of regularity.

Other regular cycles that are often referred to are the five-year and
three-and-a-third year cycles. In the hope that these may reveal the missing
key to unlock the future, they have also been plotted for the whole post-
war period, in Figs 10.9 and 10.10. There may be some hidden meaning in
these charts, but it is pretty well hidden. Automatic, repeating cycles over
these periods of time are not obvious. If they ever had been, it should be
clear that investors would quickly have identified it and reacted in such a
way as to change the cycle.

## Conclusion

Many non-specialists are attracted to the idea of a rigorous system that
excludes human judgement; somehow the results just pop out. This is not
really how technical analysis works, and most practitioners will emphasize
the importance of interpretation. Much economic forecasting, based on
large models, can also be equally mechanical, with the same sorts of
strengths and weaknesses. The same could be true of fundamental analysis
of companies. Most of this is fairly mechanical—here are profits, growth
rates, industry averages, relative performance; punch in the numbers and
out comes an expected price. There are, in fact, a growing number of so-
called *quants* who spend their time doing exactly that. Many fundamental
analysts will look at trends, often in the form of moving averages, in order
to determine the attractiveness of a company. However, in this case, it will
be the trend of earnings or sales that will be the focus of attention rather

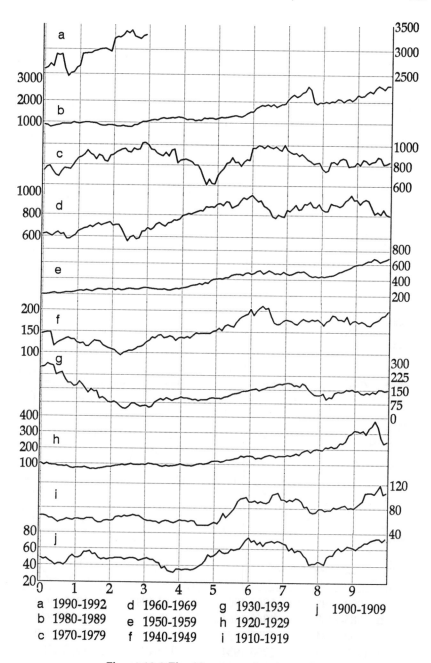

a  1990–1992     d  1960–1969     g  1930–1939     j  1900–1909
b  1980–1989     e  1950–1959     h  1920–1929
c  1970–1979     f  1940–1949     i  1910–1919

**Figure 10.8** The 10-year stock price cycle

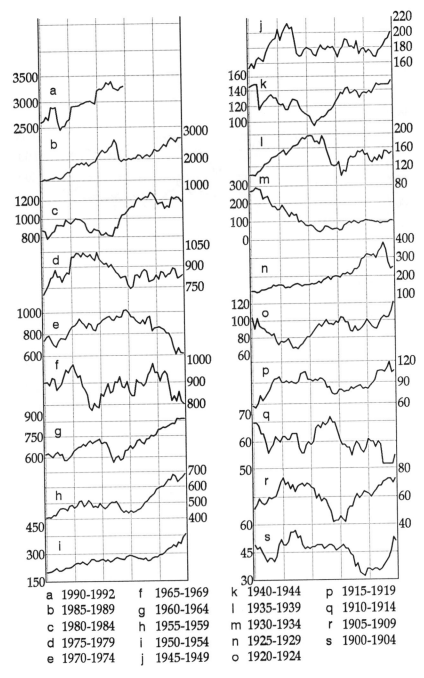

| a | 1990-1992 | f | 1965-1969 | k | 1940-1944 | p | 1915-1919 |
|---|-----------|---|-----------|---|-----------|---|-----------|
| b | 1985-1989 | g | 1960-1964 | l | 1935-1939 | q | 1910-1914 |
| c | 1980-1984 | h | 1955-1959 | m | 1930-1934 | r | 1905-1909 |
| d | 1975-1979 | i | 1950-1954 | n | 1925-1929 | s | 1900-1904 |
| e | 1970-1974 | j | 1945-1949 | o | 1920-1924 |   |           |

**Figure 10.9** The 5-year stock price cycle

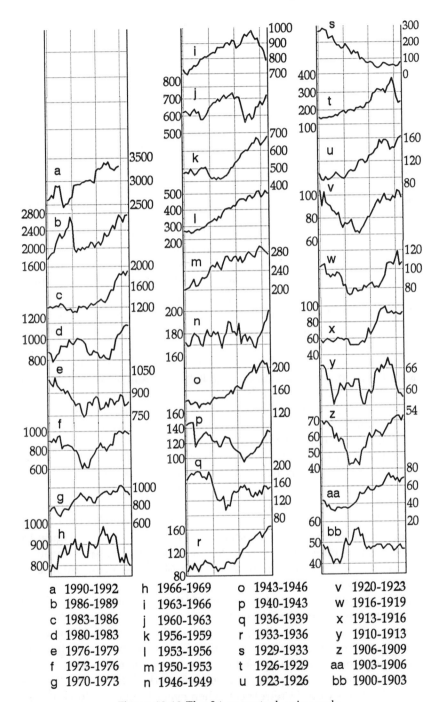

| a | 1990-1992 | h | 1966-1969 | o | 1943-1946 | v | 1920-1923 |
|---|---|---|---|---|---|---|---|
| b | 1986-1989 | i | 1963-1966 | p | 1940-1943 | w | 1916-1919 |
| c | 1983-1986 | j | 1960-1963 | q | 1936-1939 | x | 1913-1916 |
| d | 1980-1983 | k | 1956-1959 | r | 1933-1936 | y | 1910-1913 |
| e | 1976-1979 | l | 1953-1956 | s | 1929-1933 | z | 1906-1909 |
| f | 1973-1976 | m | 1950-1953 | t | 1926-1929 | aa | 1903-1906 |
| g | 1970-1973 | n | 1946-1949 | u | 1923-1926 | bb | 1900-1903 |

**Figure 10.10** The 3+-year stock price cycle

than the final market price. This is rather like technical analysis, but one step back along the decision-making chain.

Technical trading rules are presented in a way that anyone can use them, but this is not actually the case. Looking at a chart of past market action can be helpful. It shows where a stock, or currency, or whatever, has been; its highs and lows; where there was a lot of volatility and when things calmed down again. Breaking trends can be seen on a chart, and this is something that needs to be explained. When no obvious explanation can be found this should set off alarm signals.

Technical analysts are fond of saying that 'the market knows'. Market prices reflect all information in the hands of buyers and sellers and is, therefore, in some sense, correct. It is hard to disagree with that conclusion, but then neither does it represent much of a theory. The next step is to conclude that the market price today tells you something about the market price tomorrow. Interestingly, there is an influential group of fundamental analysts who say exactly the same thing, but come up with the completely opposite conclusion. There is a popular argument, backed by many statistical studies, to the effect that stock prices incorporate all known information and, therefore, follow a random walk. In this view, the market is so efficient that there is no room left for an individual to beat the market on a consistent basis. It might be possible to beat the market a hundred times in a row, in the same way that it is possible to get a head every time on a hundred flips of a coin. It is possible, but it is very unlikely, and is all down to luck. These people argue that the same rule applies, i.e. the price movement on any one day is independent of the price movement the day before.

On the one hand, there are the technicians who say that because the market embodies all known information it is a good predictor of the future, and, on the other hand, the random walkers who say that for the very same reason there is absolutely no predictive value in market prices. Even fundamental analysis is a waste of time according to them, since everyone will know new news at the same time and prices will move instantly to discount it. However, part of that news will be forecasts of what the outcome will be, which seems to make research essential. It does seem logical that all *widely known* information is reflected in the price. That has to mean that there is no predictive value in the price itself, otherwise not all information has been included in the price.

Taking a position somewhere between these extremes, it does seem possible to forecast market prices to some extent, but it is not easy, and there is more to it than adopting easy to follow rules that are widely known, either technical or non-technical. Charts can be very helpful, but they require individual interpretation based on personal experience. The proof is whether the interpretations derived worked, or not, as a forecast. They will always work in retrospect, when everything is obvious. The key is whether they consistently put you on the right side of the market before-hand. Pat formulas do not pass the test. Simple rules are just that—simple.

There are always things happening that only very few people will know, and certainly not the average investor. This information will be reflected in market prices to some extent. In addition, people can be wrong, and those views will also be reflected in market prices. However, there are also things that are known, and it would be wrong to ignore these just because they are *fundamental*. Investors can never be too well informed. Technical analysis can be seen as a way of making up for some of the gaps. In that role it can be very useful, but why throw away what is known in the process? That is too high a price to pay.

Technical analysis requires jumping on board a moving train. This action can potentially be very dangerous, and great caution should be used in timing such jumps. Technicians essentially want to see the train pull out of the station in a given direction, i.e. provide some sort of signal of trend, before committing themselves. There is one element in the technical approach that always seems to say that someone else knows better than you do. See where the basic trend is going, i.e. see what the majority are doing and then follow on. Sentiment indicators adopt a similar approach. One favorite is to find out what the insiders are doing and copy them, since they must know something the rest of us do not. Sometimes this works and sometimes it does not. A good example of it failing badly was in the case of the Bank of New England. In 1989, 10 insiders bought stock at prices between $14.13 and $23.73. Anyone who jumped on board that train could then have ridden it all the way down to nowhere.

There is definitely danger in letting others make decisions for you. There are no simple rules that provide easy profits on a consistent basis. A technical approach, properly applied will be hard work. Simple trend-following techniques are exactly that. If they are very easy to understand and create they may well be used as a substitute for thought, turning investors into sheep. And sheep get savaged by both bulls and bears.

To invest without looking at charts is like driving somewhere you have never been before without a map. You may get there, but it will depend on a lot of luck. Equally, to look only at charts is like driving with your eyes fixed on the map while never even glancing at the road, which is hardly very sensible. To ignore the fundamentals altogether can be hazardous to your financial health.

## Postscript

The data series contained in Figs 10.1 and 10.2 are not stock or bond prices but were generated as random series on the computer. How then is one to interpret the results? One possible conclusion is that technical analysis is very powerful since it can even identify trends in random series; another is that technical analysis can have little use since technical patterns show up even in random series, so evidence of past chart patterns does not mean the price series are anything but random. I leave the reader to decide.

# 11

---

## *FORECASTING METHOD AND MADNESS*
### *(crystal balls and glass-houses)*

Chapter 9 showed that expectations, or forecasts, are an essential part of every decision that is made. Very often the forecasting process is ignored in favor of *practical assumptions*, or something similar. These are just another name for a forecast, and recognizing that might improve decision-making. The objective of this chapter is to take a closer look at how specific forecasts are made for the macro economy, with particular reference to the business cycle. Such a task is obviously difficult, and the results will never be totally accurate, but it is still an essential part of trying to make the best *guess*. Some forecast is necessary to follow, like a path through a minefield. Almost every day, new statistics explode on the screens around the world, officials lay trip-wires for the unwary, and it is easy to become confused and lost without some basic guidelines.

Everything depends on everything else. What separates the events is time. Without time everything would collapse into a single moment, and all things would be known with certainty. Time introduces uncertainty into the relationships, and makes the outcome of events unknown. That unknown future creates great risks for those who get it wrong, and great potential for those who get it right. Lucky guesswork can prove successful over a period of time, and the odds favor some individual experiencing an extended winning streak; it happens. However, consistent success requires a more reliable approach. It requires careful consideration of the probabilities of gain and of pain, and this can only be done by adopting a disciplined approach to forecasting the future.

Great care has to be used in deriving forecasts of the future. While past statistical relationships are essential in building a model for the future, there are many potential traps along that path. There is a major flaw in the widespread belief that if some statistical relationship has had a close fit with actual data in the past it will satisfactorily predict the future. The data employed are seriously flawed and frequently revised. What is more, proving the existence of a close relationship, even with lags, is no proof of causality. The statistical techniques are potentially extremely sophisticated, but that should not be allowed to give a false appearance of sophistication to the results obtained. It is necessary to understand the strengths and limitations of the techniques and data employed, and ensure that the result is consistent with the underlying theory.

Intelligence-gathering type operations form a large part of the work of professional forecasters. Weather forecasters collect more and more information on anticyclones, winds, air turbulence, etc., employing increasingly sophisticated equipment, which is then churned around inside ever more complicated and faster computers in order to provide predictions which still fall well short of perfection. Something similar is happening in making forecasts about the economy and about financial markets, but in this case there is a major additional problem, quite apart from the obvious one, that human behavior is much more difficult to predict than physical. The equipment and statistical techniques have become increasingly sophisticated, but the data that are put into the machines are flawed. The amount of information becoming available is increasing exponentially, but the quality of the vast majority of it is extremely poor.

The first part of this chapter discusses some of the problems facing forecasters, and some of the methods employed. This is followed by a presentation of the methods employed here, and the cyclical indicators derived. The emphasis here is on the economic indicators. Many of these are then used as inputs into the market indicators that are introduced in the specific chapters that follow.

## Gathering intelligence

The forecasts that are made can be broken down into two types. The first depends on gathering available information on order flows and backlogs, inventory levels, current costs, etc., and talking directly to management. This is not so much research as intelligence gathering, and dominates short-term views. There is some scope for independent conclusions, but we should not be surprised to find that a consensus usually develops fairly quickly. The same approach can be used with macro-economic variables, like inflation, but only over the very short term. Analysts will collect the latest information on energy prices, food prices, and the various components making up the consumer price index. On this basis it is possible to build up a picture of the likely inflation number due out in the current month.

The results of such research are quickly discounted in market prices. As information gathering proceeds, with the help and encouragement of companies or government agencies, so expectations and market prices are updated. This is what is meant by efficient markets. Not that prices somehow discount the immediate future; only that they discount what information is already available. Where less is known, as with the longer-term trends of macro-economic variables or the development of new companies, so there is likely to be a wider spread of opinions, greater uncertainty and greater opportunities to beat the market, both on the up-side and down-side.

Every major broker and most large institutions will cover the largest companies and sectors, and the economy. So that is where the greatest concentration of manpower and information is, and, not surprisingly, where the greatest consensus exists. These short-term forecasts are updated constantly as new information becomes available, are widely circulated, and are generally very close to the actual results when they are published. Occasionally something goes wrong and the outcome deviates from the forecasts. Since these forecasts, in the case of company results, were built on close contacts with the company itself, it usually means that the company made a mistake in its calculations.

Once the time-frame is extended beyond the next reporting cycle, then the forecasts take on a more subjective character; this is the second type. The companies and industry organizations, etc., will still provide a wealth of information, but the opportunities for error, excessive optimism and pessimism, are much greater, and there is greater scope for different assumptions about the future. However, even over these longer timeframes, the forecasts tend to be similar. Here again the companies will feed information to the analysts. They will understand what they are doing, but tend to take the macro-environment as given, extrapolating economic demand from the recent trend. As a result, the background economy is seen to be strongest when it is already growing rapidly, while the weakest forecast will be found at the bottom of a recession.

The macro-economic context in which companies operate is the weakest link in the forecasting chain. Each industry and company will be affected differently, but all will be affected. Not surprisingly, market prices deviate most markedly from forecasts at the time of business cycle turns. These are the times of the greatest risk and opportunity, and yet are the very time when the detailed company forecasts are least helpful, and earning revisions are most frequent. Individual company forecasts are dependent on correct identification of the way in which the business cycle is progressing. This is also essential to provide forecasts for bonds and the overall movement in stock prices. To be useful, forecasts of the business cycle are required that extend out several months, even years. This is a task that is surprisingly well done, but with limited success; the reason being that it is very difficult to tell the future.

## Data reliability

A problem with using statistical techniques to make forecasts is that the original data are of dubious quality. The accurate recording of the number of widgets produced depends on true reporting by the producers. It is the same when it comes to measuring sales, and there are nearly always problems in making production and sales add up. The problem is greater still when trying to measure services, which represent by far the largest part of the economy. What form this work is reported as, in what way and even whether it is reported at all, will all affect the final outcome. Not much has changed from the time when Harold Cox quoted some Indian statistics in court. Sir Joshua Stamp (1929) reported the judge's reply:

> Cox, when you are a bit older, you will not quote Indian statistics with that assurance. The government is very keen on amassing statistics—they collect them, add them, raise them to the Nth power, take the cube root and prepare wonderful diagrams. But what you must never forget is that every one of those figures comes in the first instance from the chowty bar (village watchman) who just puts down what he damn pleases.

As if these problems with the economy and reliability of the data inputs into the forecasting process were not bad enough, there is the added problem that the past is frequently revised. The numbers on economic growth, money growth, the balance of payments, the leading economic indicators, profits, etc., nearly always go through some revision after they are first estimated, and sometimes these changes can be very great indeed. Samuel Butler said, 'God cannot alter the past, but historians can'. That, however, is too narrow a list. Government statisticians certainly qualify to be included.

The sort of confusion that can be created is illustrated with the GNP figure for the second quarter of 1986. For years that was reported as an increase, but has since been turned into a decline. The economy was clearly much closer to recession than recorded at the time. Consider also the case of the amazing disappearing trade deficit. When the Commerce Department revised the balance-of-payments statistics in June 1989, they reported that US exports in 1988 had been under-recorded by $20.9 billion, and that exports in the first quarter of 1989 had been understated by $25.4 billion at an annualized rate. These gains also carried over to net exports, exports of good and services less imports of good and services, reducing the 1988 deficit from approximately $95 billion, depending on which revision you use, to $74 billion. In real terms the improvement was even greater, going from a deficit of $100 billion to one of $75 billion. Trade statistics are notoriously difficult to keep track of, and all countries suffer from under-recording, misclassifications and deliberate avoidance. Most countries periodically report significant revisions incorporating new information and improved estimates of what really happened.

An additional complication comes with the definitions of the series used. The Commerce Department, in the summer of 1991, announced that the United States was shifting away from GNP as the main measure of economic performance, to GDP, gross *domestic* product. GNP measures output (and income) produced by workers and capital *supplied by* US residents, while GDP measures output produced by workers and capital *located in* the United States. Most countries emphasise GDP over GNP, and so the United States was only conforming to the rule. However, while there is normally little difference between the two series, it so happened that GNP fell 0.5 per cent in the second quarter of 1991, while GDP increased by 0.7 per cent—the difference between recession and recovery. In reality, the difference was insignificant. The habit, in the United States, of annualizing minute changes and drawing big conclusions, as in the case of the 0.5 per cent (annualized) fall in GNP, is unhelpful and inappropriate. What is more, those were the first estimates. Subsequent revisions have shown that GNP also showed positive growth in the second quarter, although below GDP. Sometime in the future, who knows, they may both turn negative.

It sometimes seems that there is a conspiracy involved. That politicians are playing with the numbers in order to achieve some Machiavellian objective of their own. In reality, the collection process is so involved and complicated it is doubtful that many politicians understand enough to be able to carry through such a plan. Within a democracy it is difficult to see even how it could be accomplished. The problem is that the sources of the data are not necessarily very reliable. The same restraints do not apply within a totalitarian regime, and history has shown that gross distortion of the facts, to the extent they are known, is commonplace in such systems.

Over time, additional information becomes available, the statisticians understand the existing information better and so think they can make better estimates of what is missing. Improved collection procedures result in a truer representation of the economy and it may be possible to make adjusted estimates of the past. New weightings are given to different sectors, goods or commodities in constructing a particular index, or new additions made to an existing index. For example, in measuring bank credit, only banks over a certain size are included. If a number of new banks are added at one time then there is a sudden jump in the published statistics. In reality, credit did not jump that much, since all the past growth is included at this one time. In order to better understand the true growth rates it is necessary to adjust the past data to include these banks when they were growing but were still too small to be included in the published statistics. Something similar can happen with the economic numbers.

With the speed of communications these days we have become accustomed to instant results and instant analysis. However, allowances should be made for dealing with people. The information is obtained from forms filed with government agencies or professional organizations, e.g. tax returns, import/export documents, etc. If someone files late, a not uncommon occurrence, or does not file at all, or makes an error on the form, also not uncommon, this will distort the numbers and make them subject to subsequent revision.

Some people, nursing a deep mistrust of quantitative forecasts, may see in these problems a reason to justify their view. To some extent they are correct, but they will also have to recognize that there really is no other sort of forecast. Any forecast/expectation/prediction/or whatever has got to say something about the direction of the market in the future, and at least something about the magnitude. Furthermore, those forecasts will have to be based on existing information about what has happened and what is happening. Anyone who does not have to rely on actual reported data is in a special superhuman category that knows more than anyone else will ever know. In practice, the only thing that can be done is rely, wherever possible, on the most reliable data, as discussed later in this chapter.

## Imperfect correlation

It is not necessary here to judge or criticize the data problems, only to recognize that they exist, and the difficulties that this creates for those using this information to forecast the future. If you are facing south it becomes very hard to see what lies to the north, but that is exactly what is likely to happen if the data point you in the wrong direction. This is worth remembering when the heavyweight statistical techniques are brought out to massage, manipulate and manufacture explanations of the past for use in forecasting the future.

In addition to the data problem, there is also the question of misspecification. The statistical methods used to identify correlations between series assume that the data are accurate, that the explanatory series are independent of each other and of the influence of the series to be explained, and that the relationship which has been defined is the true one. Every one of those assumptions has to be wrong. The data are inaccurate and subject to revision; practically everything depends on everything else, as shown in earlier chapters; and reality is far too complex to be exactly represented by a limited number of inaccurately measured economic series. If the basic assumptions for the analysis are not satisfied, how much confidence should be placed in the results?

What has been identified are problems, not reasons why all analysis should be thrown away and no attempt made to use what information there is. It is still necessary to attempt to forecast the future. To make the best *guess* possible. The conclusion should be that it is necessary to consider the evidence very carefully. Shoving all the data into a black box and accepting whatever it throws out at the end is hardly inspiring. There is a tendency to assume that sophisticated techniques produce sophisticated answers. That is not necessarily the case. Improved techniques should help, but not if they are substituted for rational thought.

The real world is highly complex, and that is extremely inconvenient for people trying to make a model of the world. In order to do that it becomes necessary to force free markets into the theoretical equivalent of a cardboard box. Any inconvenient bits left hanging outside are simply lopped off. What remains is neat and may be elegant, but may be no more useful than a gelding in mating season. Not much may have been removed, but it really can make a lot of difference.

The real world is likely to be very poorly represented if there is excessive insistence on elegance, rigor and analytical purity at the expense of the behavioral reactions, instincts and luck that actually lie behind the decision-making process. This is the economics of the ex-Soviet Union, not of free markets. Such models deal with final outcomes, but do not really investigate the reasons why. Models of this type can be very helpful, in the same way that a color-chart is useful when deciding to redecorate a room. But the decision will depend on many other factors.

Businessmen tend to take the opposite approach, often basing very important decisions on nothing more than a hunch. Years of experience may make that a good guess, but often history has shown that this is nothing more than the extrapolation of recent trends. Entrepreneurs will generally recognize the importance of intuition and luck in their decision making, and that often makes them very nervous about the whole economic system. It will often seem nebulous and hazardous, as if held together by nothing more than chewing gum and sealing wax.

That general randomness is, however, exactly what gives strength to the economic system. Practical men and women want to know where the next super widget will come from. What will be the next high-selling item? They want a precise answer. To the mathematician, the next one will be just like the last one, or will at least be some derivative of it; how boring. The truth is that no one knows. There will be many, many attempts to find the key to success and the great majority will fail. But somewhere, someone will hit on the something that will ignite the imagination of enough people to be successful—usually in a totally unexpected direction. This is not something that can be worked out in advance, planned with a slide rule or modelled mathematically. It evolves out of imagination, luck, intuition, competition and a lot of hard work. It means taking risks. Not the measurable sort of standard deviations of income so beloved of mathematical model builders, but real risks of total failure, bankruptcy and despair.

What is frequently found is that near perfect explanations in terms of statistical fit, or correlation, over the past provide very poor forecasts of the future. Part of the reason might be changes in data which invalidate the estimation. That happens all the time, but is not the main reason for the poor forecasting performance. The more usual cause is the fact that the correlation discovered has little if any explanatory power. Correlation is not proof of causality, nor that the estimated relationship will continue into the future. Most econometric models are better at extrapolating trends than forecasting turning points. Moreover, they often take many of the important influences, like interest rates, as predetermined. A classic example of mistaken causality is the relationship between the stock market and the economy which was discussed in Chapter 1.

There will be many times when the lack of causality will not matter and the correlation will hold up. However, the occasions when correlations will not be enough are likely to prove extremely important. There are many other cases where correlation has even less validity. There are thousands upon thousands of past statistical relationships that have failed to predict the future. These include economic models of all sorts, and a wide variety of technical rules and relationships. Personal experience has shown that it is possible to *prove* a whole mass of correlations without necessarily being able to forecast, or explain, anything at all.

Correlations that exist for particular periods do not necessarily persist over time. That applies further into the past as well as into the future. The first rule is to make sure that any estimated explanation is tested over the longest period possible. The last few years, or the last 10 years, is not enough. There are a great many correlations that are very close over particular periods of time, often over several years, and for very special reasons in some cases, only to cease to exist when conditions change. The longer the period of time over which it can be shown that a particular relationship has persisted, the greater the degree of confidence one can have that it will persist into the future. Correlations that are shown to exist over the period of a few months are particularly suspect, but you will frequently find them presented as evidence of how the world works.

The key is to build confidence that the relationships that have been identified will persist into the future. Another way of doing that is to examine the same behavior in the same markets overseas. There are institutional differences due to different tax regimes, national characteristics, history or geography, but the basic rules of markets still apply. The underlying laws of supply and demand are in operation in all market economies. If people are paid more they will tend to spend more. The relative amounts spent and saved may differ across countries, but the response at the margin works the same way. Equally, stock prices are related to corporate profitability, the growth of profits and the rate at which these are discounted.

Very often, relationships are proposed to explain inflation or money growth or some other variable in the United States, or somewhere else, that are unique to that country. If a unique explanation is to be provided then great care should be made to explain why. Human behavior is very similar under similar conditions. The specific incentives created may be different, and this accounts for the observation of different patterns of behavior, but the underlying set of responses are very similar.

A third rule is to use good quality data wherever possible. The greatest reliability is found in things like stock prices, bond prices, short-term interest rates, exchange rates, etc. These are well known, available quickly, are not seasonally adjusted and are not revised. These data are extremely reliable, but they will not be sufficient to meet all needs. Some monetary data are quite good, particularly when you get down to the level of reserves. Industrial production and inflation are altered, but are generally pretty good. Balance-of-payments data, on the other hand, are constantly being revised. This relative reliability is common across countries too. With things like the balance of payments, where the numbers tend to be both volatile and adjustable, it often helps to use a moving average of the data in order to smooth out the lumps and bumps.

## The importance of time

In a complex world, where everything depends upon everything else, time becomes a crucial element. Removing time produces an absurd situation in which all reactions are compressed into a matter of moments. For example, rising interest rates slow down the economy thereby reducing interest rates which would speed up the economy which would raise interest rates, which would slow down the economy . . ., and so it goes.

Time is not only necessary in order to tell an interesting story, but is an essential part of the decision-making process. Changes in the economy usually take place slowly, thereby gradually changing behavior. In order to influence a major decision it is necessary to believe that a change will be sustained, or even that the trend will be continued. For long-lasting investments, a small change in interest rates will not be relevant, particularly if it is expected to be reversed in the near future.

In the 1970s, governments responded to accelerating inflation by increasing interest rates slowly, so that real interest rates remained negative, thus contributing to the acceleration of inflation. Had individuals thought that interest rates were going to be pushed up rapidly in order to stop inflation that belief would have influenced their behavior. Some people undoubtedly did adjust in this way, and quickly found themselves falling behind both relatively and absolutely. What they could also observe was that those sceptics who borrowed in the belief of continued inflation were benefiting handsomely.

Over time, therefore, more and more people came to believe that inflation would continue, and get worse. That represented a deterioration in inflationary expectations in aggregate. The time it takes for people to adjust their thinking produces lags in the formation of expectations. This cumulative process is a major way in which the influence of time is incorporated in the macro-economy. In this context, we are concerned not with the behavior of a single individual, but the behavior of large groups. The process by which particular influences feed their way through to the rest of the economy is very important in explaining timing in markets.

Time is important in a number of different ways. As relative prices or incomes change so individuals will react with different speeds. The aggregate reaction will be the average of all the individual responses. The reaction is made up of a number of lags that are at work. There are lags in perception, or recognition, since it takes time for people to be sure what has happened and whether it is likely to be permanent. There is also likely to be a lag in the speed it takes to react. This is most obvious in the case of purchases of durable goods where it may be necessary to obtain finance, or save the full amount. For example, a shift in relative prices may make it attractive to change from oil heat to some other alternative. Such a shift, however, requires a significant investment, and, as might be expected, this takes time. However, non-durable consumption patterns will also change slowly. Rising living standards are likely to lead to changes in the types and quality of food consumed. These do not happen overnight, and there is likely to be a long learning, or adjustment, process involved, both on the part of consumers and suppliers. Then there is a lag as these reactions feed back to the rest of the economy.

Further complicating the picture is the fact that the lagged effects will all overlap each other, setting up highly complex lag structures and interactions between decision makers. As one effect starts to take hold, so reactions are set off elsewhere, and these continue as the lags work their way through the various markets. While it is true that things normally happen slowly in the economy, there are times when sudden, dramatic changes take place. These could be the result of natural forces, such as an earthquake, or to non-market intervention, as in the case of the OPEC oil price increases in the 1970s. In such instances, the normal recognition lags are absent and reactions are accelerated as far as possible. On the other hand, adjustment is much more difficult and results in very long lags.

The example of the Second World War shows the extent of the lags that can be involved following a large shock to the system. Post-war reconstruction should be measured in decades rather than years. Normal life was wrecked and it took a very long time for it to be restored. The banks came out of the war with a very high proportion of government debt on their balance sheets, reflecting the pattern within the economy. For a long time this was thought to be natural, and a great many learned papers were written expressing concern at the deteriorating state of banks' balance sheets as the proportion lent to the private sector increased. What was really happening was that the banks were returning to a more normal structure. At the same time, the private sector was achieving a similar objective, and in the process pushing up share prices dramatically.

What we have are a lot of different lags, each of different lengths, all working simultaneously and, therefore, making the sum of any reaction extremely complex. These are what lie behind the behavioral lags discussed in Chapter 1. Action and reaction, separated by time, explain the cyclical pattern of the economy. The behavioral links explain the cyclicality, while the different shocks and disturbances provide the difference in the final, observed outcome.

## Public intervention and interference

So far we have been talking about responses within the private sector, but there are also those within the public sector to be taken into account, and these are very important in explaining the cyclical behavior of the economy and financial markets generally. To some extent, policy actions are determined outside the economic system, at least in terms of its short-term reactions. However, even decisions on the building of roads and bridges, and the quality of health care, depend on the long-run prosperity of the economy.

Other policy actions are deliberately designed to be different from the behavioral responses within the private sector, the intention being to stabilize the economy. That is the objective with the payment of unemployment benefits. Left to itself, the private sector will generate much wider swings in the economy. A fall in aggregate demand that results in large-scale layoffs will be followed by further reductions in demand and further layoffs. Payments to the unemployed help them to maintain demand and reduce to some extent the follow-through effect. Consequently, you do not have to be concerned about the welfare of the individual in order to support the case for unemployment benefits, although it helps. In this case, the total benefits are greater than the sum of the individual parts. Unemployment benefits are an example of automatic stabilizers. These have the advantage of being automatic, and so do not depend on the dubious process of political decision-making in order to be implemented. The problem, however, is that human ingenuity finds ways to take advantage of the situation.

Other policy actions are taken in response to what is happening in the economy. Fiscal policy responds at different speeds—all of them relatively slow. What is more, the responses are highly politicized which is not always an advantage. The normal response time for fiscal policy is one year, at the annual budget process. At such times, expenditure and tax changes are implemented, but normally these actions are fairly cautious. There are also long lags involved. First, politicians have to be convinced of the need for action; this so-called recognition lag can be quite long. Then there is the lag before action is taken, and a further lag before the actions take effect. Only at that point do the private sector lags, referred to above, come into play.

There is also an aspect of fiscal policy that involves much longer lags, as structural problems are encountered, or political philosophy changes. An example is provided by the attempt to reduce marginal tax rates in the United States, a policy that has been copied around the world. The lags in action and reaction in this case have been very long. It has taken very many years to reach the conclusion that high marginal tax rates have a negative effect on the growth potential of the economy, and then to attempt to correct the situation, and now the policy is reversing.

Monetary policy, on the other hand, is much more immediate in its effect, and less politicized. The role of the monetary authorities in trying to steer a stable course can be compared with the captain of an ocean liner. No matter how good the captain may be, he cannot completely control events since he has to accept, and deal with, the waves created by the great swell of private sector competition. There are many who would eliminate such inconveniences with controls and restraints. The Soviet Union went the furthest in that direction, essentially putting the boat in dry dock—not surprisingly they did not go anywhere.

Introducing policy in this way produces another source of lags within the economy that has to be taken into account. The intention has been to improve stability and dampen swings, but within certain restraints imposed by the political system and policies taken elsewhere. These restraints were very apparent in the 1970s as central banks fought to gain control of inflation, while avoiding major recessions, within the context of expansionary fiscal policies. The path of compromise that was chosen, and was probably unavoidable under the circumstances, resulted in much longer lags in the struggle to gain control.

Many forecasters take government and central bank actions as separate from, and independent of, the rest of the economy. The reason for this is that most quantitative forecasting has grown up within government or universities, with the objective of influencing decision making. That has meant looking at what would happen in the event of no change in interest rates or tax rates, and then what would happen when these are changed. As far as changes in tax rates are concerned, putting them outside the system is less important since they are subject to longer-term trends, but in the case of more direct reactions and, in particular, changes in interest rates, the approach is seriously flawed. Interest rates are the major connecting rods, like sinews, within the economy.

Without the reaction of interest rates to the rest of the economy, the different parts are left standing in splendid isolation. If the model is defined incorrectly it will not provide insights into the operation of the economy that will be of any value to anybody. In particular, such an approach does not even start to address the needs or concerns of investors. To be helpful, any forecasting model must include the action, reaction and interaction of interest rates and exchange rates, and the part played by governments in these and other markets. Government reactions have got to be part of the process. Policies are not decided in a vacuum, but as a result of the pressures from developments within the rest of the economy.

## Making forecasts

All of these considerations have been taken into account in developing the indicators used here. Even more important, however, is the actual approach employed. The typical procedure used elsewhere is to estimate a relationship over a given period, employing current variables, and then to extrapolate that into the future. There are two problems with that approach, apart from the data problems already discussed.

The first is that in order to forecast the series that you are interested in it is also necessary to forecast the series that are used in making the prediction. For example, suppose you have a relationship that explains inflation in terms of present and past changes in the money supply. In order to forecast inflation in three months' time, it is also necessary to forecast the growth of money in three months' time. At the time of making such a forecast, neither inflation nor the money supply for the present month will be known. Any success in forecasting inflation will not only depend on the dubious quality of the estimated relationship, but also on the ability to forecast the supply of money. The chances of success are not very high.

The second problem is that a misleading impression of the degree of accuracy involved is created by plotting actual inflation, in this example, along with the estimated inflation rate. A reasonably competent analyst will have no trouble obtaining a close fit, which will look good and be accompanied by suitably impressive statistics to prove how good it is. This really proves nothing about how well such a relationship will forecast. As an illustration of this point, consider Fig. 11.1, which shows two estimates of the Deutschemark/dollar exchange rate, but with dramatically different forecasts for the out-of-sample period. Shown simply over the estimation period, it would have been difficult to distinguish one from the other. These are not necessarily the best estimates possible, but are introduced

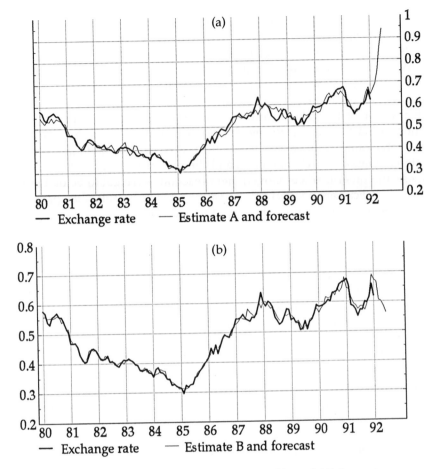

**Figure 11.1** (a) Model A forecast and (b) model B forecast

here only to show how easy it is to be misled by the power of statistical techniques. The moral of the story is not to be convinced by simple in-sample comparisons. The same is true of evidence of how good an investment strategy would have been over past market behavior. It is possible, *in retrospect*, to produce models generating spectacular returns, only to find that future returns fail to live up to the promise. The only way to test a forecasting model is by how it works in the future, beyond the period over which the model was estimated.

In constructing the indicators presented here, only information that is already known is used. Anything that is to be forecast in three months' time will depend only on information that is known at the time the forecast is made. In the case of the longer-leading indicators of the economy, the lead time on the forecasts are between six months and one year. Those indicators, however, are based on data that are already well known. The different approaches employed are designed to improve decision making under conditions of uncertainty.

Not only are forecasts of the future based on known information, the same is also true in the past as well. The past relationship between the actual series and the estimate is also a forecast, in the sense that the estimates were known ahead of time. All the lines plotted are totally independent, in the sense that the estimated lines were known at the time, and do not depend on information that would only be known later. The estimates are, therefore, completely different from the normal display of an estimated relationship.

There is another sort of forecast used for the market indicators, and this places the emphasis on identifying turning points. A correlation tries to fit a relationship over the whole estimation period, giving equal weight to all points along the way. If part of the true explanation is missing, the fit will not be good, and what there is will be a half-hearted compromise. It is a tall order to try and explain every little movement, and there are a great many different influences, not all of which can be included. Not all points in time have the same significance; changes in direction are much more important than movements along a continuing trend, and yet are treated equally by correlation programs. An alternative approach is, therefore, just to concentrate attention on the major turning points. In this case the approach is quite different, with the emphasis on isolating the distinctive occurrences that happen around such turning points. The forecasts arrived at this way point to the direction to be followed, with particular emphasis on the cyclical turning points, but have less to say about the magnitude of the move.

There are a number of things that may repeat sometimes, even fairly often, but not always. The proximate cause of a turn may well be different between cycles, depending on exactly what else is happening. In order to obtain confidence in such an approach, it is necessary to employ a number of different indicators so that, like a good detective, it is possible to judge the weight of evidence. This approach to turning points has been employed in constructing market indicators for the stock and bond markets. These composite indicators incorporate a number of separate influences that have little general predictive or explanatory power except in determining the important cyclical turning points.

*Official leading indicators*

A convenient place to start, and a useful point of comparison, is with the official leading economic indicator (LEI) produced by the Commerce Department. The leading economic indicator is made up of a number of different series based on their correlation with the economy in the past. No one, however, seems to have asked whether these relationships are very sensible or not from a behavioral point of view. There are 11 series altogether making up the LEI, which are listed below. The index was first constructed in 1968 using 12 indicators, of which only three are still included; these are the average workweek, building permits and stock prices:

1. Average weekly hours of production of non-supervisory workers in manufacturing.
2. Average weekly initial claims for unemployment insurance.
3. New manufacturing orders, in constant dollars, in the consumer goods and materials industries.
4. Index of stock prices, S&P 500.
5. Contracts and orders for plant and equipment in constant dollars.
6. Index of new private housing units authorized by local building permits.
7. Vendor performance, slower deliveries diffusion index.
8. Index of consumer expectations as computed by the University of Michigan.
9. Change in unfilled orders for durable goods in constant dollars.
10. Change in sensitive materials prices.
11. Money supply on an M2 definition.

The emphasis is on the interest-sensitive areas of the economy, which is fair enough since that is where the initial effect is felt, although the selection chosen seems arbitrary. The inclusion of the stock market is evidence of a purely statistical approach, with the potential for misleading signals; as, for example, happened in 1987. The question of causality between the stock market and the economy was considered in detail in Chapter 1. There is a statistical leading relationship, but it is not causal. Stock prices move to anticipate economic developments, but these can in turn change events in the opposite direction, thereby destroying the supposed relationship.

Figure 11.2 shows the 12-month rate of change of the LEI, together with measures of economic growth and the economic activity index (EAI). The EAI, described below, is an alternative measure of economic performance with similar characteristics to the official leading indicator series, but is constructed differently. Figure 11.2 shows that neither series really qualifies as a leading indicator of the economy.

In most instances, the two indicators provide very similar measures of the cyclical movements of the economy which accord with actual experience.

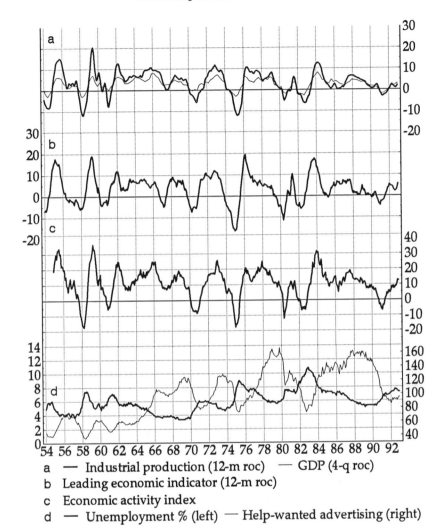

a  —  Industrial production (12-m roc)   —  GDP (4-q roc)
b   Leading economic indicator (12-m roc)
c   Economic activity index
d  —  Unemployment % (left)  — Help-wanted advertising (right)

**Figure 11.2** Economic activity and the leading economic indicator

There is, therefore, clear evidence that the cycle shows up in a variety of data. However, when there have been deviations, the EAI has provided the more accurate measure of actual and future economic performance. For example, in 1966 and 1985 the official leading indicator became weaker than the economy, and again in 1987. Each time there were widespread predictions of impending recession. Wider use of the economic activity index would have shown that these predictions were wrong and that the official LEI warnings were misleading.

## Economic activity index

Having seen how the EAI relates to the economy and to the official leading economic indicator, the time has come to see how it has been constructed. One lesson to come from this is the discovery that things are not always what they seem. The index is simple to construct, but there are lags in data availability. Despite the data delay, the index can still be put together before the final version of the LEI, and a preliminary indication could be produced much earlier.

Everyone knows that employment lags the economy and is, therefore, of no use as a leading indicator of the economy. This view is both true and false. Employment does lag economic activity in absolute terms, but important changes start to take place in the employment data much earlier. Some people have looked at hours worked, or overtime, as ways to get earlier information out of the labor market. However, even the unemployment series itself contains useful, early indications on the economy.

The EAI takes two simple series that look at the overall labor market from different sides. The series are help-wanted advertising and the percentage of the labor force that is unemployed. An important aspect of these series is that they cover the whole economy, and do not put emphasis on the manufacturing sector, as so many cyclical indicators do. Manufacturing will normally be more sensitive to the cycle, but not necessarily and not always. The service sector is continuing to grow in importance, and this should be allowed for when looking for ways to anticipate the growth of the economy. Assuming a fixed pattern, with manufacturing always leading, risks getting it wrong when conditions change.

The first step in constructing the EAI is to take the deviation from trend of both series. These deviations are then combined to produce the index; very simple and easy to do, and the result is more reliable than the official leading indicator series. The time frame of the EAI is approximately the same as the LEI, as shown above, and is not really a leading indicator of the economy. The series provides more up-to-date information on the economy than current published data, but that is all. There are other indicators that do provide more of a lead on the economy, and a true longer-leading indicator is described later in this chapter. A number of separate indicators are presented here; some are components of the leading economic indicator and some are used in the individual market indicators developed in later chapters. Naturally, there is some overlap.

## The yield curve

One measure of tightening credit conditions is a less positive yield curve. The curve, in this sense, is the ratio of short-term interest rates and long-term bond yields, making sure to use market rates of similar types. The introduction of different credit qualities into the relationship makes it harder to interpret the result. The ratio of Tbill rates to Treasury bond yields, or commercial paper rates to AAA corporate bond yields, will tell similar stories, but the comparison of Tbills to corporate bonds is not a good idea. Figure 11.3 uses rates on private sector paper.

Short-term interest rates are more volatile than longer-term bond yields. When rates are rising they will move up more quickly at the short end than the long end, thereby narrowing the ratio between the two. In an environment of free credit markets, the period of credit tightening is not usually complete until the yield curve has become inverted, which is the point at which short-term interest rates rise above bond yields, but such a development is not necessary. The actual outcome will very much depend on whether the monetary authorities tighten late or early. If they are late, and inflation has taken hold, then the yield curve is more likely to become inverted, and stay that way for longer. Early action, taken before conditions deteriorate, can head off trouble before it gets too bad.

At times when credit controls have been in force there has been a rationing effect, switching off the flow of credit to the economy without interest rates having to rise so far, or the yield curve inverting. The problem with controls of this sort is that they are unfair and distortionary, and extremely inefficient as a long-term means of control. Eventually, credit starts to flow around the obstacles, seeking out the path of least resistance.

Long-term yields reflect many influences, but are dominated by where investors think inflation is headed, while the influences affecting short rates are more heavily weighted by the business cycle, and what is happening in the real economy. A comparison between the two is, therefore, a reflection of what *is* happening in the economy, and also what is likely to happen in the *future*. The importance of interest rates and the yield curve was emphasized in earlier chapters, and there is further discussion in Chapter 12, on the bond market. The yield curve is shown in Fig. 11.3. The leading relationship is emphasized by advancing this series so that it leads the growth of GNP and industrial production by 12 months. The same 12-month lead is used with all the component series described below. This is only intended to be indicative of the approximate lead time, rather than an exact description. It will be seen, however, that the relationships with the economy are much closer on that basis than with no lead.

## Interest rates

Changes in the yield curve are not the only way in which interest rates influence the economy. The yield curve could narrow because short-term interest rates have risen, or because long-term bond yields have fallen, and

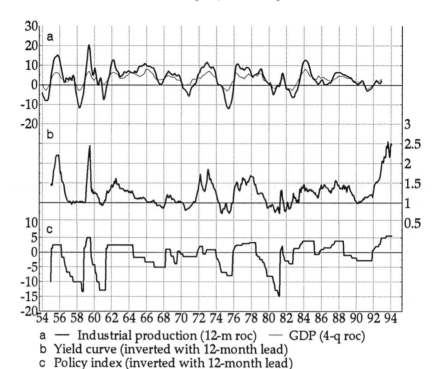

a   —  Industrial production (12-m roc)   —  GDP (4-q roc)
b  Yield curve (inverted with 12-month lead)
c  Policy index (inverted with 12-month lead)

**Figure 11.3** Yield curve and policy index

it makes a difference which it is. The simplest way to take account of this added influence is to include the rate of change of interest rates. Changes in short-term interest rates are the most volatile and sensitive to economic conditions, while long-term bond yields more closely follow the underlying trend, missing out some of the short-term variation. In Fig. 11.4, both series are inverted, so that rising interest rates are related to lower economic growth and lower interest rates with higher growth, and have been advanced by 12 months, i.e. changes in interest rates are shown leading economic growth.

This is the simplest way of taking account of changes in interest rates. However, simplest is not always best when it comes to forecasting the economy. The importance of taking account of inflation when considering the effect of interest rate changes was discussed earlier. A 10 per cent increase in interest rates will have a different effect on behavior depending on whether inflation is 100 per cent, 10 per cent or −10 per cent. The obvious solution is to create a real interest rate series. Unfortunately, that is not as easy as it seems.

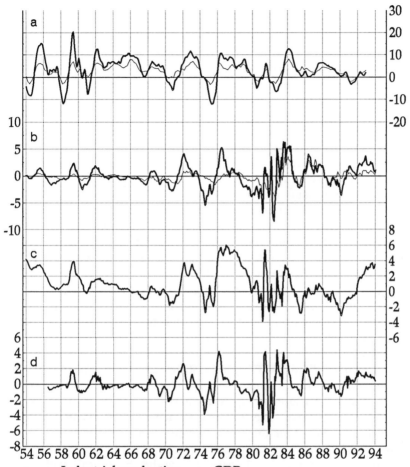

a — Industrial production  — GDP
b — Change in 3-month rate (inverted and advanced 12 mths)
   — Change in bond yield (inverted and advanced 12 mths)
c  Cost of credit index (advanced 12 mths)
d  Federal Reserve funds - deviation from trend (advanced 12 mths)

**Figure 11.4** Interest rates and the economy (monthly)

## *Cost of credit index*

The real interest rate that affects decisions depends on *expectations* of future inflation. That expectation will be heavily dependent on past and present inflation, but it is unlikely to be the same as the actual measured rate of inflation. A rise in reported inflation may be largely ignored if it is widely perceived as temporary. Alternatively, a loss of confidence in the monetary authorities may well mean that even a small increase in inflation will lead to a widespread expectation of even higher inflation. A real interest rate of the type normally seen, the current interest rate minus the current rate of consumer price inflation, does not correlate well with the economy; nor should it be expected to do so.

In making a decision to borrow today, an individual or company has to compare the cost of that borrowing with the income or other benefits that will result, and the cost or value of waiting to make that purchase/investment in the future. What is important in this calculation is not the current rate of inflation but the rate expected in the future. The present rate is important only to the extent that it influences that expectation. The solution adopted here is to measure expectations by an exponential moving average of actual inflation. The idea is that past inflation can have a long, lingering effect, but that recent experience has a much bigger effect. This is not perfect, but gives a better underlying trend to bond yields than other inflation choices; this is discussed further in Chapter 12.

The cost of credit index (CCI) is constructed by taking the specially constructed index of the theoretical, or expected, cost, based on the expected rate of inflation and subtracting the actual cost of money, in the form of the three-month money rate. The attempt is to identify a real cost that is relevant for borrowers at the time they make the decision to take out a loan. Given the way the CCI has been constructed, a positive reading means that credit is relatively cheap, the actual cost is below the theoretical level, while a negative reading implies that the cost of credit is relatively high. The series is shown in Fig. 11.4.

When the expected rate of inflation is above the current cost of borrowing this is likely to be associated with an optimistic outlook, high credit demand and an expanding economy. The prospect of higher prices means that companies can expect to raise prices sufficiently to offset the cost of borrowing. Equally, for both investors and consumers of durable goods, there is an added incentive to accelerate purchases, using borrowed money, when the cost in the future is expected to rise by more than the present cost of borrowing.

## Credit supply conditions

The supply of credit is something that cannot be measured directly, but the Federal Reserve does have control over the conditions under which short-term credit will be supplied. The basic determinant will be the Federal Reserve's willingness to supply liquidity to the banking system. The supply of reserves can be measured directly, but that is not necessarily the same as liquidity, which depends on the perceived need for reserves, and that can increase dramatically at times of emergency, as the banks need for reserves changes. Also, other financial institutions can change the velocity of circulation. The choice has been made in favor of the price at which liquidity is provided.

The market is liquid, in this sense, when there are ample reserves to finance the loans the financial system wishes to make. The market is *highly* liquid when the supply of funds exceeds demand at the short end of the market. It is impossible to measure demand and supply directly, but certain indicators are helpful in judging the situation. For example, when supply exceeds demand for any commodity the price should fall; the price in this case is the short-term interest rate. As pressure comes off the short end, short-term interest rates should fall, not only relative to long-term bond yields but also relative to their recent trend.

The market rate most directly under the control of the Federal Reserve is the federal funds rate. On an intra-day basis, the federal funds rate can be extremely volatile, but the trend can be, and is, determined by the Federal Reserve. The measure of credit supply conditions compares the most recent federal funds rate with a moving average of past rates. This shows which direction the federal funds rate is headed and, therefore, whether credit conditions are being eased or tightened. Increased restraint will push interest rates progressively higher, producing a distinct upward trend. Eventually, the restraint will produce lower interest rates, but not before the higher rates have slowed the economy and reduced the demand for credit. Once demand eases relative to supply, interest rates drop, and the monetary authorities will inject additional reserves. Suddenly the supply/demand equation reverses and interest rates will drop below the rising trend, and will continue falling. In Fig. 11.4 the relationship has been inverted and advanced 12 months.

## Policy index

It is not possible to judge the monetary authorities by what they say, only by what they do. Politicians are always talking down interest rates, and central banks are always opposed to any acceleration of inflation. Despite that, interest rates do not always fall and inflation has been known to accelerate. Even when the authorities tighten, and more often when they ease, they provide misleading explanations for what they are doing. The true test of a tight monetary policy is in the extent to which reserves are cut back, market interest rates are allowed to rise and the willingness of the Federal Reserve to raise the official discount rate. It is market rates that have the greatest impact on decision making and therefore the economy, but the discount rate still has an impact on the financial markets, as a *statement* from the Federal Reserve.

The last of the interest rate based indicators is the policy index. This index is based on the discount rate, taking cumulative changes from the last change in direction. The index, shown in Fig. 11.3, is therefore negative if the discount rate is falling, and positive if the discount rate is rising. Changes in the discount rate have very little direct effect on market liquidity, reserves or interest rates generally. Moreover, the discount rate does not anticipate changes in market rates, but lags behind. Changes in the discount rate, therefore, provide confirmation of trends already in place, rather than early warning that a shift in direction is about to happen. However, this confirmation is still useful information, and is the clearest statement made by the Federal Reserve. As shown here, in Fig. 11.3, the index is inverted and advanced 12 months.

## Real money

The growth of money reflects a number of different influences, primarily the demand for credit and the supply of bank reserves. Money is used in all transactions. The number of barter deals, where goods are swapped directly for goods, is so small as not to be relevant. The use of money covers a lot more than the final total of goods and services produced, since it is also used in financial transactions, the buying and selling of stocks and bonds, and all intermediary transactions. There is a tendency to concentrate attention on industrial production—autos, steel, etc.—but this is a small part of the overall economy and it is getting smaller. Money provides a wider perspective on the economy as a whole. Even more importantly, changes in the growth of money provide early warning of changes that will only show up in the economy later on.

The amount of money in existence reflects the demand for credit, and that depends on the cost of money, i.e. short-term interest rates, consumer confidence and business conditions generally. The influence from the supply of reserves comes through the rate of interest. The Federal Reserve has the ability to control the supply of reserves and, therefore, the growth of money. There are lags in this relationship, and the exact response depends on what else is going on in the economy, and which definition of money is being considered. The monetary authorities may raise interest rates, but not enough to slow down the growth of money. That does not mean they do not have the ability to do so, only that they have refrained from doing so. The growth of money provides a confirmation of what is actually happening, rather than what officials say is happening.

In order to be stimulative, the growth of money needs to exceed the rate of inflation. Otherwise the real stock of money outstanding will be falling, which is not a situation that encourages the growth of consumption and investment. The relationship between real money growth and the economy was discussed in Chapter 4 (see Fig. 4.1) and it is this that makes real money an essential ingredient in forecasting movements in stock prices.

### Loans velocity index

This index measures the relationship between bank debits, i.e. the total amount of all checks drawn on checking accounts, and the total of short-term business credit. Bolton (1967), called this 'the single most useful index of economic data available for the interpretation of the stock market economic environment'. That is hardly surprising given the close correspondence between the rate of change of debits and the stock market, and the economy, in the 1929–33 period. This can be seen in Fig. 11.5.

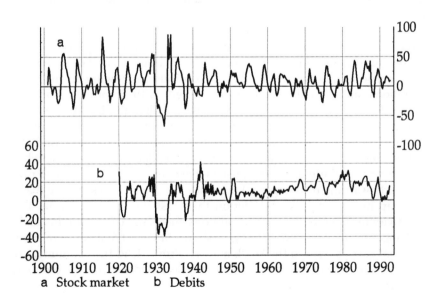

**Figure 11.5** Stock market and debits (four-quarter rates of change)

Bank debits are closely related to the economy, and even better con-
nected to the value of turnover within the economy, since it measures the
value of all monetary transactions passing through the banking system; a
lot more than just final sales by businesses. Also included are all financial
transactions and all intermediary transactions that take place in the process
of production. Up until the middle of the century, debits were extremely
closely matched to the movement in stock prices, and to changes in industrial
production. The relationship still existed following the war, but it ceased to
be quite so good.

The loans velocity index (LVI) is based on the ratio of a moving average
of debits and short-term loans to the corporate sector. The loans series
consists of short-term business credit, which is bank loans to companies
plus commercial paper outstanding. One way of interpreting the resulting
ratio is as the velocity at which loans are turned over, or used, much like
the velocity of money.

Bolton emphasized the relationship between a version of the LVI, which
he called the debit loan, and the inverse of the inventory–sales ratio, i.e. the
sales–inventory (S/I) ratio. However, the LVI has much wider coverage.
The S/I ratio measures only the relationship between business sales and
inventories, whereas the LVI includes the value of all major monetary
transactions compared with short-term credit to all businesses. As a result,
the LVI remains representative of the business cycle in an increasingly
service-based economy. Moreover, changing technology has allowed
improvements in inventory control that have modified the relationship
between inventories and the economy.

As the economy moves into recession, transactions will typically decline
but business loans will stay relatively high or, at least, not fall as quickly,
since corporations will be forced to continue borrowing to maintain
operations and swelling inventories. Even with improved controls,
inventories will still increase. The net result is a fall in the LVI. As the economy moves into recession, corporations will cut costs and reduce borrowing.
At some point during this process, demand will start to pick up and this
will be reflected in the turnover of deposits, i.e. debits. The ratio of debits
to loans should, therefore, be extra-sensitive to the business cycle, and provide early warning of changes taking place. It is, in fact, so sensitive that it
picks up more changes in direction than just the business cycle. The
sensitivity to changing financial conditions makes the LVI a good indicator
of changes in corporate profitability, as shown in Fig. 11.6. It is this relationship that carries over to the stock market. Profits lead the economy, not
follow it, so it is no use waiting until there is clear evidence that the economy
has recovered.

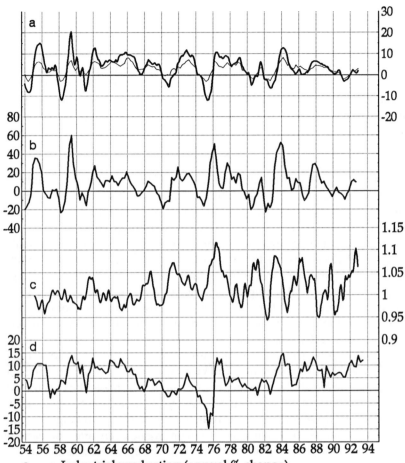

a — Industrial production (annual % change)
  — GDP (annual % change)
b  Company profits (adjusted) (annual % change)
c  Loans velocity index
d  Cash flow index (advanced 12 months)

**Figure 11.6** Loans velocity and the economy (monthly)

## Loan demand

A direct measure of credit conditions is provided by including an actual series of loan demand. In this case the growth of short-term business credit, as defined above, is combined with the expansion of consumer credit. This is averaged and smoothed in order to provide an indicator of broad credit conditions, as reflected in the actual numbers borrowed. Such an indicator is essential to identify any credit contraction or expansion that may be due to influences other than interest rates, and to provide confirmation that interest rate changes are having the expected effect. The growth in the combined and individual series is shown Fig. 11.7.

Typically, consumer credit demand turns ahead of business credit. The slower response of business credit is because it is less sensitive to interest rates in the short term. However, once the effect takes hold, the response is usually much greater. The delay is due to two things. First, businesses pay more attention to profits than interest rates when it comes to making investment decisions, so the slowdown of demand for their products is actually the main way that interest rates impact investment spending by corporations. Second, companies very often are forced to borrow, even when they want to cut back. As spending slows down, so companies sell less; inventories build up and the same workforce brings in less revenue. The biggest effect will generally be on the manufacturing sector, but other areas will also be affected. Companies will start to cut back, after a delay, and will still be trimming costs and cutting inventory when demand picks up again. The effect of a recovery in demand is to achieve the cuts in inventory to the extent of creating shortages. At that point, revenues will improve, allowing companies to reduce their bank borrowings. For these reasons, business borrowing will remain weak even after demand has started to pick up again after the bottom of the cycle. And as demand and incomes improve, so will consumer confidence and consumer borrowing. This pattern can be seen in the figure.

If business loans are slow to respond, and consumer loans are quick to respond, this raises the question of why not just use the latter? After all, the objective is to get the earliest indications possible. The reason is that we are measuring the pressure on the credit markets and interest rates. The forced borrowing by the business sector is one of the reasons why monetary policy remains tight so long, and helps explain the extent and duration of the downturn. To look only at consumer credit demand would mean being too early, and also occasionally getting a false signal.

## Cash flow index

There is a strong leading relationship running from net corporate cash flow to profits and the economy. The index, shown in Fig. 11.6, takes cash

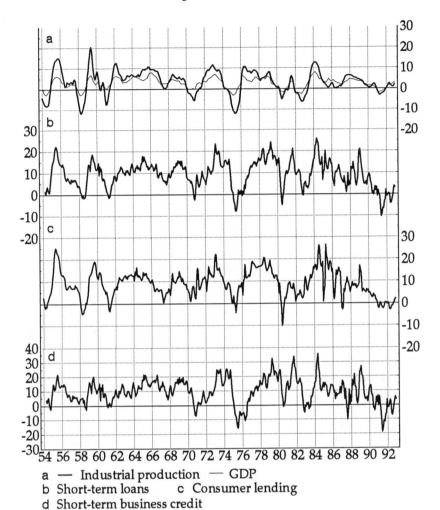

a — Industrial production — GDP
b Short-term loans      c Consumer lending
d Short-term business credit

**Figure 11.7** Economic activity and credit growth (12-month rate of change)

flow divided by GDP, and is shown with a 12-month lead. Companies typically do not cut back operations until they are actually in a recession. It
would, therefore, seem that they ignore the warning signals provided by
the cash flow numbers. Partly it is a squeeze on financial resources, and
partly it is companies overextending themselves. This happens when
optimism is high and everything looks good, but the signs of impending
problems are there for those who care to look.
The data come from the quarterly flow of funds statistics, which means

that the information is quarterly and late. To complicate matters even further, the figures are frequently revised, and more than once. These problems make it hard to rely on the cash flow index (CFI) on its own. However, it does provide some insights to the future which it would be foolish to ignore. When used in conjunction with other indices, the CFI provides important corroboration of where the economy is headed.

The cyclical nature of this indicator is quite clear, and it has provided early warning of most cyclical turning points. The one major exception was the latest recession which began in 1990. As far as the CFI was concerned, it never happened. This evidence might be used to argue that the recession was caused by Iraq's invasion of Kuwait, except that the rest of the evidence argues strongly against it. Another interpretation is that the financial condition of the corporate sector was in better shape than generally perceived at the time, which may explain why the stock market suffered a relatively mild decline and quickly recovered.

## Longer-leading economic indicator

This indicator is a composite made up of a number of different influences discussed earlier. The emphasis is on financial conditions; not just bank credit but credit generally. The result is a genuine leading indicator that projects into the future. This is shown in Fig. 11.8.

The longer-leading indicator illustrates the points made earlier. The forecast is independent of the series it is designed to predict. In addition, emphasis should be put on the fact that the forecast relationship exists all along the plotted line. This is completely different from the plot of an actual series together with an econometric estimate over that same period, including current values. By doing that it is possible to demonstrate a very close relationship in the past, but it really tells you nothing about how well that model will forecast the future. There are endless examples of econometric relationships that have withered and died as soon as they were exposed to the harsh climate in the real world—as demonstrated earlier in this chapter. The presentation here is quite different.

To give an example, at the low point in the economy early in 1975, the forecast of a sharp recovery into 1976 was already known. The economy was still showing considerable strength early in 1979, at the same time that the forecast was indicating a sharp weakening in early 1980. Now that is the sort of information which can really help in making decisions. Given this information, it was clearly suicidal to have attempted to introduce credit controls at the beginning of 1980; the economy at that point was already about to fall into recession. What resulted was a policy debacle that reduced confidence in the monetary authorities and increased the cost of reducing inflation. No forecasting model of the future will ever be 100 per

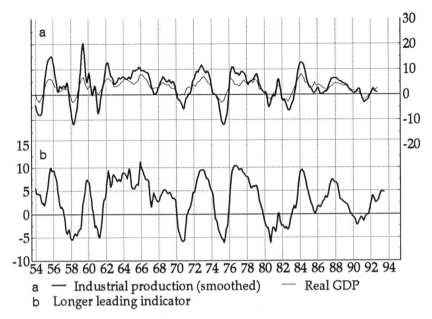

**Figure 11.8** Forecasting the economy (12-month rates of change)

cent accurate, but this longer-leading indicator has been very helpful. The approach has been tested over history and across countries. Figures 11.9 and 11.10 show longer-leading indicators that have been developed for a number of other countries. These forecast lines have the same characteristics as the one for the United States, and have proved very accurate at identifying the business cycle in each of these countries, including the latest cycle.

The forecasts have performed very well in *true* tests. The sharp downturns in the United Kingdom and Japan, for example, were forecast exactly, well in advance of the actual event. In both cases, domestic forecasters failed to anticipate the extent of the weakness. Some examples from *The Financial Economist* are included as illustrations, starting with forecasts for the United Kingdom.

> The economy is expected to remain weak throughout 1990, getting the new decade off to a very poor start. (December 1989)

> The new forecast shows the economy stumbling along into the final quarter of the year, but then finally becoming weaker. The subsequent decline is later, more sudden and also steeper than previously shown. (June 1990)

> The economy is about to enter a recession according to our indicators. (October 1990)

And, in the case of Japan:

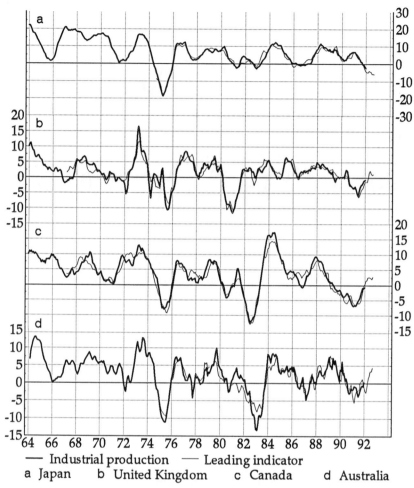

**Figure 11.9** Production forecasts (12-month rate of change)

Everyone expects continued growth, a slight slowdown this year, and a pick-up again in 1992. Our leading indicator suggests that the economy could be much weaker in the latter part of the year than currently expected. (May 1991)

In the United Kingdom, the Treasury conducted a study to explain the forecast failure, and concluded that it was the result of insufficient under-standing of the way the real economy works. Rigid computer models containing hundreds of equations and thousands of variables are not well

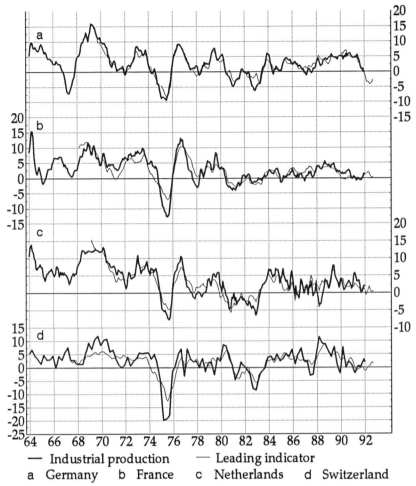

**Figure 11.10** Continental Europe (12-month rate of change)

suited to explain macroeconomic behavior. Apart from anything else, the models become so complicated that no one is able to understand how it all works. As a result, the machine takes over. Complexity is mistaken for sophistication, and the conclusions have to be accepted without qualification or understanding. The indicators presented here are simple and reasonably easy to understand. Some people see that as a weakness, but logic and the actual forecasting record suggest a different conclusion.

# Section III

## *THE MARKETS*

Just as there are many different approaches to investment, so too there are many markets to trade in. There are stocks, bonds, and commodities, and these can be broken down into their individual elements. People may concentrate on a particular group of stocks, e.g. only gold, or only high technology, or only low P/Es etc., or they could look at an individual or small group of commodities. In this way it is easier to gain the knowledge to become an expert in that particular area. In addition, there are all the foreign markets, which can also be broken down into their constituent parts, and the currencies that link them together. There are futures and options, and enough other derivative products to enable investors to specialize in one of over a hundred ways.

This book is about the broad market trends of the main markets. In the following chapters you will discover cyclical indicators that have had a documented history of success in predicting market turns. The indicators are all composites, formed from a number of different measures of underlying cyclical pressure. They refer to periods of time usually extending over many months, often years. The indicators are designed to identify the underlying trend at an early stage, and provide early warning of impending turning points.

Stocks and bonds are discussed in Chapters 12 and 13, with emphasis on the main characteristics of each market, and the presentation of composite cyclical indicators. Bonds are dominated by inflation and inflationary expectations. Investors in bonds need to understand how the yield curve varies over the business cycle, adjusting the maturity, or duration, of the portfolio to take advantage of the changing environment, while reducing risk. The quality spread, the differential between high and low quality bond yields, also varies over the business cycle.

The demand for stocks is based on the expectation of future profits, discounted by expected interest rates. Interest rates, therefore, become the key ingredient, since they will also affect profit forecasts as well. The stock market is a highly sensitive antenna that picks up any signal affecting the economy and corporate profits. There is no value in waiting for economic conditions to become clear; the obvious will have long since been discounted in market prices. The stock market offers tremendous potential but also substantial risk. Fortunately, the main cyclical indicator presented here shows that it has been possible to identify the major turning points ahead of time.

International markets offer opportunities that do not exist at home, and the ability to reduce risks through diversification. Part of any return, and risk, will be derived from changes in exchange rates, which are dealt with in Chapter 15. The exchange risk can be avoided by hedging the exchange rate forward. This can be thought of as a play on relative yield curves, and makes more sense for bonds than stocks. The different influences on exchange rates are also discussed, as inputs to developing a leading indicator.

The final chapter, Chapter 16, is devoted to gold. Gold performed spectacularly well in the 1970s, but extremely badly in the 1980s. It is important to understand that the 1970s provided a unique set of circumstances that will not be repeated. Part of the gold lore considers gold to be the one and only true money, and that price stability was, and will again be, achieved only under a gold standard. There are serious flaws with both these arguments. A chart is included that shows the real price of gold, i.e. the price deflated by the consumer price index, over the past 170 years. This comparison emphasizes just how dramatic the price increase was in the 1970s, and also how exceptional.

# 12

## THE BOND MARKET
### (the borrowing and lending of money)

In the early part of this book, interest rates were shown to play a central role in determining the business cycle. The emphasis there was on the cost of credit, and the way in which changes would have a wide-ranging impact on demand and the costs of production. It was shown that it was not only the level of interest rates that were important but also relative movements across different maturities, i.e. the yield curve.

The purpose of this chapter is to look at interest rates from the other side of the street; from the perspective of the lender or investor. Here again, the yield curve will be important, since a major choice facing investors in bonds is the maturity of the paper they decide to hold. When interest rates are expected to fall, the place to be is out at the long end of the maturity spectrum. On the other hand, if interest rates are expected to rise, emphasis on the long end will carry the risk of capital losses. Under those circumstances the emphasis will be on short-term paper.

Borrowers and lenders in the bond market will interpret news about the economy very differently—up to a point. Evidence of a strong economy will be good news to the borrower, who will generally have borrowed in anticipation of higher profits or rising asset values. If interest rates are pushed up as a result, that is not so bad, since the borrower at the long end has already locked in a lower rate. A strong economy is not such good news for the lender, particularly if demand is so strong as to result in rising inflation. Rising bond yields will result in a capital loss.

Interest rates will tend to fall during periods of economic weakness. As a result, signs of recession are usually greeted gleefully by bond holders. This negative orientation can make bond-market participants appear unpatriotic and cold-blooded, with their obvious joy at rising levels of unemployed. There is, however, a limit to this glorification of bad news. If the news gets bad enough, the danger of defaults increases, threatening the very existence of the corporate bond market. At such times, quality concerns become paramount. The Treasury may have a lot of debt outstanding, and this may be criticized widely, but there is nothing like owning some of it when the props under the economy look like they are about to give way.

Rising inflation is the deadly enemy of bond holders. Bonds can be indexed against inflation, as in Brazil and in some cases in the United Kingdom, but bonds with a fixed coupon and fixed capital value are at risk. For example, the acceleration of inflation in the 1970s caused losses to bond holders to become acute. Those who bet on the government, and price stability, were badly burnt, while the cynics prospered. Bonds were supposed to be conservative and safe. It is not surprising, therefore, that people felt cheated when it turned out that they were in the middle of a crap shoot, and they were the ones being shot at. Their *safe* bonds were, in fact, highly speculative, and they were on the wrong side of the trade.

There are two key questions facing investors in bonds: what to buy or sell? and when to buy or sell? Timing will depend on the movement of interest rates and the yield curve over the business cycle, and also needs to take account of any longer-term inflationary trends. As far as the 'what' is concerned, the main choices are maturity and quality. There are other considerations such as foreign bonds, which are dealt with separately, and convertibles, which share characteristics with equities.

The extensive interrelationship between economic behavior and the cost of credit, itself imparts a significant cyclicality to the economy and interest rates. High real interest rates raise costs and lower demand, leading eventually to a decline in loan demand and a fall in interest rates. Low real interest rates stimulate spending, investment and borrowing, leading to expansion and, if carried too far, inflation. This inflation, or even the expectation of it, will cause investors to lower their demand for bonds, thereby pushing up long-term bond yields. There are, therefore, automatic forces at work within the financial markets that will tend to bring excessive expansion under control. However, the monetary authorities can play a major role in the timing and precise details of the cyclical pattern through their control over the reserves of the financial system. It is necessary to understand the motives of the authorities in order to understand cyclical movements in interest rates.

There are many different interest rates and, for analysis to be of any use, it is important to make at least broad distinctions between short- and long-term and between high- and low-quality. Other concerns, such as different tax treatment, and the effect of varying tax rates, which can be very important to particular individuals and institutions, are not dealt with here. It is not only short-term interest rates and long-term bond yields that change over the business cycle, but also the yield curve; i.e. the relationship between short-term interest rates and long-term bond yields. This relative movement in interest rates is a key relationship in the link between interest rates and the rest of the economy, and, one step removed, on the price of bonds.

Another change in relative interest rates associated with the business cycle, which it is also important to note, is quality rather than maturity. Spreads between high- and low-quality paper of similar maturity can change a great deal depending on economic conditions and the confidence of the financial community. A major factor affecting quality spreads is the growth of debt during good times. Debt becomes top-heavy and fragile as the economy moves into recession, thereby changing the conditions and assumptions on which the debt was originally built up. Not only are borrowers less able to repay but, at such times, lenders suddenly become risk-averse and see the advantages of liquidity as overwhelming.

## Short-term versus long-term

Short-term interest rates and long-term bond yields are closely related, but not so close that the spread between different maturities remains constant over the business cycle. The relationship between interest rates over different maturities is known as the yield curve. Figure 12.1 shows the yield curve in US Treasury debt at the end of 1990, and in June 1991, from 3 months to 30 years. A certain yield curve exists at a point in time. It is like taking a snapshot at one particular moment, and the picture will change over time. Sometimes the yield curve will slope down, with each successive interest rate below the earlier one. That relationship is referred to as a negatively sloped, or inverted, yield curve. At other times it will slope upwards, in what is called a normal or positive yield curve, when interest rates move steadily higher as maturity is extended. These are the two extreme possibilities but other variants are possible, containing combinations of negative and positive yield curves. A humped yield curve would rise for a while but then start to fall over longer maturities. The exact shape of the yield curve will depend on economic conditions, and will offer different opportunities to investors.

Looking at Fig. 12.1, it can be seen that, in both cases, the yield curves were steeply positive over the first five years, after which they flatten out. The curve became much steeper during the first half of 1991, as short-term interest rates fell but bond yields went up. A snapshot taken later in the summer would have shown bond yields coming down as well.

In an important sense, the yield curve reflects expectations about what will happen to interest rates in the future. Anyone wanting to invest money for six months, for example, has the choice of buying one-month paper and rolling it over five times, three-month paper rolled over once or a single six-month bill or deposit. Taken literally, if the six-month rate is above the three-month rate, that implies a rise in interest rates in the second three months to a rate even higher than the current six-month rate in order to produce the same yield at the end of six months. A literal unwinding of

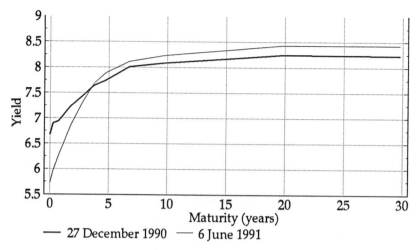

**Figure 12.1** Yield curve

the yield curve in this way is not possible because of other factors. The existence of transactions costs suggests that the future rate should be even higher. However, the desire for liquidity is likely to swamp that effect, with investors receiving real, or perceived, benefit by having more immediate access to their money.

While these temporal choices are a factor in determining the yield curve, there are other, more powerful, forces at work. Some forecasters have tried to use the yield curve to predict interest rates in the future only to be continually proved wrong. A negative yield curve is supposed to imply falling interest in the future, but short-rates remained above long from 1978 to 1981, except for a brief moment in 1980. Equally, there are a great many times when a positive yield curve has been followed by lower interest rates not higher rates. Examples include the yield curves shown above. These were both steeply positive but short-term interest rates still fell later on and, even after June 1991, rates fell across the whole spectrum. The dynamics of the economy overwhelm such naïve forecasting methodology.

The yield curve that was shown in earlier chapters was of a simpler variety, just the ratio of short-term interest rates to long-term bond yields. This reduces a complex relationship to a single dimension and allows it to be plotted over time. Some of the subtlety is lost, but the gain in being able to look at how the yield curve changes over time, and in relation to other economic developments, is worth the loss as far as macro-economic analysis is concerned. A more detailed yield curve is still necessary when it comes to making investment decisions about which maturity to buy.

The main influences on interest rates at all maturities are inflationary expectations and the strength of the economy, but the effects work in different ways. There are no absolutes but, in general, short-term interest rates will be influenced more by the economy than inflation, while the relative balance is reversed for bonds. Inflation has become more important since the sharp acceleration in the 1970s, and, at times, has been the dominant influence on monetary policy. Controlling inflation, however, is not the only objective of the monetary authorities. They are also concerned about the level of employment, economic growth, the exchange rate and health of the financial system. Sometimes these objectives will not be in conflict, and the balance of policy will simply be a question of emphasis. At other times, the existence of major conflicts requires much more difficult decisions to be made.

The point to make about inflationary expectations is not that they are unimportant in determining short-term interest rates, only that they are absolutely crucial at the long end of the market. The supply of bonds will matter, but not as much as demand. Supply has a habit of fluctuating with demand; strong demand will quickly bring out new issues tailored to the particular maturities in demand, whereas weak demand will see supply dry up very quickly. The supply of government debt is not so flexible, and this often dominates national bond markets. What seems to happen is that the supply of private sector bonds is forced to adjust to the supply from the public sector. Long-term, structural borrowing needs will affect long-term, real bond yields, as a reflection of real investment opportunities. This provides the underlying trend around which business cycle influences play a dominant role.

Short-term rates and long-term yields will move differently, but they are not in opposition. It is more that they are competing in a race. Bonds are the tortoise, moving more slowly, while short-rates are the hare, racing up and down much more quickly, and passing the tortoise on the way. The short end of the market is where all residual demands find their way. If bond yields rise to a level which borrowers think is too high and will not be sustained they will stop issuing bonds, preferring instead to borrow short term. That sort of behavior will tend to push up short-term interest rates towards the end of the cycle. At the higher levels of interest rates, the desire to borrow is likely to slow down, but the need to borrow will increase. The opposite behavior will be observed when bond yields seem low.

Exaggerating these moves is the fact that the short end of the interest rate spectrum is where the central bank can have the most influence. The Federal Reserve can exert no direct influence over long-term bond yields through manipulation of reserve levels. There will be an influence, but it will work indirectly through the effect on inflation and inflationary expectations, and may well be in the opposite direction to that intended. The speed of the reaction will depend on how much confidence investors have in the anti-inflation resolve of the central bank, but it will never be as immediate or extensive as the effect at the short end of the market. The combination of a concentration on short-term borrowing and restraints on the supply of reserves is capable of forcing short-term interest rates up sharply during the latter stages of the business cycle. In the absence of non-market credit controls, this will often be accompanied by an inverted yield curve. How inverted, and how long it will last, will depend on how ingrained inflationary expectations have become, and how resistant demand remains in the face of higher interest rates. Early action by the monetary authorities will avoid the extremes that characterized business cycles in the 1970s and early 1980s when, for a while, it seemed that conditions were getting out of control.

During the terminal phase of the business cycle there is increased concern about the continued viability of the economy, and long-term investments start to look less attractive. The rush for liquidity results in a fall in short-term interest rates which is often quite sharp. This important feature of the economic cycle occurs after the onset of recession, when it becomes clear that continued restraint will jeopardize the very existence of the economic system. Not only is there a heightened demand for liquidity, but also the authorities will relax the tourniquet on the financial pipeline, thereby permitting an increase in the supply of reserves.

Each cycle has its own unique characteristics, but interest rates tend to rise gradually to start with, often resisted by the monetary authorities who continue to supply excessive reserves. Towards the end of the cycle, the rise in rates tends to accelerate sharply. The exact pattern will depend crucially on the actions of the central bank. Since the inflationary experience of the 1970s, the Federal Reserve has tightened policy much more quickly, and as a result has started to ease before the onset of recession. Even so, sure signs of economic weakness will still bring forth a sharp drop in short-term interest rates. By that time, optimism has turned to pessimism, and finally to fear. Once the conditions have been established, the trigger is generally supplied by some domestic or international event which suddenly focuses attention on the new reality.

An increase in inflation will result in an increase in long-term interest rates, as lenders seek compensation for the loss of principal and real interest income resulting from the higher inflation rate. If short rates do not change, borrowers will turn to the short end of the market where costs are cheaper. This, in turn, will push up short rates. Short-term rates will be held down only if the monetary authorities pump in large amounts of additional reserves, and there are limits to how long that can continue in the face of a deteriorating bond market. Once tightening is under way, short-term interest rates will rise even further in the attempt to bring inflation under control. The only way that the authorities can maintain an easy monetary policy under these conditions is if bonds are indexed to inflation.

The extent to which short rates rise relative to long yields will depend on the resolve of the monetary authorities, while the level interest rates will have to reach will be determined by the rate of inflation itself, and its recent history. The level of nominal interest rates is generally meaningless as a measure of tightness or ease. An interest rate of 20 per cent has very different implications for policy and the future course of inflation, depending whether inflation is running at 5 per cent or 40 per cent. Real interest rates will provide a useful guide to policy, and it will also be instructive to watch the behavior of the yield curve. Relative interest rates reveal a great deal about the tightness of monetary policy.

Within a market environment, operating monetary policy means squeezing reserves in order to put up the price of money at the short end of the market. This squeeze on reserves may or may not be reflected in changes in the measured reserves of the banking system. Distortions are created, particularly in the short term, when rapid institutional changes are taking place within the financial system, and when transfers between different deposit categories imply different reserve requirements. Under such circumstances, the most reliable guide to monetary policy is the price of money, and in particular the price of short-term money, relative to the rate of inflation and the long-term bond yield. The relationship between money growth, the yield curve, and economic growth, is shown in Fig. 12.2. The yield curve here is measured by the ratio between the three-month money rate and the Aaa corporate bond yield.

Two major technical advantages of the yield curve as a measure of policy and indicator of the future are (a) the speed with which the information becomes available, that is, instantly for the yield curve, and with a lag for the money supply and other statistics, and (b) the reliability of the information. There are no seasonal adjustment problems and the data are not continually being revised and amended, as are other statistics on money and the economy. Which is not to say that these other measures are not valuable indicators of changes in credit conditions. These technical considerations are only important because of the role interest rates and the yield curve play in the economy. If these were random variables, it would not really matter whether they were reliable, or even available.

When short-term interest rates rise significantly above long-term rates and remain there, they make short-term credit expensive and raise doubts about whether the increased cost can be passed on. As long as rates are expected to fall quickly, the contractionary effect is slight. Short-term interest rates have to remain high and the yield curve has to remain inverted long enough to create the expectation that they will stay that way for a long time. At some point, there will be a sharp rise in risk and uncertainty, credit demands will be slashed, and demand for certain goods and services

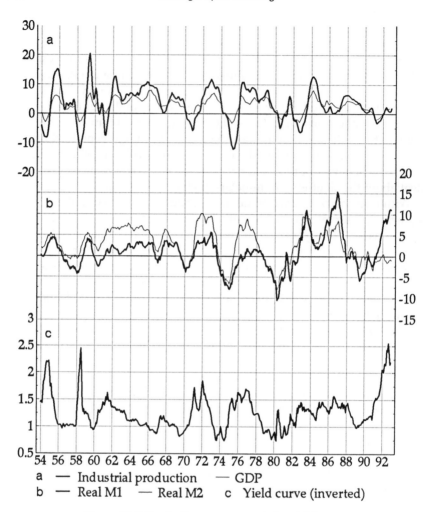

a   — Industrial production    — GDP
b   — Real M1    — Real M2    c   Yield curve (inverted)

**Figure 12.2** Production, money and the yield curve

will evaporate. Then, in a domino effect, the decline in activity and disruption of balance sheets is transmitted through the rest of the economy,
leading to lower inflation and inflationary expectations. It is important to
recognize that monetary policy will only put downward pressure on inflation
by first depressing demand—there is no other way. And it is only then that
interest rates can be allowed to come down and the yield curve can
unwind. Very often, unless policy is managed with perfect timing, which
means anticipating events before they happen, such times will also be
associated with recession.

How much time it takes to reach this position, where expectations in the private sector are turned around, and demand and output are lowered, depends on many different factors. Three major influences are discussed briefly below.

First, inflation itself delays the process. The longer inflation has been a problem, the more persistent it becomes and, therefore, the harder reversing the trend becomes. Inflationary expectations are built more strongly into the decisions of government, workers, business people and investors. New contracts are structured in such a way as to provide protection from the inflation expected in the future, and this increases downward resistance and puts a floor under the rate of inflation. As a result, it becomes harder and harder to break expectations and get inflation to turn down. Under these conditions a recession is very likely.

Second, the more quickly policy has been reversed in the past, leaving inflation unscathed, the harder it becomes to reverse expectations. Rates cannot fall until they are expected not to fall, and weakness on the part of the monetary authorities in the past will only increase the problems of achieving control in the future. The situation is analogous to that of the little boy who cried 'Wolf!' so many times that finally when a wolf did appear no one came to his rescue. Monetary authorities may start with a good deal of credibility, but once credibility is lost it is hard to win back; to do so then may well require excessively tight policies. Under such conditions, a recession is virtually inevitable in order to break expectations.

Third, credit controls, interest-rate ceilings and restraints on competition have been gradually dismantled in recent years. This process has been speeded up in the 1980s, putting more pressure on interest rates to clear the financial markets. The overall effects on demand may be the same, but the process will be different, and the visible signs of stress will also change. With more emphasis on the price of credit, interest rates may have to be pushed higher and stay there longer.

In sum, all these forces were working in the same direction through the 1970s, to make the yield curve more inverted and to keep it that way for longer. The main periods of tight money are clearly visible in Fig. 12.2, in each case preceding the major downturns in economic activity that have occurred since 1952. During this time, the peaks and troughs of money supply growth have tended to become more pronounced, while the yield curve, at least up until the latest cycle, became less positive during periods of monetary ease and more negative when monetary policy was tightened. These trends were related to the gradual acceleration of the underlying rate of inflation, which became embedded in expectations, as well as to disillusionment with official policy, and the removal of constraints on competition between financial institutions. The latest cycle has reflected the early action by the Federal Reserve to ease monetary policy before the economy fell into recession. There were also signs of improving inflationary expectations, although there remained some suspicion.

The yield curve is a valuable summary of a great deal of behavior and information. It is important both in explaining the cyclical behavior of the economy, as discussed in Chapter 11, and as a basic guideline to the bond market. A simple rule has made a lot of money for investors, while enabling them to avoid substantial risks during the postwar period: stay in bonds as long as the yield curve is positive, and go short as soon as the yield curve becomes inverted; that is, as soon as short rates rise above long bond yields. This rough rule of thumb is very crude, but it has proved very effective. It has allowed investors to earn the higher bond yield as long as short rates were lower, but still to avoid the worst of the bond market crashes that have occurred. While this easy-to-follow rule would have improved performance beyond a simple buy-and-hold strategy, it still left some money on the table, and should be expected to become less effective as understanding of that relationship becomes more widespread. The indicators discussed later help to improve performance even more, and on a more consistent basis.

## Maturity and duration

The maturity of a bond is the date at which the principal is paid back. If a bond has a call option on it, the final maturity may not be very important. If current yields are higher than they were at issue when the call time arrives, the bond will be allowed to run. On the other hand, if yields are lower, it is likely that the bonds will be called, since the borrower will be able to reborrow the money at lower cost. Call provisions favor the borrower at the expense of the lender, and should be viewed with extreme scepticism. That factor alone justifies a higher yield. More advantageous to the lender are put provisions that allow the bond holder to sell the bonds back to the borrower at a particular price at, or after, a specific date, i.e. the lender has the right but not the obligation to shorten the maturity of the bond. It is possible to calculate yields to maturity, to call or to put.

Typically, investors should extend maturity the more confident they are that inflation and yields will fall in the future. By doing this they will be able to lock in a higher yield for the whole life of the bond. For example, a bond that was bought with a current yield of 14 per cent will continue to provide that higher return even if market yields fall to 7 per cent. The price of the bond in the meantime will have risen so that the yield, to anyone buying after yields have fallen, will only be 7 per cent. This produces a substantial capital gain to the holder of the bond. The gain will be larger the longer the term, maturity, still to run, since the longer the term the greater the benefit from receiving the higher yield.

The greatest leverage will be obtained with long-term, zero coupon bonds. These bonds pay no income over the life of the bond, and all the return is in the price. As a result, the price of these bonds will fluctuate substantially as yields change. US Treasuries are systematically stripped down to provide a zero coupon bond and a stream of coupons with no final payment. A disadvantage for US investors is that the phantom yield on zeros is taxed in the year it accrues even though it is not received. There are one or two exceptions, but that is the normal status. One advantage of these bonds is that they will lock in a true yield to maturity. For normal bonds, the yield to maturity is calculated on the assumption that coupon payments are reinvested at the same yield existing at the time of the calculation. If interest rates fall, this will not be possible, and the yield to maturity will actually be less than it seemed to be when it was bought.

The concept of *duration* is used by professional bond managers to fine-tune maturity decisions. The risk of holding a long maturity is, to some extent, offset if the yield is also high. That is because it will take less time for the price of the bond to be repaid in fall. In addition, money received before final maturity has a higher present value, i.e. it is worth more than payments made much further in the future. As a result, a long-maturity bond with a high yield may have the same duration as a short-maturity bond carrying a lower yield. The idea of duration was developed separately by two economists, F. R. Macaulay and J. R. Hicks, in the 1930s (Macaulay, 1980; Hicks, 1939).

An approximate way of thinking about the duration of a bond is as the average life of all future interest and principal payments associated with that bond. Duration brings out an important feature of the relationship between price and yield, which is that price volatility is reduced as yields increase. This can be seen in Table 12.1, which shows that as yields rise so maturity has less and less influence on duration. This is important. Hicks demonstrated that duration measures the sensitivity of a bond's price to changes in the yield. To give an example of what happens as duration changes, consider the price change needed to generate a full percentage point change in bond yields. At a five-year duration the price change would be five points; three-year duration, three points and two-year duration,

Table 12.1 Duration of a 10 per cent coupon bond

| Yield | Maturity 5 year | Maturity 10 year | Maturity 30 year |
|-------|-----------------|------------------|------------------|
| 10% | 4.05 | 6.54 | 9.94 |
| 15% | 3.95 | 5.96 | 7.23 |
| 20% | 3.83 | 5.38 | 5.56 |

two points, i.e. the price change is less the shorter is the duration of the bond.

In the example shown, the risk characteristics of the 10-year and 30-year maturities are virtually identical at a 20 per cent yield, but much higher at the long end with a 10 per cent yield. The risk considered here is just the price risk. Event risk, the risk of default, is separate from the issue of maturity or duration. One way of interpreting this aspect of duration is that it becomes increasingly attractive to extend maturity as yields rise, particularly if yields are highest at the longest end of the spectrum. Price risk will be very similar if yields rise further, because durations are already very close, and partly because they will move even closer. On the other hand, if yields fall, durations will widen out again, which is another way of saying that the price of the longer-maturity bond will rise faster than in the case of shorter-maturity bonds.

The principle is still the same: hold long-duration bonds when yields are expected to fall, go short when yields are expected to rise. Medium maturities are for those with a less certain outlook. Medium-term bonds will not gain as much if yields fall, but will not lose as much if yields rise. The slope of the yield curve may be such that medium-term bonds become particularly attractive, but in general investors trying to maximize the benefits of the business cycle will need to emphasize the two extremes.

The apparent safety of intermediate maturities/duration is often deceptive. If inflation picks up, yields will tend to rise faster at the long end, imposing potentially significant capital losses on bond holders. However, if monetary policy is then tightened, which would be the normal response, the yield cure will flatten, and is likely to invert. What that means is that yields at the short to medium end will increase more than at the long end. This yield curve effect tends to offset the greater capital stability of shorter maturities; that only applies for equal changes in yield.

## Quality spreads

Another aspect of interest rates that investors should take into account is the movement of the spread between high- and low-quality financial instruments. Quality spreads can be used in two ways: first as a guide to investment, either in staying with quality or playing the spread, and second, as a confirming indicator of a turning point in the economic cycle and the level of yields. Liquidity, as discussed earlier, is a function of confidence, dependent basically on the perceptions of investors and potential investors. The trouble is that these perceptions can change dramatically over the economic cycle. Confidence is generally built up only gradually, but it breaks suddenly. At such times, the mass of investors demand only the highest quality, and the spread between high- and low-risk paper can widen dramatically. Even without actual bankruptcy and repudiation of debt, the investor in low-quality paper is likely to see the value of the investment decline sharply, even as the price of high-quality paper is increasing. When this happens, investors who took lower-quality paper in order to earn a higher return will remember what they really always knew—that return and risk are positively correlated.

It is not simply that expectations change against a constant background. Typically, what happens is that debts accumulate during periods of easy money and favorable expectations of the future. Creditors are inclined to see their own claim in isolation from the many other claims that are also mounting up. However, when money tightens and liquidity becomes more highly valued, individuals lower their expectations about the future, and closer examination reveals the huge stock of debt which has been built up.

Two things happen then which together make creditors very nervous. First, the economic assumptions that were made to justify the original loan are found to be excessively optimistic. An example is the widespread assumption in 1980 that the price of oil would rise continuously, in both nominal and real terms, throughout the 1980s. It is one thing to lend to oil producers under that assumption, but quite another if there is a glut of oil and the real price starts to fall. Another example would be the excessive lending on commercial real estate in the late 1980s. Each project may have made sense on its own, but collectively they created huge excess capacity. Second, the situation is made far worse by the huge buildup of debt, and often a problem of gigantic proportions is created. Each individual loan becomes lost in a sea of credit, which only adds to the cash-flow problems of the debtors. Under these circumstances, creditors' concerns about relative returns are replaced by a deep-seated fear for the safety of their capital.

A conservative measure of riskiness is provided by the average quality spread for the United States, as shown in Fig. 12.3. Two versions are presented, one in terms of the straight difference between Baa and Aaa yields, and the second as the ratio of Baa to Aaa yields. The pattern of both series has been broadly similar from 1953 or 1991. On the basis of differences alone, it is possible to argue that there was a significant increase in risk over the 1980s, and some people made that point at the time. However, it should be recognized that the level of interest rates had also risen strongly. Consequently, for any given percentage difference, the absolute difference would be greatly expanded. It is not possible to say how investors actually perceive quality spreads, but it is likely that the absolute difference over-states expectations at times of high nominal interest rates such as those recently experienced.

The concerns expressed at the time about the rise in the risk premium were based on a short-term horizon. The chart shown here goes back far enough to bring history into focus. One thing this suggests is that at times

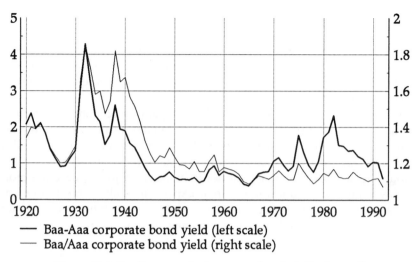

Figure 12.3 Quality spreads: long-term bond yields (annual)

of low interest rates the ratio series almost certainly overstates the degree of perceived risk. The true measure most likely lies somewhere in between, but at least the direction of movement in both series is the same. Also, it would clearly be wrong to suggest that the quality spread through the 1980s was at all comparable to what happened in the 1930s.

There is a clear cyclicality in quality spreads which is closely related to the level of rates at the high-quality end. Quality spreads are narrowest when interest rates are low and the economy is growing—basically when liquidity and confidence are both running at a high level. The existence of only one of these conditions is not enough. In the 1930s, the rate on high-quality bonds was very low, but the quality spreads rose to astronomical levels because of the perceived risk of default. Also, even with high growth, quality spreads start to widen, if only gradually, as interest rates begin to firm up.

While the early widening of spreads is only gradual, the final move up at the end of the cycle is usually explosive. This last convulsive move is closely associated with a crack in the market, the collapse of loan demand, and a sharp, often dramatic, fall in interest rates at the high-quality end. At this point, risks of a cumulative collapse, which could prove uncontrollable, seem highest. At the lowest end of the quality spectrum yields rise, while yields on medium-quality paper do not change much either way, always assuming that a major collapse is avoided, whereas the high-quality end shows sharp improvement. This divergence widens the spreads dramatically, just when rates start down, and the economy is still in recession.

It is at this point that the Federal Reserve must step in to maintain confidence. To do otherwise would risk a repeat of the devastation of the 1930s. The Federal Reserve will, therefore, provide added liquidity, just at the point when interest rates were to start coming down anyway. However, the Federal Reserve is acting for other reasons, to protect confidence and the financial system, and there really is no alternative. The operation of this support function does help to explain why interest rates fall so dramatically when perceived risks in the survival of the economy become extreme, and why more of the same can be expected in the future.

The spread between Aaa and Baa bonds is a very technical measure of risk. It has the advantage of being comparable over time, but does not take account of the particular circumstances of different business cycles. For example, the emphasis on credit risk shifts through time. Texas suffered badly in the early 1980s along with the Latin-American debtors, then there was farming. In the early 1990s, it has been the turn of commercial real estate, the S&L industry, banks and insurance companies. Through the center of that financial mess, ran the so-called junk bond mania. Junk bonds is the name given to high-yield bonds with a credit rating of BB or below.

The low rating has typically been earned because of the huge amounts of debt taken on. Partly for that reason it seems there has been too little discrimination between the debt of different companies. For example, the Campeau debt for Federated and Allied department stores and RJR Nabisco debt both earned a junk rating, making it seem as if they were in the same sinking boat. This comparison was misleading, since RJR had/has a much greater cash flow and underlying profitability to service the debt. High leverage can be a problem, but it does not have to be.

In 1989 and 1990, the spread between high-quality and junk bonds widened out substantially, particularly as the economy and the stock market turned down. But the weakness did not last, despite some extremely large and well publicized defaults. Using such an index of lower-rated bonds would have shown wider spreads over this cycle, but that would also be true in other cycles as well. What can be seen in the charts here is that concern shows up even where the risk difference is not very great.

## Inflationary expectations

The overriding long-run influence on bond-market yields is provided by expectations about inflation. Economic journals are full of attempts to explain exactly how inflationary expectations are formed, but there are many problems. It would be naïve to believe that a single factor determines expectations of inflation, or for that matter expectations about anything; but people do learn from the past. Bond yields in the 1970s typically undershot the actual rate of inflation, strongly suggesting that the view of investors about the future course of inflation was too optimistic. The persistence of inflation, however, gradually pushed up the trend of long-term bond yields until, as shown in Fig. 12.4, the rate was pushed well above inflation, where it subsequently stayed throughout the 1980s. The process is cumulative. Investors eventually demanded a real return on their assets—to compensate them not only for current lending but also for losses on past lending.

It is necessary to go beyond the actual measured rate of inflation and try to understand people's expectations about future inflation. Expectations are strongly influenced by the past trend, and are slow to adapt to a change in that trend. However, people do adapt as experience shows that they have been wrong. And once expectations have adapted to the new trend, they will be slow to change again. History shows that actual expectations follow the theoretical level as long as the trend rate of inflation changes only slowly. When the shifts in inflation are more dramatic, bond yields can deviate quite a long way from the theoretical level. At such times, this is a sign of exceptional opportunity or exceptional risk, depending on whether inflation is being under- or over-estimated.

Long-term bond yields tend not to rise as fast as inflation when the inflationary trend is accelerating, nor do they fall as fast when the trend of inflation is decelerating. Irving Fisher argued that the lags in the full adjustment of inflationary expectations could be very long (Fisher, 1930). The lags certainly seem to far exceed anything normally assumed.

One thing to make absolutely clear is that bond yields are not related to the level of prices, or the level of any nominal series. It is only the rate at which prices change, and are expected to change, that really matters. This is not a subject that warrants discussion, except that such relationships have been claimed between prices, particularly commodity prices, and bond yields. Such correlations may seem to exist over relatively short periods of time, but they have to be spurious. The idea is so illogical that it is not even worth including a chart to demonstrate the point. After all, a nominal series may increase a very long way; look at wholesale prices in Chapter 6. The price level may double, triple, quadruple or go up 100 times, but when prices stabilize, at whatever level, bond yields will still be in a reasonable range. Bond yields will be affected by the rate of change of prices, not the level.

Figure 12.4 shows the corporate bond yield together with three different ways of measuring an expected yield based on inflationary expectations, calculated from past inflation. A constant has been added to each series in order to reflect the reasonable expectation of a positive real yield on bonds. The first measure, at the bottom of the figure, shows the actual rate of consumer price inflation on an annual basis. This rate picks up some of

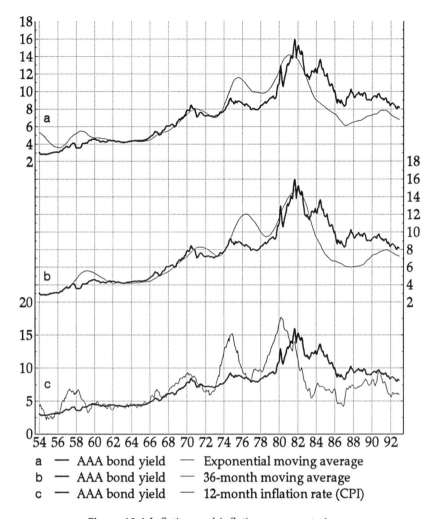

a  — AAA bond yield    — Exponential moving average
b  — AAA bond yield    — 36-month moving average
c  — AAA bond yield    — 12-month inflation rate (CPI)

**Figure 12.4** Inflation and inflationary expectations

the short-term moves, but exaggerates the movement and some of the
turning points. The middle series takes out the volatility from the original
inflation series by smoothing it over 36 months. The smoothed series does
a better job of reflecting the underlying trend, but there are times when it
is a little slow in changing direction.

    The top series tries to retain the benefits of smoothing over a long time
period, while speeding up the reaction time to sudden changes in direction.
This is done by calculating an exponential moving average, giving greater
weight to the latest information than to old news. Through the 1950s and

1960s, and on into the 1970s, the exponential moving average tracked out a pretty reasonable path for bond yields. The one major deviation, in 1957–58, when actual yields and expected inflation went sharply in opposite directions, was soon followed by a period of readjustment during which bond yields moved back towards inflationary expectations.

As inflation took off in the second half of the 1970s, inflationary expectations failed to keep up. The conclusion has to be that bond holders were too optimistic, seriously underestimating how high inflation would go and how long it would stay there. As a result, bond holders suffered a period of negative real returns. The crisis of confidence that followed eventually pushed yields up above the level required by this measure of inflationary expectations. Now investors were suspicious and demanded exceptionally high real yields to compensate for the increased risk. In fact, risks had fallen, with the result that bond holders achieved exceptionally high real yields over an extended period of time.

Simply telling people that inflation will fall, and that the right policies are being taken, will bring down neither inflationary expectations nor long-term bond yields. It would be strange if they did, and yet that is what some economists and politicians argued on both sides of the Atlantic, as the United States and the United Kingdom embarked on their *fight against inflation* in the early 1980s. This view was based on a naïve version of *rational* expectations. Events proved otherwise; only a sharp fall in inflation and a deep recession were capable of bringing down yields, as indeed should have been expected, after the years of persistent monetary ease and inflation, and even then bond yields stayed above the trend suggested by historical relationships.

Here is an influence that is longer than the business cycle, and the information it provides is an important supplement to the cyclical indicators. In broad terms, returns will be above normal if yields are above the theoretical level, and will be sub-par if yields are below the theoretical level. In the latter case, the bond market will be much more vulnerable to any deterioration in the cyclical indicators. In interpreting cyclical influences it is, therefore, also necessary to pay attention to the expected bond yield.

It is also important to take account of the level of government expenditure, and the size of the budget deficit. Government spending has been a major factor contributing to the pressure of excess demand, which has led to accelerating and sustained inflation. Consequently, government spending has now become an important factor in influencing expectations about inflation. The pressure on financial markets coming from massive government demands for funds has also directly resulted in higher interest rates than would otherwise have been necessary—although that has not prevented interest rates from falling at times of very weak private sector financial demands.

As long as bond yields remain above the exponential moving average, this provides a positive bias to the bond market. It means that investors are still sceptical and there is no danger of overconfidence. The two lines are slowly moving closer together, and will eventually come back into line. Investors have come to expect high real yields as the normal situation, but that has to change. The 1980s was an exceptional opportunity for investors in bonds, but that cannot last forever.

## Bond cycle indicator

This brings us to the cyclical influences on bond yields, which operate about the longer-run trend of inflation. First, there is the impact of liquidity conditions on short-term interest rates and the relationship between short- and long-term rates, as measured by the yield curve. The process of tightening monetary policy by raising short-term rates and inverting the yield curve will have an adverse effect on bond prices by restricting the liquidity of the market. If cash is yielding more than bonds, this reinforces the downward pressure on bond prices. Bond dealers are faced with a negative cost of carry on their inventory of bonds, i.e. the financing cost exceeds the yield earned, so they are suffering losses on a current basis. Such a move will, however, help to establish the conditions under which bond yields will fall in the future.

Continued easy money and rising inflation will eventually accelerate inflationary expectations, which will also cause bond prices to fall. However, a standard feature of the cyclical behavior of bond yields is that they are also forced higher by attempts to correct the inflation that accounts for the longer-term deterioration of fixed-interest asset values. If investors had complete confidence in government policy, their confidence would help greatly to offset the negative impact of reduced market liquidity. In fact, quite the opposite generally occurs. The government action to stop inflation actually seems to increase investors' awareness of the problem, resulting in rising bond yields. A number of the indicators developed in Chapter 11 can be used to measure the influence of tightness or ease of monetary policy.

Credit conditions generally are also important in determining bond yields. In a period of economic expansion, private-sector credit demands grow rapidly. After a time, this results in a tightening of monetary policy, which pushes up interest rates as liquidity is drained out of the system, and interest rates remain high as long as demands for bank credit are excessive. Not until these demands fall are interest rates able to come down in sustainable fashion. That is the first stage. In the second stage, liquidity is added aggressively when credit demand turns negative and starts to fall.

Another way of approaching the bond market is to look directly at the strength of the economy. Such an indicator is useful on the grounds that a weak economy tends to bring down interest rates. In fact, history shows that it is a weakening economy, rather than one which is simply weak, that is more important. The most useful indicator of economic activity in this case has proved to be the economic activity index (EAI) presented earlier in Chapter 11.

The EAI provides early warning of decisive moves by the economy into recession and back to recovery. This indicator is important in triggering buy signals, but generally returns to strength at a time when there is still the potential for further improvement in the bond market. That is because loan demand does not pick up so quickly in the early stages of recovery, and the initial strengthening of the EAI should be treated as an early warning signal. The EAI represents a highly conservative measure. Economic strength tends to indicate that bond yields are unlikely to fall. Whether there is pressure for yields to rise very much depends on the level of *real* yields; if these are high it will tend to limit any increase. This is less important when real yields are high, and inflation is reasonably under control, but was crucial in the less favorable circumstances that typified the 1970s and early 1980s.

The most that such indicators can do is explain broad cyclical movements, and in this they have been very successful. The result of combining and weighting the indicators discussed above produces the composite cyclical bond market indicator shown in the BONDMETER in Fig. 12.5. This indicator is designed to identify major turning points only, and does not track the detailed path of bonds. It provides warning of pressure on bond yields, as opposed to the total return on holding bonds. Bonds may provide a reasonable return even under conditions where yields are moving sideways or even rising slightly. Whether that justifies holding bonds in the portfolio will also depend on the level of short-term interest rates. The leading indicator is shown in Fig. 12.5, together with bond yields, the expected yield and the change in the total return on bonds.

The serious investor will also pay close attention to other economic and political developments that may change the timing, and under unusual circumstances even the trend of bond prices. The advantage of an indicator such as this is that it provides a useful summary of the main cyclical forces that are likely to influence bond prices. An anchor to reality can prove invaluable when fear and uncertainty are strongly suggesting selling not buying. Or, when complacency has set in and no one can be bothered to look up and see the gathering storm clouds.

The indicator should be interpreted in conjunction with the expected real yield, which is also shown on the chart. When real yields are high, as they have been through most of the 1980s, this imparts a positive bias to bonds. Risk is significantly increased when the real yield is too low. This combination has identified all major turning points in bond yields. For

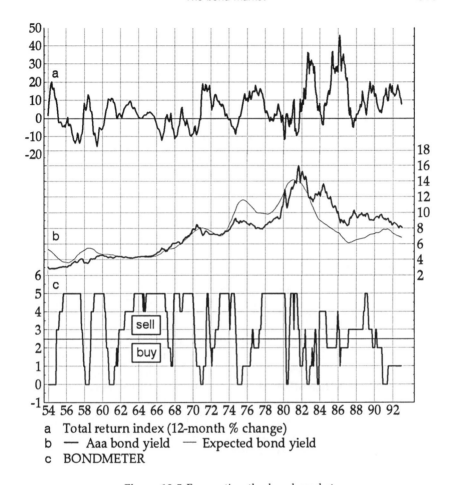

a   Total return index (12-month % change)
b   — Aaa bond yield    — Expected bond yield
c   BONDMETER

**Figure 12.5** Forecasting the bond market

example, the indicator was bullish through 1982, apart from a brief time
when it turned negative in the middle of the year, but went positive again
ahead of the sharp fall in yields that started in August of that year. Extracts
from *The Financial Economist*, below, show that the indicator stayed bullish
into 1983, but turned negative ahead of the correction that extended into
1984:

> The desire by governments to ease further and bring down interest rates is
> increasingly running into the obstacle of reality, which suggests caution, and
> increasing rates. (May 1983)

The importance of looking at the expected inflation rate was apparent in 1984 as yields backed up, and created attractive buying opportunities ahead of an actual turn in the BONDMETER:

> The gap between the actual yield and this expected yield has now equaled the maximum spread reached in 1958, and this provides the possibility of a significant rally around present levels. (July 1984)

And favorable conditions continued through 1985:

> The greatest potential exists in the US where real yields are still the highest. Any significant weakness in oil prices will be capable of producing a good rally in prices. (February 1985)

> The long-term outlook remains highly favorable as the trend of inflation comes down and so do real interest rates. (October 1985)

Conditions remained favorable, apart from a temporary blip in early 1986, until early in 1987:

> We expect the upward pressure on bond yields to dominate the months ahead as the economy picks up further. The BONDMETER has now turned bearish. (February 1987)

The stock market crash in October 1987 improved the outlook for bonds, but the cyclical indicator remained negative for yields, although total returns were favorable. That was reflected in the interpretation of the positive relationship between actual and expected yields. The crash opened up a window for bonds, that quickly closed again. The resilience of the bond market was illustrated when yields hardly rose as short-term rates increased through 1988 and into early 1989. Under these circumstances the cyclical indicator became significantly negative, but it was also clear that bonds were becoming attractive, e.g.:

> We continue to recommend the gradual build up of bond positions on price weakness. (May 1989)

The outlook for bonds remained cautiously optimistic through 1989 and into 1990. The BONDMETER went positive at the end of 1989, suffered a brief reversal early in 1990, but by the end of that year had become significantly positive. In mid-1991 there was also a renewed downturn in the expected bond yield, which had been a factor preventing a big move in bond yields. Conditions, therefore, improved on both fronts, and remained positive well into 1992 and the latest cut-off date.

The underlying trend in the level of interest rates is related to inflation, while the shorter-term movements are determined by the business cycle. The yield curve is also cyclical in its behavior. These movements create some excellent investment opportunities for investors, particularly those prepared to take a two- to three-year view when making decisions. This does not mean that actual holding periods have to be the same. However, even short-term traders should try to look beyond their own trading horizon to establish the underlying trend.

Cyclical and secular trends may also be discerned in quality spreads. These widening spreads reflect increased risks for those taken by surprise, and opportunities for those who anticipated what would happen. Under normal cyclical conditions, the gap will quickly close again once confidence is restored. However, a cumulative decline would set off a mass of defaults, resulting in an explosion in the quality spreads on a scale not seen since the 1930s, and the whole invested capital of many investors would be wiped out. This is obviously a matter of concern for investors, which is why the subject was dealt with in detail in Chapter 5.

# 13

## THE STOCK MARKET
### (owning the assets)

There are many theories about why stock prices rise or fall. Explanations range through the phases of the moon; sun-burst activity; the breaking of trend lines; a whole slew of indicators of market psychology; changing interest rates; to this, that and the other thing. However, reducing the analysis to basics takes you back to the growth of profits. It is only to be expected that the value of claims on a company will depend on the income stream that can be earned by that company. The expected future income stream from operations will be the greatest determinant of a stock's price, but consideration also needs to be given to the value of the assets owned.

Investors are not very concerned with current earnings, much more important is what the future stream of profits is likely to be. About that, however, there is great uncertainty, and investors will base their expectations on the most recent experience and the latest information. For this reason, prospects over the next quarter or two, at the most, generally carry the greatest weight in valuing individual stocks. The latest reported profits will be important only to the extent that they influence these expectations. Stock prices on average will lead the economy and profits. As pointed out earlier, this is not because the stock market is a major determinant of the economy, but because investors as a group succeed in anticipating what will happen. Consequently, investors who wish to maximize gains and minimize losses must also anticipate the major turning points.

Stock prices fluctuate in the short term but, on average, follow a rising trend over time; in line with the growth of earnings. Some stocks will do better than the average and some will do worse, and not all sectors will act in the same way. In all cases, the current and expected future profitability of the underlying company will be the determining force. Movements in the broad market indices are the sum of the changes in individual stock prices—the result of many, many different influences. Information about current developments in individual companies is quickly discounted in market prices, particularly for the large, widely covered companies. The price of a small, relatively unknown company could, however, get out of line with the fundamentals for some time. There are also larger events that affect whole sectors, or all sectors. Inflation, interest rates, taxation and government policies generally, all fall into this category, as does the overall business cycle.

This chapter starts by providing some historical background to the stock market, outlines a structured way in which to discuss valuation and focuses on the importance of interest rates and inflation. This leads to the development of a composite indicator which can be, and has been, used to identify turning points in the stock market. This indicator is not hypothetical and unproved, but has actually operated successfully through the 1980s; predicting, among other things the upturn in August 1982 and the market crash of October 1987.

## Potential for profits

The stock market has traditionally provided the best long-term investment performance for individuals either directly, or through their pension funds or mutual funds. There is often much talk about the absence of the individual investor, but that is only a discussion of what form the transactions take. The ultimate owner of stocks is the individual. There is no reason to believe that the stock market will not continue to provide significant returns.

Each separate stock price is highly volatile, but as a group they offer the ability to participate in the growing wealth and earning potential of a country. Other investments will do better over particular periods of time, but nothing offers the long-run performance and liquidity of stocks. During the 1970s, gold and commodity prices rose more quickly, but the 1980s were less kind. Such investments require special circumstances in order to do well, and they carry no yield to compensate for the times when prices fall. Even at those times, equity in the producers of such commodities generally provided a better vehicle for investors.

Many collectible items, in particular impressionist art, have performed spectacularly. But the dealing costs are high, the items are typically non-liquid and require specialist knowledge. There is no way that the majority of individuals can invest in such items. Some art categories have fallen in price, and many have underperformed inflation. There is really no way of telling the fads and fancies of tomorrow. Investments in antiques or pictures yield a return in the pleasure of looking at them, or using them, in addition to any potential monetary gain. However, the basis of a growth portfolio is still going to depend heavily on stocks.

Over the 1980s the New York Stock Exchange provided a return of 404 per cent, including capital gains and dividend payments. The returns on gold and silver were −32 per cent and −63 per cent respectively. Bonds

Table 13.1 Investment returns over the nineteenth century (%)

|  | Common stocks | Corp bonds | Gold | Silver | Cash | Real estate | Consumer prices |
|---|---|---|---|---|---|---|---|
| 1900–09 | 133.68 | 34.31 | 0.00 | −15.91 | 72.38 | 6.35 | 8.00 |
| 1910–19 | 58.14 | 39.62 | 6.00 | 107.45 | 65.76 | 26.28 | 92.00 |
| 1920–29 | 335.19 | 69.60 | −24.53 | −48.44 | 64.13 | −2.63 | −1.50 |
| 1930–39 | −28.34 | 34.17 | 68.75 | 2.34 | 5.67 | −12.62 | −19.00 |
| 1940–49 | 140.47 | 23.86 | 0.00 | 106.29 | 4.17 | −97.58 | 71.64 |
| 1950–59 | 486.56 | 25.20 | 0.00 | 22.85 | 20.31 | 24.97 | 22.28 |
| 1960–69 | 112.07 | 6.99 | 21.75 | 97.70 | 46.31 | 31.56 | 25.76 |
| 1970–79 | 76.69 | 71.13 | 1121.22 | 1232.72 | 84.38 | 142.17 | 98.00 |
| 1980–89 | 403.67 | 227.79 | −32.27 | −63.27 | 134.33 | 49.68 | 69.00 |
| Total return | 306654 | 3872 | 1915 | 877 | 3826 | 671 | 1361 |

Compound returns assuming reinvestment of interest and dividends.

did well over the 1980s, in sharp contrast to their performance in the previous decade, providing a total return of 228 per cent. Table 13.1 shows how these different investments have performed during this century, together with cash. Stocks have clearly provided the most spectacular returns even allowing for the depression and other well-documented downturns that have occurred. Nothing else comes close to the gains stocks have made.

These returns are for the average of stocks as measured by the New York Stock Exchange. Certain groups have done better or worse depending on economic conditions. In the 1970s, it was hardly surprising that commodity-related companies did a lot better than the average, since they provided compensation for the rampant inflation at that time. This is shown in the relative performance of the AMEX index, which has a heavy weighting of such companies, and the New York average; up 112 per cent and 21 per cent respectively over the decade. The average return can therefore be exceeded easily by selecting the right sectors to be in. In this case just the appreciation in price is taken into account, unlike the table which shows total returns.

Figure 13.1 shows how the main indices have fared over the post-war period. The Dow Jones Industrial Average (DJIA) is the narrowest index, consisting of only 30 stocks, and is potentially quite misleading. The point about looking at an index is to measure what the overall market is doing, as opposed to a particular company, small group of stocks or particular sector. The DJIA was first constructed by Charles H. Dow in 1884, when it consisted of only 11 stocks; but then that was 11 out of a smaller number. The 30 share average dates from October 1928.

Since then, the composition has been changed many times. Not only do the companies change over time, but the emphasis on different sectors is also adjusted. The latest change, in May 1991, removed Navistar, Primerica and USX Corp, and replaced them with Caterpillar, Disney and J. P. Morgan. This gave a greater weight to the service sector, and included a bank for the first time. Clearly, the DJIA can become very unrepresentative of the market overall. An added problem is that there is a tendency to take out stocks that have done badly, for obvious reasons, and put in stocks that have done well. Given this retroactive reasoning, that tends to give a downward bias to the index at certain times, and will tend to overstate the P/E; in the first case because earnings are non-existent, and in the second case because the stock price has already risen strongly before being included.

Consideration also has to be given to the fact the DJIA is a price-weighted index not value-weighted. What that means is that one or two high-priced stocks will be capable of having a disproportionate effect on the index. A good example of what can happen is provided by the example of Disney. David Shulman of Salomon Brothers, pointed out in a note, *Disney and the Dow*, 19 February 1992, that at the start of 1992 Disney accounted for 8.1 per cent of the index. Disney's price for the year to that date had risen 32 points which accounted for all of the 56-point gain in the index. At that time, Disney had just announced its four-for-one split. That change would reduce the weighting to only 2.2 per cent of the index. Had that change been introduced earlier the DJIA would hardly have risen at all. The other effect was to reduce the divisor of the industrial average from 0.559 to 0.525, thereby tending to make the index more volatile. The Disney announcement was followed by the announcement of stock splits by both Coca Cola and Merck, further changing the nature of the index.

The DJIA was invaluable in the nineteenth century, and even for a large part of the twentieth century, when calculations were all done by hand. It enabled a reasonable approximation of market behavior to be derived relatively easily and quickly. Now, however, computers are capable of calculating the whole index instantly, while the DJIA is probably less representative than it was. Either way, there is something odd about such heavy reliance on what is, at best, an approximation of the stock market, when much more comprehensive measures are readily available.

The Wilshire index, by contrast, contains 5000 stocks, and thereby provides a much broader view of *the* stock market. Somewhere in between are the S&P series and the New York Stock Exchange index. These are calculated throughout the day, and provide a much more accurate picture of what is really going on. During the early part of 1991, there was extensive debate over whether the DJIA would make a new high or not, despite the fact that all the other major indices had already done so, quite conclusively. What really is the significance of these 30 stocks? They are just a sub-index of the market, and no more important than that.

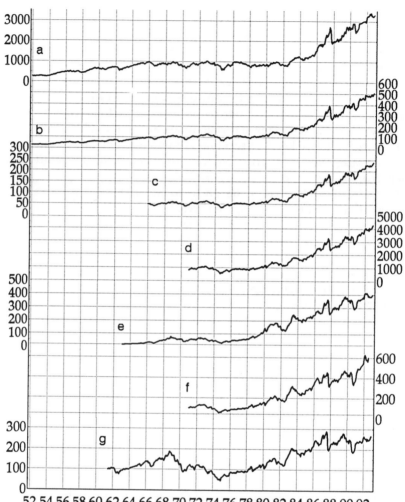

52 54 56 58 60 62 64 66 68 70 72 74 76 78 80 82 84 86 88 90 92
 a  Dow Jones Industrial Average      b  S&P 400 Industrials
 c  NYSE Composite    d  Wilshire 5000 Equity Index
 e  AMEX Composite   f  NASDAQ Composite  g  Value Line

**Figure 13.1** Major stock market indices

Another index shown here is the AMEX, the stocks listed on the American Stock Exchange. In the 1970s, this index did much better than the rest because of the heavy weightings given to oil and commodity stocks. Now, the index contains a lot of derivative products, including such things as put warrants on the Japanese and British markets. This index is, therefore, capable of behaving quite strangely. Even the NYSE now includes a large number of foreign stocks, in ADR form, and is no longer simply a measure of how US companies are performing.

The NASDAQ lists over-the-counter stocks. Normally, these are smaller companies, trading over the counter, but the index is dominated by technology in the form of Apple, Microsoft, Intel and Sun Microsystems. These are not small cap companies. The 1990s has also seen rapid growth in the importance of biotech companies. Over-the-counter stocks underperformed badly following the 1987 crash, until 1990, when they started to outperform. The Value Line index is an unweighted index and, therefore, gives the same weight to a one dollar change in a small stock as in a large cap company. As a measure of the impact of price changes on portfolio values it is totally misleading. This is the only index that, by 1992, had not managed to rise above the peak level reached in 1987.

Despite the very positive long-term performance of stocks on average, there have also been times when it would have been good to be out of the market altogether. The most striking example was during the period from October 1929 to May 1932. Actually it paid to be out in the early part of this price collapse, but the rewards were enormous for those who bought when prices were down, even if this was before the final bottom. There have been other times when it was good to be out of the market, and two of the best were in 1973/74, and the short period from August 1987 to November of that same year.

Such times are not random events, but coincide with severe liquidity pressures and the danger of an economic downturn. The greater the recession or potential disruption, and the greater the prior run up in stock prices, the greater the subsequent decline will be. The long-term return from holding stocks will be greatly increased if these periods of weakness can be avoided. The way to do that is to develop indicators that accurately anticipate the pattern of the business cycle. The government tries to do this with its leading economic indicator, but this is (a) not particularly reliable, (b) not a true leading indicator, and (c) anyway includes stock prices as one of the components, as explained in Chapter 11. It was shown there that it is, in fact, possible to develop a true longer-leading indicator of the business cycle. The stock market does not follow this by an absolute fixed rule, but it is possible to identify a large part of the cyclical influences that determine stock prices, as is demonstrated below.

## Owning the assets

Of all investment vehicles, the stock market attracts the most attention. Even when interest in other assets is running at fever pitch, happenings in the stock market still dominate the news media. The main reason is the range of diversity involved. Stocks, and the companies they represent, touch the lives of everyone in the country. Bonds are abstract, and gold is no more than a yellow metal, while each stock has its own story, which is capable of capturing the attention.

The stock market provides a way for individuals, either directly or through one institution or another, to invest in the productive potential of the country. Each stock represents a share in the ownership of a company. Stock markets evolved in order to spread the risk of raising capital. By providing a secondary market for the paper claims, individual investors would obtain liquidity and thus enable companies to attract money from a wide range of individuals. A liquid, active stock market is a central pillar of a capitalistic system. Capitalism is built on the freedom of choice, on the freedom to hold capital, to create new businesses, to grow and to prosper— but also the freedom to fail. This freedom creates a tremendous dynamic that raises wealth for the whole community. Success, however, often requires taking great risk, and there will be many failures.

The innovators and entrepreneurs require a source of capital, but the individual investor does not want to accept the risks involved. The stock market provides liquidity to the investor by allowing the pooling of small amounts while at the same time permitting the individual to hold a diversified range of investments. By doing this, the stock market increases the amount of money available for equity investment.

The raising of new capital is still the primary function of the stock market. Sometimes this is hard to recognize because of the attention now given to short-term trading and the explosive growth in the creation, and use, of derivative products. The revolution in electronics, and communications generally, has resulted in much shorter-term horizons. Modern emphasis on speculation and hyperactive trading sometimes gives the impression that the major stock exchanges are nothing more than casinos, but without the dancing girls.

Rising wealth and incomes require rising investment possibilities. Part of the new wealth created can go in the form of lending, either to the banks to lend on to others, or directly in the form of notes or bonds. This results in a rising trend in the quantity of debt outstanding—the inevitable counterpart of the rising assets. Increasing leverage is certainly one way for an economy, and companies, to grow, but only at the expense of raising the risk involved. The way to spread the risk is through widening the ownership of the assets. If others are to share the business risks, they also need to share in the profits that are earned. By diversifying the ownership it is possible to raise capital while, at the same time, spreading the risk.

This was a basic lesson that went unheeded by the less developed countries (LDCs) in the 1970s. They wanted to grow, but wanted to retain all the benefits themselves. What they failed to appreciate was that they were also taking on all of the risk. Consequently, they borrowed extensively, with predictable results. The point is that companies, and countries, can spread the risk by diversifying the ownership, and the same is true for the equity holders; risks are reduced by holding equity in a variety of different companies.

When buying stocks it is worth remembering that you are taking ownership, in some small way, of a productive enterprise. Many reasons may be offered to justify owning a particular stock, and it is helpful to ask yourself whether that is a business that is likely to do well, and better than the average. That after all is what constitutes value. Mistakes are still possible, but at least such a discipline should eliminate some of the more obvious ones.

There are a great many different influences that will affect stock prices, and this variety can often be confusing. People will emphasize different aspects at different times. There are questions of valuation, profitability and liquidity, foreign competition, new businesses, political issues, new taxes, technical breakouts and no end of individual hooks to get hung on. The weight of money is another argument that is brought out when nothing else seems to work. The suggestion in this case is that demand is so high that prices have been pushed beyond any realistic fundamental valuation. Stock prices are determined by the intersection of supply and demand, and so it is possible for demand to rise because of a high level of savings. However, there are a wide range of other investments, including overseas investment, which should reduce the possibility of overvaluation. Overvaluation is most likely in developing countries, where investment options are limited, and on those rare occasions when expectations get out of control.

Most of the influences listed above will vary between sectors and/or individual securities, but some will influence the market generally. It is these latter influences that are the focus of attention in this book. Individual stock selection will be significantly affected by macroeconomic considerations, but it will also be necessary to take more specific considerations into account. Mutual funds, and the existence of composite indices, provide a more direct way to take positions based on the movements of the business cycle.

Under normal circumstances, the weight of money can be combined with liquidity, and taken into account through changes in interest rates. Most other influences, including the effect of interest rates changes, will show up on the bottom line, in profitability. The sustainability of earnings growth combined with interest rates, as a discount factor, provides a valuation measure. Value depends not only on profits, but the durability of profits, which in turn depends on product, management, price, competition, etc., and also on the macroeconomic environment. Buying value does not mean buying a stream of high *past* earnings, but a stream of high *future* earnings.

## An outline model

In trying to determine value, and to understand and interpret stock price movements, it is helpful to develop a basic framework in which the main elements can be identified. The intention is not to capture all the intricacies of stock market behavior, but to aim only at the more modest objective of identifying the major elements in a stock valuation model. The starting point is to define the expected return on equities (*re*) as equal to the current dividend yield (*d/p*) plus the rate at which these dividends, and earnings, are growing (*g*):

$$re = d/p + g$$

The next step is to define the nominal or observed rate of interest (*rb*) that provides the main alternative to investing in stocks. The default-free bond yield that is relevant for discounting future income streams consists of the real rate of interest (*i*) and the expected rate of inflation (*x*):

$$rb = i + x$$

Investors are constantly having to make choices between alternative investments. When comparing bonds and equities, they have to take account of the additional risk involved in actually owning the assets. Returns are, therefore, equalized after taking account of this additional risk premium (*R*), i.e:

$$re = rb + R$$

Combining these relationships produces an equation for stock prices (*p*):

$$p = \frac{d}{i + x + R - g} = \frac{ae}{i + x + R - g}$$

where *a* is the dividend payout ratio, *d/e*, i.e. dividends divided by earnings.

Stock prices, therefore, depend positively on dividends or earnings, and the rate at which these are growing; and negatively on the level of risk associated with equities as compared with government bonds, the real rate of interest and the expected rate of inflation. The real world is clearly more complicated than this, but most of the important influences are captured. Here is a framework with which to assess how macroeconomic developments affect stock prices.

One point to note is that the various influences are not independent, and it is necessary to take account of the widespread interrelationships that exist when applying the model to the real world. For example, a shift to tight money might raise the real rate of interest, raise the risk premium, lower expected growth rates, lower dividend payments as cash flows of corporations are cut, but at the same time, lower the expected inflation rate. Hence, the net impact on stock prices is complex, particularly as the short-term effects of any change may be the opposite of the long-run implications.

The price equation above shows why quite small changes are capable of having large effects on stock prices. For example, if the dividend is $5, and the risk adjusted growth of the dividend is 5 per cent, then an interest rate of 8 per cent will produce a price of $166. If interest rates now rise to 10 per cent, and everything else stays the same, the price will fall to $100. A further increase to 12 per cent will knock the price down to $71; i.e. down over 50 per cent from the initial price. The result of relatively small interest rate changes can, therefore, be quite large. In addition, it should be recognized that higher interest rates are likely to slow the economy down, thereby slowing the expected growth of dividends, possibly raising perceived risks, and could even result in a cut to the dividend.

Interest rates are important, because of the extensive effects they have on the economy. Once interest rates have changed, investors will immediately try to discount the expected effects. Attempts will also be made to anticipate future interest rate movements. That, however, will add to the volatility of interest rates themselves. When it comes to expected growth rates, allowance will have to be made for the likely volatility of those earnings and dividends. If a company is in a highly cyclical industry then it has to be expected that higher earnings will not be sustained, but also that low earnings will be followed by a recovery.

What then is value? A company may well have a low price/earnings ratio, and, consequently, appear to offer good value, just at the point when earnings have hit their peak. Consequently, there are high risks associated with following simple rules such as buying low P/E stocks. Value does not reside in what has happened in the past, only in what will happen in the future. Part of that future will depend on the particular products and management skills of each company, but will also depend on interest rate developments and other economic factors.

The question of value, in a broad sense, has received increased attention since 1987. After the crash, people looked around to see what might have warned them it was coming. One of the most visible signs was the low earnings yield (and dividend yield). Ever since then the earnings yield has been watched closely, and warning signals have increased as it approaches the 1987 level.

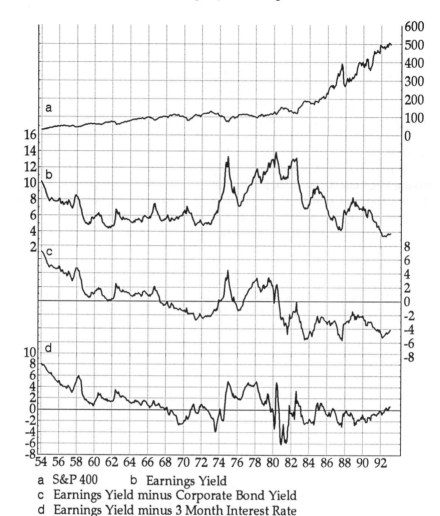

**Figure 13.2** Valuation measures

a  S&P 400        b  Earnings Yield
c  Earnings Yield minus Corporate Bond Yield
d  Earnings Yield minus 3 Month Interest Rate

   The earnings yield was low in 1987, but what made it really dangerous was the fact that interest rates were rising sharply. If a low earnings yield is compared with slippery conditions at a sharp bend in the road, then interest rates represent the speed going into the bend. In 1987, the speed was very high and still accelerating. However, it is not the case, as is sometimes implied, that slippery conditions must inevitably result in a bad accident. A cautious approach, i.e. low and falling interest rates, will lower the risk considerably. Figure 13.2 shows the earnings yield, together with alternative measures that take account of changes in interest rates.

Valuation in this sense is a relative concept. Not only will low interest rates raise the discounted value of current and prospective earnings, and dividend, flows, but they should also improve expectations of growth in the future. Consequently, it makes no sense to look at stock yields without considering the interest rate environment. An added complication is the measurement of earnings themselves. The earnings used to calculate the P/E ratio is one possibility, but there is also the adjusted profits series provided as part of national income accounts. The growth rates of these two series can diverge significantly, as shown in Fig. 1.5, with the adjusted series generally leading by as much as a year. As a result, the P/E ratio is likely to appear much higher before a recovery, and much lower before a recession, than if adjusted profits were used as the denominator.

The movement in stock prices is never obvious. Moreover, as pointed out in earlier chapters, a certain amount of confusion and uncertainty has its advantages when it comes to making money. The classic example is that a recession does not necessarily mean that stock prices will fall. The actual outcome will depend on many other things but in particular whether interest rates are rising or falling. Interest rates, it turns out, are the key ingredient. Before explaining why that should be, we shall briefly discuss the effect of changes in inflation.

## Inflation and the stock market

At the beginning of the 1980s there were serious doubts being expressed as to whether stock prices really could keep up with inflation. In an earlier time, the standard view had been that equities were the perfect hedge against inflation. The argument was simple enough; consumer prices were charged by corporations, so they also represented revenues. Consequently, both should rise together.

In the 1970s, as inflation accelerated and stock prices fell further behind, the view developed that stocks were not a good hedge against inflation. Theories followed the fact, and provided belated justification for what was happening. Unfortunately, these had more of the characteristic of ex-post rationalization than predictive theory that could explain market behavior over different periods and different countries. These are important criteria, too often neglected in the attempt to explain particular circumstances. The development of specific theories or explanations is not unique to the stock market, but can be found in most areas of market behavior, economics, politics and life itself. However, general applicability should provide the ultimate test of any such model. While the main emphasis here is on the United States, examples from other countries are also used. The proposed explanation of the relationship between the stock market and inflation is general enough to cover a wide range of different experiences without being a tautology.

An interesting aspect of the serious alternatives that were put forward to explain why the stock market was not a good hedge against inflation was that in nearly every case the conclusion was very bullish for when inflation stopped accelerating, and finally came down. For that reason, it is of interest to review the main theories that were proposed, and how stock prices have performed with inflation at different times and places. The explanations vary from the assumption of irrationality on the part of investors to rationality in the face of deteriorating conditions.

The different explanations considered here each emphasized their own distinguishing characteristics, and this helped to conceal a common thread running through all of them. All of the discussion centered around the fact that the earnings yield, as defined above, fluctuated with nominal interest rates, and inflation, as shown in Fig. 13.3. A problem arises because the earnings yield or, looked at the other way around, the price/earnings ratio, ought to be a good deal more stable if, as is generally accepted, the rate at which corporate earnings are discounted is a real rate of return, and the real rate of interest is fixed. The essence of this argument can be seen in the equations presented above: with a fixed payout ratio, a fixed real rate of interest and no change in the risk premium, then if earnings grow at the same rate as inflation, plus a fixed margin, the earnings yield should remain unchanged in the face of accelerating inflation.

One view about why stock prices failed to keep up with inflation was that *adjusted* corporate earnings did not keep up with inflation. Nominal earnings, as reported, may have kept up, but the quality of the earnings deteriorated because of the effect of rapid inflation on inventory valuation and depreciation adjustments, which carried the implication that the increases in earnings were therefore unsustainable. One problem with that approach was that the earnings did seem to have been sustained, as shown by their ability to keep up with inflation. There has been endless debate in the quality of earnings, and this is likely to continue without ever being finally resolved.

Others have argued that if true adjustment was made, including the benefits of fixed interest debt issued at lower yields, then readjusted earnings did in fact keep up with inflation. In this case, alternative explanations were required for the failure of stock prices to keep up, and one of these was based on the assumption of the irrationality of investors. The problem here was why the irrationality persists in this way. Why are investors rational sometimes, and irrational at others? Also, why have investors not always been irrational when faced with rapid inflation, since there are plenty of examples when stock prices have kept up with inflation.

Another alternative was that the dividend payout ratio had declined as a direct result of inflation. In this case there would be an increase in retained earnings which might be expected to raise the growth of earnings and

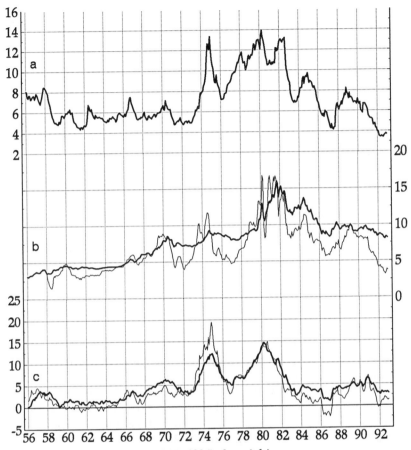

a   Earnings price ratio (S&P 400 Industrials)
b   —  Aaa corporate bond yield
    —  3-month commercial paper rate
c   —  Consumer price index (12-month % change)
    —  Producer price index (12-month % change)

**Figure 13.3** Inflation and market yields

dividends, in the future. After all, Japanese companies have very low payout ratios and yet are also highly priced. A higher growth rate should actually have the effect of reducing the dividend yield not raising it. The greatest weakness in this explanation was its failure to account for the rise in the dividend yield along with the earnings yield.

A different explanation of the observed reduction in the payout ratio is possible which reverses the causality. A reduction in the share price relative to earnings, for some other reason, raises the external cost of funds through the issue of shares, while rising interest rates raise the cost of borrowing. It becomes sensible, therefore, to retain a higher proportion of earnings for investment purposes.

The final, specific, explanation of the rising earnings yield put the blame on increases in the risk premium. Certainly that would do it, but no justification was provided as to why the risk premium should move so closely with inflation. An even greater problem with the argument that there was some automatic link between the risk premium and inflation in the United States in the 1970s, was that in other countries, and at other times, the relationship has been absent. This was a problem with all those explanations that sought to establish an automatic link between inflation and the earnings yield.

What is needed is an explanation that covers all behavior—one that allows stock prices to go up with inflation under some circumstances, but which also explains why sometimes, particularly in the developed countries, stock prices fail to keep up. The possibility has to be considered that it is not inflation that is holding back stock prices, but something else. The key factor, I believe, is whether the inflation is unrestrained or whether attempts are being made to control it. In the first case, money is pumped in to keep the level of activity up and fuel further price increases. Under these circumstances of easy credit, stock prices will keep up with inflation. If, on the other hand, the monetary authorities are trying to restrain inflation, so that credit becomes expensive and real interest rates increase, then stock prices will lag behind inflation. This explanation is consistent with the facts, and general enough to explain behavior in different countries and over different times. I first developed this alternative explanation in Boeckh and Coghlan (1982).

The assumption made above, and the assumption generally made by economists, is that the real rate of interest is very stable, with wide fluctuations only in nominal yields. This alternative view of the way in which inflation affects the stock market lifts that assumption and allows the real rate of interest to vary. That, in turn, would also explain increases in the earnings yield, but not automatically with inflation, only when monetary policy is tight.

In addition, there is likely to be a systematic relationship between risk and attempts to control inflation, as distinct from inflation itself. Once it becomes clear that the monetary authorities are going to push interest rates up in order to bring inflation under control, this leads to the expectation of weakening economic activity, falling profits and the increased possibility of bankruptcies. Rather than wait for this to happen, investors are likely to anticipate events by lowering the price they are prepared to pay for the present inflated stream of profits. Therefore, since earnings are still rising with inflation, the earnings yield will be pushed up even faster. Instead of assuming that investors are irrational, this approach assumes a very rational form of behavior.

For all these theories, a fall in inflation is good for the stock market. However, there is an important distinction between the general explanation suggested here, and the alternative theories. In the case of the alternatives, declining inflation is all that is needed to bring down the earnings yield. According to the general theory, falling inflation only creates the conditions for the relaxation of monetary policy, and it is this that will bring down the earnings yield. The distinction may seem slight, but, as discussed later, can be very important, as, for example, in the period from 1980 to 1982. Inflation peaked at the beginning of 1980, but the stock market did not bottom out until there was a significant change in monetary policy in August 1982.

Looking at the way stock prices have moved at times of very rapid inflation contradicts the theories which say that there is something inherent in the process of inflation that requires stock prices to lag behind. What we find, in fact, is that stock prices have typically kept up easily. In Israel, over the five years from 1980 to 1984, consumer prices rose 56 times, which definitely counts as high inflation, and stock prices rose 57 times.

The classic inflation period was that in Germany after the First World War. The experience of stock prices at that time showed that they will rise with general prices no matter how fast inflation accelerates; after all, why not exchange rapidly depreciating paper money for claims on real assets? It also showed that there must be sufficient liquidity available. The stock market was disorientated by the war and the chaos that followed, and this helped produce major fluctuations in prices. The behavior of the economy at that time was discussed earlier in Chapter 7.

In 1920, stock prices (+65 per cent) outpaced wholesale price inflation (+14 per cent) and the depreciation of the mark (+13 per cent rise in dollars) by a substantial margin. In 1921, the increase in stock prices (+163 per cent) fell just short of the decline in the exchange rate (+196 per cent rise in dollars), but still did better than wholesale prices (+142 per cent), and substantially better than consumer prices. 1922 produced a very different response. Share prices ended the year 12 times higher than they had been at the start, but wholesale prices, and the dollar/mark exchange rate, had risen 40 times. There was, therefore, a substantial decline of share prices in real terms.

The classic illustration of what happened, also referred to earlier, is that given by Constantino Bresciani-Turroni (1937) with his reference to the Daimler car company which had a total market value equivalent to only 327 cars at that time. The economy was weak, with production 30 per cent below what might have been considered normal, but the undervaluation of corporations was clearly extreme. Bresciani-Turroni draws attention to the fact that, whereas there had been easy money through 1921, conditions tightened considerably in 1922. Bank credit slowed and the quantity of money increased only 65 per cent over the first seven months of the year. At the same time the government had tried reducing expenditures and raising taxes. The discussion above suggests that this restriction in money growth was even more significant than allowed for by Bresciani-Turroni.

Towards the end of the year there was a dramatic shift in monetary conditions. Note issues increased rapidly and the floodgates were opened wide. During 1923 stock prices increased an incredible 83 000 times, compared with an increase in the cost of living of *only* 16 500 times. A buying panic developed, encouraged by foreign exchange constraints. In November 1923, the gold price of shares had risen above the pre-war level for the first time; the ratio of the share price to gold was 39.4 compared with only 16 in July of the same year, and 18 in October 1921. At this point, stock prices had become overpriced, given the fragile economic structure.

The main conclusion to be drawn from a review of such experiences is that stock prices will rise at times of rapid inflation by an equal, or even greater amount, as long as monetary policy is easy and credit is readily available. Runaway inflation is no problem for real stock values. However, attempts to stop inflation will typically lead to high real interest rates, and it is these that will prevent stock prices keeping up with inflation. This experience, to varying degrees, has been repeated many, many times in the United States and around the world and the evidence seems very clear. Stock prices keep up with, or exceed, inflation when it is accompanied by easy money, but fall well short in periods of tight money.

## Real stock prices

Inflation also has the effect of distorting price comparisons. When looking at stock prices over any length of time it is important to take out the effect of inflation. The subject was discussed in Chapter 6, in order to show how easy it is to be misled by looking only on nominal prices. This is so important, and so widely ignored, that some repetition is justified.

The conventional wisdom is that stock prices in the United States rose between 1966 and 1982. In nominal terms it was true, but that was far from being a bull market. The value of stocks fell in terms of real purchasing power. If the bundle of stocks bought in 1966 was sold in 1982, the money received would have purchased less of the bundle of goods making up the consumer price index. The section above explained how this could have happened, but it is also necessary for investors to recognize that it did happen. The period from 1966 to 1982 represented a major bear market, and yet, as pointed out earlier, much of this period has been categorized by history as a bull market.

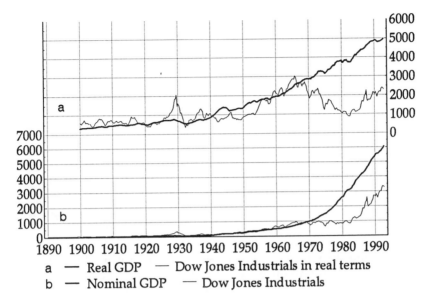

**Figure 13.4** The stock market and the economy (quarterly)

Figure 13.4 shows the Dow Jones Industrial Average over the whole of the twentieth century, both in nominal and real terms. When it comes to interpreting what stock prices have done in the past, as a guide to what they might do in the future, it makes a lot of difference which series you look at. In nominal terms, stock prices went sideways between 1966 and 1982, but there was a very clear bear market when measured in real terms. Inflation disguised a huge bear market which is not recognized even now with the benefit of hindsight.

To add injury to insult, there is an aspect of this inflation illusion that hits hard on the bottom line. The IRS only recognize nominal capital gains. As a result, the purchasing power of the inflation gains is reduced by even more. To give an example. If a stock goes up from 100 to 200 over five years, and inflation also doubles, the proud owner of a stock that doubled in price will actually have lost money, ignoring the dividends received. At a tax rate of 30 per cent, the investor will keep only 70 per cent of the gain versus the 100 per cent rise in prices, ending up with a real reduction in the value of his or her wealth. Part of the price appreciation in stock prices is due to inflation—in this example, all of it was—and to tax that as if it were a capital gain is unfair and unproductive.

There has been a heated debate within the United States over the question of capital gains tax. The Bush Administration fought hard to get some cut in the rate at which capital gains are charged, and had to face defeat and charges of favoritism. Whatever the rate charged, a minimum requirement should be to cut the inflation gains from the tax net, as has been done in the United Kingdom. There is not much point complaining about the low level of savings, if those doing the saving are going to be so heavily penalized.

## Interest rates

One thing to emerge from the analysis of inflation is the importance of interest rates. How stock prices will react to rising inflation depends crucially on whether it is accepted, or whether monetary policy is tightened in order to slow the economy down as a way of controlling inflation. As already pointed out, the way that monetary policy works is through raising interest rates and narrowing, possibly inverting, the yield curve.

Without any monetary restraint, earnings will, on average, rise with inflation, and stock prices will increase in line. That is what is implied by the simple model developed earlier and will, in fact, be the case. When interest rates rise at a faster rate, stock prices will underperform. The effect comes through not only directly, as a result of a higher rate of interest used to discount future returns, but also by reducing demand for what companies have to sell, while at the same time raising their costs of production. It was shown earlier that changes in interest rates would have a major impact on the economy, and through that, on inflation and corporate profitability.

There are, of course, other influences at work, such as changes in tax rates, new inventions, immigration, etc., but nothing is as all pervasive as interest rates. While interest rates are generally seen as important, the true significance has been missed. Immediate effects are expected, in a direct, visible way, and other influences are ignored. When interest rates have not shown up as the only and obvious determinant of stock price movement, the role they play has been downgraded.

A classic example of this all-or-nothing approach was provided by a Brookings Institute study (Owens and Hardy, 1925). The authors claimed that accepted theory was that high interest rates caused stock prices to fall, while low interest rates caused prices to rise. Specifically, when credit became cheap, particularly in relation to the dividend yield, speculators were supposed to borrow in order to buy stocks. This borrowing would then fall when interest rates rose, and the buying would turn to selling.

Owens and Hardy compared interest rates and stock prices over the prior 50 years in order to test the theory, and concluded that 'neither economic analysis nor historical research reveals any foundation for the accepted theory'. However, what they did not do was as important as what they did. They did not allow for other influences, such as changes in the expected rate of inflation, the earnings yield, the growth of earnings, money growth, the change in interest rates, real interest rates or the yield curve. These were just some of the likely candidates whose absence was likely to distort the results obtained.

They did, however, uncover a very interesting result which they mistakenly dismissed as unimportant. When they looked at the correlation between interest rates and stock prices, allowing for both leads and lags in the relationship, they were forced to conclude that 'the relationship between stock prices and interest rates is not a random one'. But the influence worked in both directions. As a result the significance was dismissed. 'The data . . . afford no more conclusive evidence that advances in interest rates cause declines in stock prices than they do that advances in stock prices cause advances in interest rates'.

The right conclusion should have been that both results are valid, each feeds on the other. That is exactly the basis of a behavioral business cycle as described in Chapter 1. Everything depends on everything else, and there are important lags before the full effect is felt. That is exactly the true regularity in cycles. Owens and Hardy stumbled on an important truth, but threw it away.

The influence of interest rates on stock prices is not simple and one-dimensional. Changes in interest rates have their effect through many different channels and as the result of interacting with many other influences. The idea that interest rates only affect stock prices as a cost of margin financing is altogether too narrow, and is the least interesting channel of influence. As explained in Chapter 1 on the business cycle, higher interest rates affect both the demand for goods and the costs of production, and in that way impact on profitability. Market prices do not respond after these effects have been recorded, but move in anticipation of them, i.e. there is a parallel impact on expectations. The influence on profits will also depend on other developments within the economy. Once a wider perspective is employed, it is possible to identify the true, absolutely crucial, role played by interest rates. It may seem paradoxical that the importance of interest rates only shows up when other influences are taken into account, but then life is often like that.

## Exchange rate effects

The way in which changes in the exchange rate influence stock prices provides an interesting illustration of how different forces interact. This interaction can, in fact, prove to be extremely confusing, to the point of providing misleading conclusions. A reading of the financial press frequently makes it seem that a lower exchange rate will be bad for stocks. If the dollar starts to fall, there is always someone who will raise a warning flag over the stock market. While there are circumstances under which pressure on the exchange rate might raise concerns about stock prices, that is really because of reactions elsewhere to the change. A change in the exchange rate will not affect all companies in the same way, and some will be impacted negatively, but, in general, a lower exchange rate will be a beneficial influence on the stock market.

The pluses, and minuses, of a change come through the interaction with external markets. A lower exchange rate makes domestic companies more competitive. This will be particularly important if the exchange rate had previously been so overvalued as to make it difficult for companies to compete in foreign markets, which was the situation facing US companies in the middle of the 1980s. At that time, US producers, and products, were made out to be so inferior to the foreign competition that it was hard to imagine who would buy anything in the future. The deficit, it seemed, would remain forever. The sorry situation was attributed to the greater quality of goods produced in other countries, and to such things as weaker productivity and management skills. Much of this was justification after the fact.

The exchange rate effects take a long time to work through. So, even when the dollar was falling, the companies were still finding it hard to compete abroad. Domestic costs will go up to some extent when the exchange rate falls, and it takes time before foreign sales pick up in response to the improved competitiveness. The lags are long because it takes time to set up a foreign sales operation. For a company not selling in an overseas market it takes a substantial price differential, sustained for a long time, in order to go to the trouble of investigating the possibilities and setting up the infrastructure to export. In the case of companies already selling in foreign markets, it takes a sustained squeeze on profits to convince them to close up the operation and get out. For companies that have gone through this once, it only makes the lags even greater when circumstances reverse.

A declining exchange rate will be the single largest influence, but as the trade account improves there will suddenly be interviews with successful exporters. They will be doing what they have been doing for years, only now they will be more successful and their efforts will be newsworthy. In addition, success breeds success. If there are profits to be made in a particular area, this will attract new entrants, both people and companies, and all of a sudden there will be expertise where there was none before. In all the excitement, the influence of the exchange rate will be forgotten about.

The example of what happened in Germany in the late 1970s and early 1980s is instructive. At that time, the German current account plummeted into deficit and there was extensive debate, inside and outside Germany, that the miracle was over. And there, clearly leading this collapse in competitiveness and confidence, was the overvaluation of the Deutschemark against the dollar in the late 1970s. Then suddenly in the mid-1980s the miracle was reborn, the external balance improved and stock prices soared, and surprise, surprise, this was preceded by the sharp undervaluation of the Deutschemark.

The United States, in the first half of the 1980s, experienced strong domestic demand and progressive overvaluation of the exchange rate. Originally, this was bad for the balance of payments but good for corporate profits. Profits suffered relatively later on, when domestic demand had to slow down in order to improve the external balance. Continued world-wide growth helped to hide this relative deterioration for a long time, but it was real enough. An extended period of overvaluation will hold back industrial growth and lower relative living standards. In which case, exchange rate effects can extend beyond the business cycle. Later on, the situation reversed. Between 1985 and the first quarter of 1991, the United States experienced the fastest growth of exports of any country, more than twice as fast as the average for all industrialized countries; benefiting from a 40 per cent decline in the trade-weighted exchange rate.

The strong influence of the exchange rate played an important, and generally unrecognized, role in the depression of the 1930s. The details have been presented in earlier chapters, but it is worth emphasizing the specific effects with respect to the stock market. Between 1929 and 1932 the dollar rose by 48 per cent against the pound sterling, thereby crushing international competitiveness. Moreover, the Federal Reserve tightened monetary policy sharply in 1931, apparently in response to a drain of gold reserves. Companies had no chance under the circumstances. In 1932, the dollar hit its high point at $3.28 and dropped swiftly to $5.15 early in 1934. A number of conditions had improved for the stock market by late in 1932, and the exchange rate was certainly one of them.

## The composite cyclical indicator

The point has been made over again in this book that the business cycle is not an automatic, mechanical repetition of itself. Each cycle is different from the one before. Tax rates may be different, liquidity constraints will vary, the structure of the economy changes over time, fashion and fancy change, and so on. A major reason why the next cycle will differ from the one before is that people learn from what has happened, but the learning process is dominated by the most recent experience. Many of the mistakes of the future are made in the attempt to avoid the mistakes of the past.

As a result, there is no single influence that will capture all turning points. On one occasion the emphasis may be on the economy, next time it may be on measures of liquidity, interest rates or some other leading indicator of economic activity. Investors' expectations about inflation will also vary

with actual inflation and other political, monetary and economic considerations. Consequently, it is necessary to focus on a number of different
aspects of the economy in order to pick up these different influences. That
is the approach employed here in developing the composite cyclical indicator.

The separate indicators presented in Chapter 11 cover a wide range of
early pressures on the economy, with particular emphasis on conditions in
the credit markets. Since the stock market itself reacts to these same pressures,
in anticipation of the effects showing up in economic performance, these
series form the basis of a composite indicator of cyclical movements in
stock prices. Emphasis in this case has been placed on identifying the turning points, rather than trying to explain every point along the way. The
indicator, therefore, triggers buy or sell signals, but has less to say about
the exact path that prices will follow. The index does have a range of values,
depending on how many components are positive or negative, but it needs
to be interpreted in the light of what else is going on. The index has been
called the STOCKMETER, for want of a better title, since that seems to
reflect the objective. The composite indicator is designed to measure the
outlook for stock prices, from good, through fair to stormy, based on fundamental forces. The composite index is plotted in Fig. 13.5 together with
the real and nominal value of the S&P 400 stock index.

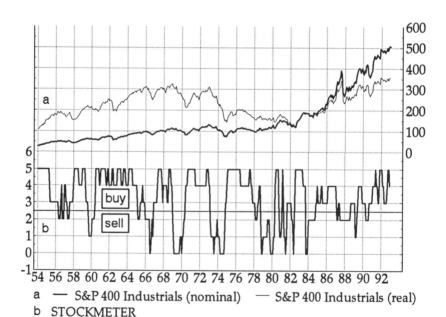

a — S&P 400 Industrials (nominal)    — S&P 400 Industrials (real)
b  STOCKMETER

**Figure 13.5** Forecasting the stock market (monthly)

The only true test of any indicator has to be based on how well it has forecast outside the estimation period. As a result, it is necessary to provide some documented evidence of how this indicator has performed under those conditions. These are not *what if* examples that include the period of estimation. There are many published examples of how a forecasting model, or indicator, would have done over a particular period had it been used. Such comparisons are generally not very helpful, since the model was explicitly designed over that period, when the outcome was already known. And it is amazing how often the forecasting models change with each new cyclical downturn.

The indicators discussed here have been employed in *The Financial Economist* since 1982. As far as the stock market is concerned, the composite cyclical indicator went bullish in July 1982, just in time to catch the start of the strong bull market that started then. The strength of this signal was reinforced by the longer-term view that a long-wave cycle bottom had passed, and that the economy and stock market were about to embark on a major up-move. The reader is also directed to the leading indicators for the economy contained in Chapter 11.

The composite cyclical indicator turned bearish in January 1984 and bullish again in November of the same year. By the time 1985 was over, everyone was a bull, but expectations had been quite different at the beginning of the year. The January 1985 issue of *The Financial Economist*, published in mid-December 1984, concluded that:

> Good quality stocks should perform well in this environment. A further fall in short rates should set off a general upmove in stock prices—just at a time when a number of forecasters have lost faith.

The next major signal came in July 1987, just ahead of the market peak that came in August. Cycle risks seemed particularly high at that time, and *The Financial Economist* warned in September 1987 that:

> There is the risk of a sudden sharp drop in prices under conditions of extreme concern, i.e. A CRISIS.

It did not take long for that warning to be turned into reality. When the market crashed on 19 October 1987, most people chose that time to become bearish on the stock market and the economy. However, the right time to become nervous about the economy was prior to that decline. The crash in stock prices happened so fast that anyone unprepared had no chance to get out, and many high quality stocks hit their lows on the day of the crash. Immediately afterwards there was time to panic, and by far the greatest damage to portfolios was done subsequently. A time of crisis can also be a time of opportunity, and so it was in this case, although not many people cared to notice. Once stock prices around the world came crashing down, it was quite clear that the monetary authorities would relax policy and allow interest rates to come down. The more rational conclusion about the market was:

> We expect the stock market to recover. If it is not the end of the world, stocks should be bought on major sell-offs. This is not the end of the world. The lower price levels offer good buying opportunities. (October 1987)

> It is likely that the US witnessed a six month bear market collapsed into six hours. (November 1987)

It is much easier becoming bullish immediately following a crash like that if you are bearish beforehand. And that is exactly the point. Most forecasters had been bullish up to then, and sentiment following the fall was overwhelmingly bearish. Such timing was not entirely helpful.

The next time the indicator went bearish, in June 1990, circumstances did not look so bad and the decline in prices was not expected to be very great. The indicator went bullish again in October 1990, and remained bullish through 1992. Both changes coincided with movements in the stock market in the same direction.

> There is need for short-term caution . . . the STOCKMETER is signalling a warning. (June 1990)

> The composite indicator has now turned bullish again. (October 1990)

Experience shows that a broad cyclical indicator of the type presented here can help investors avoid cyclical corrections in the markets. The signals identified the major changes in direction over the 1980s and into the 1990s. This record is not the result of wishful thinking, nor was it constructed with the benefit of hindsight. Perfect success is not necessary in order to improve investment returns, but it can be seen that these *documented* turning points have established a consistent record.

# 14

---

# INTERNATIONAL MARKETS
## (the world is your oyster)

International diversification offers great advantages to investors through reduced risk, and by widening the range of opportunities. New and different areas of investment carry new and different risks but, by combining investments from different areas, it is possible to reduce the risk of the overall portfolio below that of any single investment. International markets increase the potential for doing just that. They offer opportunities that do not exist in a single domestic market, and different economic conditions.

All domestic markets are impacted by developments in other parts of the world. Consider how the stock market crash in 1987 sped around the world; or the effect of the Iraqi invasion of Kuwait; or the brief coup in 1991 in the Soviet Union. A less dramatic but more durable effect has come from Japanese competition in cars, cameras, watches and consumer electronics. The greatest single influence has been, and remains, the United States; what happens there sends shock waves around the world. But even the largest economy in the world is not immune from what happens elsewhere, as illustrated by the examples above.

If the activities of foreign markets, economic developments and politics, are going to influence investment outcomes, it is only sensible that those same actions should play a part in making the original investment decisions. Once the logic of that sequence is recognized, it is only a small step further to investing directly in foreign markets. When foreign markets are taken into consideration, an investor may well recognize a superior product, a more efficient means of production, higher growth trends, better economic management, etc. And with each increase in awareness comes the possibility of improving investment performance.

Opportunities in foreign markets exist not only at the micro-level, from the operation of individual companies. There are also differences in the way the macro-economy works. Tax policies are different between countries, the degree of fiscal and monetary stimulus or tightness varies and political developments can play a role. Because of these various possibilities, business cycles will sometimes be in synchronization, while at other times they will be out of phase. As a result, exchange rates will be affected, offering different opportunities for returns in domestic currency terms from bonds and stocks. These returns will partly be determined by changes in the exchange rate directly, and partly by the effects of the currency changes on profits, monetary policy, etc. Exchange rate changes can play a very important part in investment decisions and the final returns achieved, and for this reason are dealt with separately in the next chapter.

## Widening horizons

To see the advantages, imagine that your investment potential is restricted to the neighborhood in which you live. It might prove a little restrictive, with a severe lack of liquidity and high risk. Expanding the geographic area will also expand the investment potential. The smaller a country, the more limited will be the potential, and performance will be tied closely to how well the economy performs—good or bad. Opportunities will be greater in a large, diversified, economy, and this will also allow risks to be reduced. Returns will no longer be dependent on a narrow range of options. Not surprisingly, small, developed economies have shown a greater propensity for investing in foreign markets. Investors in large economies such as the United States have been much more insular, because of the greater possibilities at home. These investors have been able to have most of the options at home that foreign investors have had to go outside their own country to obtain.

The United States still offers great opportunities for domestic investors, but there are limits. Even in this case, returns will be increased and risks reduced by including world markets in the range of possibilities. The tremendous improvements in communications and in the growth of world trade have made people much more aware of the potential that exists in other markets. It has become easier to obtain up-to-date information on companies, countries and different economic trends, and also to execute orders in foreign markets. Investors operating in much smaller domestic markets have always been aware of the possibilities that existed in other countries. Now their task has been made easier, and the requirement to look for opportunities in these other markets has never been greater.

Consider, for example, the predicament of an investor in the United States, the largest automobile market in the world, investing only in domestic automobile stocks. Such a strategy would have missed entirely the growth in that market through the 1980s, which essentially all flowed abroad. Honda, Toyota, Nissan, Mitsubishi, Mercedes, BMW—these were the car companies that expanded rapidly in the US market, and became household names. A purely domestic horizon was too restrictive and narrow in focus. What is more, to the extent that Ford and General Motors had any success in the 1980s, it was to some extent based on their European operations. And the foreign influence is not restricted to the automobile market. automobile market.

The Japanese have dominated the home electronics market in most countries. Televisions, VCRs, video cameras, miniature radios, etc. have been supplied from Japan in increasing quantities. An investor in the United States, or Europe, who wanted to participate in these booming new markets was compelled to buy stock in Japanese companies. Many drugs sold around the world are made by European pharmaceutical companies. The floating glass process was developed by Pilkington in the United Kingdom. High-speed trains are being produced in France, Germany and Japan, but not in the United States. The United States has, however, been dominant in computers and aircraft manufacture. Non-US investors who ignore these crucial sectors simply because the companies are not European, or Japanese, or whatever, are reducing their own potential for profit.

New discoveries, new developments or new processes are being made or introduced around the world. Competition is now more than ever a global concept. The result is companies striving to compete in new markets world even by restricting investment to domestic markets. Foreign companies will compete in that domestic market and domestic companies will compete in foreign markets. Even where there is no direct competition, the influence of events elsewhere in the world is likely to be felt through commodity prices, interest rates and exchange rates. Inflation, in the short term at least, will not only be determined by domestic influences, but will also be affected by the price of oil and other prices determined in world markets.

Foreign markets partly offer similar types of investments that may be better for one reason or another—the product, the production etc.—and partly they offer diversity, i.e. investment in areas that is not possible in the home market. The second case would include much of the home electronics business, at least for the non-Japanese investor, or major integrated oil companies for Swiss investors.

The economic development of post-war Japan provided exceptional investment opportunities that were not available within the western economies. More recently, the growth of the Asian Tigers, Hong Kong, Taiwan, Singapore and South Korea, has opened up new potential for profits. Other countries in that area are also industrializing rapidly, e.g. Indonesia, Thailand and Malaysia. At the start of the 1990s, attention has turned to the Latin-American countries in expectation of improved economic management and recovery from the debt-induced collapse of the 1980s. In some of these cases, the risks are high, but there are also recognizable opportunities that are not open to investors within more developed markets.

The benefits of a rapidly changing environment adding to the possibility of higher economic growth are not restricted to the peripheral markets. Europe is embarked upon a path towards complete economic unification. Most people think this will also mean monetary union before too long, and some even anticipate political union. Monetary union seems a possibility unless something goes seriously wrong, but political union has to be a long way off. Having said that, there is clearly a trend towards greater political cooperation. The European Economic Community is inching towards a common foreign policy, a united defence policy etc., but the sovereign governments are reluctant to let too much power pass to the elected representatives in Strassburg, or the bureaucrats in Brussels.

The greater integration of European markets, with the removal of technological, economic and political barriers to free trade, will reduce marketing and production costs, thereby increasing growth and profitability. The benefits accrue not only to European companies, but also to foreign companies operating in Europe. Instead of having customized products for particular national markets, it should be possible to develop products for a pan-European market. For a more detailed discussion of the beneficial effects of European unification, see Coghlan (1991).

As markets move closer together, and macro-economic policies move into line with each other, so they offer less potential for diversification. The basis of risk reduction through international diversification is that market price movements are less than perfectly correlated. Stock markets and bond markets will become more highly correlated, i.e. are more likely to move in the same direction at the same time, as the macro-economic conditions within which they operate become more similar. Europe provides an extreme example of this development, particularly as integration continues, but the whole world has been moving in this direction. On the other hand, the advantages of diversification across individual assets will be increased, as it becomes easier to trade in a wider range of securities.

Figures 14.1 and 14.2 show how inflation rates are moving closer together, following the extreme volatility, and deviations, during the 1970s. There is a tendency to discuss this convergence in terms of European unification, and that undoubtedly has been an influence, but the trend extends over a much wider area than that. It is hard to make a case that European convergence, up to now, has been any greater than between all the major industrialized countries of the world. Partly what has happened is that inflation has risen in the traditionally low-inflation, strong-currency countries and has fallen elsewhere. Over the 1990s, it is likely that inflation rates will come more into line, while also achieving a lower average.

The changes taking place in Europe bring into question what exactly is international diversification. At present, a German stock held by a UK fund manager is just as much part of the international category as the holding of

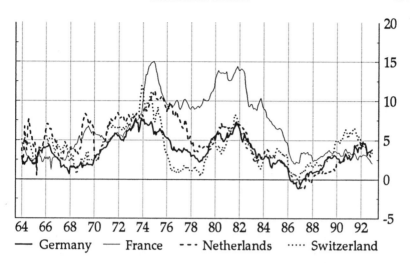

**Figure 14.1** European convergence of inflation

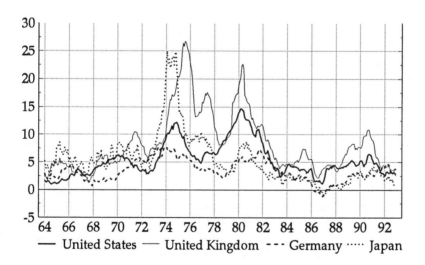

**Figure 14.2** International convergence of inflation

a US stock. Some time in the future, however, it may be necessary to think of such a position as no different to the holding of a Pennsylvania company in a portfolio managed out of Texas. That is the direction being traveled, but it will still take a long time before that destination is achieved. Along the way, more emphasis will undoubtedly be placed on European-wide indices, for both bonds and stocks.

The unification of western Europe is not the only major event impacting on investment decisions in that part of the world. There is also the complete disintegration of the communist empire. The rising living standards across their borders to the west could not be ignored by the impoverished and repressed populations in the communist countries. The comparison revealed the lumbering inefficiency of the centralized system and also the widespread corruption. Communism, as it worked in practice, was less organized along the lines of 'by the people, for the people', than 'by the people in charge, for the people in charge'. The communist rhetoric has really been nothing more than a justification for dictatorship.

Gorbachev loosened the chains and even opened the door to freedom. However, he must have been surprised at the mad rush to escape and, a number of times, was in danger of being trampled underfoot. The communist regimes suppressed ideas, incentive, freedom and living standards. The Russians had a long history of communism, and a *glorious* revolution, which helped to sustain communism through the most absurd contradictions. No such historical tradition existed in the satellite countries, nor in many of the Soviet Republics. These then quickly took over the lead from Gorbachev. The Russians had trouble facing the inevitable progression to a free-market economy, and as a result the economy was sliding into depression in 1991 with no obvious way out. The failed coup against Gorbachev put the final nail in the coffin of the communist monster that ruined so many lives for so long. The ex-communist countries such as Hungry, Poland and Czechoslovakia have suffered severe costs of adjustment, but at least quickly made the necessary changes to enable free markets to start providing a solution.

These countries provide enormous new markets for the products of existing companies, but also have a huge appetite for capital. Part of this will inevitably have to come in the form of aid from western governments. Part will come from direct investment from companies, and part through financial investment, in this case more like venture capital than normal portfolio diversification. The risks are high, as they have to be for something so new and revolutionary, but the potential rewards are also very great. On the consumer side, the early beneficiaries should be companies selling low-priced products that will easily, and cheaply, raise living standards. Only later will the market develop for higher-priced luxury goods. Capital goods industries should also be early beneficiaries given the need to raise quality, productivity and output generally.

To take advantage of these dramatic developments taking place in Europe, investors need to follow what is going on, and be aware of the ramifications for domestic companies. Many of the main beneficiaries are in Europe. German companies, in particular, are faced with more choices than they can ideally cope with. East Germany is a natural, almost captive, market at this point, in terms of direct investment, on top of which are the other East European countries. The changes have also had a major impact on government finances. The federal government has had to increase the budget deficit significantly, while at the same time raising taxes. The state of the Eastern economy was much worse than anticipated. Products were inferior, and production techniques were not only inefficient but also harmful to the environment, and in some cases, as with the nuclear power stations, extremely dangerous. As a result, reconstruction and reform has required much more money than had been anticipated at the time of reunification, and as well the old East German exchange rate was badly overvalued. While it is possible to focus on the negatives, these developments also offer tremendous potential for the future.

Companies have the advantage of a wider market for just about everything; machine tools, infrastructure, power plants, modern factories, consumer goods, banking and financial services, etc. At the same time, the increased investment needs raised the cost of capital, and the financial position of the federal government has deteriorated. This deterioration is in conventional terms, which views a higher budget deficit and rising expenditure as a percentage of GNP as a bad thing. In this case, however, such a perspective is much too narrow. The West German government has acquired an expanded tax base, more land and property and greater production. The costs are showing up in the present, while the benefits will accumulate in the future. Too great an emphasis on one side or the other distorts the picture.

In the first half of 1990, only the benefits were seen, and then, for more than a year after that, it was as if there were no benefits, only costs. One of the most important roles of government is to fill the gaps created by such temporal displacement. Here is a valid role for government; it should not be confused with the more normal distortions caused by excessive interference in the market economy, and obvious inefficiencies. Even so, there is no mistaking the conflict created by high capital needs in the near term and the long-term benefits to corporate profits. Investors, therefore, have to pay close attention to the time-scale of what is happening.

The developing countries of Europe, Portugal, Greece and Turkey provide yet another area of diversification opportunities. Elsewhere, Mexico has led a recovery of the Latin-American countries which suffered so badly from the debt crisis, and there is a lot of pent-up potential there once each country gets its financial house in order. The smaller Asian developing countries continue to demonstrate their amazing capacity to industrialize rapidly. At their shoulders stands China, increasingly looking as if it will develop a market economy. China suffered a series of catastrophic revolutions, but never really embraced communism as a philosophy in quite the way the Soviets did.

All around the world there are opportunities that will be partly reflected in domestic markets, but more importantly will benefit markets in other countries. An awareness of international developments is an indispensable ingredient in the modern investor's bag of tricks, even if the intention is never to venture outside the borders of the domestic economy. There are potentially great rewards for those prepared to be more adventurous. It may seem that this requires taking on more risk, but that is not how it turns out. The risk of the whole portfolio will actually be reduced, and return increased, through appropriate diversification.

## International stock markets

Attention has already been drawn to the potential and risks that exist in some of the developing markets. The risks are very much higher because the financial systems are normally not very well developed, accounting systems are often no better than basic and regulations can be extremely lax. In addition, reliable economic and financial data are usually very hard to come by so that it is difficult to judge the true state of the economy, or the corporations operating there. In this section, attention is concentrated on more established markets within developed economies, since these are where it is possible to employ the type of analysis presented in this book. Business cycles can be identified, with consistent implications for the financial markets. The same relationships will exist in the developing markets, but they will not be so easy to identify, and possibly next to impossible.

Essentially, the same influences will bear on market values in other developed countries as in the examples used for the United States. The business cycle operates in similar ways, with similar relationships existing between the economy and the different financial markets. The structure is the same, but some of the details are different. Too often, attention focuses on the differences that exist, to the extent that the domestic economy and financial system are presented as unique, implying that there are no lessons to be learnt from looking at market behavior in other countries.

There are no end of examples to illustrate this tendency to emphasize the uniqueness of one's own domain. National taxes and tax rates will make a difference, as will the particular accounting rules that are applied. Differences in national temperament and attitude may account for some differences in the propensity to consume, although that is more likely to be due to different historical perspectives and institutional structures. Faced with broadly similar circumstances, people are likely to react in the same way. To the extent that differences exist, these will generally not change reactions at the margin to a significant degree. There is a lot of evidence to support that general conclusion. Expectations of profit cause people to buy, and expectations of losses cause people to sell, and that seems to be true just about everywhere.

A classic example of the uniqueness approach was apparent following the collapse of stock prices on 19 October 1987. In the United States the blame was initially placed squarely on the failure of Congress to cut enough off the budget deficit. Two trillion was wiped off asset prices around the world because the budget deficit was $20 billion higher than what was thought acceptable. It really does not add up, and never did. This idea survived for quite some time, but was then superseded by the Brady Commission, which pointed a crooked finger at the existence of derivative products—options and futures. These, supposedly, opened the window so that the stock market could fall out. What was not satisfactorily explained is why, if that was the true explanation, the German stock market, for example, where there were no derivatives at all, fell by an even greater percentage.

Proponents of these ideas failed to take the international aspects into account. Earlier in 1987, there had been a lot of discussion about the lack of liquidity in, and vulnerability of, the German market, exactly because derivatives did not exist. Many signposts leading down blind alleys and off the edge of cliffs could be avoided if greater attention was paid to the consistency, historical and international, of the arguments employed. As explained earlier, there were clear signs that the market was under siege and was about to collapse. As it was, the United States was no more vulnerable to special circumstances than any other country at that time.

Taking the top 17 markets of the world as classified by Morgan Stanley Capital International (MSCI) we find a total market capitalization of $8 444.3 billion, at end-1990 exchange rates. The total size was magnified by the weak dollar at that time. A stronger exchange rate would lower the dollar value of foreign stock prices denominated in other currencies. Table 14.1 shows market valuations and gross domestic products (GDP), in dollar terms, along with dividend yields, earnings per share, money market rates and bond yields, where available. The market indices for the major industrialized countries are shown in Fig. 14.5, in both real and nominal terms.

One feature that stands out is the low level of dividend yield and earnings per share in Japan, as compared to the other countries. The low dividend yield is partly explained by the fact that there is no significant capital gains tax in Japan, so there is real incentive for companies to reinvest profits, thereby converting them into a higher stock price. An essential requirement for such a process to work is for there to be plenty of good investment

Table 14.1 International stock market indices

| Country | MSCI market value $ billion | Weight in MSCI index | Total market value $ billion | Market value weights | GDP $ billion | GDP weights | Market value as % of GDP | Dividend yield | Earnings yield | Money† market rate | Government† bond yield |
|---|---|---|---|---|---|---|---|---|---|---|---|
| Austria | 15.5 | 0.3 | 24.5 | 0.29 | 155.8 | 0.9 | 15.7 | 1.7 | 3.0 | 8.87 | 8.80 |
| Belgium | 37.4 | 0.8 | 65.2 | 0.77 | 192.4 | 1.2 | 33.9 | 5.8 | 11.1 | 10.05 | 9.99 |
| Denmark | 23.9 | 0.5 | 39.5 | 0.47 | 131.0 | 0.8 | 30.2 | 1.8 | 6.9 | 10.40 | 10.80 |
| Finland | 10.2 | 0.2 | 22.9 | 0.27 | 144.4 | 0.9 | 15.9 | 3.9 | 11.4 | 14.30 | 13.23 |
| France | 169.0 | 3.4 | 296.5 | 3.51 | 1 264.5 | 7.6 | 23.4 | 4.0 | 10.8 | 10.27 | 10.53 |
| Germany | 205.7 | 4.2 | 341.7 | 4.05 | 1 625.8 | 9.7 | 21.0 | 4.0 | 7.9 | 9.21 | 8.90 |
| Italy | 75.3 | 1.5 | 148.2 | 1.76 | 1 090.8 | 6.5 | 13.6 | 3.9 | 9.6 | 12.96 | 11.96 |
| Netherlands | 85.5 | 1.7 | 114.3 | 1.35 | 279.2 | 1.7 | 40.9 | 5.0 | 8.5 | 9.34 | 9.06 |
| Norway | 15.1 | 0.3 | 25.7 | 0.30 | 105.8 | 0.6 | 24.3 | 2.5 | 9.8 | 11.66 | 10.61 |
| Spain | 54.6 | 1.1 | 105.1 | 1.24 | 491.2 | 2.9 | 21.4 | 5.6 | 11.5 | 15.12 | 14.54 |
| Sweden | 48.2 | 1.0 | 93.0 | 1.10 | 236.9 | 1.4 | 39.3 | 3.4 | 11.0 | 14.36 | 12.30 |
| Switzerland | 95.9 | 1.9 | 162.8 | 1.93 | 241.1 | 1.4 | 67.5 | 3.0 | 8.9 | 8.82 | 6.68 |
| United Kingdom | 537.2 | 10.8 | 882.4 | 10.45 | 1 060.9 | 6.3 | 83.2 | 5.7 | 9.2 | 13.31 | 10.42 |
| Europe | 1 373.5 | 27.7 | 2 321.8 | 27.50 | 7 019.8 | 41.9 | 33.1 | 4.6 | 9.3 | 11.65 | 10.17 |
| Australia | 68.2 | 1.4 | 105.9 | 1.25 | 293.3 | 1.7 | 36.1 | 6.7 | 9.3 | 12.05 | 12.05 |
| Hong Kong | 43.3 | 0.9 | 83.5 | 0.99 | 65.5 | 0.4 | 127.5 | 5.5 | 10.4 | 6.45 | |
| Japan | 1 548.0 | 31.2 | 2 805.5 | 33.22 | 3 189.5 | 19.1 | 90.0 | 0.8 | 3.2 | 7.61 | 7.06 |
| New Zealand | 5.4 | 0.1 | 8.0 | 0.09 | 32.5 | 0.2 | 24.6 | 7.8 | 17.2 | 12.05 | 12.26 |
| Singapore/ Malaysia | 33.9 | 0.7 | 67.7 | 0.80 | 32.5 | 0.2 | 208.3 | 1.9 | 6.4 | 5.05 | |
| Pacific | 1 698.9 | 34.3 | 3 070.6 | 36.40 | 3 613.3 | 21.6 | 85.0 | 1.2 | 3.8 | 7.72 | 7.29 |
| EAFA | 3 072.4 | 62.0 | 5 392.4 | 63.90 | 10 633.1 | 63.5 | 50.7 | 2.7 | 6.2 | 9.48 | 8.58 |
| Canada | 138.6 | 2.8 | 222.4 | 2.63 | 578.8 | 3.5 | 38.4 | 3.7 | 6.6 | 11.23 | 10.41 |
| United States | 1 734.0 | 35.0 | 2 813.5 | 33.32 | 5 513.8 | 33.0 | 50.8 | 3.7 | 7.1 | 7.82 | 8.31 |
| World Index | 4 954.5 | 100.0 | 8 444.3 | 100.00 | 16 725.7 | 100.0 | 50.5 | 3.1 | 6.5 | 8.95 | 8.54 |

opportunities. These have existed, and have generated high growth of earnings, and the economy, over time. That, combined with relatively low interest rates, has helped to explain the high valuation of the Japanese stock market. Other considerations include the 100 per cent depreciation rate used by companies, which depresses current earnings, and the habit of presenting results on an unconsolidated basis. Making adjustments for such institutional factors helps to produce a more reasonable valuation for the market. Even taking such institutional considerations into account, there is no doubt that the market became extremely expensive in the late 1980s, and early 1990s.

When making international comparisons, it is necessary to take account of differences in interest rates and growth rates. Within a domestic market there is nothing unusual about a company with very high growth of earnings having a high/price earnings ratio, i.e. a low earnings yield, even if the company pays out no dividend. This is the normal relationship that is found. If allowance was not made for the high growth rate then the price/earnings ratio would quickly become too low, as earnings kept growing. Investors are bound to anticipate future earnings and thereby bid up the price.

The influence of interest rates can also be observed within the domestic market. There is a close relationship between high interest rates and a high earnings yield. Likely reasons for the existence of such a relationship were discussed in Chapter 13, and these apply in all countries. Sometimes, the true costs of finance may not be very well measured by published interest rates so that the linkage is not so clear. That is not a suspension of economic rationality, but simply a measurement problem; not an uncommon problem in the real world. Investors should beware of glib comparisons of price/earnings ratios, or other so-called valuation criteria, that ignore such basic points of analysis. There is no sleight of hand involved, no attempts to deceive; quite the opposite in fact. The deception is in ignoring such inconvenient complications.

What we find is that the same basic valuation criteria that were important from a domestic perspective also apply when making international judgements. An added advantage of looking at markets in other countries is that comparisons can be made not only over history, but also across a single point in time. This can be extremely helpful, even if the intention is only to invest in the domestic market, since it provides a point of comparison with alternatives. Of course, if it shows that other markets are cheaper, with better future prospects, then the logical next step is to take advantage of it by investing in those markets.

Taking a closer look at the German stock market, this has not risen in value as much as might have been expected given the spectacular performance of the economy. There are three possible explanations. First, there is the fact that a large number of fast-growing smaller businesses have remained privately owned, and do not, therefore, show up in the index. Second, there is the treatment of dividends. In Germany, the relative attractiveness of dividends versus capital gains is the exact reverse of the situation in Japan. In Germany, domestic investors receive a credit on dividends which makes them particularly attractive to pension funds etc., which do not pay tax. This arrangement makes a high dividend payout ratio an attractive feature of a stock. And, since capital gains are subject to tax, there is a preference for dividends over capital gains. Another consequence of this situation is that there is an incentive for foreign investors to sell a German stock over the dividend period and buy it back ex-dividend. At the same time, it is attractive for domestic investors to do the opposite. This coincidence of wants creates a potential market in which both parties can benefit, and, therefore, helps to generate volume in stocks paying high dividends.

The third possible explanation is the effect of the changing value of the exchange rate. Over time, the Deutschemark has appreciated against the dollar, reflecting Germany's better inflation performance. This rise has helped to keep down the profits of German companies from external trade. However, US holders of German stocks still benefited through the currency appreciation.

The reverse, however, was the case for German holders of US stocks. These investors found that the Deutschemark value of their holdings failed to keep up with the rising market. The two cases are shown in Figs 14.3 and 14.4. Looking at the German market in domestic terms, an investor might conclude that performance was very poor, since it lagged badly behind the US market. However, converting the US market to Deutschemark terms shows that the German investor did much better, from 1970 to 1991, in Germany than in the United States. And that is without taking dividends into account. Also, it turns out that the US investor would have done much better in Germany, once stock prices were converted back into dollars.

On the face of it the US stock market did much better than the German market since 1970, which makes it seem that US investors did much better by staying at home and that German investors did relatively badly. Appearances, however, are deceiving, and the reality is quite the opposite. The truth is that the German market did better than the US market when converted into Deutschemarks, i.e. from the point of view of a German investor, while the German market outperformed the US market in dollar terms. Even after these adjustments, it still seems as if the US investor did very much better in the German market than the German investor did, but even that is deceptive.

A large part of the better performance in favor of US-based investors is just a reflection of higher inflation in the United States. The returns shown

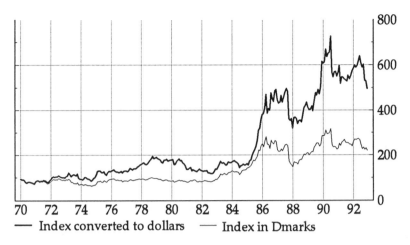

**Figure 14.3** German stock market index (domestic and dollar)

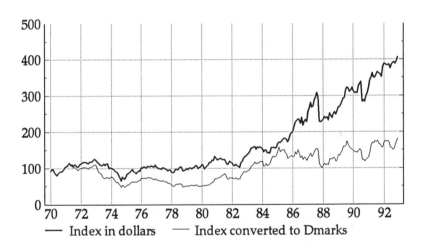

**Figure 14.4** US stock market index (domestic and Deutschemark)

are measured in nominal terms, but would be much closer if converted to real terms; over this period US prices increased by 263 per cent while German prices increased by 125 per cent. The fact that US investors in Germany did a little better in relative terms is because the Deutschemark rose more than relative prices.

The German investor wishing to avoid the currency loss could consider hedging the dollar position back to Deutschemarks through the forward market. The way that market works is discussed in Chapter 15 but the main point is that the forward rate will reflect the difference between interest rates in each country, and such insurance could prove expensive. Under normal circumstances, interest rates will be high in the higher inflation country. If one year rates in the United States are 8 per cent, and they are 5 per cent in Germany, for example, then the forward rate for a year for Germans will be 3 per cent below the spot rate; i.e. the forward cost of cover, apart from any transaction costs, will be 3 per cent. The existence of this cost often makes it difficult to hedge stock portfolios, but it can be done, and the benefits of diversification still hold. Where hedging is much more normal is in the case of international bonds.

Going back to Table 14.1, another feature to note is the wide difference between the market valuation and the size of GDP for different countries. The ratio of market value to GDP varies from a low of 13.6 per cent for Italy to 208.3 per cent in the case of Singapore/Malaysia. In terms of the larger markets, the ratio for Germany is only 21 per cent, but is 90 per cent for Japan, a little higher than the United Kingdom. The ratio for the United States comes in at around 50.8 per cent which is almost the same as the world average.

The MSCI market weightings are important since they are widely used to measure the performance of international fund managers, or performance generally. However, there is a question as to whether market capitalization is the best measure. There are two issues. One is whether it might be more realistic to use GDP weights and, second, concern over the effect of a strong exchange rate in raising a country's weighting. To deal with this second question first, a very strong currency against the dollar will raise the market capitalization, or GDP in dollars and thereby raise the index weighting, whether this is justified by what else is going on or not. Even more worrisome is the fact that the higher exchange rate will have the effect of reducing competitiveness of corporations, making them less attractive, right at the time the weighting is being increased. There is a need to take account of changes in relative price levels over time, but without stacking the odds against the investor. A strong case can be made for using purchasing power parity rates, instead of exchange rates, for deciding market weightings, in order to get around this problem.

The other concern regarding market weightings is even more of a problem, and is harder to resolve. Using market-value weights, Singapore/Malaysia has virtually the same weight as Belgium despite the fact that GDP is only 16 per cent of the Belgian level. Hong Kong is the other country with very high relative weighting. There are two main reasons why market value is likely to be high relative to GDP. First, more companies are listed in such countries than in many other countries. There are still many large family-owned businesses in Europe. That may just be an institutional characteristic, in which case market value is probably the right choice, or it may be that many more marginal businesses have come to the market for finance, making GDP weights a better choice. Second, it could be that the market is trading at a high price/earnings ratio and, thereby, a high market value/GDP ratio. In that case, a GDP weighting might be more justified. One factor accounting for the relatively low market capitalization in Italy has been the extremely weak market conditions that have existed for some time. These have resulted in the *real* value of the market falling to one third of its value in 1968. This relatively poor performance can be seen in Fig. 14.5.

The combined market value weight of Japan, Hong Kong and Singapore/ Malaysia is 32.8 per cent. The GDP weight for the same three countries is 20 per cent. Because of the perceived high risks associated with these markets, international fund managers tended to underweight these markets, particularly Japan, in the second half of the 1980s and, because of that, underperformed the world index. As a consequence, there was considerable debate as to why international fund managers had done such a poor job. However, the outcome may have been very different if alternative weights had been used for the base index.

International fund managers and their clients need to pay very close attention to the base that is used to measure performance. A cynical view might be that managers want to choose an index that is reasonably easy to beat, but that is not the real point. The base index will determine how much risk the manager will take, and that is what is really important. As discussed in Chapter 8, it is essential to decide a basic approach, or philosophy, to investing. That means selecting low-risk positions that will form a base at times of great uncertainty, and provide a foundation for consistent asset allocation decisions. The individual investor is not as tied to official indices, and it is not clear that institutions have to be either.

A small investor is likely to invest overseas only on a selective basis, and the idea of using market weights will seem unimportant. However, even in that case it will be helpful to look at market valuations of the alternative markets before settling on a final investment choice. An extremely wealthy individual should pay much greater attention to market weights, since diversification is crucially important. These weights need not be any of those discussed here, but could be customized to individual preferences and perceptions of risk. That is much harder to do in the case of a large institution, but not impossible.

The question of the correct market weights becomes extremely important when international portfolios are run on an indexed basis. This type of auto-pilot management received a large boost in the second half of the 1980s when all international fund managers consistently underperformed the international index. Part of the reason for that has already been discussed. It is strange, but true, that there were many institutions who were happy to be underweighted in Japan, but who, at the same time, were attracted to indexation because of the better performance. The fact that indexation meant taking a full weight in Japan seemed to be forgotten, or maybe the decision was easier if it did not have to be thought about explicitly. Full indexation has its advantages under certain circumstances, but as a general rule is not a good idea. The problem, in the case of international accounts, is really with the index being chosen. The index is acceptable as a black box as long as the internal details are not inspected too closely, and as long as it performs well. Indexation is a sign of a bull market. No one wants to be indexed to a falling market.

The weights used by large institutional managers can affect all investors, particularly if there is a major change. For example, changing from market-value weights to GDP weights would result in a substantial increase in flows to the German market, for example, and out of Japan, the United Kingdom, etc. The market that would be least affected would be the United States, where the two weights are very similar.

In choosing between market-value and GDP weights, a case can be made for selecting some form of compromise. The very high market-value weights for Singapore/Malaysia and Hong Kong are worrisome. Assuming these economies grow faster than the world average, it is likely that the market value will rise even faster, thereby raising their weights even higher. Investors want to participate in such high-growth markets, but need to recognize the high risks involved. The market-value weights are fine as long as prices are rising, but the risks are also higher than average when prices turn down.

An example of the risks in these markets was provided by events in Hong Kong in 1987. The market ran up strongly until the world-wide collapse on 19 October and then the gates slammed shut, locking investors out of the market for a week. Stock prices in Hong Kong fell more than the average, by nearly 50 per cent, and took a very long time to recover. The Taiwanese market is not in the MSCI index, but generated similar sorts of problems. In 1990, that index fell by 80 per cent in one year, from a high of 12 495 to a low of 2560, between February and October—a fall to match the total decline of the US stock market from 1929 to 1932. This mighty crash took place with hardly a comment, and yet it was devastating for those investors who held stock there. Fortunately for international investors it is not easy to invest in Taiwan stocks, but there are authorized funds through which it is possible to gain exposure.

What we are talking about here is not a small, insignificant market, although clearly smaller than it was. The market capitalization in February 1990, prior to the collapse, was over $300 billion. Comparing that with the market capitalization for other markets as of the end of 1990, we come up with the startling conclusion that this was higher than all but the four largest markets, in the United States, Japan, the United Kingdom and

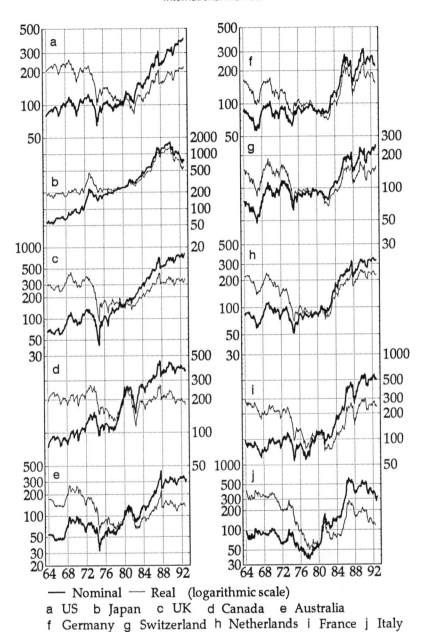

**Figure 14.5** International stock markets
*Source:* Morgan Stanley Capital International

Table 14.2 Latin-American stock markets at end 1990

| | Market capitalization US $ billion | GDP* US $ billion | Market value as % of GDP |
|---|---|---|---|
| Argentina | 3.3 | 14.2 | 23.2% |
| Brazil | 16.4 | 112.7 | 14.5% |
| Chile | 13.6 | 21.9 | 62.1% |
| Columbia | 1.4 | 35.1 | 4.0% |
| Mexico | 32.7 | 187.1 | 17.5% |
| Venezuela | 8.4 | 44.4 | 18.9% |

* Latest available

Germany. One reason for this high valuation was the high price/ earnings ratio. The ratio of market capitalization to GNP had reached 158.4 per cent by the end of 1989, compared with only 17.1 per cent at the end of 1985.

Taiwan is not the only large market missing from the MSCI market classification, and many of these have a lot of potential to grow, particularly in Latin-America, which is totally unrepresented. In 1990, the eight top performing markets were all in developing countries; with the percentage change shown in parentheses, these were Venezuela (+572), Greece (+90), Zimbabwe (+84), Chile (+31), Columbia (+27), Mexico (+25), Nigeria (+24) and India (+16). For all emerging markets, market capitalization was $470 billion at the end of 1990, compared with a market value of $67 billion at the end of 1982. The main Latin-American markets are contained in Table 14.2 (Salomon Brothers, 1991). GDP figures have been added to show how low market capitalization is on a relative basis. For all markets, capitalization as a percentage of GDP increased from 6 per cent in 1980 to 32 per cent in 1990.

## International bond markets

Bonds in the major industrialized countries are subject to very much the same forces they are in the United States. Inflation is a large influence, with the strength of the economy within the business cycle also being important. Fiscal policy, and size of the budget deficit, will affect the supply side, in addition to issues from other sources. However, since this latter group tends to follow demand, there is little identifiable effect on price. Tax laws will play a role, and from an international perspective may make a particular market attractive or not. For example, when the German government proposed a domestic withholding tax in the late 1980s, the effect was to push up bond yields on domestic issues sharply.

International fund managers are very concerned about liquidity, so the size of the market is also of concern. This is also a question to which individual investors should pay attention. There is a sort of catch-22 at work. A market needs to be large enough to make it easy to buy and sell on small spreads, but not for the government or companies to be heavily indebted. That requires a large country. This is a problem with the Swiss government bond market; it really does not have the liquidity to make it attractive to international fund managers. The size of the central government bond market was only $8.6 billion at the end of 1990, out of a total public issue size of $190 billion. In addition, the conservative investment policies of Swiss domestic institutions ensures that the yield on the few government bonds that are issued is kept very low. The largest component in the Swiss franc market is made up of foreign bonds.

Bond issuers have much greater potential to customize offerings to the desires of investors than in the case of stock issues. For a while, in the second half of the 1980s, Japanese companies were issuing bonds, often in Swiss francs, that carried extremely low coupons, because they were accompanied by a warrant on the stock, and warrants were in demand. Bonds have been issued in bearer form in the Euro markets, providing anonymity for purchasers. Issuers will use different countries, and currencies, in order to reduce the expected cost of the bonds, and vary maturity in order to meet investor demand. The French government issued bonds linked to the price of gold in the 1970s, the Giscard bonds; these backfired badly, turning out to be probably the most expensive bonds ever issued.

There are also many issues by supernational institutions in various currencies, and issues by developing countries, usually in dollars. There is no international bond market in the more peripheral currencies, like australs or pesos. These countries will borrow internationally in dollars, if at all. That might seem to give the lenders an added degree of security, but the potential costs that are pushed on to the borrower can be so high as to force effective default—exactly what happened in the 1980s in Latin-America. Had these countries borrowed in domestic currency, the lender could have got back the full amount of the money lent, but it would have been worth only a fraction of its original value in dollars.

The main international bond markets are included in the Salomon Brothers world bond indices. The market sizes contained in Table 14.3 are based on Salomon Brothers' 1991 update, with values as of the end of 1990. A number of points stand out in this table. One is the extremely small percentage of government bonds outstanding in Switzerland. The percentage is increased if state and local issues are added, but it is still very low. In many cases, for the other countries, the inclusion of all forms of government and government-guaranteed debt changes the picture considerably. Central government debt is usually the most marketable, and in some countries, such as the United States, state and local bonds carry special tax advantages available only to domestic residents. As a result, yields are so

Table 14.3 International bond market indices

| | Total public traded issues $ billion | Market weight | Central government | Central government as % of total | Total* government related | Total government as % total | GDP $ billion | Market as % GDP | Total government as % GDP | Government bond yield | Inflation† |
|---|---|---|---|---|---|---|---|---|---|---|---|
| US dollar | 5 388.9 | 44.8 | 1 668.4 | 31.0 | 3 873.8 | 71.9 | 5 522.2 | 97.6 | 70.2 | 8.31 | 5.3 |
| Japanese yen | 2 221.9 | 18.5 | 1 163.9 | 52.4 | 1 365.8 | 61.5 | 3 141.5 | 70.7 | 43.5 | 7.06 | 3.1 |
| Deutschemark | 1 123.7 | 9.3 | 295.3 | 26.3 | 365.6 | 32.5 | 1 490.2 | 75.4 | 24.5 | 8.90 | 2.8 |
| Italian lira | 755.4 | 6.3 | 596.7 | 79.0 | 620.9 | 82.2 | 1 089.1 | 69.4 | 57.0 | 11.96 | 6.4 |
| French franc | 575.3 | 4.8 | 240.8 | 41.8 | 458.8 | 79.7 | 1 191.4 | 48.3 | 38.5 | 10.53 | 3.3 |
| UK sterling | 361.3 | 3.0 | 219.6 | 60.8 | 219.8 | 60.8 | 978.4 | 36.9 | 22.5 | 10.42 | 9.5 |
| Canadian dollar | 312.4 | 2.6 | 119.2 | 38.2 | 215.6 | 69.0 | 578.6 | 54.0 | 37.3 | 10.41 | 4.8 |
| Belgium franc | 270.6 | 2.3 | 135.1 | 50.0 | 212.9 | 78.7 | 194.8 | 138.9 | 109.3 | 9.99 | 3.5 |
| Danish krone | 213.0 | 1.8 | 66.5 | 31.2 | 66.5 | 31.2 | 130.9 | 162.7 | 50.8 | 10.80 | 2.6 |
| Swedish krona | 208.5 | 1.7 | 75.0 | 36.0 | 76.2 | 36.5 | 230.2 | 90.6 | 33.1 | 12.80 | 10.5 |
| Swiss franc | 190.0 | 1.6 | 8.6 | 4.5 | 19.1 | 10.1 | 223.4 | 85.1 | 8.6 | 6.68 | 5.4 |
| Dutch guilder | 186.1 | 1.5 | 119.8 | 64.4 | 122.9 | 66.0 | 276.9 | 67.2 | 44.4 | 9.06 | 2.5 |
| Spanish peseta | 90.4 | 0.8 | 49.6 | 54.9 | 53.3 | 59.0 | 491.3 | 18.4 | 10.8 | 14.68 | 6.7 |
| Australian dollar | 80.8 | 0.7 | 24.8 | 30.7 | 44.4 | 55.0 | 298.2 | 27.1 | 14.9 | 12.05 | 7.3 |
| Norwegian krone | 46.7 | 0.4 | 12.9 | 27.6 | 20.9 | 44.8 | 105.7 | 44.1 | 19.7 | 10.72 | 4.2 |

* Central government, agency, guaranteed, state and local.
† Averages for the year.

low as not to be attractive to international investors. Even so, it is useful to get an idea of total government involvement.

In the United Kingdom, for example, the central government does all the borrowing for all levels of government, so that comparing only central government issues overstates the relative size of the government sector: central government issues as a percentage of total issues is the third highest after Italy and the Netherlands, but when the same comparison is done using total government issues there are seven countries with higher percentages than the United Kingdom. An even more realistic way to judge government debt issues is as a percentage of GDP. In that case the percentage for the United Kingdom is only 22.5 per cent, coming 11th down the list. The Swiss percentage is extremely low at only 8.6 per cent, while Belgium leads the field with 109.3 per cent.

As everyone knows, the United States has accumulated a lot of debt, but it is still not the highest as a percentage of GDP. That title is taken by Denmark. Central government bonds are in the middle range as a percentage of GDP, and the really big market is made up of mortgage bonds. This is a very unusual situation that has taken the bond market to 163 per cent of GDP, and gives Danish bonds an international importance greater than suggested simply by looking at the size of the economy. Bond yields in Denmark were exceptionally high in real terms going into 1991. The other market offering very high real yields was France.

France has been one of the major success stories of the European Monetary System. Traditionally a high-inflation country, France has steadily reduced inflation down close to the German rate, typically used as the benchmark for Europe. In 1991, French inflation fell below the German rate, and remained below through 1992. The Italian inflation rate has also moved down, but not with quite the same success yet. These examples encouraged talk about *convergence* as a general investment approach in Europe, and sometimes even the world.

The idea behind convergence is that the countries of Europe will do everything in their power to maintain fixed, or nearly fixed, cross rates, against a German base. As a result, inflation rates will move closer together, and the high bond yields will fall towards the German average. Figures 14.1 and 14.2 showed inflation for some of the main countries, with prospects for greater convergence through the 1990s. This argument resulted in international funds flowing to the higher-yielding countries of Europe, providing a justification for investing in Italian and UK bonds. Then attention, and money, was directed towards the Spanish, Swedish and Portuguese markets. This worked well until the summer of 1992 when the Bundesbank refused to reduce interest rates and precipitated a series of currency crises, leading to major realignments of exchange rates within the EMS.

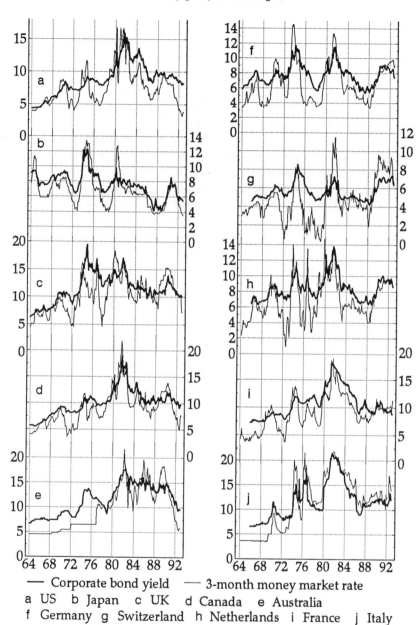

— Corporate bond yield    — 3-month money market rate
a US   b Japan   c UK   d Canada   e Australia
f Germany  g Switzerland  h Netherlands  i France   j Italy

**Figure 14.6** International interest rates

Investors have become used to high real interest rates through the 1980s, but these are likely to trend lower through the 1990s. Capital requirements have been increased by the opening up of eastern Europe, and to a lesser extent by the turmoil in the Middle East, and this will add something to real interest rates. However, rates through the 1980s were much higher than average, and followed the negative real returns that were available through much of the 1970s. This compensation effect is likely to be reduced further on average, and should be only partly offset by the higher capital needs. Capital needs were huge in the 1980s as well, as the world economy moved into higher gear and asset values were pushed up, after having been severely depressed. The higher capital needs in eastern Europe are only part of the story, and should not be allowed to obscure the rest of the picture.

Figure 14.6 shows how bond yields have acted in the main international markets over the 26 years from 1964. The charts show the movement of interest rates over time, short and long, the difference between them being the yield curve. When considering bonds as an investment it is important to take account of the yield offered, since this will typically be a large part of the total return. With international bonds it is also necessary to include the effect of exchange rates. Figure 14.7 shows the total return in dollars for some of the main countries. These total return indices include interest, capital gains and changes in the exchange rate.

Over time, total returns on an international basis should equalize. Domestic bond yields should reflect inflationary expectations, while exchange rates should eventually move to discount changes in relative prices; either that or relative prices need to adjust. These are long-term relationships, but they provide a reason to become suspicious when returns move substantially out of line for an extended period of time. When making such comparisons it is, however, necessary to bear in mind that the base year is unlikely to represent equilibrium at that time. An important conclusion that follows from this long-term tendency to equalize, is that there is less advantage to running an international bond portfolio on a fully indexed basis than in the case of equities. There is still the benefit that the standard deviation of return will be reduced, and that is worth having, but over time you are likely to get the same return as the domestic market. As a result, the case for active management is even stronger in the case of bonds than for equities.

It can be seen from Figure 14.7 that the Japanese index return moved up very high in 1988 and, at the time, these bonds were widely expected to continue to outperform. That was a bet against the odds. What happened was that the index fell back towards the average in late 1989 and early 1990. The more similar the countries the closer the returns should be expected, and this relationship can be seen in the index movements for the

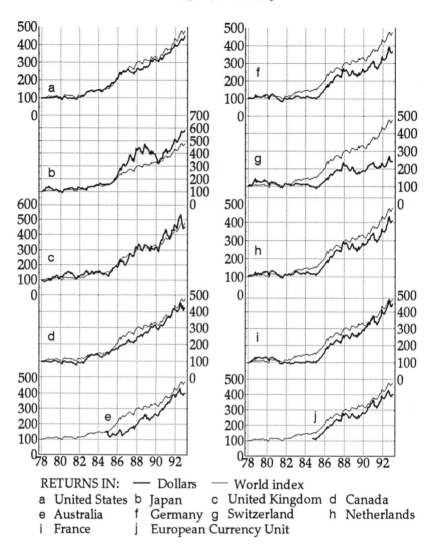

**Figure 14.7** Total returns from government bonds.
*Source:* Salomon Brothers. 30 December 1977 = 100 except e and j

United States and Canada. Bond returns in Australia have also been similar; the Australian index started in 1984 (September 1984 = 100) and has been rebased to the world index to make it comparable.

The return on German bonds had lagged behind, caught up with the United States in 1987 and stayed close through 1988, but then fell behind again. The gap has closed up to some extent but will require a further improvement in German bond prices. Market returns within continental Europe remained close up to 1985. They have stayed reasonably close since then, although the Swiss return has consistently lagged behind, reflecting reasonably stable exchange rates but below-market yields. The special situation of the Swiss government bond market was discussed earlier.

## Hedged bond returns

A hedged bond portfolio is much easier to organize and run than a hedged equity portfolio, and there is more reason to consider it. A weaker currency will generally be beneficial to exporters in that country, thereby raising the likely profit. As a result, stock prices may well move to offset any currency weakness. The actual outcome will depend on the circumstances surrounding the currency weakness. Such offsetting behavior is unlikely in the case of bonds, and bond yields may even be forced up above where they would otherwise have been in the face of currency weakness. To put that in a slightly more technical form, there is more likely to be a positive correlation between bonds and the exchange rate than is the case for equities, where the correlation is more likely to be negative.

There is also a more natural fit between international bonds and currency hedging. Firstly, currency movements are partly determined by interest rates, secondly, bond hedging can be interpreted as a play on relative yield curves. A hedged portfolio continues to provide the benefits of an internationally diversified portfolio, but without the added currency risk. This makes a hedged portfolio a good choice as the base index against which to measure performance, and Salomon Brothers produce hedged-return indices that can be used for that purpose. Doing that still leaves open the possibility of unhedging parts of the portfolio to take advantage of expected favorable exchange rate changes, while hedging back to the base index at times of uncertainty. There is further discussion of forward exchange rates, and how these are set, in the following chapter on the exchange rate. The main point to note here is that the forward rate will be equal to the interest rate differential for that maturity; i.e. the three-month forward will be equal to the three-month interest rate differential.

Through means of currency hedging it is possible to set up a synthetic country bond. This is a bond that is effectively denominated in one currency, but has the capital gains features of another country. To show this, take the example of UK gilts at the end of 1990. At the time, these were widely recommended as attractive, with the 10 years yielding 10.93 per cent. UK inflation was expected to fall to 5 per cent or below, from a high of over 10 per cent, and it was thought that the weak economy would cause the Bank of England to ease monetary policy. There was, however, a better alternative that received hardly any attention. It was possible to buy French government bonds yielding 10 per cent and hedge that back into sterling for one year to pick up an additional 2.1 per cent in yield, for a total yield of 12.1 per cent. Using French franc Euro bonds, the comparison was even more favorable, since French Euro 10-year bonds yielded 11.4 per cent, compared with sterling Euros yielding 11.28 per cent. A three-month hedge, instead of 12 months, improved the yield even further, because of the steepness of the yield curve at that time, producing a yield pick-up of 3.5 per cent at an annual rate. On a yield basis, the sterling synthetic created out of French bonds was certainly attractive, with a potential yield close to 15 per cent.

Before deciding on the trade there was still the capital gains potential to consider. The improving UK inflation outlook was a plus, and was the main focus of attention. However, French inflation was already close to 3 per cent and was not expected to increase significantly. The French economy was also weak, although not in the same devastated state as in the United Kingdom. Even on the most optimistic assumptions, UK inflation was unlikely to match the French rate for some time. What mattered in making a decision was not what would finally happen, since that was not known, but the expectations at the time. The synthetic created a much better *expected* return, and that, in fact, is how it turned out.

What made the trade attractive was the fact that the yield curve was negatively sloped in the United Kingdom and positively sloped in France. This situation produced higher short-term interest rates in the United Kingdom than in France and, therefore, a positive pick-up on the hedge, while at the same time long-term bond yields were reasonably close. Doing the hedge the other way, against the yield curve, from sterling to francs would have been extremely expensive and made no sense. *As a general rule, it is profitable to hedge on a yield basis if the yield curve is more positively sloped in the foreign market.* Under those conditions there may be a cost to the hedge, but it will still be worthwhile. The most favorable case is where domestic short rates are above foreign short rates, and particularly if the domestic yield curve is inverted, as in the UK example above.

Consider an example where 10-year bond yields in Japan and Germany are 6 per cent and 8 per cent respectively, while the interest rate on one-year Euro-deposits is 5 per cent and 6 per cent. Because of the steeper yield curve in Germany, measured in basis points, the Japanese investor can pick up a yield of 7 per cent on German bonds hedged for one year—

the 8 per cent, less the 1 per cent cost of the forward hedge. Had Japanese short rates been even higher in this example, the benefits from the hedge would have been increased. For example, if one year Euro-yen rate had been 7 per cent while all other rates stayed the same, i.e. an inverted yield curve, the Japanese investor could have achieved a hedged return of 9 per cent; the 8 per cent, plus the 1 per cent pick up from the hedge.

Yield is not the only consideration. The expected change in the exchange rate and the two bond prices will also be important in deciding whether to do the trade. The synthetic will not be very attractive if domestic bond yields are expected to fall, and they are expected to rise in the foreign country. That would mean sacrificing an expected capital gain and accepting an expected capital loss. Similarly, if an investor has a strong view that the foreign currency will appreciate over this holding period, a hedge will not look attractive. To protect against an expected appreciation of the domestic exchange rate may require putting on hedges even when these are expensive.

Hedged bonds offer the significant advantage of diversification without currency risk. Even in those cases where there are suitable opportunities to diversify within the domestic market, there is still the problem that the return on different categories of bonds will be highly correlated. There is no reduction in the risk that all bond prices will fall together if conditions deteriorate. Bonds are sensitive to macro-economic conditions, particularly inflation, and the only way to reduce the standard deviation significantly within a bond portfolio is through international diversification. Some countries also offer limited choice in types of bonds, so that international diversification is the only way to gain access to a variety of different issuers. Table 14.4 shows the correlation between different bond market returns over the period 1978 to 1989.

Figure 14.8 shows what happens to the return and standard deviation of return for a yen bond portfolio as hedged international bonds are added, 10 per cent at a time, gradually replacing the domestic component. In this

Table 14.4 Correlation coefficients of local-currency bond returns

|  | US | JP | UK | GE | SW | NE | FR | CA |
|---|---|---|---|---|---|---|---|---|
| United States | 1.00 | | | | | | | |
| Japan | 0.39 | 1.00 | | | | | | |
| United Kingdom | 0.37 | 0.35 | 1.00 | | | | | |
| Germany | 0.51 | 0.58 | 0.33 | 1.00 | | | | |
| Switzerland | 0.35 | 0.37 | 0.29 | 0.48 | 1.00 | | | |
| Netherlands | 0.55 | 0.48 | 0.35 | 0.76 | 0.48 | 1.00 | | |
| France | 0.29 | 0.35 | 0.25 | 0.43 | 0.27 | 0.52 | 1.00 | |
| Canada | 0.78 | 0.37 | 0.33 | 0.58 | 0.42 | 0.55 | 0.41 | 1.00 |

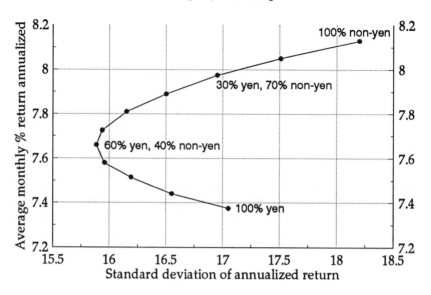

**Figure 14.8** Risk and return on a hedged yen portfolio

case, the standard deviation was reduced to the point where 60 per cent was in domestic bonds and 40 per cent in international hedged bonds. The return continued to rise up until the point where 100 per cent was in hedged bonds and nothing in the domestic market. Figure 14.8 shows that for the same standard deviation that existed for the 100 per cent yen portfolio, investors could have received a much higher return; approximately 8 per cent compared with 7.37 per cent.

These examples use a hedged portfolio that is weighted according to Salomon Brothers' international average. However, there will usually be a combination of good, not so good and downright bad opportunities at any one time. The point is that active portfolio management ought to be able to do even better than these averages indicate, thereby further enhancing the benefits from including hedged bonds in the portfolio. Such techniques are not widely employed, but are increasing in popularity—a trend that is likely to increase through the 1990s.

# 15

## *EXCHANGE RATES*
### *(markets in money)*

The exchange rate clearly affects the return available from investing in foreign markets, but it also has wider implications for domestic investments. All investors need to have some understanding of world developments and currency movements in particular. Restricting investment to domestic markets will be no protection against influences from abroad. Most important markets are interconnected, and no investor should ignore what is happening on the foreign exchange markets. Exchange rates are sensitive to changes in different countries and will feed back on to the decisions that are made in a variety of markets, helping to determine the returns that will be realized.

Foreign exchange transactions make up the single largest financial market. Latest estimates published by the Bank of England put the daily turnover in April 1992 at about $1000 billion, many times the value of international trade and central bank reserves. Turnover had been estimated at $650 billion in 1989, which was more than double the figure for three years earlier. This is a true 24-hour market, with activity transferring between London, New York and Tokyo as the main centers. London is still the largest, accounting for $303 billion of the total. The market is still expanding rapidly according to traders, with the majority of all business being transacted in dollars. The most activity is in the dollar/Deutschemark, followed by dollar/ yen, dollar/sterling and dollar/Swiss. The first cross-rate, the yen/ Deutschemark, comes in fifth place.

The scale of activity is many times what would be required to finance the transfer of goods and services. Even if bond and equity transactions are taken into account, that still leaves a considerable proportion that are of the short-term and speculative variety. In addition to ordinary spot transactions there are also trades in forward contracts, futures, options and even long-term warrants that trade on the stock market. This concentration of attention tends to produce a highly efficient market, but it can also result in some extreme movements.

The world has become accustomed to floating exchange rates, but that

375

has not been the normal state of affairs through most of history. Strong arguments were made under the old system of fixed exchange rates in favor of floating rates. In general, the experience has not lived up to expectations and, in many instances, the effect has been the opposite of what had been expected. Partly in response to these negative effects, there has been a movement towards currency blocs. The European Monetary System is the best known, and other groups are moving in that direction in North and South America. Other countries have decided to tie their currencies to that of a larger country, either absolutely as in the case of Hong Kong, or with a little more elasticity, as in the case of Canada.

As a background to understanding exchange rate movements, it is helpful to trace the development of the present *ad hoc* arrangement of semi-floating rates from the old system of fixed exchange rates. That experience demonstrates what is possible, what is not, and what sort of forces influence exchange rates. The final section in this chapter looks at the main determinants of exchange rate movements.

Before getting into these discussions it is necessary to briefly define what we are talking about here. An exchange rate may seem to be a simple enough concept, but it is an area where confusion can easily take hold. There is not one exchange rate, there are many. There is an exchange rate between every single currency: the dollar/pound, dollar/yen, yen/Deutschemark, etc. Also, it is possible to quote exchange rates in either of two ways. There is the dollar/pound rate, which is the number of dollars to a pound, for example $1.75, and there is the pound/dollar rate, which in this case would be £0.5714, the inverse of the dollar/pound rate. And just to add to the confusion, all the cross-rates can be quoted on either side. When someone says that an exchange rate went up, it makes a lot of difference which way round they are quoting it.

The banks tend to quote the European way, which is the number of domestic units to the dollar, so that the Deutschemark might be shown as DM1.6. However, just to confuse matters, the dollar/pound rate, what is conventionally termed *the cable* in the currency markets, is nearly always quoted in terms of dollars to the pound, i.e. $1.75. The futures markets are more consistent and put all currencies into dollar terms, which makes the $/DM rate quoted above, 0.6250. The inclusion of a currency denomination along with the quote helps in interpretation, but very often it is not given.

In addition to the currencies, there is also the European Currency Unit, ECU, to be taken into account. This consists of a weighted basket of European currencies and is becoming increasingly popular as a means of diversifying currency positions. The ECU officially came into existence in March 1979, as a replacement for the European Unit of Account (EUA), which had been created in 1975. The issue of ECU denominated bonds and short-term paper proceeded slowly for a long time, but more recently has picked up rapidly. It is becoming increasingly likely that the ECU will be the key that will unlock the door to full monetary union in Europe; if the door actually exists. In the meantime, the ECU provides a way to invest in European currencies, providing a reasonable combination of stability and yield, although its relative attractiveness will vary with market conditions.

## Fixed exchange rates

The old Bretton Woods Agreement that existed up until the early 1970s imposed a system of fixed exchange rates on countries. Attempts by governments to expand demand too fast resulted in a rising current account deficit. The deterioration resulted both from the excess demand itself, and the resultant higher level of inflation that reduced the competitiveness of domestic companies. If governments did not act to slow demand an old-fashioned currency crisis quickly developed, and interest rates were forced up. Sometimes, when competitiveness had deteriorated far enough, the country would devalue. France did this often and was able to maintain rapid growth.

The alternative was to cut demand, usually by tightening fiscal policy; notably through higher taxes rather than cuts in government expenditure. This was the slow growth, stop-go approach adopted by the United Kingdom. The demand side was corrected temporarily, but the loss of competitiveness became institutionalized. As time went by many governments became disillusioned with the system of fixed exchange rates, seeing it as a constraint on their independence. In addition, there was concern that fixed exchange rates did not reflect changing fundamentals, and were therefore distortionary.

Floating exchange rates were offered up as a solution to these and the other operational limitations of fixed exchange rates. This was a wonderful ideal that made some sense at the time, but it is a view that is impossible to sustain given the evidence of how the system has actually worked. One will search in vain to find any semblance of reality with this ideal. It is not simply that there is a poor fit between the system as it now works and the original blueprint. There is, in fact, not even the remotest similarity. What has actually happened in practice is that exchange rates, instead of moving to improve competitiveness, have gone in the opposite direction, at least temporarily, thereby increasing the overvaluation in the deficit countries. In addition, higher interest rates have had the effect of reducing competitiveness.

What happened at the start of the 1970s was not the normal impatience of politicians to keep growth going in the face of business cycle constraints. There was also growing evidence that we were approaching a turn in a much longer-term, secular or super-cycle, trend. Post-war reconstruction had taken a long time to satisfy even the basic needs of consumers, and had provided a powerful motor for real economic growth. At the same time, the role of government spending during the war, and subsequently, had created the belief that the economy could in fact be controlled. The lever-pulling mentality was encouraged by the long period of growth through the 1960s.

Natural growth potential, and the opening up of international markets, were mainly responsible for keeping the economy growing. The excess growth of governments contributed, but also helped to make the level of demand unsustainable. When the world economy slowed down in 1969 this was considered unacceptable and unnecessary. The demand boost that followed quickly met with balance-of-payments constraints. As these became restrictive so they were removed, with the United States finally shifting to a floating exchange rate.

The reasoning was plain enough. Under fixed rates, a current account deficit generally resulted in fiscal and/or monetary restraint which lowered demand until a balance was restored. But the price level did not fall back, deflation was now unacceptable, so there was generally a sustained loss of competitiveness. Eventually, a devaluation was necessary, and those who resisted the move experienced slower growth rates. There is a clear trade-off between growth, the balance of payments and the exchange rate. Faster growth can be achieved for a lower level of domestic demand the lower the exchange rate is relative to its purchasing power parity rate. With an overvalued exchange rate, demand is likely to be higher but the average growth rate will be lower.

Typical symptoms will be periodic balance-of-payments crises, a tendency towards stop-go policies and the widespread belief that the propensity to import is too high to allow sustainable growth. In that case, why not devalue immediately? France had been much less reluctant to devalue, and had one of the fastest growth rates in Europe through the 1960s. The answer, as much by default as by intent, was to shift to a system of floating exchange rates; the object being to keep competitive without cutting back on demand. The inflationary implications were not fully appreciated, but at least the market response was expected to be consistent with adjustment towards maintaining equilibrium exchange rates.

## Floating exchange rates

The idea behind floating was that flexible exchange rates would avoid the regular balance-of-payments crises that plagued countries through the 1960s. Once it became clear that the current account was deteriorating to any significant degree, speculators would sell the currency, thereby improving competitiveness before the imbalances became too bad. Typical of the arguments made at the time is the following statement (Johnson, 1969):

> A freely flexible exchange rate would tend to remain constant so long as underlying economic conditions (including government policies) remained constant; random deviations from the equilibrium level would be limited by the activities of private speculators, who would step in to buy foreign exchange when its price fell and to sell when its price rose. On the other hand, if economic changes or policy changes occurred that under a fixed exchange rate would produce a balance-of-payments surplus or deficit, and, ultimately, a need for policy changes, the flexible exchange rate would gradually either appreciate or depreciate as required to preserve equilibrium.

According to this approach, exchange rate movements should be smaller, as should the current account imbalances. Subdued movements meant greater stability in international trade and financial markets, and greater confidence which would, in turn, encourage greater international trade. The way in which floating rates have actually worked has differed remarkably from the optimistic expectations expressed by the theorists. Instead of smoothing out disequilibrium on the current account, exchange rate movements have actually exaggerated them.

The political leaders of the Group of Seven leading industrialized countries, meeting in Paris in 1989 did promise to 'keep under review steps that could be taken to improve the coordination process, exchange market cooperation, and the functioning of the international monetary system'. Our leaders receive high marks for identifying a problem, and even higher marks for swiftly stepping around it as if it was not there. Such sleight of hand is to be admired, but it does leave a nagging worry. Not only would some further statement on the dollar have been welcome then, and at other times, but, perhaps even more importantly, so would some recognition of the frequently perverse behavior of floating exchange rates.

Early in the 1970s, around the time that floating exchange rates came into general use, the change was justified in terms of reduced adjustment costs. Despite the overwhelming evidence to the contrary, this view seems still to be accepted, if only by default. The argument was that exchange rates would adjust gradually at the first hint of any current account imbalances. As a result, adjustment would be smoother and quicker, and the imbalances would be smaller. Well, exchange rates do seem to adjust more quickly, but the direction is the opposite of what was expected. The outcome is more extreme trade deficits and surpluses, and increasingly unrealistic exchange rates that make conditions worse not better. Risks to domestic and international stability are actually increased as a result. One conclusion is that there should be less reliance on monetary policy, and a better balance between monetary and fiscal policies.

The original proposals for floating exchange rates were based on the idea that the needs of trade dominated exchange-rate transactions. Under fixed exchange rates that may well have been true, at least under normal circumstances. However, the emphasis quickly changed once exchange rates became unfixed. Not only did investment demand become more important, but exchange-rate trading in its own right became a major activity. All of the major banks, and many other financial institutions, now have large departments that do nothing but trade currencies, and these are often major profit centers for the organization.

From an investment point of view, it is necessary to appreciate the long-term nature of the disequilibrium that can, and does, exist. It is not that the markets are being irrational. What is rational is to try to make money and not lose it. People respond to incentives. If the resulting actions prove to be destabilizing it is no good complaining about irrationality, or trying to force changes in behavior. Instead, changes should be made to the incentives facing investors.

## Floating down the river

The perverse reaction of floating exchange rates can be seen in the recent history of a number of countries. The classic example was that of the United States in the period up to February 1985; the current account deficit was increasing substantially while, at the same time, the dollar kept going up. By 1985, credibility had been stretched to its limit, and the dollar started back down the road to where it had begun its long climb. Whatever one may think about the significance of the events, it is not possible to argue that they represented greater stability. There is no evidence of improvements in the adjustment process. In the 1960s, currency movements and trade imbalances were considered extreme. From today's perspective such volatility seems slight. The problems arise from the interest rate sensitivity of capital flows. The early discussions of floating exchange rates assumed that equilibrium in currency markets reflected equilibrium in the underlying current account. That is clearly not the case.

It might seem reasonable to assume that relative interest rates between any two countries represent the market's expectation of where the currency is going; i.e. if the three-month rate in the UK is 13 per cent and it is 5 per cent in Germany, then the exchange rate between the pound and Deutschemark should be expected to fall by 8 per cent at an annual rate over that three months. That is borne out by the fact that the three-month forward exchange rate is the same as the three-month interest rate differential. This relationship is enforced by the ability to arbitrage these markets without taking any currency risk at all. For example, if the forward rate assumed only a 7 per cent decline in sterling, a bank would be able to borrow

Deutschemarks, convert the proceeds into sterling and hedge that back into Deutschemarks, thereby achieving a risk-free Deutschemark return of 6 per cent—a full 100 basis points over the domestic market.

What happens if the actual exchange rate in three months' time is higher than that implied by the forward rate three months ago? Those institutions or individuals who hedged their currency exposure receive exactly the return they expected. However, anyone who bought dollars or pounds with Deutschemarks and did not hedge, made a much higher return. If this happens enough times people may come to expect it to continue. This will particularly be the case if the government in the high-yielding country commits itself to holding up the exchange rate. The only alternative equilibrium then is for interest rates to become equalized, but interest rates will be determined predominately by domestic considerations.

Money flowing from the low-interest country to the high-interest country will be directed towards short-term instruments. Assuming no intervention, the exchange rate will be pushed up instead of down, quite the opposite reaction to that predicted by the theory. If the buying continues, the exchange rate may well get pushed up to completely unrealistic levels. In this case, there is no tendency for interest rates to fall, and the process can continue for a very long time. The high relative returns become reinforcing, and tend to attract increasing flows from other investors, and countries.

Eventually, the high interest rates and the overvalued exchange rate will result in a substantial weakening of economic activity. At that point, interest rates will finally come down, and they will do so at a time when the investment potential in the country is looking at its worst. The exchange rate will consequently start to come down. Once confidence starts to ebb, it can quickly turn into a flood. The chances are that the exchange rate will overshoot on the downside, unless held up artificially by official buying. One thing should be perfectly clear: there is no smooth adjustment process. There are signs that the monetary authorities in different countries have become aware of this problem, and have become more cautious about reducing interest rates.

The problem created by relative interest rates is partly due to the emphasis placed on monetary policy. In some ways that is inevitable. There used to be extensive controls and limitations on credit creation and the international movement of funds. The development of free financial markets has inevitably changed the old responses, and exaggerated movements. In addition, there has been a greater emphasis on monetary policy for control purposes. The old focus on fiscal policy to influence demand was discredited by the acceleration of inflation through the 1970s.

The shift to greater emphasis on monetary policy meant higher interest rates. Those countries with the highest level of demand ended up with relatively higher interest rates, and at times of perceived exchange rate stability this resulted in an inflow of foreign money, which, in the absence of sustained intervention, pushed up the exchange rate. What resulted was the opposite of what was required. The countries with the highest level of demand had the highest inflation, and were, therefore, losing competitiveness. At the same time, the relatively higher level of demand was pulling in imports and diverting potential exports to the domestic market. If the exchange rates now went up instead of down, this made imports even more attractive and exports less attractive.

The responses are all wrong, but the full effects take a long time to show up. In the meantime, the belief takes hold that somehow the laws of economics have been suspended in this one case. This has been made plain over and over again in the United States and United Kingdom. By the end of 1984, there were many commentators in the United States who claimed that the dollar would stay high or even go higher because now everyone wanted to invest in the United States. What was required was a better balance between monetary policy and fiscal policy, and recognition that intervention to stabilize the exchange rate need not always be wrong. A major factor behind the unfortunate rise in the dollar in the first half of the 1980s was the highly expansionary nature of fiscal policy at that time, which had to be offset by tighter monetary policy, i.e. higher interest rates, than would otherwise have been necessary.

The spending boom in the late 1980s in the United Kingdom partly came from a different source, with the government finally running a budget surplus, at least temporarily. This surplus was a recent phenomenon and was partly the result of asset sales of one form or another. Even so, it did mean that it was not possible to put blame on an excessive fiscal policy. Which only goes to show that stereotypical views of economic growth and cycles cannot be applied blindly.

Governments could offset the effect of the inflow of money on the exchange rate through intervention. The usual objection has been that this will inflate the money supply, but that is not necessary. It is also possible to neutralize the domestic monetary effects of these inflows. That has not always been done, which would anyway be inconsistent with freely floating exchange rates. Over the past few years there has been increasing concern about the volatility of exchange rates, and the potential for extreme reactions. The G7 countries agreed in Paris in February 1987, the so-called Louvre accord, to try and stabilize the dollar. The main concern was with preventing the dollar falling, and initially the central banks were called upon to intervene to buy dollars in large amounts.

Through these actions, the monetary authorities were able to build some sort of floor under the dollar. However, that immediately changed the nature of the game. If the dollar was going to be artificially held up then there was very little risk in buying dollars. There was no point in doing that just for the sake of it, but relatively high interest rates provided the necessary incentive. Furthermore, as trends build so they start to bring in other participants. Psychologists might call this a reinforcement effect; in the markets it is known as technical confirmation. Chart points are reached and passed, and this creates *buy* signals long after the original turn has taken place. What resulted was an unsustainable rally in the dollar. The higher the dollar went so the risks of a movement in the other direction increased. So these movements became reasonably predictable, which was quite the opposite effect desired by the monetary authorities. Central banks like to burn speculators, not reward them.

The monetary authorities in the United States have to take much of the blame for generating the extreme volatility, by allowing the dollar to rise unopposed in the first half of the 1980s. As a result, the dollar became extremely overvalued, thereby contributing to the continuing current account deficits. If it were decided to attempt to target particular exchange rates as an alternative to free floating, this should be done in terms of real exchange rates. In doing so, however, it is essential to ensure that the real exchange rates which are chosen to stabilize really do reflect underlying competitiveness.

## Exchange rate forecasting

There are forecasts of every shape and size when it comes to currencies. Here is a market with massive two-way activity on a daily basis. There are short-term traders, long-term investors, holiday makers, buyers and sellers of goods and services, people hedging future transactions or existing assets and others unhedging. All sorts of motives and approaches exist, and there are as many different forecasts as there are ways to forecast.

Exchange rates are determined by a mixture of short-term influences, cyclical developments and long-term trends. For example, the pound sterling fluctuated between one and two dollars per pound throughout the 1980s, and on into the 1990s, and there were a number of different forces that accounted for the wide variation over that time. However, there has also been a long-term trend of higher inflation in the United Kingdom than in the United States, and this has produced a downward bias to the exchange rate. Long-term, in this case, means really long-term. To put recent events into perspective, there were as many as $14 to the pound at the time of the American Civil War.

It is easy to be wrong when it comes to forecasting exchange rates. In the early years of the 1980s, the dollar staged a spectacular rally, even as the trade account softened and finally deteriorated dramatically. Almost all the way through that rise, the consensus forecasts were that the dollar was too high and was about to fall. That is until the end of 1984, when many people concluded that there had been a fundamental change and the dollar would continue to rise. Professional forecasters were not alone in this change of heart. The *New York Times*, on 27 February 1985, reported that:

> R. T. McNamar, the former Deputy Secretary of the Treasury suggests that the dollar will stay permanently strong . . . Mr McNamar suggested that the dollar's strength, despite the record United States trade deficit, was due to the preference of investors all over the world to put their money here more than any other country.

To be fair, the same article also noted that many forecasters had changed their minds, and 'have now begun to say it (the dollar) may stay up for years to come'. The front cover of the 8 October 1984 issue of *Business Week* carried the headline, *SUPER DOLLAR*, and concluded that it 'could last a decade'. These are good examples of forcing the explanation to fit the facts; of forecasting the past, and assuming it applies to the future.

There are some who have argued that it is not possible to forecast exchange rates; that currency movements are random, arbitrary, even vindictive. Certainly, there have been few claims that exchange rates follow fundamentals of any sort. The natural result of such scepticism is that technical rules have dominated the market. While such rules may help in the short term, and in following an established trend, there is no evidence that they have successfully forecast the market. The emphasis on technical rules helps explain the recent volatility of the markets. The dramatic rally in the dollar against the Deutschemark in early 1991 can best be understood in those terms. If the dollar was at the point of moving into a new uptrend, as seemed likely at the time, then there was no point in waiting. The result was a widespread reversal of expectations, and a rush into the dollar. Later in the year this was largely unwound, as the pendulum swung back again.

However, it is not true that the currencies have a life of their own, independent of the underlying economic fundamentals. It is true that there are influences that are not known, or not measured, and that forecasts are never perfect, but there is still a rational order to the universe. Short-term influences can create major distortions to the underlying trend, but these generally do not last for long. Before going on to discuss what to look at in making exchange-rate forecasts it seems necessary to provide some proof that there is actually some value in the exercise. Figure 15.1 shows the movement in the trade-weighted dollar.

The period from 1982 to 1992 witnessed dramatic variations in the value of the dollar. There were a number of broad trends and sharp turning points. Invariably, these turning points took the markets by surprise, and yet they were not totally unpredictable. The strength of the dollar was fore-

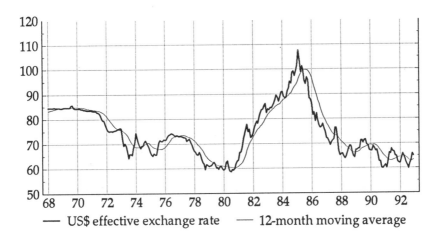

— US$ effective exchange rate     — 12-month moving average

**Figure 15.1** Trade-weighted dollar

cast, as well as the sudden change in direction when it came. The May 1984 issue of *The Financial Economist* claimed that 'under these circumstances the dollar should remain strong for some time to come'. In August that year, I discussed the reasons why the dollar should remain strong for the time being, but that it was being set up for a fall of major proportions (Coghlan, 1984). The conclusion was:

> In these circumstances the dollar could remain strong for some time to come. At present the cost of selling the dollar is high, in terms of the United States interest income given up. However, there is a persistent build up of potential selling pressure, so that when confidence turns, it could turn very fast.

By the beginning of 1985, time was running out for the dollar, despite the fact that the dollar had an explosive rally in January and February 1985. The following quotes from *The Financial Economist* spelt out the danger:

> There are a number of fundamental indicators that are signaling the need for caution ahead. According to these measures, the dollar could come under pressure in the new year. Investors should diversify on extreme dollar strength. (January 1985)

> The exchange rate has now completely parted company with the fundamentals . . . the dollar has finally run out of steam. (February 1985)

Even now, most people date the turn in the dollar from the G5 meeting in September 1985 at New York's Plaza Hotel, that gave the official stamp of approval to the dollar's fall. By then, however, the dollar had already dropped precipitously from its February peak. It had fallen 26 per cent against the Deutschemark between February and September, and 31 per cent against the Swiss franc. The dollar did not collapse because of what was said at the G5 meeting, but because the fundamentals had turned against it, and the fragile thread of confidence that held it up had, by February 1985, finally been stretched to the limit.

The dollar fell steadily until the end of 1987. In December of that year, there was another sharp move down in the dollar. There was little talk at that time of a reversal in the downtrend that extended back to early 1985, but there were signs that conditions were changing, if only you knew where to look:

> The dollar fell sharply over the latest month, continuing the adjustment that followed the drop in stock prices. A rally in the dollar is likely in the first two months of the year. (December 1987)

The dollar then rallied strongly right from the start of 1988 into the end of February, retraced a good part of that move into April, and then resumed its rally into August. From that point there was a significant correction that lasted into December, only for the dollar to take off again and peak in June 1989. These were volatile times with a lot of potential distortions, false leads and fast-moving markets. Forecasting in such an environment is never easy. Consider what conclusion the indicators came to at each of these points along the way:

> Central banks around the world have been getting some practice selling dollars. This so far has taken the form of warning shots across the bows, rather than an actual declaration of war. There is no major constituency in favor of a sustained rise in the dollar. On the other hand, it is still reasonable to believe that the dollar is in a trading range. The dollar is expected to trade towards the lower end through the latter part of the year. The yen is likely to make a new all time high against the dollar [it did in December]. (August 1988)

> We had been looking for a temporary rally in the dollar, but this had been slow in coming and we had just about given up on it. As we said last month, 'the dollar is due for a rally, but could manage nothing more then stability'. (January 1989)

> This indicator suggests that the dollar has experienced a recent high, and is likely to trend lower over the balance of the year. (June 1989)

The next turn came in February 1991, when the Deutschemark hit an all-time peak only to collapse by over 20 per cent in little over a month. The suddenness of the move took investors by surprise, but here again there were clear warning signals that a turn was coming. In December 1990, the conclusion in *The Financial Economist* was:

> Our view is that the dollar will weaken into February, and then start to rally. From a risk/reward perspective time starts to run out pretty early in the new year . . . The strong European currencies should continue to rally into February,

but that looks like a peak. In the months following that point the dollar is likely to gain ground.

In the January issue the warning was repeated. The dollar hit its low point in February, and the rally that followed lasted into the summer, but then reversed in the second half of the year. Again, the change in trend was identified beforehand:

> The dollar managed to break out to new recovery high during June . . . (but) time is rapidly running out, and we expect the trend to reverse sharply in the second half of the year. (June 1991)

These forecasts should demonstrate the advantage of looking at the fundamentals that underlie exchange-rate movements. Random guesswork, or following trends, could not have proved that accurate. Not that it is possible to forecast currency movements with absolute accuracy; that will never be the case. For example, the rally in the dollar in the early part of 1991 was stronger than had been anticipated by the indicators, and was due to a number of exceptional factors. Partly, it was due to the psychological impact of the easy victory in the war against Iraq, and partly to the huge transfer payments made by the allies to pay for the war: $38.5 billion by the end of May 1991. In addition, there was the effect of events in eastern Europe, and the problems West Germany was having digesting East Germany, but that was of lesser importance. On the basis of this evidence, and the accompanying caveat, let us consider the major influences on currency movements that can be used to forecast currency trends.

## Purchasing power parity

There are various changes that will cause exchange rates to move, but what if there are no changes? What determines the underlying benchmark for an exchange rate, in the way that stock prices will be related to the discounted earnings flow? The underlying base level in the case of exchange rates is provided by the level of competitiveness between countries. In theory, this should relate to all levels of actual and potential competition over all goods and services. In reality, attention is concentrated on relative domestic price levels with little if any consideration of other developments.

Support for this emphasis on relative prices comes from the well-known theory of purchasing power parity. The internal value of a currency depends on the price level within that country; the higher the prices the less the money is worth. From there, it is a short step to equate the external value of a currency with the relative price levels existing in one country compared with another. A simple example will help to clarify the point.

The value $(Va)$ of the currency $(Ca)$ in country $a$ depends upon the price level $(Pa)$, in that country, i.e.:

$$Va = Ca/Pa$$

The value ($Vb$) of the same currency in country $b$ will depend on the rate at which one currency is exchanged for another ($r$) and the price level ($Pb$) in country $b$, where the money is spent, not on the price level in $a$, i.e.:

$$Vb = r \times Ca/Pb$$

The value of the currency will be the same in both countries when the exchange rate is equal to the relative price levels. In order to see that make $Va = Vb$, i.e.:

$$Ca/Pa = r \times Ca/Pb$$

$$r = Pb/Pa$$

If the domestic currency does not go as far in another country, i.e. is not worth as much as it is at home, this will be because the exchange rate is less than would be implied by the relationship between relative prices, i.e.:

$$Ca/Pa > r \times Ca/Pb$$

$$Pb/Pa > r$$

In this case, the exchange rate is below the level indicated by relative prices, so the currency is undervalued. Travelers from $a$ to $b$ will find that the things they buy will be expensive, and imports from $b$ to $a$ will also tend to cost more. This is the situation the United States was in over the second half of the 1980s and into the 1990s. While it seems that domestic residents suffer in this situation, it is also true that domestic companies will find it easier to sell in foreign markets, and foreigners are more likely to come and visit. A key distinction is that existing wealth is not worth as much, at least in foreign markets, but it is easier to create incomes and wealth.

In a competitive world, it would be reasonable to expect the same tradeable good to sell for the same price in all countries of the world. There are a number of qualifications required to bring theory into line with reality. The goods must be tradeable, not necessarily traded, but at least capable of being exchanged freely. Clearly, buildings and land do not fall into this category. Even with a fixed exchange rate, and uniform laws and taxes, as within a single country, property prices will vary widely depending on location.

Differences in laws and taxes need to be taken into account, as well as transportation costs. Other factors include national tastes. The prices of some things will differ simply because there is more demand in some countries than in others. In principle, exchange rates should adjust to even out *general* price differences. This does not mean that the prices of all goods will be equalized. That would only occur if *relative* prices were the same in every country, and that is not the case, for the reasons cited above. Prices differ even within a single country. There is not a separate exchange rate for each commodity, good or service, but a single one between countries that will have to balance these differences. What this means is that there will always be plenty of examples where prices of particular goods are not equated by the exchange rate, even on average over time, but this is not evidence that purchasing power parity (PPP) is invalid.

An advantage of PPP is that it does take account of changes in productivity, since that will have the effect of making prices more competitive. The disadvantages are that it is only a long-term, equilibrium, condition, and it cannot be measured perfectly. In the real world, there are barriers to trade; quotas, domestic subsidies, packaging restrictions, language and cultural differences. These can be particularly noticeable in the case of developing countries, but trade restrictions between the industrialized countries have been reduced, thereby improving the operation of PPP. That still leaves questions of quality and problems of identification. It can be argued that luxury car prices must be equalized, and in a competitive market it is hard to imagine otherwise, but how does one compare a Cadillac with a Mercedes-Benz, a Jaguar or Lexus, and how does this relationship change over time?

Then there is the problem of how to measure relative prices. There are any number of candidates—consumer prices, wholesale prices, export prices, wages, etc., and a case can, and has, been made for each of these. It is misleading to look only at the items that enter into trade, since that misses the potential for new trade, and may end up comparing very different things. For example, Japan's imports are still dominated by commodities, while exports are predominantly manufactured goods. Wages do not allow for improvements in productivity. Consumer prices include prices for domestic housing and sales taxes which can be highly distortionary, as in the case of the United Kingdom. That leaves some form of wholesale prices, or producer prices, as the best choice.

Deciding on what price indices to use is only the first problem solved. Dividing one price index by the other will provide a ratio that should have the same trend as the exchange rate, but is unlikely to have a value anywhere close to the actual exchange rate, or any future or past exchange rate. The ratio will depend on the base levels of the two price indexes, and these will change over time. What is needed is some factor to bring the ratio into line with the exchange rate. Deciding on that factor has been a constant thorn in the side of those trying to make sensible use of PPP.

The choice has often been completely arbitrary. The present is seldom seen as equilibrium, but the recent past frequently is, despite clear evidence to the contrary. Another approach is to take a long-term moving average to establish a base equilibrium level. That makes a little more sense, but there have been very long periods when PPP has not held and external payments have been out of balance. The longer the moving average, the closer it is likely to be to some reasonable equilibrium level.

Figure 15.2 shows two different PPP measures for the Deutschemark/pound exchange rate based on the same relative price indices. The top line is simply the result of dividing the German price index by the UK index, and basing the line on the value of the exchange rate in 1966. This is related to the Deutschemark price of pounds, i.e. how many Deutschemarks to the pound, which falls, in theory at least, if prices rise faster in the United Kingdom than in Germany.

The index of international competitiveness (IIC) is the line that I have calculated using the same price ratio and an attempt to identify reasonable equilibrium levels for all the main exchange rates. This was an involved process that looked at periods of approximate trade balance, when there was little tendency to change, low interest rate differentials and relatively calm economic and political conditions. In addition, I looked at all cross-rates in order to achieve reasonable consistency between all countries, not only each one on a bilateral basis. The second line tells a much more plausible story when looking back over recent history.

A close look at the difference between the 1966 estimate and the structural estimate (IIC) will help in understanding the function and value of

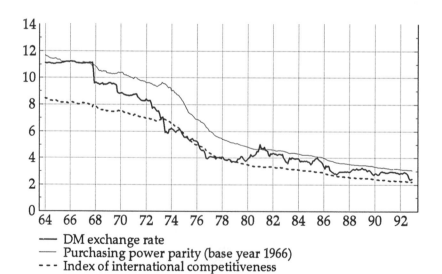

Figure 15.2 Deutschemark/sterling exchange rate (alternative PPP levels)

PPP. The 1966 estimate has basically acted as an upper bound for the exchange rate, touching in 1966, 1980/81 and 1985. These points look very much like times when sterling was overvalued, not in equilibrium. For practically all of this period, UK interest rates were substantially above those in other countries, and particularly those in Germany. In the 1980s the United Kingdom became a net oil exporter, and the net balance for manufactured trade moved into deficit for the first time in 100 years. These are not the sort of conditions consistent with the exchange rate remaining persistently *below* its PPP.

It is quite clear that the United Kingdom chose a high value for the exchange rate at the end of the Second World War in order to maximize purchasing power, while Germany suffered the indignity of an under-valued exchange rate. By doing this, the United Kingdom was putting the emphasis on wealth effects, but the income effects, i.e. the ability to earn income from selling goods abroad, was quite the reverse. This continued a long tradition that includes Winston Churchill's ill-timed, and ill-fated, attempt in April 1925 to put the pound back on the gold standard at \$4.25.

North Sea oil came on-stream in the late 1970s, and that alone should have given a boost to the exchange rate. The steady overvaluation of sterling from that point can be seen in Fig. 15.2, assuming that IIC represents a reasonable equilibrium valuation. The only way to protect the manufacturing base would have been to cut interest rates below the international average. What happened was that UK interest rates remained relatively very high. The combination had to result in a substantially overvalued exchange rate, at least in terms of manufacturing competitiveness. The argument seems so obvious that it is really hard to understand how so many people thought that a PPP rate of over DM3 was appropriate in October 1990, when sterling was finally slotted into the EMS exchange rate mechanism at a rate of DM2.95. That sort of valuation was more consistent with the 1966 estimate of PPP, which surely cannot be right.

The exchange rate should settle around the PPP when interest rates are roughly in line with their international counterparts, the balance of payments is in reasonable equilibrium, and the North Sea has run out of oil. If the exchange rate is already at that level, it means no change in the exchange rate, assuming no change in PPP, when these positive props to sterling are taken away. When that happens it is much more likely that the exchange rate will move down. As shown in Fig. 15.3, relative interest rates are a very potent influence on exchange rates. To ignore these other effects when establishing a PPP level risks absurd results when conditions change, the point at which getting the right answer is most important. The only alternative, at least that is consistent with free markets, is for prices to rise more slowly in the United Kingdom than in Germany, thereby improving relative price competitiveness. These inconsistencies finally

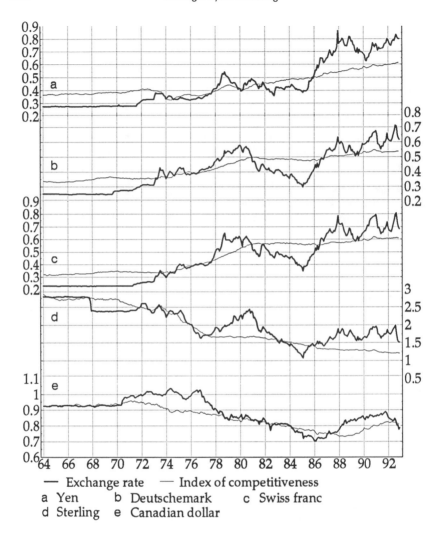

**Figure 15.3** US dollar exchange rates

proved too much in the second half of 1992, and the UK government gave in to external pressure by taking sterling out of the EMS, allowing it to fall steeply against the Deutschemark.

Figure 15.3 shows a number of exchange rates in US dollar terms, together with their purchasing power parities, calculated on the structural basis outlined above, and, therefore, called indices of international competitiveness. It is quite clear from these that, on their own, such equilibrium values are not much use in forecasting the exchange rate in the short term, or even in the long term, although it does establish the broad trend that is followed. In the case of the dollar, there was the massive distortion created in the 1980s, initially by the run up in the dollar and then its subsequent collapse, and adjustments are still taking place.

The closer two countries are in economic structure, monetary policy and political and social attitudes, the closer the exchange rate between their currencies will be. Therefore, the exchange rate between the US and Canadian dollars is closer to parity than for most other currencies, with the major deviations explained by large interest rate differentials. For the same reason, the Swiss franc and the Dutch guilder stay close to parity with the Deutschemark. The French have always tended to devalue whenever there was any danger that the franc would become uncompetitive against the Deutschemark. Allowing for that pattern of behavior, the French franc has closely followed the Deutschemark. That tie has become even closer in recent years as domestic policies have moved more into line, and should become even closer as the European Monetary System moves towards monetary union.

Too much can be claimed for purchasing power parity, and too little. Frequent reference will be found to the uselessness of PPP because it is not the same as the exchange rate. There is no point trying to rely on the PPP to forecast the exchange rate. Equally, it is no use trying to forecast exchange rates without it. PPP provides the underlying equilibrium around which other influences push and pull. Saying that an exchange rate is overvalued on the basis of its underlying competitive level is not the same thing as forecasting that it is about to fall. There are other important influences at work around that equilibrium level.

## Relative interest rates

The importance of relative interest rates was in dispute for a long time, but the evidence over recent years has now convinced most people that high interest rates can play a significant role in holding up an exchange rate. There are many examples of exchange rates held above their competitive level by high relative interest rates, despite the existence of a significant deficit on current account. This is contrary to what was once thought likely, or even possible. The implications are still not fully understood, and take the story back to the way flexible exchange rates are supposed to work.

Before anything else, it is necessary to show how relative interest rates determine forward exchange rates. For example, if the interest earned over three months in the United States is 3 per cent and is 1 per cent in Germany, then the three-month forward Deutschemark, i.e. Deutschemarks bought for delivery in three months' time, must be 2 per cent higher than the spot rate. At that forward rate, the expected return on holding three-month money is equalized within each country. An investor in the United States will get 3 per cent in the US, and also 3 per cent in Germany on a hedged basis: 1 per cent income and 2 per cent on the currency. A German investor will get 1 per cent from investing in US three-month money hedged back into Deutschemarks; 3 per cent, less the 2 per cent loss on the currency forward. Any deviation from this relationship will set up the potential to improve on the domestic return through riskless arbitrage. Taking advantage of that opportunity will have the effect of closing the gap.

A comparison of forward rates with interest differentials shows that the markets work exactly as they are supposed to. For example, at the end of June 1991 the three-month rates in the United Kingdom and Germany were 11.3 per cent and 9.25 per cent, producing an annualized differential of 2.12 per cent. The forward premium quoted in *The Financial Times* for that day was 2.05 per cent on an annual basis which on a closing basis of DM2.93 represented a forward rate of DM2.86. The additional income earned by investing in UK paper was exactly offset by the cost of forward cover. On that same day, the three-month interest differential between the United Kingdom and the United States was 5 per cent, and the forward premium quoted in the paper was 4.94 per cent. This market tends to be very efficient.

The next step, a step too far, has been to argue further that the forward rate represents the market expectation of where the exchange rate is headed in the future. If this is not true then investors would get different returns in different markets, and maybe even would not arbitrage the forward market. As a result of this argument, forecasters have been known to use the forward rate as a prediction of the expected future rate. The persistent failure of events to ratify this expectation usually forces them to find some alternative means of forecasting pretty quickly. Typically, exchange rates in countries with high interest rates are more likely to rise than fall. What is more, this does not seem illogical.

Simple logic suggests a fundamental flaw in the forward expectation argument which says that currencies with high interest rates will fall over time. Not only that, but, on that argument, as long as relative interest rates stay high the exchange should continue to fall. Any rational thinking individual should have a horrible tingling feeling running up his or her spine at the mere suggestion that reality would be anything like that. The mistake is in confusing riskless arbitrage with foreign currency investment decisions which are far from risk-free.

When domestic interest rates rise, so that the international differential widens out, the spread between the spot and forward rates will also have to widen out. This can happen through a fall in the forward rate or a rise in the spot rate, denominated in foreign currency terms, or a combination of the two. As experience has been gained with floating exchange rates, the effect has increasingly been felt on the spot rate. Market participants try to beat the market by making forecasts of where interest rates are headed. This greatly increases the volatility of the market, as forecasters are not always correct. The main influence still comes from actual interest rate differentials, except where there is a very clear trend to interest rates.

The supporting role of relative interest rates can survive small, and sometimes quite large, changes in interest rates, particularly in the case of countries with very high relative interest rates. For example, UK rates fell relative to European rates in 1990 and early 1991, but the exchange rate did not fall, although there was some reaction later in the year that effectively halted the decline in interest rates. The reaction came later, in 1992, and was quite dramatic. Also, Australian interest rates fell sharply in 1990, from over 18 per cent to under 12 per cent, without causing a collapse in the exchange rate. There was some adjustment, but the point seems to be that, although interest rates came down, they continued to attract investors' funds, as long as they remained well above rates in other countries. Investors were encouraged by the fall in inflation and the continued commitment to bring it down further. That implied that there would not be a repeat of the cut-and-run tactics sometimes adopted in the past. Of course, there was also a reaction in the Australian dollar in 1992, although there were other factors to take into account in addition to relative interest rates.

So far, the discussion has been in terms of nominal interest rate differentials. In the case of forward arbitrage, the rate of inflation in the foreign country makes no difference. The interest return has been hedged back into domestic currency terms, which will be affected by domestic inflation but not inflation in the other country. Even in the case where the currency is not hedged, the inflation rate in the country of origin is what matters. If an investor measures return in US dollars, then US inflation will affect the real return achieved. The fact that inflation may be soaring in another country need not matter at all, unless it is intended to make purchases there, or that fact is expected to affect the exchange rate.

While domestic inflation is the only concern in terms of the final return achieved, inflation in other countries will matter if it affects the expected return itself. One way it can do this is through expectations of future interest rates and future exchange rates. In one sense, lower inflation means a higher exchange rate through the effect on international competitiveness. On the other hand, if it means lower interest rates, then that will tend to have the more immediate effect of lowering the exchange rate. If lower inflation remains a major objective of the monetary authorities then real interest rates might be expected to remain relatively high.

There is some lagged effect from interest rates on the exchange rate, but there is also an effect from expected interest rate changes. Forecasts of interest rates, or influences on interest rates, also have to be taken into account. Looking at official action, it is possible to identify a number of potential influences. One is the prospects for inflation. In addition, the economic outlook, particularly unemployment, will also be of concern to the monetary authorities. These considerations were discussed in Chapter 12 and the effects need to be carried over to the exchange rate market. All markets are interrelated, and, as discussed earlier, the exchange rate and balance of payments will feed back into interest rates as well, thereby closing the circle.

## The current account

The external balance on trade and services plays both a direct and indirect role in determining the exchange rate. The direct influence comes from the financing needs of a deficit, or inflow from a surplus. Starting from a point of current and capital account balance, an increase in payments out of the country is likely to put additional downward pressure on the exchange rate. The trade and current account balances are outside the direct control of investors and speculators, and can therefore produce an independent demand for or supply of currency. Nothing is really independent, and there are linkages here, but at least the decisions in the short term are based on very different considerations.

The dominant influence of real flows has not worked the way proponents of floating exchange rates had expected, but there is still an influence that needs to be taken into account. It is not that the real flows are not important, only that other influences such as relative interest rates can be more important, particularly in the short term. The balance of payments effect tends to build up if substantial disequilibrium persists for a long time. If the imbalance gets bad enough for long enough, even high relative interest rates will lose their potency.

The external balance can also influence the exchange markets indirectly by feeding into the decision-making of investors. The current account represents the net external saving or dissaving of a country. As with an individual, any deficit can be financed by selling assets or borrowing money. In the case of a wealthy individual, or country, there is no reason why the process of asset sales cannot continue for a long time. At some point, however, it is necessary for lenders to know that asset cover is not likely to run out in the near future. This situation was discussed further in Chapter 3.

Certain countries can finance a deficit more easily than others, and this has to be taken into account when looking at the likely effect of a change in the balance of payments. The markets will adjust to a given situation, and it is changes in that which will have the major impact on the exchange rate. A persistent balance-of-payments deficit is rather like having persistently higher inflation, as pointed out in Chapter 3. The balance-of-payment implications do not seem to be quite so bad, and in the same way are generally offset by relatively higher interest rates. Examples of persistent deficit countries would be Canada, Australia and Denmark. In each case, interest rates have been kept relatively high, even when inflation has come down below the world average.

## A model forecast

The following forecasting model incorporates the main elements discussed above. The trade-weighted exchange rate for the dollar is not something most investors or businessmen are very worried about. It provides a single measure of *the* exchange rate, but that is all. Decision-making in the real world will be concerned with a particular exchange rate. The single exchange rate used here to demonstrate the methodology set out above is the Swiss franc against the dollar. This has provided an accurate leading indicator of trends, and, more importantly, provided advance warning of turning points. The leading indicator, together with the actual exchange rate, is shown in Fig. 15.4. Other leading indicators have been developed for all of the main exchange rates on the same basis.

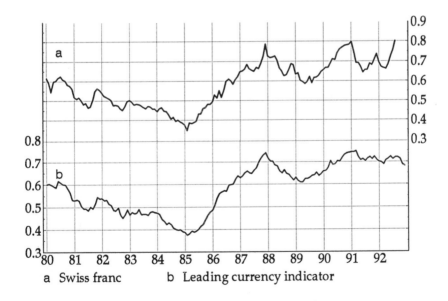

**Figure 15.4** Forecasting Swiss exchange rate

Once again, emphasis needs to be placed on the fact that the leading indicator, shown in Fig. 15.4, is a forecast over the whole length of the line. At any point in time, and actual exchange rate, there was a forecast of the future as shown by the leading indicator. That value did not change when the actual exchange rate became known, and the value of the leading indicator now shown is the same as when it was a forecast. It can be seen that the leading indicator has been extremely successful in identifying all of the major turning points in the exchange rate, and most of the minor ones, ahead of the event. This is the basis of the forecasts included earlier in this chapter.

# 16

## *GOLD*
### *(glittering surprises)*

There have been times when gold and other precious metals have provided dramatic returns to investors. There have been other times when the returns on such investments have been disastrous, and there has been little in between. The return on gold has been either spectacularly good or spectacularly bad, with the emphasis on the latter. In a situation of such great volatility, the timing of buy and sell decisions is crucial, and yet this has proved very difficult. In order to make money investing in gold it is necessary, at a minimum, to understand why conditions were favorable in the 1970s and why they turned negative in the 1980s. There is a great deal of myth and mystery surrounding gold, and it is essential to cut through this to discover the underlying fundamentals that drive the price.

Part of the controversy surrounding gold concerns its role as a form of money, and the possibility of a return to a gold standard. Such arguments have become inseparable from the use of gold as a form of investment. The argument is often made that gold is the only true money, and should form the basis of the world monetary system. While not as popular as it was in the early 1980s when inflationary expectations were still very high, this view still has its advocates. The supporters argue that the only road to price stability and sustained growth in the future is paved with gold. According to this argument, these conditions existed under the gold standard. On the one hand, gold is so important, unique among assets, that its price is bound to keep rising; the dramatic price rise during the 1970s was just a prelude to even greater prices rises in the future. On the other hand, the price of gold is about to be fixed as the US/world embarks on a new gold-standard era.

The truth, however, is that gold does not perform the functions of money, nor would it be very efficient at doing so. The idea that prices were stable under the gold standard is one of the great myths of all time. That may seem to be a strange claim given the widespread claims to the contrary, but the evidence is quite incontrovertible—prices were extremely volatile over that period. The conditions for a return to a gold standard do not exist. A gold standard requires the political will to do whatever is necessary to sustain it; but if the political will existed a gold standard would not be needed. In addition, the investment outlook is far more mixed than generally realized. There was a unique set of circumstances, both economic and political, favoring gold in the 1970s that will not be repeated.

Gold is an attractive metal that has fascinated people since early times. There is little likelihood that it is about to go out of favor. However, gold is not alone in having aesthetic appeal to the senses; there are other precious metals and stones that fulfil that same role. There are also human creations that have great appeal and are extremely rare. These include paintings, sculptures, buildings, books, cars, furniture. To put gold in the right perspective, it does have a rarity value and is attractive, but on both counts there are other commodities or goods that fulfil those objectives to a much greater degree. None of this excludes gold as a potential investment vehicle, but it is necessary that such investments are based on realistic expectations.

## Gold as money

The claim is often made that gold is the only true money. Those green pieces of paper that circulate around the United States, and the multicolored pieces floating around in other countries, are not considered to be worth the price of the paper, let alone the denominations printed on them—or so the story goes. There are some people who believe that it is only a matter of time before gold returns to its rightful place on the throne, and resumes its monetary rule.

The use of language means accepting certain conventions as to the meaning of words. For example, if someone says there is a cow in a field we all, hopefully, know what to expect to see. Money also has its definition in terms of certain characteristics. Money is a means of exchange, store of value and unit of account. Gold fails to satisfy the definition of money on two characteristics absolutely, and does a poor job in the third.

Gold is not acceptable as a means of exchange. Gold cannot be exchanged for goods in any of the main areas of exchange. It is not possible to fill up a gas tank with gas and pay with gold dust, gold coins or bars of gold. No main department store will accept payment in gold, and so on. The cashier cannot make a phone call to check the true value of gold-colored metal offered in exchange for goods or services. The person with only gold in their hand is likely to go hungry.

Gold may be accepted under extreme circumstances, but never at face value. A credit card will buy a ticket out of trouble, while the equivalent value of gold will not. It is almost impossible for the average person to check the value of gold in its various forms, or even to know that it is what it is *claimed* to be. Gold can perform the role of a store of value, but it has not done a very good job lately. Measured in terms of those old despised pieces of green paper, gold declined substantially in value over the 1980s. Stocks also provide a store of value, a function which is not unique to money, and on that comparison gold did extremely badly. The ratio of stock prices to gold prices rose seven times over the period of the 1980s, and that is without taking dividends into account. That is a huge difference.

A good store of value in a monetary sense should have liquidity and maintain its purchasing power over time. Through the 1980s, bank accounts, which perform that function, and other liquid assets that are money or near money, performed that job very well, since interest rates were generally above the rate of inflation.

The unit of account employed in the United States is the dollar. Accounts are presented in dollar terms, and that is what is expected. A set of accounts, or financial records, maintained in terms of ounces of gold would not be well received. Money provides a common standard by which to make comparisons; this is what makes it so useful as a means of exchange. Gold does not satisfy that condition. Gold does not satisfy the basic condition of money, and is not money.

The argument might be made that *true* money means something different. True money, presumably, is much better. However, it is hard to see how such a view can be justified when gold fails to perform even the most basic functions of money. Maybe the argument is that gold *ought* to be money, and that the monetary system should be changed in order to bring this about. That possibility is considered later in the chapter.

## Price stability

The main reason put forward to justify a return to gold is as a means of returning to the price stability that existed during the gold standard. Evidence of this price stability is derived from the experience over the nineteenth century. Over little more than a hundred years, consumer prices ended up at almost exactly the same level they started at. However, to conclude from these facts that prices were stable over the period in between depends upon fallacious reasoning. The fact that there is a road on one side of a river, and a road on the other side, does not mean that there is a bridge in between. So it is with this price experience. The price level was above and below the starting and end points, to a considerable extent, throughout the hundred years.

Between 1791 and 1902 there was effectively no change in wholesale prices. A more convenient comparison would be between 1800 and 1900. Unfortunately, while the time frame is not very different, the price level fell by 40 per cent. This rather large difference gives an indication of the volatility of prices over this period. Just to give some examples; prices rose by 58 per cent between 1808 and 1814, 28 per cent between 1834 and 1837, 48 per cent between 1843 and 1857, 117 per cent between 1861 and 1864, and fell 50 per cent between 1814 and 1834, 35 per cent between 1837 and 1843, 54 per cent between 1864 and 1879 and 37 per cent between 1882 and 1896. This was hardly an example of price stability. This historical pattern was shown earlier in Fig. 2.6. The real economy, as measured by the growth of industrial production, also fluctuated widely at this time. These extreme fluctuations can be seen in the figures in Chapter 6.

There is no evidence from history that the gold standard produced greater stability, prevented wide fluctuations in inflation or prevented financial crashes. Monetary policy, as now operated, is far from perfect, but then that is an essential part of the human condition. The gold standard has also had a mixed history, and many failures to its credit. Figure 2.4 shows inflation and output growth over the period since 1900, which provides an interesting background against which to consider the question of stability. The fluctuations have been more subdued in the post-war period, but it is the earlier period that was on some form of gold standard. Here again, it is worth recalling the quote from Hickernell in Chapter 2 on the historical instability of prices.

The point about the gold standard was not that it produced stable prices, since it clearly did not do that. Prices rose and then fell by very large amounts. It is not clear whether prices fell back down because of the gold standard, or because such a move was seen as politically desirable. In fact, political support was essential whatever the monetary mechanism. Ultimately, it was not gold that brought prices down, but a government run by, and on behalf of, wealthy individuals.

Stability would, therefore, not really seem to be the issue here. The times in which we live will always seem unstable to a certain degree, since this is an integral part of a freely competitive economy. There are many people who would like to control the climate, or their total environment, and even more who would like to control the economy. But in all cases the implications of trying to do so would be unacceptable if realized and, in the end, such attempts must anyway be unsuccessful. It is better to recognize the need for change and adapt to it, rather than to be always trying to turn back the clock. In reality, an automatic pilot like the gold standard will not take us where we want to go.

Throughout history, rulers have constantly been faced with the problem of finding enough money to spend. At any one time, there are always unsatisfied wants, a crying need for things to be done, thereby raising the possibility of expansion, but the money has been lacking. Sophisticated trading relies on the lubricating properties of a generally accepted means of exchange. For more than 2000 years, until recently, money was based on the precious metals of gold and silver. Much of the time the quantities of these metals did not increase as fast as output and were, therefore, a restraining influence. Over time, banking systems developed that substituted paper for coins and helped raise the velocity of circulation of monetary coins. The existence of a sophisticated financial system, including extensive credit availability, electronic transfers, credit cards, etc., would greatly complicate the operation of a new gold standard. These are the sorts of inconvenient details that have to be faced when discussing this subject.

In addition, there is the issue of maintaining confidence in the financial system. A gold standard has the prime objective of restoring confidence in the purchasing power of the currency, but it does not improve the stability of the financial system. All the great financial crises in history, including the 1930s depression, occurred during periods of a gold standard. It is unrealistic to assume that the monetary authorities would stand by and allow the financial system to collapse in order to preserve a gold standard. That totally ignores the political reality.

The monetary authorities have the power to limit the growth of money and credit without using gold as a base. It would also be possible to have a golden base but no effective control over money and credit growth. The key to price stability is not gold but the political desire and will, as expressed through the electorate, to make that 'the' prime objective. As John Maynard Keynes pointed out nearly 70 years ago (Keynes, 1923):

> In truth, the gold standard is already a barbarous relic . . . Advocates of the ancient standard do not observe how remote it now is from the spirit and the requirements of the age. A regulated non-metallic standard has slipped in unnoticed. It exists. Whilst the economists dozed, the academic dreams of a hundred years, doffing its cap and gown, clad in paper rags, has crept into the real world by means of the bad fairies—always so much more potent than the good—the wicked ministers of finance.

Gold is not the rock that will protect, and support, the free markets of the world. It is, in fact, quite the opposite; it is the rock against which the ships of the free world could founder. It is appealing to believe that there is some automatic rule that will serve the good of mankind under all circumstances. It is like the belief that fate rules our lives. But no matter how comforting the belief may be, it is safer to adapt to changing circumstances, and to recognize the dynamic, ever-changing nature of the world, and the economy, in which we live.

## Supply of gold

One feature about gold is that it stays around. Most of the gold that has ever been mined is still around in a reasonably accessible form. New supply each year adds only a fraction to that total. However, this fraction tends to be very influential in determining the price of gold. The main supply of gold on to the market each year comes from new production. In 1991, western mine production was estimated to be 1782 tonnes, or 57.3 million ounces. On top of that there was production from the communist countries, notably the Soviet Union, China and North Korea. These countries typically sell about 300 tonnes a year, with a similar amount coming on to the market through the recycling of scrap metal.

The production and supply of gold has increased significantly (Fig. 16.1), as might have been expected following the sharp run-up in the price in the 1970s. One of the conditions that encouraged speculation in gold in the 1970s was the low level of production and supply in the early 1970s. Producers were in a difficult position at that time. The price of gold was fixed, but mine costs were being pushed up sharply by the accelerating inflation. Western mine production hit a low of 946 tonnes in 1975, according to *Gold Fields Mineral Services*, with total supply to the private sector shown as 1104 tonnes. Private sector supply is estimated to have peaked at 2913 tonnes in 1990, falling slightly in 1991 to 2815 tonnes. Supplies from the ex-communist bloc fell to 226 tonnes, from 425 tonnes in 1990, and there was less forward selling by producers.

Having risen sharply through the 1980s, the growth of non-communist production slowed to only two per cent in 1991, and this slower growth is expected to continue to 1993, at which point many analysts think production may actually start falling. South Africa is the world's largest producer, and that is also where the highest-cost mines are located. Some of these mines have had to close production. What will happen to mines in that country in the future is highly uncertain given the rapid political changes that are taking place. It is quite likely that there will be periods when production will be interrupted; also, wages may well be pushed up sharply. Despite that, there will be a desperate need for money, and it is possible that gold sales will increase, even if that means producing at a loss. Economic rationality may not be the most potent force at work.

Most producers continued to make handsome profits through the 1980s even though investors were suffering huge losses. The gold price at this time held above the costs of production in most cases, while improvements in technology lowered production costs further. By the early 1990s, the supply situation was tightening with more than one third of production unprofitable.

A restraining force on the price of gold over recent years has been the tendency for producers to take advantage of price rallies to sell their production forward. Some have just sold futures, while others have used option strategies, allowing the producers to take advantage of the time premium involved, in addition to the attractive forward price resulting from

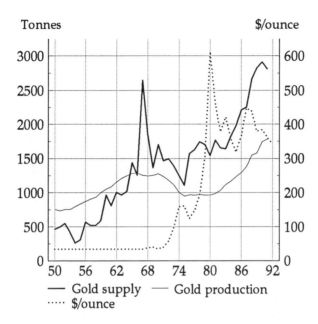

**Figure 16.1** Gold production and supply (annual)

high interest rates. There have been complaints from the investment side that these sales have deterred investment demand, but the producers have benefited substantially. Since nothing succeeds, or persuades, like success, it is reasonable to expect them to continue, although lower interest rates and lower volatility reduce the potential for such action. Anyway, the investor argument can easily change. When these sales first came to be noticed in the late 1980s, the view was that these were very bullish for the price since it meant that supply had already been taken off the market.

In any one year, a fall in investment demand can increase the supply of gold into the market. Gold is the ultimate durable good, easily recyclable and environmentally friendly. There is a lot of gold in hoards around the world that potentially could be put up for sale. It has been estimated that the total production of gold over all time has amounted to something in the region of 120 000 tonnes, of which 90 per cent still exists in the form of bars, jewelry and coins. The largest hoards actually belong to governments, in the form of official reserves. This harks back to the old days when gold was used as backing for the currency issued by the government. Gold has also been transferred to official bodies, like the IMF, as part of each country's contribution.

When the price of gold was fixed, these gold reserves provided an incentive for central banks to maintain price stability. High inflation meant that the value of the gold reserves would keep falling. Now that the gold price is floating, these gold reserves provide no incentive against inflationary policies. In the meantime, the income that is being foregone by holding reserves in non-interest bearing form is significant.

Official gold reserves held by the world's central banks are equal to approximately 35 000 tonnes, i.e. 1125.3 million ounces. The bulk of this is held by the developed countries, and that total has been declining steadily since 1965. Since that time, the developing countries have, on average, been building up their official reserves; the increased demand for gold reserves has essentially come from Asia and the Middle East. Official holdings might seem to be a stable component in total demand, included here among supply factors because it affects supply to the private sector, but it can be highly variable. For example, there were net official sales of 105 tonnes in 1991, net purchases of 66 tonnes in 1990, net sales again in 1989 of 225 tonnes and purchases of 285 tonnes in 1988.

As long as countries maintain such huge hoards of gold, it will encourage private investors to hold gold. It is hard to argue that gold is a risky, speculative investment if that turns out to be the investment of choice by governments. The central government, after all, is generally held to be the most conservative sector of the economy, and certainly should be. The question then has to be asked, is this situation ever likely to change?

At a time when governments everywhere are trying to cut costs, raise money and balance their budgets, there is increasing interest in realizing some of the value of the gold stored in the vaults of the central banks around the world. The Netherlands sold 400 tonnes during 1992. This represented a quarter of the bank's gold holdings and brought in over $4 billion. It was the equivalent of 20 per cent of all Western mine production for the year. Earlier in the year the Belgian central bank had sold 202 tonnes, continuing its policy of reducing its large gold reserves.

There was some satisfaction that the market was able to absorb these sales so well. On the other hand, the size of the potential overhang could dampen speculative demand. The problem from a government perspective is that the gold is not serving any purpose sitting in dusty vaults. Had the gold been sold ten years earlier at $460 an ounce, and the proceeds invested at 10 per cent, which was not difficult at the time, the value by the end of 1992 would have been $1200 instead of $330. If the Swiss gold reserves were sold and reinvested in bonds, they would provide a return of $550 for each citizen every year. It has been estimated that the gold reserves of the eight largest holders would produce revenue of $20 billion every year if invested at end 1992 market yields.

Official sales were made in the 1970s as a matter of policy, and could be again. One possibility is that the IMF, and the industrialized countries, could recommend gold sales to be used to finance development in the old communist countries of Europe. The collapse of communism is an event of historic importance. There are tremendous transitional costs involved, after years of corruption, inefficiency and bad management. Investment demand, and potential, is very high and it is at least plausible that gold sales could be used, in part, to help finance this major reconstruction. One way of viewing such a move is the conversion of dead money into productive potential that will benefit many people directly, and the whole world indirectly. To some, that might seem like a good use for gold.

## The demand for gold

Gold will remain an interesting investment vehicle in the future, because it will not be fixed in value. As long as central banks continue to store gold in their vaults it is hard for wealthy individuals to resist the temptation to do the same. However, most gold supporters hold the view that the Treasury does not know what it is doing. So why do the same thing? Central bank holding of gold goes back to the days when gold was money. One reason why gold is attractive in this role is that it is neutral and therefore carries no political implications, nor any inference about which currencies are expected to be weak or strong. These are issues that the individual investor does not need to be concerned about.

Precious metals exploded onto the investment scene in the 1970s, when Nixon took the dollar off the gold standard at the start of the 1970s, and US citizens were legally permitted to own gold. Investors initially seemed too stunned to take advantage of the situation, but rising inflation soon spurred them into action, and the Ayatollah provided the high octane to launch the price of gold and silver into the outer stratosphere. By the time it was all over, gold had hit $850 an ounce in January 1980, and silver had topped the $50 an ounce level.

Now, every time the gold price shows any signs of life, enthusiastic supporters jump on board and extrapolate the price rise back up into outer space. When the price jumped up to $425 from $360 in the final quarter of 1989, the expectation quickly developed that this was only a temporary pause on the way to $500, and then on to $1000, $2000 and beyond. This was not the first time that forecasts had raced ahead of events in this way. Gold, and silver, did experience rallies in the 1980s, at times quite large, but each time the price fell back. Like punch-drunk boxers they had their odd successes, only to be knocked down once more just when it may have seemed they were on the point of making a comeback. Over the decade of the 1980s gold provided an average return of −3.1 per cent per year, while silver returned −15.7 per cent per year.

The most stable demand component is for jewelry, although even that can vary sharply. Jewelry demand increased by 4 per cent in 1991 and 6

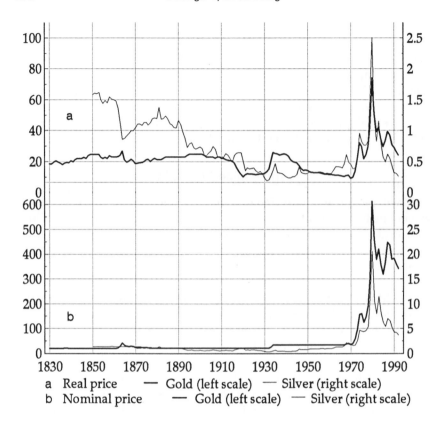

**Figure 16.2** Gold and silver prices (annual)

per cent in 1990, following two years of 25 per cent increases, which brought the total to a record 2111 metric tons (where one metric ton equals 32 151 ounces). Investment demand is a relatively small percentage of the total, but can be extremely volatile. Jewelry demand and investment demand will sometimes reinforce each other, and at other times will be off-setting. If the price is rising gradually these separate demands will often reinforce each other, since jewelry can act as a form of investment. How-ever, when the price rises rapidly on strong speculative demand, jewelry will become extremely expensive, inventory costs will rise and become increasingly risky, with the net result that demand falls.

The price of gold since 1830 is shown in Fig. 16.2, along with the price of silver since 1850. Prices are shown in nominal terms in the bottom half of the figure, and in real terms, deflated by the consumer price index, in the top half. What this figure shows clearly is that the surge in prices in the 1970s was unique. It is an extreme understatement to say that prices rose sharply; they exploded. Prices soared to levels that were unheard of, that had no historical basis, no logic and ultimately no support.

The price of gold had been held down artificially, and this distortion was bound to result in a sharp rise in price once the restraints were removed. In addition, there was an exceptional combination of negative forces that came together to influence expectations and send the prices of gold and silver soaring. What should also have been clear was that those prices could only be justified if the world had changed dramatically for the worse.

The nominal price of anything can be very misleading, as argued throughout this book, since its significance depends on what is happening to the price of everything else. In a hyperinflation, the price of all goods will be rising exponentially. That is not what happened in the case of gold and silver. These prices rose relative to everything else. This can be seen by looking at what happened to the *real* price of gold and silver.

Even in real terms, the prices of gold and silver rose dramatically, representing a radical departure from the historical trend and rationality. Since the bubble burst in January 1980, real prices have gradually been returning to longer-term historical levels. The price of silver has already come into range, but the real price of gold is still too high. Continued inflation will slowly bring it down, but that will be a long drawn-out process as long as inflation remains subdued. If this idea of a long-run equilibrium price ever took hold in the market the price would adjust downwards immediately. A comparison between the two prices, shown in Fig. 16.3, shows how silver has depreciated in terms of gold since 1979. That partly reflects the excessive speculation in silver in the 1970s, but also the fact that the real price of gold has been slow to fall.

The figure shows very broad swings in the silver/gold ratio. The relative improvement of silver in the 1970s, was, in historical terms, only a slight recovery against a much more substantial downtrend that started in 1969. Alternatively, one could go back and find a longer downtrend extending back to the 1850s. The only substantial rally, that extended from the early 1940s practically through to the end of the 1960s, was due to the persistence of inflation, combined with a fixed gold price, and legal restraints on the ownership of gold. In that sense, it can be viewed as a measure of the disequilibrium, pent-up demand for gold that was created over that period. On that basis, it could be argued that the imbalance had just about worked itself out by 1991. However, that assumes the long-term downtrend in the relative price of silver has ended. That is a hard call to make. There was a time when the silver/gold ratio was 1:2, so the downtrend has been going a lot longer, and from a much higher level.

In order to justify the much higher prices that occurred in the 1970s, something very exceptional must have happened at that time. There were many at the time who did, and who still do, expect that experience to be

**Figure 16.3** Silver/gold ratio (annual)

repeated. What has to be realized is that the 1970s represented a unique period for gold, an exceptional set of circumstances that will not be repeated. The mistake was not made by those who took advantage of the massive run-up in price at the time, but by those who expected the conditions to be repeated, and even built upon, sufficient to carry prices much higher still. It never could be.

First, the price of gold had been fixed for years. On 15 August 1971 the price of gold was unpegged. There was, therefore, tremendous potential for gold to seek out a true equilibrium level after years of controls. Second, by 1970, gold in real terms was as cheap as it had ever been, at least since 1830, as can be seen in Fig. 16.2. Third, at the end of 1974, US citizens were allowed to hold gold legally for the first time since 1933. Fourth, the world was at the threshold of a huge acceleration of inflation in 1972. Money, government spending, commodity prices and oil prices all rose dramatically through the 1970s. Even if the gold price had started off in equilibrium it would have had to go up considerably, just to keep up. As it was, there were increasing concerns that inflation was out of control. Fifth, there was concern that debt levels were too high and there was a real danger of financial collapse.

Sixth, there was extreme political uncertainty surrounding the Middle East. There was a resurgence of Muslim fundamentalism that included the overthrow of the Shah of Iran and the setting up of a Muslim state. American embassy workers were taken hostage and the power and prestige of the United States was called into question. Seventh, the Vietnam experience created a period of uncertainty and disillusionment, and widespread talk about the end of American power. Eighth, there was a crisis of confidence surrounding the President of the United States. President Carter was perceived as a good man, but without the qualities to make a good president. There was weakness at the center and consequently a lack of leadership.

A ninth factor, not unrelated to the conditions at the time, was the attempt by the Hunt brothers, with a little help from their friends, to corner the silver market. In the process, they pushed the price of silver up from $2 in 1969 to over $50 at its high point in 1980. At that rarified level, people were lining up to sell the family silver, or anyone else's for that matter. One of the laws of economics is that supply is not independent of price, and at $50 an ounce there was a lot of silver on the market. The price of gold never kept up with silver, as seen by the improving silver/gold ratio in Fig. 16.3. However, the enthusiasm was infectious and encouraged the buyers of gold. Silver subsequently went into a deep swoon, but still only recently reached levels that look reasonable in real terms. Finally, the supply/production of gold fell sharply in the early 1970s from the high levels reached in the mid to late 1960s. This was discussed in the previous section on supply.

This is quite a list. Never had there been more fertile ground in which to plant the subversive ideas of the potential for the price of gold to rise. The combination of inflation, political uncertainty and fear of the unknown, starting from a position of extreme disequilibrium, propelled the gold price ever on to record levels. But that was then. As the 1970s gave way to the 1980s, conditions changed dramatically. Inflation peaked out in January 1980, and so too did the price of gold, although the coincidence was missed at the time, and still seems to be overlooked. More important still was the change in attitude that meant that inflation would be kept down.

The change in attitude to inflation was not just a business cycle reaction. Just as inflation had built up over a number of cycles, so the new-found religion was bound to last for a number of cycles. The lags in these types of trends and reactions are very long indeed. As a result, the overall trend of inflation remained down, despite temporary moves in the opposite direction, and inflationary expectations were dragged down in response.

There were clearly forces that combined to provide an exceptionally bullish environment for gold in the 1970s. But these were temporary. It is worth considering whether there are more permanent changes that will have longer-term effects. One thing that has happened is that the character of inflation has changed. There was inflation in the past and, at times, very high inflation, but it did not continue. Eventually, prices fell back down again, although the lags involved were very long, extending over several decades. The likely continuation of inflation is an important change that would seem to give an added boost to gold's prospects.

A reasonable starting point is to consider how the price of gold is likely to respond to inflation. Inflation continued through the 1980s, but the price of gold fell. The difference can be explained by the fact that gold started from a position of extreme overvaluation. What the 1970s showed is that the price of gold is likely to rise faster than consumer prices if it looks as if inflation is accelerating out of control. The consequence of a more gradual inflation rate is much less clear. From a position of equilibrium, wherever that is, the gold price might be expected to rise along with inflation. At times, the price might move ahead more strongly and at other times fall behind, but, on balance, maintain a relatively stable real rate. Movements in interest rates would affect the cost of holding gold, by changing the return on alternative assets. The point is that precious metals do not seem to gain a relative advantage from the trend towards continuous inflation. The return from holding cash or bonds has also increased to compensate for this expected outcome.

Other changes have taken place that work against precious metals: the increase in political stability that has occurred, although it is sometimes hard to believe, and a significant increase in the availability and liquidity of alternative investments. In the nineteenth century, there were very few investment opportunities and much less liquidity. Even more significant has been the increased role of governments in ensuring financial stability and preventing a major economic collapse. This is the ultimate form of collective insurance, with the premiums paid in taxes. Imagine what would have happened in the United States under nineteenth-century rules when faced with the collapse of oil prices in the second half of the 1980s, the farm crisis in the first half, the S&L debacle, or the actual and potential failures of banks and insurance companies. A sudden demand for liquidity cannot be met, even in the best of times, even under the strongest rules, without the direct intervention of the monetary authorities. To the extent that such intervention is successful in maintaining confidence in the overall system, the role for gold as a security blanket is greatly reduced.

From the demand side, there has been a major population boom in the twentieth century, thereby potentially adding to the demand for gold. However, most of these people live at basic subsistence level and are hardly a major influence on the gold price. Within the industrialized world, wealth has risen rapidly and become more widely spread. This might result in an increase in demand, but there are many alternative assets to buy, and it is not clear that overall demand is higher than it was when wealth was more heavily concentrated in fewer hands. Gold after all, has always been a luxury item.

There was a time when gold was seen by many people as the ultimate safe haven in case of war or financial crisis. Even people who did not like or understand gold, respected it for its *insurance* characteristics. *The Economist* for 16 June 1990, began an article on gold by saying, 'What the gold market needs now is a good war'. As if on cue, Saddam Hussein marched into Kuwait and set up what might have been considered ideal conditions for gold. The price did rally a little, but enthusiasm petered out quickly. By the third quarter of 1990 there was the very real potential for war, there were American hostages in the Middle East and rapidly rising oil prices. If that was not enough, there was also the ongoing S&L crisis and the threat of a collapse of the banking system. In sum, it was an ideal environment for gold, but the response was only half-hearted. Gold did provide some insurance protection when uncertainty was at its highest, but it also proved untrustworthy even in that role. At the point where war became a reality, the price fell by $30 in one day. On the day it was announced there had been a coup in the Soviet Union, in August 1991, the gold price could manage to rally by no more than a dollar or two at best, and closed the day virtually unchanged.

The lesson should not be that gold is not a form of insurance. It clearly does have a role to play under adverse circumstances, but the coverage is expensive. Conclusions drawn from the 1970s experience do not really apply, since conditions at that time were so exceptional. A key factor in gold's limited response to crises in the 1980s and early 1990s has been the fact that the price has remained at a relatively high real level. This is generally ignored, but is likely to have been a major restraint on the price.

There is a tendency to look at gold only in terms of US dollars. The truth is that the greatest part of investment and industrial demand comes from other countries. As a result, the price of gold in other currencies is also likely to be an influence. There is some relationship between gold and the dollar, but it is far from perfect. Two explanations for a link are possible. The first is that gold is like a currency, an alternative to the dollar. However, on that argument, why does it work only for the dollar and not other currencies. Second, as the dollar rises, gold gets more expensive in foreign currency terms, depressing demand, while a weaker dollar means that the foreign currency prices fall; thereby increasing demand and tending to raise the dollar price.

Figure 16.4 shows the price of gold in dollars, Deutschemarks, yen and pounds. Gold seems cheapest in yen, with the price back at mid-1970s level. In real terms, the yen price is much lower. The price has tended to remain higher in countries that have the higher rates of inflation, the United Kingdom in particular. This gives support to the idea that investors should look at the real price of gold as a guide to whether it is cheap or expensive.

The cycles change and gold will have its turn again. Precise timing with gold will always be unpredictable given its very nature. The point to be made here is that gold offers no automatic return in excess of that available elsewhere. In fact, it frequently provides no return at all, or only one that is negative. Gold provides no interest return, and there is normally a cost of storage. The price of gold is always likely to remain highly volatile because

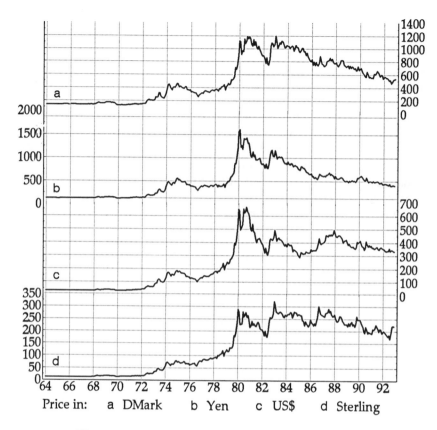

Figure 16.4 Four measures of the gold price (monthly)

it has no yield, therefore the only return is through price appreciation. To the extent that such calculations can be made, potential investors need to anticipate that the price will rise by at least the rate of interest, plus a pretty hefty risk premium. If that is not expected then the price should fall until such a point is reached. That is because of the income forgone by holding gold.

Within the context of such marginalist decision making, a fall in interest rates should boost the price of gold a little. However, the reason why interest rates fell is likely to be even more important. A fall in inflationary expectations, for example, will probably have a larger negative effect on the price of gold than the resulting change in interest rates. The low-risk time to buy gold is when it is cheap in real terms. That was the situation that existed at the start of the 1970s, when the real price of gold was at its lowest level for at least 150 years, and possibly for all time. On that basis, gold was not cheap at the start of 1990, even after a ten-year bear market.

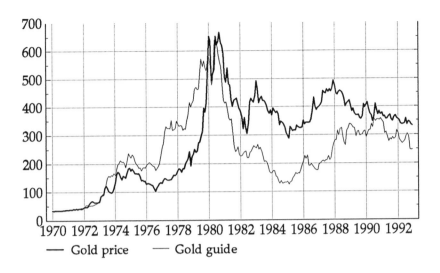

**Figure 16.5** Gold guide (monthly)

Despite the negative pressure from the high real prices of gold, there have been rallies through the 1980s in response to changing economic conditions. The short-term changes that are likely to impact on the gold price were briefly discussed above. Figure 16.5 shows the price of gold together with a guideline that provides a distillation of these separate influences. The guideline is not itself a forecast of the gold price, but does identify the conditions that would be necessary to support another strong rally. The inputs include commodity prices, a measure of inflationary expectations, the strength or weakness of the dollar and the effect of changes in interest rates. No attempt has been made to fit a perfect line. The objective instead nas been to provide a logical structure and see to what extent the gold price has conformed to that basic outline.

Considering the limitations of this approach, the results are highly encouraging. An interesting conclusion is that the gold price surge in the 1970s was not as unlikely as thought at the time. There were strong short-term influences at work, due partly to the structural changes already discussed. If anything, the gold price seems to have lagged the fundamental forces pulling it up. Summarizing those forces as inflationary expectations, it can be argued that these lead on the way up, and also lead on the way down. When the price of gold peaked early in the 1980s, the price was slow to fall, holding well above the theoretical guideline. This outcome is very similar to that experienced in the bond market, where inflationary expectations lagged on the way up and also on the way down. In addition, there is the time it takes to recover from the sort of major disruption that occurred in the 1970s. Expectations do not immediately settle back down, having been pushed to such extremes.

On the basis of this model, a surge in commodity prices would bring about an increase in the price of gold, as long as nothing else changed. Inflationary expectations should continue to improve for a while longer which will help to keep the price down. All of the variables are inter-related. Rising commodity prices will tend to raise interest rates which will raise the exchange rate, at least as long as relative prices do not diverge too much. Higher interest rates and a higher exchange rate will have a negative effect on the gold price. However, inflationary expectations will eventually turn up if inflation stays high for very long, and that will be positive for the gold price. To some extent, conditions for gold have improved, but the price is still some way from the bargain basement level of the early 1970s.

# REFERENCES

Boeckh, J. A. and R. T. Coghlan (eds), 1982, *The Stock Market and Inflation*, Dow Jones-Irwin, Homewood.

Bolton, H. (1967), *Money and Investment Profits*, Dow Jones-Irwin, Homewood.

Bresciani-Turrone, C. (1937), *The Economics of Inflation*, Augustus M. Kelly (originally published in Italian, Universita Bocconi, 1931).

Brooks, J. (1969), *Once in Golconda: A True Drama of Wall Street 1920–1938*, W. W. Norton and Co., New York.

Coghlan, R. T. (1981), *Money, Credit and the Economy*, Allen and Unwin, London.

Coghlan, R. T. (1984), 'American locomotive races towards a dollar crisis', *The Times*, August 1984, London.

Coghlan, R. T., (1987), 'Friday 13th', *The Times*, November 1987, London.

Coghlan, R. T. (1991), 'European investment opportunities', in J. Lederman and K. K. H. Park (eds), *The Global Equity Markets*, Probus Publishing Co., Chicago.

Dewey, E. R. (1971), *Cycles: The Mysterious Forces that Trigger Events*, Hawthorn Book Inc., New York.

Fisher, I. (1930), *The Theory of Interest*, Macmillan, London.

Freeman, C. (1977) 'The Kondratiev long waves, technical change and unemployment', in *Structural Determinants of Employment and Unemployment*, OECD, Paris.

Friedman, M. (1968), 'The role of monetary policy', *American Economic Review*, March.

Friedman, M. and A. Schwartz (1963), *A Monetary History of the United States, 1867–1960*, National Bureau of Economic Research, Princeton University Press.

Galbraith, J. K. (1954), *The Great Crash 1929*, Houghton Mifflin Co.

Gann, W. D. (1942), *How to Make Profits Trading in Commodities*, Lambert-Gann Publishing Co. Inc., Pomeroy.

Granville, J. (1976), *Granville's New Strategy of Daily Stock Market Timing for Maximum Profit*, Prentice-Hall, Englewood Cliffs.

Hawtrey, R. G. (1928), *Trade and Credit*, Green & Co. Ltd.

Hickernell, W. F. (1928), *Financial and Business Forecasting*, Bureau of Business Conditions, Alexander Hamilton Institute.

Hicks, J. R. (1950), *A Contribution to the Theory of the Trade Cycle*, Oxford University Press, Oxford.

Hicks, J. R. (1939), *Value and Capital*, Oxford University Press, Oxford.

Homer, S. (1963), *A History of Interest Rates*, Rutgers University Press, New Brunswick.

Jevons, W. S. (1875), 'The Solar Period and the Price of Corn', paper read at the British Association in 1876, and printed in *Investment, Currency and Finance*, 1884, Macmillan, London.

Jevons, W. S. (1878), 'The Periodicity of Commercial Crises and its Physical Explanation', *Nature*, vol. 19, pp. 33–37.

Johnson, H. (1969), 'The case for flexible exchange rates', in H. G. Johnson and J. E. Nash (eds), *UK and Floating Exchanges*, Institute of Economic Affairs.

Keynes, J. M. (1919), *The Economic Consequences of the Peace*, Macmillan, London.

Keynes, J. M. (1923), *A Tract on Monetary Reform*, Macmillan, London.

Keynes, J. M. (1936), *The General Theory of Employment, Interest and Money*, Macmillan, London.

Keynes, J. M. (1940), *How to Pay for the War; A Radical Plan for the Chancellor of the Exchequer*, Macmillan, London.

Kindleberger, C. P. (1978), *Manias, Panics and Crashes*, Basic Books, New York.

Kindleberger, C. P. (1984), *A Financial History of Western Europe*, Allen and Unwin, London.

Lynch, P. (1989), *Once up on Wall Street*, Simon & Schuster, New York.

Macaulay, F. R. (1980), *Some Theoretical Problems Suggested by the Movements of Interest Rates, Bond Yields and Stock Prices in the United States since 1856*, Arno Press (originally published 1938).

Mackay, C. (1932), *Extraordinary Popular Delusions and the Madness of Crowds*, Farrar, Strauss and Giroux Inc., New York (originally published by Richard Bentley, New Burlington St, 1841).

Mitchell, W. C. (1941), *Business Cycles and their Causes*, University of California Press (originally published in folio form, 1913).

Owens, R. and C. Hardy (1925), *Interest Rates and Stock Speculation*, Brookings Institute Study, Washington.

Pring, M. (1991), *Technical Analysis Explained*, McGraw-Hill, New York.

Roach, S. S. (1991), 'The Leveraging of Corporate America: Fact and Fallacy', Morgan Stanley Report, 21 June.

Rodgers, D. I. (1971), *The Day the Market Crashed*, Arlington House, New York.

Salomon Brothers (1991), *Emerging Markets Factbook.*

Schumpeter, J. (1912), *The Theory of Economic Development*, trans. Opie, R., Cambridge, Mass., Harvard University Press, 1934.

Schilling, A. G. (1991), 'Exits and entrances', *Forbes Magazine*, 16 September.

Smith, A. (1776), *An Enquiry into the Nature and Causes of the Wealth of Nations*, Campbell, R. H. and A. S. Skinner, (eds), Liberty Press, New York, 1981.

Stamp, Sir J. (1929), *Some Economic Factors in Modern Life*, P. S. King and Son, Westminster.

Thomas, G. and M. Morgan-Wills (1979), *The Day the Bubble Burst*, Doubleday and Co, New York.

Toynbee, A. (1947), *The Study of History*, Oxford University Press.

Wheeler, R. H. (1983), 'Climate—the key to understanding business cycles', in M. Zahorchak (ed.), *The Raymond H. Wheeler Papers*, Tide Press, New Jersey.

de la Vega, J. (1688), *Confusion de Confusiones*, trans. H. Kellenbenz, Baker Library, Boston, Harvard Graduate School of Business Administration, 1957. Publication of the Kress Library of Business and Economics.

# INDEX